VERBA NOMINALIA;

OR,

WORDS DERIVED FROM PROPER NAMES.

BY

RICHARD STEPHEN CHARNOCK, Ph.Dr.,

F.S.A., F.R.G.S., F.R.S.S.A., F.R.S.N.A.,

FELLOW OF THE ANTHROPOLOGICAL SOCIETY OF LONDON;
FOREIGN ASSOCIATE OF THE ANTHROPOLOGICAL SOCIETY OF PARIS;
CORRESPONDING MEMBER OF THE NEW ENGLAND
HISTORIC-GENEALOGICAL SOCIETY.

"Nomina si nescis, perit cognitio rerum."
COKE ON LITTLETON.

GRYPHON BOOKS
ANN ARBOR, MICHIGAN • 1971

This is a facsimile reprint of the
1866 edition published in London
by Trubner and Company.

Library of Congress Catalog Card Number 78−145522

PREFACE.

It must, without any research, have been apparent to most people that many well-known words have had their origin in Proper Names; but whoever has made even a slight study of the various branches of etymology will have discovered that the number of words so derived is very large indeed. The ordinary reader of history may know that " to roam " is to wander about on the pretence of a pilgrimage to Rome; that the word calico is derived from Calicut; humbug from Hamburg; or that bayonets are supposed to have first seen the light at Bayonne. He will doubtless be further interested in finding dimity referred to Damietta, marigold to the Virgin, mayduke to Médoc, fuchsia to Dr. Fuchs, coffee to Káfa, quince to Cydonia. This latter class of names, however, not being usually met with in the narrative of great and exciting events, required an independent chronicler, and I determined to volunteer my services to investigate and register them. The chief difficulty lay in deciding where to stop. Should the work be confined to the most common words found in a dictionary of the English language? or should it embrace also those used in the Arts and Sciences? On the whole, I was inclined to think that these also should be included, since terms technical in their origin frequently force themselves into general use, after which there is, through lapse of time, a difficulty in framing for them an accurate genealogy. To remedy the errors, omissions, and defects unavoidable in the first issue of such a work, I beg the corrections, additions, and suggestions of etymologists, with a view to a more complete edition. In carrying out my design, I have availed myself of all information within reach, and have, I believe, generally acknowledged my authorities. To the Rev. S. F. Creswell, M.A., of Lancaster School, Fellow of the Royal Astronomical and Geographical Societies, I am indebted for some useful information and many hints and corrections. My learned friend also, at my request, suggested the title, " Verba Nominalia," and he is quite willing to father it. Some additions and corrections will be found at the end of the work.

R. S. CHARNOCK.

GRAY'S INN,
    1st October, 1865.

VERBA NOMINALIA.

———◆———

ABDERIAN. Foolish or incessant laughter is so named, from Abdera, in Thrace, the birthplace of Democritus, who was much given to laughter, and who was styled the Abderite. See Whitaker; Webster.

ACADEMY (L. *academia*, Gr. ακαδεμια). A school, or seminary of learning, holding rank between a university or a college and a common school; also, a school for teaching a particular art, or particular sciences, as a military academy; so named from the Academe or school of Plato, originally, it is said, a garden, grove, or villa near Athens, where Plato and his followers held their philosophic conferences.

ACONITE. The herb wolfsbane or monkshood, a poisonous plant; so named from Acone, a place in Pontus famous for poisonous herbs.

ADAMIC. A term given to common red clay, from the mistaken opinion that *Adam* signifies "red earth."—*Webster*.

ADANSONIA. The Ethiopian sour gourd, or African calabash-tree, a native of Africa, and one of the largest of the vegetable kingdom; named from M. Adanson, who has given a description of it.

ADONIA. In ancient history, festivals held in honour of Adonis, principally celebrated by females among the Egyptians and the Greeks, who spent two days in lamentations and infamous pleasures.

ADONIC. A name given to a verse consisting of a dactyl and spondee, in which was bewailed the death of Adonis, son of Cinyras and favourite of Venus. Among the Anglo-Saxons

B

the Adonic verse was a poetic verse consisting of one long, two short, and two long syllables.

ADONIS. In botany, the generic term of bird's-eye, called also pheasant's-eye, and so named because its flowers resemble those of the anemone, into which flower Venus changed Adonis.——A term applied to a youthfully handsome man, more graceful than vigorous. George IV. was contemptuously called " a fat Adonis " (*S. F. Creswell.*)

ADULARIA. A mineral, a variety of orthoclase found in granitic rocks, occurring in great perfection in the high districts of Savoy. The name is derived from Adula, one of the highest peaks of St. Gothard. The Valencianite Breithaupt is a variety of adularia, and was named from the Mexican mine Valencia.

ÆNEID (L. *Æneïs*). A heroic poem, written by Virgil, in which Æneas is the hero.

ÆOLIAN. Pertaining to Æolus, god of the winds; as Æolian harp.

ÆOLIST. A devotee of Æolus; a pretender to inspiration.

ÆOLIPILE. A hollow ball of metal, with a pipe or slender neck having a very small orifice, used in hydraulic experiments ; named from *Æolus*, and *pila* a ball. Bailey renders *œolopyle*, an ancient device to prevent smoking chimneys, from Αιολου πυλαι, the gates of Æolus.

ÆSCHYNITE. A black or dark brownish yellow ore from the Ural Mountains ; an ore containing titanium, zirconium, and cerium (*Dana*) ; probably named after Æschines, the Greek orator, though for no better reason than that other celebrities have been commemorated in the naming of metals, &c.

AFFENTHALER. A celebrated red wine made from grapes, and growing in the Affenthal, near the Rhine.

AGARIC (Gr. αγαριχον, L. *agaricus*). In botany, the generic term for the mushroom tribe of the fungi which grow in decaying animal or vegetable matter, and said to be from *Agaria*, in Sarmatia. (See Dioscorides.) In pharmacy the term is applied to two species of fungi belonging to the Linnæan genus *Boletus*, the one used as a cathartic, the other as a styptic,

and also for tinder and dyeing. The agaric mineral is one of
the purest of the native carbonates of lime; it is found in clefts
of rocks, and is named from its resemblance to the agaric in
texture and colour. It has been considered as a variety of
meerschaum. The Germans call it *bergmehl,* mountain meal;
the Italians, *latte di luna,* moon-milk.

AGATE (L. *achates, gagates,* Gr. γαγατης). An ornamental
stone used in jewellery, and for some purposes in the arts;
sometimes called Scotch pebble. Bochart deduces the word
from the Punic and Hebrew עקד *âkad,* with a different prefix
Heb. נחד *nakad,* spotted. Others derive the word from the
Greek αχατης, a stone described by Theophrastus, and which,
according to him, was brought from the river Achates, in
Sicily; now the Drillo, in the Val di Noto. Pliny (33, 10)
tells us achates (agates) were once in great demand; that
they were found first in Sicily, near a river of the same name,
but afterwards in many places; and he says there are many
varieties, as *Phass-achates, Sard-achates, Hem-achates, Leuc-
achates, Dendr-achates, Ant-achates,* and *Carallo-achates.* (See
also Solinus and Isidore.) There was also a river of Lycia
called Γαγης, and Γαγγης is the Greek name for the river
Ganges.

AHRBLEICHART. A strong red highly-prized wine made
from Burgundy grapes, growing in the neighbourhood of
Ahrweiler, in the Ahr Valley, in Rhenish Prussia. The last
part of the name is probably derived from *bleich-roth-art,* pale-
red-like.

ALALITE. A crystallized mineral first found by Bonvoisin
in the black rock at Musa, near the village of Ala, in Piedmont,
whence its name. See Cleveland.

ALCAICS. Several kinds of verse, so called from their inventor Alcæus, a lyric poet of Mitylene, in Lesbos, who
flourished about the 44th Olympiad. One kind consists of five
feet, a spondee or iambic, an iambic, a long syllable, and two
dactyls.—*Encyc.*

ALCANTARA. A Spanish military order, so named from
Alcantara, in Spain.

ALCHORNEA. A genus of plants named after Mr. Stainsby Alchorne, apothecary, of London.

ALDINE. A term applied to those editions, chiefly of the Classics, which proceeded from the press of Aldus Manutius of Venice, for the most part in the sixteenth century. The term has also been lately applied to certain elegant editions of English works.

ALDROVANDA. A genus of plants, of which there is but one species, found in marshes in Italy and India ; named by Monti after Ulisse Aldrovandi, prefect of the botanic garden at Bologna, a great traveller, naturalist, and collector, styled the modern Pliny, who was born in 1552, and died at Bologna in 1605.

ALEXANDERS. An umbelliferous plant of the genus *Smyrnium*, found upon rocks on the sea-shore, and blossoming in May and June. According to Pliny it was so called because in Italy and Germany it had been denominated *herba Alexandrina*, having been supposed to be brought from Alexandria.

ALEXANDRINE or **ALEXANDRIAN.** A kind of verse consisting of twelve syllables, or of twelve and thirteen alternately ; so called from having been used in a French poem on the life of Alexander. This species of verse is peculiar to modern poetry, but well adapted to epic poems, and is less current in English than among the French, whose tragedies are generally composed of Alexandrine. See Webster.

ALGAROT or **ALGAROTH.** The name of an emetic powder, a compound of the sesqui-oxide and sesqui-chloride of antimony, obtained by pouring water into a solution of the sesqui-chloride of that metal ; named from Algarotti, a physician, who first applied it as an internal medicine. He was born at Padua in 1712, and died at Pisa 1764.

ALICANTE. A sweet wine made at Alicante, in Spain.

ALLANITE. An ore of the metals cerium and lanthanium having a pitch-black or brownish colour ; first discovered as a species by Mr. Allan, of Edinburgh.—*Dana.*

ALLEMANDE. (Fr.) A slow air in common time; or grave solemn music with a slow movement. Also, a brisk dance, or a figure in dancing (*Dictionary of Music*). Originally from *Allemagne*, *i. e.* Germany.

ALMAGRERITE. A mineral, an anhydrous sulphate of zinc, occurring at the mine at Barranco Jaroso, in the Sierra Almagrera, in Spain.

ALPHONSIN. A surgical instrument for extracting bullets from wounds ; so called from its inventor, Alphonsus Ferrier, of Naples. It consists of three branches which close by a ring, and open when it is drawn back (*Encyc.*)——A name applied to certain astronomical tables which were published in 1252 under the patronage of Alphonso X., King of Castile and Leon (*P. Cyc.*)

ALTAITE. A mineral occurring with telluric silver at Savodinsky, near Barnaoul, in the Altai Mountains, which form a boundary between the Russian and Chinese dominions.

AMADOT. The name of a French pear ; a corruption of *Damoudet*, the name by which it is known in Burgundy ; and so called from Dame Oudet, who first cultivated it, and who lived at Démigny, between Beaune and Châlons. See Ménage; also J. Ferrand, Traité des Espaliers.

AMBROSIN. In the Middle Ages, a coin struck by the Dukes of Milan, on which St. Ambrose was represented on horseback, with a whip in his right hand.

AMMONIA. An alkali (often called *volatile alkali*) composed of three equivalents of hydrogen and one of nitrogen. Some derive the word from Gr. αμμος, sand, because originally found in sandy ground. According to others it was named after Jupiter Ammon, near whose temple in Egypt it was generated, or from Ammonia, a Cyrenaic territory.

AMMONITE. The serpent-stone or *cornu Ammonis*, a fossil shell curved into a spiral form like a ram's horn, of various sizes, found in strata of limestone and clay, and in argillaceous iron ore ; named from Jupiter Ammon, who was represented in statues as having ram's horns.

AMONTILLADO. A wine, so named from its resembling, in a peculiar bitter-almond dry flavour, the wines of Montilla, near Cordova, which are so much sought after. It is dear, and used in enriching poorer and sweet wines.

AMPHITRITE. A genus of marine animals of the order *Mollusca*, very common about the southern coasts of Devonshire; named from Amphitrite, wife of Neptune and goddess of the sea.

ANACREONTIC. A poem composed in the manner of Anacreon, a Greek poet, whose odes and epigrams are celebrated for their delicate, easy, and graceful air, and for their exact imitation of nature. The Anacreontic verse consists of three feet and a half; the first foot is either a spondee or iambus, or an anapest; the rest are usually spondees or iambuses.

ANDALUSITE. A mineral, of a greyish or a pale reddish tint, sometimes in rhombic prisms; composed chiefly of silica and alumina; from *Andalusia*, in Spain, where it was first discovered.

ANDERSONIA. A genus of shrubs, natives of Australia; cl. *Pentandria*, or. *Monogynia*; named after Dr. O. Anderson.

ANDESINE. A mineral occuring in the Andes, at Marmato, in the rock called andesite, a whitish syenite; also in the syenite of Alsace, in the Vosges.

ANDREOLITE or **ANDREASBERGOLITE.** A mineral; the harmotome or cross-stone; from Andreasberg, a town of Hanover, in the mining district of Klausthal.

ANDROMEDA. A constellation containing from twenty-three to twenty-seven stars; called by the Arabians *Marah Musalseleth*, or the Woman Chained. Hence probably its Greek name of Andromeda, who, according to Greek poets, was chained to a rock by the Nereids and released by Perseus. ——A genus of plants, nat. or. *Ericaceæ*, shrubs and natives of Lapland, North America, and Russia.

ANGLESITE. Native sulphate of lead, occurring at Parry's Mine, in Anglesea, whence its name. It is also found in Cornwall, Cumberland, Derbyshire, the Hartz, the Black Forest, and in Prussia, Sardinia, Andalusia, and Siberia.

ANGOLA. The same as mohair; the wool of the Angola or Angora goat. Some derive the name from *Agnolia*. It is rather from Angora or Enguri (Ancyra), in Asia Minor, 140 miles north of Konich. At Angora stuffs and yarn are manufactured from the fine wool of this goat, of which wool 500,000 okes (11,200 cwt.) are estimated to be annually exported.

ANGOLA. The name of a pea called pigeon-pea, a species of cytisus, from Angola, a kingdom of Congo, in Africa.

ANNABERGITE. A mineral occurring on white nickel, and supposed to result from the decomposition of this ore, named from Annaberg, in Saxony, where it occurs. It is also found at Allemont in Dauphiny, at Kamsdorf near Saalfeld, at Riechelsdorf, and at other mines of mineral ores.

ANTIGORITE. A mineral, consisting of silica, magnesia, protoxide of iron, alumina, and water, from the Antigorio Valley, to the north of Domo d'Ossola, in Piedmont.

APPLE. The fruit of the apple-tree, by some supposed to have been originally from Avella or Abella, in Italy.

ARDASSINES or ARDASSINE. A very fine sort of Persian silk, said to take its name from the district of Ardeshir, in Persia. It is little inferior in fineness to the *sourbastis* or rather *cherbasses*, although it is not much used in the silk manufactures of Lyons and Tours, because it will not bear hot water in the winding. The vulgar French name was formerly *ablaque*, and it is called in German *ardassines, ardessines, ardassiner-seide, logir,* and *perlen-seide.*

ARENDALITE,. Another name of epidote or pistacite ; *epidote* being the name given to it by Haüy, and *pistacite* by Werner. The word is probably derived from Arendal, in Norway, in the district of Nedernæs.

ARFWEDSONITE. A ferruginous variety of hornblende, named after Arfwedson.

ARGAND. A name given to an improved lamp, invented by Argand, in 1780, in which, by means of a hollow wick, and a glass chimney, a strong and clear light is produced by placing the flame between two currents of air.—*Brande.*

ARGYLLIA. A genus of plants bearing beautiful flowers, natives of South America ; named in honour of the Duke of Argyle.

ARGUS. A porcelain shell beautifully variegated with spots resembling those in a peacock's tail. The mythic Argus had a hundred eyes, some of which were open while the others were closed. Juno, in recompense of his fidelity in guarding Io, fixed his eyes to the wings and tail of the peacock, and transformed him into that bird.——The name of a species of cimex found in Surinam, and of several birds, fishes, and insects.

ARIANISM. The doctrines or creed of Arius, a presbyter of the Church of Alexandria in the fourth century.

ARICINA. A vegetable alkaloid obtained from the bark of a species of cinchona, and first brought from Arica, in Peru.

ARISTARCH. A severe critic (*Knowles*) ; from Aristarchus, a critic distinguished for severity among the ancients.

ARISTARCHIAN. Severely critical, like Aristarchus.

ARISTOTELIA. A genus of plants, nat. or. *Philadelpha ceæ ;* named after Aristotle.

ARISTOTELIANISM. The philosophy or doctrines of Aristotle, a disciple of Plato, and founder of the Peripatetic school of philosophers.

ARKANSITE. A mineral ; a variety of brookite, from Magnet Cove, Hot Springs County, Arkansas.

ARMENIACA (Gr. *αρμενιαχον*). The apricot; so called from having been brought originally from Armenia. It is now a genus of plants, nat. or. *Amygdaleæ.—Crabb.*

ARMINIANISM. The doctrines or tenets of Arminius, of Holland, who flourished at the close of the sixteenth and the beginning of the seventeenth century.

ARMSTRONG. A celebrated rifled cannon named after its inventor, Mr. William (now Sir William) Armstrong.

ARRACAN. Rice from Aracan or Arracan, a British province of Further India, in the presidency of Bengal.

ARRAGONITE. Carbonate of lime crystallised in rhombic prisms, differing from common carbonate of lime, or calcareous spar, in its crystallization ; so named from Arragon, in Spain, where it was first observed.

ARRAS. Tapestry ; hangings wove with figures ; named from Arras, capital of Artois, in the French Netherlands, where it was manufactured.

ARTEDIA. A genus of umbelliferous plants, named in honour of P. Artedia, the associate of Linnæus.

ARTEMISIA (*αρτεμισια. Hippoc. et Diosc.*) The Greek

name for a plant called in English mother herb ; from *Artemis*, the Greek name of Diana, who presided over women in childbed. The name is now applied to a genus of plants, nat. or. *Compositæ*, the species of which are known by the names of mugwort, southernwood, and wormwood.——In antiquity, certain festivals celebrated yearly in honour of Artemis or Diana, in various parts of Greece, particularly at Delphi, where a mullet was sacrificed to the goddess.

ASIARCH. A term applied to the chiefs or pontiffs of Proconsular Asia, who had the superintendence of the public games.—*Acts* xix.

ASSASSIN. One who kills, or attempts to kill by surprise or secret assault ; one who takes any advantage in killing or attempting to murder, as by attacking one when unarmed. Voltaire says, " In the time of the Crusades there was a wretched little people of mountaineers inhabiting the caverns near the road to Damascus. These brigands elected a chief whom they named Cheik-Ehissisin (called by the Crusaders the ' Old Man of the Hill '), who was imagined to be a great prince because he had caused a Count Montserrat and some other crusading nobles to be robbed and murdered on the highway. These people were called Ehississin, whence the word *assassin*." Thierry (Hist. Norm. Conq., vol. 2), speaking of Philip of France, A.D. 1192, says, " He immediately assembled his barons, and showed them letters just arrived, he said, from beyond the seas, and which warned him to be on his guard, for that the King of England had from the East sent to kill him. Such was the name, then quite new in European languages, by which were designated certain Mahometans, fanatics in religion and patriotism, who thought to gain Paradise by devoting themselves to kill by surprise the enemies of their faith. It was generally believed that there existed in the defiles of Mount Libanus a whole tribe of these enthusiasts, subject to a chief called the ' Old Man of the Mountain,' and that the vassals of this mysterious personage joyfully ran to meet death at the first signal from their chief. It will be readily understood that the name of these men, who poniarded people without the slightest warning of their attack, stabbed generals of armies in the very midst of their soldiers, and who, so they had struck their victim, themselves died laughing, necessarily inspired the Western Crusaders and pilgrims with great alarm. They brought back so vivid a memory of the terror they had felt at the mere word *assassin*, that this word soon passed into every mouth, and the most absurd tales of assassination readily found in Europe people disposed to credit them." The name *haschischi*, by which the chief was designated in Arabic, is said to be derived from *hashish*, an intoxicating plant of which these people made frequent use to stupify themselves : but qu. the second form of the Arabic *hassa*, which signifies "to kill." For further information see De Sacy, Chrev. Arabe ; and Notes and Queries, 2nd S., No. 57.

ASTR CAN. The name of a scarlet shawl, and of a black jacket worn by women, and first brought from Astracan or Astrakhan.

ATACAMITE. A native chloride of copper, originally found in the form of sand in the Desert of Atacama, between Chili and Peru.—*Dana*.

ATELLAN. A dramatic representation, satirical or licentious, after the manner of the dramas at Atella, in ancient Italy.

ATHAMANTA. A genus of plants of the nat. or. *Umbelliferæ*, so called from Mount Athamas, in Sicily, where the species were first found.

ATHANASIAN; denoting a formulary, confession, or exposition of faith, formerly supposed to have been drawn up by Athanasius, Bishop of Alexandria, in the fourth century; but this opinion is now rejected, and the composition is by some ascribed to Hilary, Bishop of Arles. It is a summary of what was called the orthodox faith.

ATHENÆUM. In the United States, a building or apartment where a library, periodicals, and newspapers are kept for public perusal, so named from the Athenæum (Gr. Αθηναιον) of ancient Athens, a public school or place where poets, philosophers, and rhetoricians met for the purpose of arguing, reciting, and declaiming.

ATLANTES, ATLANTIDES, or ATLAS (called also Zelamones and Persians). In architecture, a name given by the Greeks to the figures or statues of men used to support entablatures with mutules, instead of pilasters or columns; from *Atlas*, who is fabled to have borne the heavens on his shoulders, near the Hesperides.

ATLAS. A collection of maps in a volume, supposed to be so called from a picture of Atlas supporting the heavens, prefixed to some collections. A term now also applied to works in which subjects are exhibited in a tabular form or arrangement, as a historical or ethnographical atlas; a large square folio, resembling a volume of maps, called also atlas folio. ——The first vertebræ of the neck, articulating immediately with the occipital bone, and thus supporting the globe of the head, as Atlas was said to support the world.

ATTIC. A story in the upper part of a house, with small windows in or above the cornice; a part of a building standing on the cornice, similar in form to that of a pedestal, and either broken or continued. The name is said to be derived from the Attic order of architecture, an order of small square pillars at the uppermost extremity of a building, which was intended to conceal the roof and give greater dignity to the design, and which had its origin at Athens. The Romans employed attics in their edifices, as may be seen in the remains of their triumphal arches, and in the Forum of Nerva. In the ruins of Athens no attics are to be found. There is one over a Corinthian colonnade at Thessalonica, with breaks forming dwarf pilasters over the columns, and with statues placed in front of the pilasters, as in the arch of Constantine. " The word *attic* is also now applied to a kind of building in which no roof or covering is to be seen, as was usual in the houses of the Athenians."—*Crabb*.

ATTICISM. The peculiar style and idiom of the Greek language used by the Athenians; refined and elegant Greek; concise and elegant expression.——A particular attachment to the Athenians; applied especially to the act of siding with the Athenians during the Peloponnesian War.

AUDEANISM. Anthropomorphism, or the doctrine of Audeus, a Syrian of the fourth century, who maintained that God has a human shape ; from Gen. i. 26.—*Encyc.*

AUGUST D'OR. A gold coin of Saxony, double, single, and half, reckoned at 10, 5, and $2\frac{1}{2}$ rix-dollars ; the august of 1754 being equal to 16s. 2d., that of 1784 to 16s. $3\frac{3}{4}d.$; named after August, Elector of Saxony, who succeeded his brother Maurice in 1553 ; or August Frederick, the name of two subsequent electors.

AUGUSTINE. The name of a French pear, doubtless so called after St. Augustine ; whence, perhaps, the pear named St. Austin.

AUTUNITE. A mineral found in crystals, massive, and investing other minerals, in granite at St. Symphorien, near Autun, and at St. Yrieux, not far from Limoges, in France.

AUVERNAT. A wine from Auvergne, in France.

AVELLANA, or *Nux Pontica* ; filbert. A sort of nut, so called from Avellanum, a town of Campania, where they abounded.

AVELLANE. In heraldry, a cross, the quarters of which resemble a filbert nut. See AVELLANA.

AVERNAT. A sort of grape (*Johnson*) ; properly *Auvernat*, from Auvergne, in France.

AVERRHOA. A genus of plants, nat. or. *Oxalidaceæ*, called after Averrhoes, a physician of Cordova, in Spain.

AVERROIST. One of a sect of Peripatetic philosophers who appeared in Italy before the restoration of learning ; so denominated from Averroes, a celebrated Arabian author.

AVICENNIA. A genus of plants, nat. or. *Myoporaceæ*, called after Avicenna, a Persian philosopher and physician.

AZORITE. A mineral, according to A. A. Hayes consisting of niobite of lime ; from the Azores.

B.

BABEL. Confusion, disorder (*Beaumont*); from the confusion at the Tower of Babel; a name which has been ridiculously derived from the Hebrew בלבל *bilbil*, confusion, from *balal*, to mix or confuse; but which is more reasonably from بيل باب *báb-bel*, the gate or court, *i. e.* the city, of Bel or Belus.

BABYLONICS. The title of a fragment of the history of the world, ending 267 years before Christ, composed by Berosus, a priest of Babylon.

BACALHAO (Por. *bacalháo*, Sp. *bacalláo*). The fish we call poor jack, ling, cod-fish, salt fish; so named from Bacalhoa, an island off the S.E. coast of Newfoundland, where it is found. "Llamose Bacalláo por el país en cuya mar se pesca, que tiene este nombre." (*Dicc. de la Acad. Españ.*)

BACCHANAL, BACCHANALIAN. One who indulges in drunken revels; a drunkard; one who is noisy and riotous when intoxicated; from *Bacchus*, god of wine, and son of Jupiter and Semele.

BACCHANALIA, BACCHANALE. Festivals at Rome in honour of Bacchus, celebrated in spring and autumn with games and shows, which for their licentiousness were suppressed by a solemn decree of the Senate.

BACCHANALIANS. Those who performed rites in honour of Bacchus.

BACCHARIS. A name given to a plant by the Greeks in honour of Bacchus; a genus of plants now commonly called ploughman's spikenard, nat. or. *Compositæ.—Crabb.*

BACCHIUS (Βαχχειος). In ancient poetry, a foot composed of three syllables, the first short, and the two last long, as in *avari;* so called because it was used in hymns to Bacchus.

BAECKIA. A genus of plants, nat. or. *Myrtaceæ;* so named from A. Baeck, physician to the King of Sweden.—*Crabb.*

BAGNOLS. A red wine of a rich sweet flavour, from Bagnols, dep. Gard, south of France.

BAIKALITE. A greenish variety of augite, occurring in

grouped or radiated circular prisms (*Dana*) ; from Lake Baika, in Siberia.

BAIZE or BAYS. A coarse woollen stuff having a long nap. In the singular it is *bay*, and is by some rendered "frieze of Baiæ" (It. *Baja*), an ancient city of Italy, Naples (now in ruins).

BALASSOR. An Indian stuff made of the bark of a tree; doubtless so named from Balasore, a maritime district of British India, in the presidency of Bengal, having a town of the same name.

BALDACHIN. In architecture, a structure in the form of a canopy, supported by columns, and often used as a covering to insulated altars ; the term is also used for a shell over a door (*Ency. Johnson*). The It. has *baldachino*, the Sp. *baldaquino*, a rich silk or canopy carried over the host ; the Fr. *baldaquin*, a canopy. Lunier deduces the French word from the name of a city in Babylonia.

BALDERDASH. Derived from the name of the Scandinavian god Baldur, whence also the village of Balderton, in Notts.—*S. F. Creswell.*

BAMLITE. A mineral found in long slender prisms and crystalline masses, with quartz in gneiss, at Bräkke, near Brevig, in the parish of Bamle, in Norway.

BANIAN. A man's undress or morning gown, as worn by the Banians in the East Indies, a peculiar caste or class among the Hindoos. They believe in a metempsychosis, and will neither eat flesh nor kill noxious animals. Hence it is said "Banian days," in seamen's language, are those days in the week in which the sailors have no fresh meat served out to them.

BANISTERIA. A genus of plants of the nat. or. *Malpighiaceæ*, called after the Rev. J. Banister, a botanist.—*Crabb.*

BANKSIA. A genus of plants, consisting of bushes or small trees found in Australia, where they are called honeysuckle trees; named after Sir Joseph Banks, the accomplished naturalist, &c.

BANTAM. A very small variety of fowl with feathered legs, brought from Bantam, a residency of the Dutch East Indies, forming the western extremity of the island of Java.——A kind of painted or carved work resembling that of Japan, only more gaudy.

BARALITE. Black slate with cavities filled with a black powder ; a silico-aluminate of iron found at Baralon, Côte du Nord, France.

BARB. A horse of the Barbary breed, much esteemed for its swiftness.

BARBARIAN. A man in his rude savage state; an uncivilized person ; a cruel, savage, brutal man ; one destitute of pity and humanity. The Greeks and Romans denominated most foreign nations barbarians ; and many of these were less civilized than themselves, or unacquainted with their language, laws, and manners ; but with them the word was used less reproachfully than with us. Some derive the L. word *barbarus*, Gr. βαρβαρος, Russ. *varvar*, from Heb. *bârâr* (Pip. *barbár*) " to separate," " one who is separated," " a foreigner." Passow says, " the word was used of all defects which the Greeks thought foreign to themselves and natural to other nations; but as the Hellenes and barbarians were most of all *separated* by lan_guage, the word had always reference to this: γλωσσα βαρβαρα (foreign tongue). The word is most probably derived from the Berbers, *i. e.* the inhabitants of Berbery or Barbary, in the North of Africa ; from *bar-bar*, " sons of the west," which the West Arabs, &c., call themselves. Cf. Müller, Univ. Hist. b. xxxii. s. 1.

BAREGE. A light plain woollen stuff for shawls, ladies' dresses, &c., so named from being manufactured at Barége, at the foot of the Pyrenees, famous for its mineral waters.

BARNARDIA. A genus of Chinese bulbous plants, so called in honour of E. Barnard, Esq., F.R.S.

BARNHARDTITE. A mineral composed of copper and iron, from a mine on the land of Dan Barnhardt, Cabarras County, North Carolina ; also found at other places in the same county, and in the neighbourhood of Charlotte, in Mecklenburg County.

BARRERIA. A genus of plants, whose species are shrubs, natives of Guinea ; called after Prof. Barrère, of Perpignan.

BARRINGTONIA. A genus of plants, nat. or. *Myrtaceæ*, called after the Hon. Daines Barrington.—*Crabb.*

BARTSIA. A genus of plants, nat. or. *Scrophulariaceæ*, called after John Bartsch, a physician.—*Crabb.*

BASSEIN. Rice from Bassain or Bassein, a seaport town of Pegu, taken by the British, in May, 1852.

BASSIA, a genus of plants, nat. or. *Sapotaceæ*, named after Ferdinand Bassi, curator of the Botanic Garden as Bologna.—*Crabb.*

BASSORINE. A constitutuent part of a species of gum from Bassora, in Asiatic Turkey, as also of gum tragacanth and some gum resins.—*Ure.*

BASTITE. A mineral of an olive and pistaccio green, found in the euphotide of the Baste and other places in the Harz. It is another name for schiller spar.

BATIST (Fr. *batiste*). A French linen cloth of a very fine thread and very close tissue, used for pocket handkerchiefs and body linen, chiefly made in deps. Nord, Pas de Calais, and La Somme; but also made in the Netherlands, in Bohemia, Silesia, and Switzerland, and, those most esteemed, in India. It had its name from Baptiste, its first manufacturer.

BAUHINIA. A genus of plants, shrubs, or. *Monogynia*; natives of India; named in honour of the brothers Gaspard and John Bauhin, celebrated botanists.

BAULITE. A mineral, consisting of silica, alumina, lime, soda, and potash, analysed by Genth. The name was first given by Forchammer to a greyish-white porous metal from the Baula Mountain, in Iceland, having nearly the same composition as the crystals analysed by Genth.

BAVAROY. Formerly a kind of cloak or surtout; perhaps originally written *bavarois;* from Bavaria.

BAVAROISE. (Fr.) Tea sweetened with syrup of capillaire; a kind of milk posset, first made by the Bavarians.

BAYONET (Fr. *baionette*, Sp. *bayoneta*, It. *baionetta*). A short pointed instrument of iron, or broad dagger, formerly with a handle fitted to the bore of a gun, where it was inserted for use after the soldier had fired; but now made with an iron handle and ring which go over the muzzle of the piece, so that

the soldier fires with his bayonet fixed. (*Encyc.*)   Ford says
the bayonet is said to have been first used by some Basques at
Bayonne, in the war of 1814, who stuck their knives into their
muskets' muzzles; others assert that the bayonet was first invented in 1671; but it is without doubt of a much more
ancient origin.   The word does not appear in Palsgrave's
Dictionary, published in 1530.   In Cotgrave's Dictionary, first
published in 1611, we find "*bayonnette*, a kind of small flat
pocket dagger, furnished with knives; or a great knife to hang
at the girdle like a dagger;" also "*bayonnier*, an arbalestier
(an old word)," which is rendered "a crosse-bow-man, that
shoots in or serves with a crosse-bow; also a crosse-bow-
maker."   Again, Puységur, who was sent to Flanders in 1642,
in his memoirs speaks of the use of the bayonet at Bergues,
Ypres, Dixmunde, and Laquenoc.   Miège (Great French Dict.,
Lond. 1688) renders "*bayonette* (Fr.) a dagger, or knife dagger-
like, such as the dragoons wear."   Phillips (World of Words)
gives "*bayonette*, a long dagger much in use of late, and carried
by the grenadiers."   In the Dict. Anglo-Britan., or a General
Eng. Dict. (John Kersey, 1715), we find "*bayonette* (Fr.) a
broad dagger with a round taper handle, to stick in the muzzle
of a musket."   The New World of Words (Edw. Phillips,
fo. 1720) has "*bayonette*, a broad dagger without a guard, made
with a round taper handle, to stick in the muzzle of a musket,
so that it may serve instead of a pike to receive the charge of
a horse."   Les Travaux de Mars, ou l'Art de la Guerre (par
Manusson Mallet, Amst. 1685, tom. iii. 30) gives "une
bayonette, ou une petite lame montée dans un manche de bois;
le soldat s'en sert dans quelques occasions comme une demi-
pique, en mettant son manche dans le canon de son mousquet
ou son fusil."   The name of this instrument is also found
written *bagonet*, and we find also *baggonnetts* and *bajonetts*;
indeed, as late as 1735 the word was written and printed
bagonet.   In the Glossary appended to Memoirs Historical and
Military of the Marquis Feuquière (trans. from the French,
Lond. 1735) *bagonet* is rendered "a short broad dagger made
with iron handles and rings that go over the muzzle of the
firelock, and are screwed fast, so that the soldier fires with the

bagonet on the muzzle of the piece, and is ready to act against horse." Roquefort (Gloss. de la Langue Romaine, 1808) renders *baionier* " arbalâtrier, a crossbow-man." The general opinion seems to be that the bayonet was first invented at Bayonne, in France, whence it had its name. Mr. I. Y. Akerman (Notes on Origin and Hist. Bayonet, Archæol. xxviii., 428) says, " I have sought in vain for the origin and source of the tradition that the bayonet was invented at Bayonne. The story runs that in a battle which took place in a small hamlet in the environs of that city, in the middle of the seventeenth century, between some Basque peasants and a band of Spanish smugglers, the former, having exhausted their ammunition, defeated their opponents by charging them with their long knives fastened in the muzzle of their muskets. Such an event may have occurred, but it requires authentication, and the relation begets a suspicion that the mere similarity of name has laid the foundation of the supposed connection of the bayonet with Bayonne. True or false, the story is immortalized in the verse of Voltaire, who, in the eighth book of the " Henriade," thus alludes to this occasion :—

> " Cette arme, que jadis, pour dépeupler la terre,
> Dans Bayonne inventa le démon de la guerre,
> Rassemble en même temps, digne fruit de l'enfer,
> Ce qu'ont de plus terrible et la flamme et le fer."

Voltaire, however, was not the inventor of the figment, if it is really to be regarded as such, for we find *bayonet* thus glossed in the Dictionary of Ménage, published in 1694 :— " Bayonette, sorte de poignard, ainsi appelée de la ville de Baionne." On the whole it would seem most probable that the word *bayonet* is a diminutive formed from *Bayonne* (in Sp. Bayóna). It does not follow, however, that the bayonet was invented at Bayonne in France. There are places called Bayon and Bayona in Spain, in provinces Oviedo, Pontevedra, Toledo, and Madrid.——In machinery, a term applied to pins which play in and out of holes made to receive them, and which thus serve to engage or disengage parts of the machinery (*Nicholson*).

BEAUGENCY. A fine red wine made from grapes growing in the neighbourhood of Beaugency, France, dep. Loiret.

BEAUJOLAIS. A celebrated wine made at Beaujolais, a district of France, part of the ancient Lyonnais, the capital of which was Beaujeau.

BEAUNE. A fine wine made from grapes grown at Beaune, a town of France, dep. Côte-d'Or, renowned for its vineyards.

BEAUVAIS. A beautiful tapestry made at Beauvais, in France, dep. Oise.

BECHAMEL. A fine French white sauce made of strong pale veal gravy, and now very much served at good English tables ; said to have been named after the Marquis de Béchamel, maître d'hôtel to Louis XIV. *Sauce à la béchamel: De la morue à la béchamel ; Une béchamel de brochet : Béchamel maigre.*

BEDLAMITE. An inhabitant of a madhouse; a madman ; from *Bedlam*, a hospital for lunatics in Lambeth, Surrey, properly Bethlehem, and anciently a religious house. Shakspeare used *bedlam* figuratively for a place of uproar.

BEGONIA. A genus of plants, nat. or. *Begoniaceæ*, called after Michael Begon.—*Crabb.*

BELCHER. A kind of neckkerchief of a blue colour with white spots (blue birdseye). In pugilistic encounters it is the fashion for each combatant to provide himself with a quantity of kerchiefs, which may be used either as hand or neckkerchiefs, of a different colour and pattern from those of his opponent. These kerchiefs are distributed among the supporters of each party, who after the fight pay to the successful champion a sovereign each for the same. The Belcher neckkerchief derives its name from the celebrated pugilist James Belcher.

BENEDICT. A married man ; a man newly married ; so called from Benedict, a young lord of Padua, one of the *dramatis personæ* in *Much Ado about Nothing*, who says, " When I said I would die a bachelor, I did not think that I should live to be married."

BENGAL. A thin stuff made of silk and hair, for women's apparel, so called from Bengal.—*Bailey; Johnson.*

BERAUNITE. A mineral, supposed to be a hydrous phosphate of peroxide of iron, found in limonite near Beraun, in Bohemia.

BERENGELITE. A mineral consisting of carbon, hydrogen, and oxygen, found in the province of St. Juan de Berengela, in South America.

BERENICE. In chemistry, another name for amber, perhaps from its power of attracting hair &c. Berenice, in astronomy, is a name given to seven stars in the tail of the constellation Leo, in honour of Berenice, wife of Ptolemy Evergetes, who offered her hair in sacrifice to the gods for the preservation of her husband.

BERESITE. A mineral, a fine-grained granite containing pyrites ; from near Beresof, in the Ural.

BERGAMO. A coarse tapestry manufactured with flocks of wool, silk, cotton, hemp, and ox or goat's hair, said to have been invented at Bergamo, in Italy.—*Encyc.*

BERGAMOT (Fr. *Bergamotte*). A species of pear (*Bergamotte de Hollande, Bergamotte Suisse*) ; a species of citron, at first casually produced by an Italian, who grafted a citron on the stock of a Bergamot pear-tree, the fruit of which has a fine taste and smell, and whose essential oil is in high esteem as a perfume. According to some the pear was named from Bergamo, in Italy, whence it is said to have been first brought ; others assert that the pear was first brought from Turkey, and they derive the word from the Turkish *beg, bey,* lord ; *armoud,* pear ; " prince of pears."——A species of snuff perfumed with bergamot. In France, the word *bergamotte* is also used to denote little boxes of sugar plums (*bonbonnières*), lined with the peel of this kind of citron.

BERGERA. A genus of plants nat. or. *Monogynia,* named in honour of Professor Berger, of Kiel.

BERGIA. A genus of plants, nat. or. *pentagynia,* named in honour of Dr. Bergius, of Stockholm.

BERGMANITE. A variety of scapolite, by some regarded as a distinct species, of a grayish colour, of different shades ; found in Norway ; named after Bergman, the mineralogist.

BERTHIERA. A genus of plants, of which there is but one

species, the *Berthiera Quianensis*; a shrub, native of Guinea, named in honour of Professor Berthier, of Paris.

BERTHIERITE. A mineral, consisting of antimony, sulphur, iron, and zinc; named after M. Berthier.

BERTHOLETIA. A name given to the Brazil nut tree, a tall tree of South America, the fruit of which is well known in our markets; named after M. Bertholet.

BERYTUS. A genus of hemipters, an order of insects, so named from Berytus, now Beyrout, Syria.

BERZELINE. A name for sileniuret of copper, given in honour of Berzelius. A mineral occurring in minute octahedral crystals, found in Italy, is thus named by Necker.

BESIDERY, or Le Bezi d'Hery; the wilding of Heri. A pear, so named from the Forest of Heri, in Bretagne, between Rheims and Nantes, where it was found.

BERKELEYA. A genus of small ball-shaped sea-weeds; named in honour of the Rev. Dr. Berkeley.

BERLIN. A vehicle of the chariot kind, named from Berlin, Prussia, where it was first made. Others derive the name from It. *berlina*, a sort of stage or pillory, and a coach.

BESLERIA. A genus of plants, the species of which are either shrubs or perennials; named after Basil Besler, a German botanist.

BESANT or BEZANT. A very ancient gold coin stamped at Byzantium. See Bezant.

BESSEMER. A steel invented by Mr. Bessemer.

BETONY (Fr. *bétoine*). A name common to different species of plants of the genus *Betonica*, celebrated for almost every medicinal virtue. The word *Betonica* is said to be corrupted from *Vettonica*, which is further derived from the Vettones or Vetones, an ancient people of Spain, who first used this plant. Much has been written in praise of betony; indeed, in Italy, "You have more virtues than betony" is a proverbial compliment.

BEZANT. A round flat piece of bullion without any impression, which is supposed to have been the current coin of Byzantium. The *bezant* was, in all probability, introduced into coat armour by the Crusaders. Being always of metal, bezants ought to be emblazoned *or*, or *argent*.—*Crabb*.

BEZANTY. In heraldry, an epithet for a cross composed of bezants. See BEZANT.

BIDDERY or BIDRI. A species of inlaid ware of excellent form and graceful patterns, composed of copper, lead, tin, and spelter; so named from being made at Biddree, a town of Hindustan, in the presidency of Bombay.

BIEBERITE. A mineral of a flesh and rose-red colour, found in the rubbish of old mines at Bieber, near Hanau, and at Leogang, in Salzburg.

BIGGIN (formerly *biggen*, Fr. *béguin*). A sort of female head-dress; so named from being worn by the Beguines, a religious sect in Flanders, who, without having taken the monastic vows, are united for the purposes of devotion and charity, and who live together in houses called *beguinages*.

BIGNONIA. An extensive genus of plants, consisting mostly of shrubs, natives of South America, named in honour of the Abbé Bignon, librarian to Louis XIV.

BIGOT. Derived by Ménage from "*by God;*" by others from *bigote* (Sp.) a moustache. Probably from the Beguttæ or Beguines, a religious community in Belgium.—*S. F. Creswell*.

BILBO. A sort of rapier, so named from Bilboa, in Spain, where the best were made. Hence probably *bilboes*, spars or bolts of iron, with shackles, used to confine the feet of prisoners at sea; hence, the punishment of offenders in this manner is called by the same name.

BISANTIUM, BESANT, or BESANTINE. A gold coin of Byzantium, formerly current in England, equal to half a ducane silver, or two shillings sterling. See BESANT.

BISTOURY (Fr. *bistouri*). A surgical instrument for making incisions, either fixed in a handle like a knife, or else the blade moveable like a lancet; named from Pistoria, in Italy, where it was first made.

BIVONÆA. Cruciferous plants found in Italy, named after M. A. Bivoni Bernardi.

BLAKEA. A genus of plants, nat. or. *Monogynia*, named after M. Blake.

BLANKET. A cover for a bed, made of coarse wool loosely woven, and used for securing against cold. Some assert that blankets had their name from three brothers at Worcester, by whom they were first invented; that, according to Nash's history, a family of the name resided there in the reign of Edward I., and that at Caines, adjoining the city, is a place still called the Blanquets. According to another writer, blankets were first manufactured in Bristol, and derived their name from their inventors, who lived either in St. Thomas Street or Temple Street, although the writer does not deny that the inventors may have been Worcestershire men. A correspondent of *N. and Q.* says :—" There were three brothers of the name of Blanket who were connected with Bristol in the Middle Ages. I find it first occurring in the annals of the city in the year 1340, when Thomas Blanket was bailiff ; his brother Edmund held the same office in 1349, and was member of Parliament for the town in 1369, to which dignity a third brother, Edward, who was the eldest of the three, had been elected in 1362. The trio seem to have been extensively engaged in the manufacture of coarse woollen cloths, for which at that time Bristol was much celebrated ; but to Thomas, the youngest of the three, the introduction of the article of bedding called after the family name is probably due. The cloths made by the brothers, although of the coarser sorts, were sold by them in large quantities to be made into garments for the peasantry, who until their time had worn only coarse cloths made from hemp. Blankets soon came to be used by sportsmen, soldiers, and travellers, in lieu of the loose mantle and puckered cloak and cape, which, as well as the long loose robe or gown, were inconvenient. The former could be readily thrown across the shoulders, or used to wrap about the wearer in cold or wet weather ; and Edward I. found them very useful in his army when encamped against the Welsh and Scots. When stump bedsteads came into use among the wealthy, about the reign of Edward III. (before which time they had slept on rushes, straw, or fern, laid upon the floor), blankets, soon afterwards manufactured, came to be part of the necessary furniture, and repeated mention is made of them in the Expenses of the

Great Wardrobe of Edward III., from 29 Sep., 1347, to 31
Jan., 1349." See Archæologia, vol. xxxi.   In Rymer's Fœdera,
and in the Close Rolls of 13 Edw. III., we find letters of protection given to Thomas Blanket against the burgesses of
Bristol, who had obstructed him in the manufacture of blankets.
Bailey gives also *plonkets*, a kind of coarse woollen cloth (An.
1, R. III., c. 8), " otherwise called *vervise*" (*Cowel*).——Among
printers, woollen cloths or white baize laid between the tympans
of a printing-press to produce a fair impression of the letter.
The French has *blanchet*, the blanket of a printer's press, which
would seem to be a diminutive of *blanche*, white. Bailey derives
blanket in both senses from the French *blanchet*, and gives also
blanquet as the name of a sort of pea.

BLARNEY. Smooth deceitful talk, flattery (*Irish*). Blarney
is the name of a castle in the south of Ireland, in a town of
the same name, formerly the seat of the powerful clan of Mac-
Carty, created Lord Muskerry, and celebrated from a curious
superstition.   T. Crofton Croker (Res. S. Ireland, 1824, p.
306) says, " a stone in the highest part of the castle wall is
pointed out to the visitors which is supposed to give whoever
kisses it the peculiar privilege of deviating from veracity with
unblushing countenance whenever it may be convenient—hence
the well-known phrase *blarney*."   The celebrated groves of
Blarney are about five miles from Cork. Others derive the
word *blarney* from Fr. *baliverne*, a lie, fib, gull ; also a babbling
or idle discourse.

BLETHIA. A variety of tropical bulbous plants, named
after Louis Blethia.

BLETONISM. The faculty of perceiving and indicating
subterraneous springs and currents by sensation ; so called
from Bleton, a Frenchman, who was supposed to possess this
faculty.

BLOOMER. Formerly a sort of female dress in imitation
of male attire, first set on foot by Mrs. Bloomer, wife of Colonel
Bloomer, an American.

BLUCHER. A kind of half-boot, named in honour of
General Blücher, who commanded the Prussians at Water-
loo.

BOBBY. A slang term for a policeman, because the force was introduced by the late Sir Robert Peel.—*S. F. Creswell.*

BOCCONIA. The tree celandine, a genus of beautiful plants, natives of Mexico ; named after Paolo Bocconia, a Sicilian monk, physician, and botanical writer.

BODENITE. A mineral ; colour from reddish-brown to nearly black ; from Boden, near Marienberg, in the Saxon Erzgebirge.

BODLEIAN. Pertaining to Sir Thomas Bodley, who founded a celebrated library at Oxford, in the sixteenth century.

BŒBERA. A family of plants, nat. or. *Polygamia æqualis,* found in America; named in honour of M. Bœber.

BŒHMERIA. A genus of plants, nat. or. *Tetrandria,* natives of America and the West Indies, the species of which are mostly shrubs ; named after George Rudolph Bœhmer, professor of botany at Wittenberg, in Germany.

BŒOTIAN. Stupid ; from *Baotia* (βοιωτια), a country of ancient Greece, whose inhabitants were remarkable for a natural stupidity. " In this Bœotian era of the Cæsars the prefect of police is the god of letters."—*Letters of an Englishman on Louis Napoleon in the " Times."*

BOERHAAVIA. Hogweed; a genus of exotic plants, named after the celebrated physician and botanist Boerhaave, who was born at Woarbout, near Leyden, in 1688.

BOHEA (in Chinese *woo-e-cha*). A sort of coarse or low-priced tea brought from Woo-e (called by Europeans *Bohea*) in Fo-këen, China. Indeed, black tea is chiefly brought from Woo-e. See Grosier, vol. 1, 467.

BOLDOA. A genus of Indian plants, named after Dr. Boldo.

BOLOGNA. A sausage or polony, first made at Bologna, in Italy.

BOLOGNIAN, BOLONIAN, BONONIAN, or BO-LOGNA. A variety of sulphate of barytes, found in roundish masses ; first discovered near Bologna, in Italy.

BOLOGNINO. A copper coin at Bologna and its neighbourhood, the same with the bajoccho.

BOLSOVER. A yellowish limestone combining carbonate of soda with carbonate of lime, and containing no organic remains ; from Bolsover, in Derbyshire. The new palace at Westminster is built of this stone.

BOLTONIA. A genus of North American perennial shrubs, named in honour of Mr. Bolton, a botanist of Halifax.

BOLTONITE. A granular mineral of a greyish cr yellowish colour, chiefly found at Bolton, Massachusetts.

BOMBITE. A blueish-black mineral of impalpable composition, found in Bombay ; apparently a variety of flinty slate.—*Shepard.*

BONAPARTEA. A genus of Peruvian plants, named in honour of Napoleon Bonaparte.

BONAPARTISM. The policy or manners of Napoleon Bonaparte.

BONATEA. A genus of plants, natives of the Cape of Good Hope, named in honour of Professor Bonata.

BON CHRETIEN ("good Christian"). A pear, said to have been so called from the name of a gardener.

BONDY. A fine large pear, which probably had its name from the Forest of Bondy, in France, dep. Seine.

BONNEMAISONEA. A genus of plants, nat. or. *Algæ;* named after Bonnemaison, the French cryptogamist.

BONNETIA. A tree of which only one species is known, growing in Cayenne and Guiana ; named in honour of M. Charles Bonnet, a naturalist, philosopher, and distinguished metaphysician, &c.

BONPLANDIA (Fr. *bonplandie*). A plant from which the bark angustora, used in fever, is obtained.——" The name of two kinds of American trees ; so called in honour of M. Bonpland, the celebrated traveller."—*Bescherelle.*

BONSDORFITE. A sort of mineral found near Abo, in Finland ; named after Bonsdorf, the mineralogist.

BONTIA. A plant, an evergreen much cultivated at Barbadoes for making hedges ; named after Jacobus Bontius, a distinguished physician and naturalist of Batavia, author of *De Medicinâ Indorum,* &c. &c.

BORBONIA. A genus of plants, the species of which are

shrubs, natives of the Cape of Good Hope; named after Gaston de Bourbon, Duke of Orleans.

BORDEAUX. A celebrated wine made at Bordeaux, a city and seaport of France, on the Garonne.

BORNEEN. The name given to a compound of carbon and hydrogen, found in valeric acid, and which on exposure to moisture acquires the properties of Borneo camphor ; which latter, according to Pereira, rarely comes to this country as a commercial article.

BORNEOL. Another name for Borneo camphor.

BORYA. A genus of North American shrubs ; nat. or. *Digynia;* named in honour of M. Bory de St. Vincent.

BOSCIA. A genus of shrubs or small trees, natives of the Cape of Good Hope ; named from L. Bosc, the French naturalist.——A genus of coleopterous five-jointed insects, containing five species, from the United States.

BOSEA. A genus of plants, nat. or. *Digynia,* of which there is but one species, a native of the Canaries ; named after E. G. Bose, a German botanist.

BOSTON. A complicated game of cards still played in Paris, said to have been originally from Boston, in America.

BOSSICEA. A genius of leguminous plants named in honour of M. Bossien Lamartinière.

BOSWELLIA. A genus of plants, one species of which yields the gum resin called *thus,* or frankincense, the olibanum of commerce, so much used in the Roman Catholic Church ; named in honour of Dr. J. Boswell, of Edinburgh.

BOSWELLISM. A peculiarity of James Boswell, a writer of merit, well known as the friend of Dr. Johnson.

BOULANGERITE. A mineral sulphuret of antimony and lead, occurring abundantly at Molières, in France, dep. Gard ; also in Lapland, Tuscany, &c. &c. ; named after M. Boulanger.

BOULINIS or BOULYNIS. A copper coin in Italy, answering to an English penny ; so called from having been struck at Bologna.

BOURNONITE. A mineral of a metallic lustre, found in the Hartz and in other places in Europe ; and also in Potosi, in

Mexico. It was first found at Endellion, near Redruth, in Cornwall, and hence called endellionite by Count Bournon, after whom it has since been named *bournonite*.

BOURRERIA. A genus of West Indian trees (the *Ehretia Bourreria* of Linnæus); named in honour of M. Bourer.

BOUSTRAPA. A nickname given to Louis Napoleon, suggestive of three important events in the career of the Prince; from *Bou* for Boulogne, *stra* Strasbourg, *pa* Paris. —*Times*, 11 Jan. 1853, p. 5, c. 2.

BOUVARDIA. A genus of South American plants, nat. or. *Monogynia*; named in honour of Dr. Bouvard.

BOUGIE. In Continental Europe, the name given to a candle originally and still sometimes made of wax. According to Corruvias, the Sp. *bugia* is *quasi buquica*, from *buco*, because in making the bougie it is passed through a hole. The word is more correctly derived from *Boujah* (found *Bugie*), a town of Algeria, whence the French originally imported both their wax and their bougies. The place has still a considerable trade in wax. According to Scaliger, the Moors also called a monkey *bugia*, because a great many of them were imported from Boujah. Cf. Ménage, Dict. Etym. "Bougie;" Gramaye, Afrique, liv. ii. ch. 10; Scaliger, contre Cardan, 213; Kimchi, Lex. voc. "Semamith;" Juvenal, Sat. x. "Quales, &c.;" Pierre Dau, Hist. de Barbarie, liv. i. ch. 6; Strabo, liv. xvii.; Bochart, Col. des Phœn. 539; and P. Labbe, Etym. Franç. part ii. p. 16.——A long slender instrument, introduced through the urethra into the bladder to remove obstacles. It is usually made of slips of *waxen* linen coiled into a cylindrical or slightly conical form by rolling them on any hard smooth surface. It is also made of catgut, elastic gum, and metal; but those of waxen linen are generally preferred.

BOVEY. Brown lignite, an inflammable fossil resembling in many of its properties bituminous wood; found at Bovey Hatfield, near Exeter.

BOWENITE. A mineral of a bright apple-green colour found at Smithfield, in Rhode Island, in nodules imbedded in granular limestone, analysed by Bowen.

BOWIE, BOWIE-KNIFE. A long knife or dagger used

by hunters in the Western States of America; so named from an American colonel.—*S. F. Creswell.*

BOWLESIA. A plant; nat. or. *Umbelliferœ*, named after Bowles, author of Travels in Spain.

BRAGATIONITE. A silicate in form closely agreeing with epidote; found in the Achmatowsk Mine, district of Slatoust, in the Ural; probably named after Prince Bragation.

BRADLEYA. A genus of plants, nat. or. *Monadelphia,* the species of which are shrubs, natives of India and China; named after Professor Bradley, of Cambridge.

BREGUET. In England, a term usually applied to a particular kind of watch-key and chain. The word is properly applicable to the watches made by M. Bréguet, a celebrated manufacturer, who was born in 1747 at Neufchâtel, in Switzerland, and died in 1823 at Paris. M. Bréguet rendered very great services to both astronomy, natural philosophy, and navigation; was member of the Bureau des Longitudes, and afterwards of the Institute, where he replaced Carnot.

BRAHMINISM. The religion of the Brahmins.

BREISLAKITE. A newly-discovered Vesuvian mineral which lines the small cavities in the lava of Scala, and in that of Olebano; named from Breislak, a celebrated Italian naturalist.—*Journal of Science.*

BREITHAUPTITE. A mineral consisting of nickel, iron, antimony, and sulphuret of lead, found at Andreasberg; named after Breithaupt.

BREVICITE. A mineral, a hydrous silicate, found in white fibrous subfoliated masses, probably in syenite, near Brevig, in Norway.

BREWSTERITE. A mineral found in attached crystals at Strontian, in Argyleshire; at the Giant's Causeway; at St. Turpet, in the Breisgau; in dep. Isère, France; and in the Pyrenees; named after Sir David Brewster.

BREWSTOLINE. A mineral occurring in crystal of topaz, chrysoberl, quartz, crystals from Quebec, and amethyst from Siberia, where it was detected by Sir David Brewster.

BREYNIA. A genus of plants, the only species of which is the *Breynia disticha*, a native of New Caledonia, &c.; named in honour of **J.** Breynius, and his son **J. P.** Breynius, both celebrated botanists. Bescherelle says. '' De **J.** Breynius, bot. Belge. probablement le même que Jacques Breyn de Dantzig.''

BRIAREAN. Hundred-handed, like Briareus, son of Titan and Terra, one of the giants, feigned by the poets to have had a hundred arms and fifty heads.

BRIGAND. A robber; probably derived from the Brigantes, a people of Continental Europe; or from the Brigantes, the most northern and powerful people who ravaged Great Britain in the time of the Romans, and who were subdued by Cerialis. They probably had their appellation from the W. *brig*, a top or summit, from frequenting the tops of the mountains. The **W.** *brigant* is a summit; also a highlander.

BRITANNIA. A metallic compound or alloy, consisting chiefly of block tin, with some antimony, and a small portion of copper and brass (*Encyc. Dom. Econ.*) Explains itself.

BRITANNICA (Gr. βρεταννικα). A plant, so called because it is said by the ancients to have been discovered by the Friezlanders on the coast of the British Channel.—*Crabb.*

BROBDIGNAGIAN. Gigantic; from the kingdom of Brobdignag, in Gulliver's Travels.—*S. F. Creswell.*

BROCHANTITE. A basic sulphate of copper, occurring in emerald-green crystals, at Katherinenburg, in Siberia; named by Levy after Brochant de Villiers.

BROMELIA. A genus of plants, the species of which are shrubs, natives of South America. Jamaica, &c.; named after Bromel, the Swedish botanist.—*Crabb.*

BROOKITE. A mineral consisting of titanic acid and red oxide of iron; first observed by Mr. Brooke in crystals from Snowdon.

BROUGHAM. A four-wheeled carriage named after Lord Brougham.

BROWALLIA. A genus of plants, nat. or. *Scrophulariaceæ*, named after J. Browallius, Bishop of Abo, in Finland.

BROWNEA. A genus of plants, nat. or. *Leguminaceæ*, called after Dr. Browne, the historian of Jamaïca.—*Crabb.*

BROWNISM. The doctrines or religious creed of the

Brownists, who rejected both episcopacy and presbyterianism. They had their name from Robert Brown, a dissenter from the Church of England, who left England with his congregation and settled at Middleburg, in Zealand.

BROYHAN. A celebrated white Hanoverian beer first brewed by Cord Broyhan in 1526. It is doubtless the same as that called Halberstadtische Briehan by Zedler.

BRUCEA. A genus of plants, nat. or. *Xanthoxylaceæ*, the species of which are evergreen ornamental shrubs, natives of the East Indies ; named after Bruce, the Abyssinian traveller.

BRUCITE. Native hydrate of magnesia, named in honour of A. Bruce, Esq. The name has also been given by American mineralogists to chondrodite.—*Dana*.

BRUMSFELSIA. A genus of plants, the species of which are shrubs, natives of the East Indies ; named after Otho Brunsfelsius, a monk, physician, and botanist of Mentz.

BRUNIA. A genus of plants, shrubs, nat. or. *Escalloniaceæ*, principally natives of the Cape of Good Hope ; named in honour of Cornelius Brun, the celebrated traveller.

BRUNONIA. A genus of plants, natives of Australia, named in honour of Robert Brown, the distinguished botanist.

BRUNSVEGIA. A name given to the *Amarythis orientalis*, a splendid species of the genus, in honour of the Brunswick family, one of great antiquity.

BRUTIA. A resinous pitch used to make the *oleum picinum ;* from Brutia (Brutium ?), in Italy.

BUCELLAS. A wine named from a small village near Lisbon.

BUCHNERA. A genus of plants, the species of which are shrubs, natives of the Cape of Good Hope ; called after Buchner, a German botanist.

BUCHOLZITE. A newly discovered fibrous mineral, of great hardness, consisting chiefly of silex and alumina; named after M. Bucholz. A fibrous mineral called fibrolite, brought from the Carnatic, is supposed to be identical with bucholzite. An Americn mineral so called is nothing but kyanite.

BUCKLANDIA. A fossil plant supposed to have belonged to the *Liliaceæ :* named in honour of Dr. Buckland, the geologist.

BUCKLANDITE. A silicate found in small crystals in the Neskiel Mine at Arendal, in Sweden; and also, under other circumstances, in Siberia, and at the Lake of Laach, near the Rhine; probably named in honour of Dr. Buckland.

BUDDHISM or BOODHISM. The doctrines of the Buddhists; a system of religion in Eastern Asia   It teaches that at distant intervals a *Boodh* or deity appears, to restore the world from a state of ignorance and decay, and then sinks into a state of entire non-existence or *Nirvana*, or rather, perhaps, of bare existence, without attributes, action, or consciousness. Four *Boodhs* have thus appeared and passed into *Nirvana*, the last of whom, Guadama, became incarnate about 500 years before Christ. The objects of worship, until another *Boodh* appears, are the relics and images of Guadama.

BUDDLEA. A genus of plants, shrubs, natives of Jamaica; named in honour of Adam Buddle, a botanist.

BUHL. Ornamental cabinet furniture in which mother-of-pearl, tortoiseshell, and various coloured woods are inlaid with brass; so called after its inventor, a German.

BULLACE. The wild plum (called also bullace plum and bullace-tree), the *Prunus instititia* of Linnæus. The word is found written *bullis*, and is corrupted from *burdelais* or *burlace*, q. v.——The bully-tree, a native of the West Indies.

BUNGALOW. In Bengal, a thatched cottage, such as is usually occupied by Europeans in the provinces or in the military cantonments, and constructed of wood, bamboo, mats, and thatch. The word is a corruption of the Bengáli *bánglá*, which Professor Wilson thinks may be from *Banga*, Bengal.

BUNKUM. In America, high-flown talk, bragging. The origin of *bunkum* is explained in Wheeler's History of North Carolina. "Several years ago, in Congress, the member for that state, a resident of No. 6, County of Buncombe, rose to address the House, without any extraordinary power in manner or matter to interest the audience. Many members left the hall. Very naïvely the orator told those who remained that they might go too; he should speak for some time, ' but he was only talking for Buncombe.'" Cf. Bartlett, Dictionary of Americanisms ; Haliburton ; Illustrated News for June 26, 1858 ; and N. & Q. 2nd S. vi. 92 ; 3rd S. iii. 427.

BURDWAN. An oriental dish of high savour, made with a young fowl or chicken parboiled ; named from Burdwan, a district of British India, prov. Bengal.

BURGUNDY. A celebrated wine, so called from Burgundy (*Bourgogne*), an ancient province of France, where it is produced ; a district whose soil is fertile in grain and fruits, and above all in renowned wines.

BURLACE. A sort of grape ; a contraction of *burdelais* : from the Fr. *bourdelais*, "variété de raisin à grains ovales et noirs ;" from *Le Bourdelais*, pays de Guyenne, of which the capital is Bordeaux.

BURKE. To suffocate by fixing an adhesive plaister or other obstruction over the nose and mouth ; a crime rendered notorious by an Irishman named Burke, who sold the bodies of his victims for dissection. He was executed in 1829.—— Metaphorically, *to burke* a report or an invention is to exclude it from publicity, to consign it to oblivion.

BURMANNIA. A genus of plants of which there are two species, natives of Ceylon, Virginia, and Carolina ; named in honour of John Burmann, M.D., Professor of Botany at Amsterdam, author of Thesaurus Zeylanicus, and Decades Rariorum Plantarum Africanarum.

BURSERA. A genus of West Indian plants of but one species, the *Bursera gummifera* or Jamaica birch-tree, which yields the gum elemi ; named in honour of Joachim Bursera, pupil of Caspar Bauhin, a great collector of plants, whose Herbarium, in thirty volumes, may be seen at Upsala.

BUSBY. A sort of fur hat worn by the light cavalry, copied from the Hungarian or Polish ; said to have derived its name from Dr. Richard Busby, a celebrated master of Westminster School, who wore a hat of a somewhat similar description. Dr. Busby was born in 1606 : in 1640 he became head master of the Westminster School, which appointment he retained till his death in 1695, a period of fifty-five years.

BÜTTNERIA. A genus of plants, whose species consist of shrubby perennials; named in honour of A. Büttner.

BYTOWNITE. A mineral, a silicate occurring in large boulders near Bytown, Canada West.

BYZANT, BEZANT, or BYZANTINE. A gold coin of the value of £15 sterling, so called from having been coined at Byzantium. Also a piece of gold of the value of £15, offered by the king on certain festivals.—*Camden; Ash.*

C.

CABAL. A number of persons united in some close design, usually to promote their private views in church or state by intrigue; a jumble. The Fr. *cabale* is a club, society, or combination; the It. *cabala*, knowledge of secret things; the Sp. *cabala*, secret science; *cabal*, perfect, just, exact; probably from the Heb. קבל *kabal*, to take, receive, accept, whence *cabala*, certain traditions of the Jews; but according to some, *cabal* was the appellation given to the ministry of Charles II., the initials of their names being *C*lifford, *A*shley, *B*uckingham, *A*rlington, *L*auderdale; "than which," says Hume, "never was a more dangerous ministry in England, nor one more noted for pernicious councils."

CABANNAH. A cigar originally from Cuba, so named from the manufacturer. In the "present age of progress" they are, in England, principally made of cabbage-leaves.

CACHOLONG. An opaque or milk-white chalcedony, a variety of quartz. It often envelops common chalcedony, and is sometimes associated with flint. According to Webster, the word is said to be from *Cach*, the name of a river in Bucharia (in the empire of Russia), and *cholon*, a Calmuc word for stone.

CADILLAC. A sort of pear, from Cadillac, in France, dep. Gironde.

CADMEAN or CADMIAN. A name applied to the ancient Greek or Ionic letters, such as they were brought by Cadmus into Greece from Phœnicia, whence Herodotus calls them

Phœnician letters. They were the sixteen simple letters of the alphabet as follows :—

$$\alpha, \beta, \gamma, \delta, \varepsilon, \iota, \varkappa, \lambda, \mu, \nu, \circ, \pi, \varrho, \sigma, \tau, \upsilon.$$

According to some writers, Cadmus was not the inventor, nor even the importer of Greek letters, but only the modeller and reformer thereof; and it was hence they acquired the appellation of Cadmean or Phœnician letters, whereas before that time they were called Pelasgian letters.

CÆSALPINIA. A genus of plants, the species of which are natives of hot climates, and afford the wood used in dyeing known in commerce under the name of Brazil-wood. So named in honour of Cæsalpinus, chief physician to Pope Clement VIII.

CÆSIA. A genus of liliacious plants, natives of Australasia; named by Mr. Brown in honour of Frederico Cæsio, a Roman nobleman illustrious for his patronage and cultivation of science, who founded the celebrated academy of the Lyncæi at Rome, in 1603, whence have sprung most of the scientific associations of Europe.

CÆSIO. A genus of fishes, having the dorsal and anal spines remarkably large, and their base coated with scales; probably named in honour of Cæsio. See CÆSIA.

CAHORS. A celebrated French wine made from a black grape growing in the neighbourhood of Cahors, dep. Lot.

CAIRNGORM. A yellow or brown variety of rock-crystal, or crystallized quartz, found in the mountain of Cairngorm, in Scotland.

CAJETA. In entomology, the name under which Cramer figures the Gmelinian *Noctua fullonica*. The word *cajeta* is either derived from Gaëta, in Italy; or from a surname formed from *Caius*.

CALATRAVA. A Spanish military order, named from Calatrava, in Spain.

CALCAVALLA. A kind of sweet wine from Portugal, doubtless named from a locality.

CALEDONITE. A mineral consisting of the sulphate and carbonate of lead, and carbonate of copper, occurring at Leadhills, in Scotland; named from Caledonia, the ancient name of Scotland. It is also found in Cumberland, in the Hartz, and in Missouri.

CALEMBOURG. (Fr.) A pun, witticism; from a German Count *Kahlemberg*, noted for his blunders in the French language. (*Brande*. See instance in N. & Q., 3rd S., V., 257.) Kahlenberg is the name of a hill in Austria, on the Danube, on whose side the army of Sobieski arrived to the rescue of Vienna when besieged by the Turks in 1683; and Calemberg is the name of a château near Coburg, in Germany.

CALEPIN. Formerly a common name for a lexicon, and still used in French for a memorandum-book, scrap-book, or common-place book. The word is derived from Ambrose Calepin or Da Calepio, a celebrated grammarian and lexicographer of the fifteenth century, a native of Bergamo, in Italy; author of a polyglot dictionary, of which there are many editions with the improvements of later philologists. Cf. Moreri; Tiraboschi.

CALEYA. A genus of Australian bulbous-rooted plants named in honour of George Cayley, the eminent botanist.

CALICO. A kind of cotton cloth, so named from Calicut, on the Malabar coast, where it was first manufactured. It is now also made both in Europe and the United States.

CALIPPIC. In chronology, a term applied to a period of 76 years, continually recurring, after which it was supposed by Calippus, an Athenian astronomer, that the lunations, &c., of the moon would return again in the same order; but this is incorrect, as it brings them too late by a day in 225 years.

CALUMBA, COLUMBO, COLUMBA, or COLOMBO. A root of an aromatic smell and pungent bitter taste, used as a tonic, imported from Colombo, in Ceylon. According to Webster, it is the root of the *Cocculus palmatus*, growing in Mozambique, where its native name is *kalumb*.

CALVINISM. The theological tenets or doctrines of Calvin, who was born in Picardy, in France, and in 1536 chosen professor of divinity and minister of a church in Geneva.

CAMBRIC (Fr. *toile de Cambrai*). A very fine white linen, named from Cambray, in French Flanders, where it was first manufactured by the Dutch emigrants in 1563, at which time

it was chiefly used for large ruffs.   The fabric sometimes
called cambric in England is made of cotton ; that of France
and Ireland, of flax.   Cf. also Anders. Comm. 11, 170; Stow's
Annals, 869, ed. Howes ; Strutt's Dresses, 209. ·

CAMELLIA.   A genus of beautiful flowering shrubs, the
principal of which are the *Camellia Japonica*, and the *Camellia
sasanqua*, natives of China and Japan; named in honour of
G. J. Kamel or Camellus, a Jesuit and botanist.

CAMERARIA.   A genus of plants, the species of which
are natives of South America and Ceylon; called after J. Came-
rarius, a botanist of Nuremberg.—*Crabb.*

CAMPEACHY.   A tree and wood (logwood) much used in
dyeing ; named from the Bay of Campeachy, in Spanish
America, whence it is brought.

CANAANITE.   A mineral allied to scapolite, from Canaan,
Connecticut, U.S.

CANARINA.   A genus of plants, nat. or. *Campanulaceæ* ;
so called because they come from the Canaries. —*Crabb.*

CANARY.   A wine, the same with sack, from the Canaries,
where the Spaniards first planted vines.   Hence *canary*, name
of an old dance.   Indeed, Shakspeare has used the word as a
verb for *to dance*, in a kind of cant phrase.——A singing-bird
from the Canary Isles, although now bred in other countries.
——A grass, the seeds of which are collected for canary-birds.

CANNIBAL.   A human being that eats human flesh.
Columbus, in the narrative of his discoveries, mentions certain
people called Cannibals ; but in the isles he says the natives
lived in great fear of *Caribals*, or people of Cariba, called in
Hispaniola *Carib*.   Again, in old maps the *Caribbee* Islands are
called the *Cannibal* Islands.

CANOPY.   From the L. *canopeum* or *conopeum* ; from
κωνωψ, a gnat ; or from *Canopus*, a town in Lower Egypt.
(*S. F. Creswell.*)   But qu. from κωνωπειον, a curtain to keep off
gnats ; from κωνωψ, a gnat ; or from κωνος, a cone, from its form.

CANT.   A whining singing manner of speech ; a quaint
affected mode of uttering words, either in conversation or
preaching.   "This word, which is now generally applied to
fanaticism and hypocrital conduct, is derived from two Scotch

Presbyterian ministers in the reign of Charles II. They were
father and son, both named Andrew Cant ; and Whitelock in
his Memoirs, after narrating the defeat at Worcester in 1651,
says, Divers Scotch ministers were permitted to meet at
Edinburgh to keep a day of humiliation, as they pretended, for
their too much correspondence with the king ; and in the
same month, when Lord Argyll had called a Parliament, Mr.
Andrew Cant, a minister, said in his pulpit that God was
bound to hold this Parliament, for that all other Parliaments
were called by man, but this was brought about by His own
hand " (*Timbs*).   Dr. Jamieson, under *cant*, says, " to sing in
speaking, to repeat after the manner of recitative. (Scot.)
This term is generally applied to preachers who deliver their
discourses in this manner ;" and, after referring to the above
anecdote, he says, " but there is reason to suppose that this
ungraceful mode of speaking is much more ancient, and that
it was imported by our Reformers from the Church of Rome, as
it undoubtedly bears the greatest resemblance to the chanting
of the service, and the word may have had its origin immediately from the L. *canto*, to sing, chant. Some even go so far as
to assert that Cicero and the other Roman orators delivered all
their orations in recitative."

CANTABRICA. Lavender-leaved bindweed, a herb of the
genus *Convolvulus ;* so named from having been discovered in
Cantabria, the appellation formerly given to the north-eastern
part of Spain. See Plin. 25, 47.

CANTERBURY. A receptacle for music, portfolios, loose
papers, &c., being an ornamental stand with divisions, first
made at Canterbury.——A pivot crane.

CAOUTCHOUC (found *cahuca*). Another name for India
rubber, an elastic substance impermeable to water, produced
from the *Hevea Guianensis*, and various other plants. It is
brought from the forests of Guiana, in South America, and
either the word is of native origin or the substance may have
been so named because produced in great abundance on the
banks of the Cauca, in New Granada.

CAPE. A wine of which there are two kinds, made in the
Cape Colony.

CAPORCIANITE. A mineral, a hydrous silicate occurring in geodes with calcite, in the *gabbro rosso* of Monte Caporciano at L'Impruneta, and other places in Tuscany.

CARADOC. A sandstone, a division of the Lower Silurian rocks, consisting of red, purple, green, and white micaceous, sometimes quartzose, grits, and limestones, 2500 feet thick, containing corals and mollusca ; so named from a ridge in Shropshire, on the flanks of which it is exposed. " The chief and loftiest central mass, or that of Caer-Caradoc, gives name to the whole range."—*Murchison.*

CARAWAY. A biennial ; the *Carum carui*, having a root like a parsnip, and esteemed equal to a parsnip. Its seed is a strong aromatic, abounding in essential oil. See CARUM.

CARICA. The systematic name of a genus of plants, nat. or. *Papayaceæ;* so called because it was brought from Caria.

CARICUM. A detergent ointment for ulcers, named after its inventor Caricus.

CARL D'OR. A gold coin of Brunswick, worth about five rix-dollars, or about sixteen shillings sterling ; probably named from one of the rulers of the dukedom.

CARLINA or **CARLINE.** A thistle ; a genus of plants so called from the Emperor Charlemagne, whose army is said to have been preserved from the plague by the use of its root.

CARLINO, CARLINE, or **CAROLINE.** A small coin and money of account in Naples and Sicily equal to $4\frac{3}{4}$d. In Piedmont, a gold piece coined before 1785, equal to £51 8*s.* 8*d.;* subsequently to that year equal to £5 12*s.* 3*d.;* probably named from a ruler, Carlo.

CARLUDOVICA. A genus of plants named after Charles IV. of Spain and his queen Louisa.

CARMAGNOLE. A name given to the members of a revolutionary party in France, the most exalted of the club of the Jacobins. The Carmagnoles were leagued in 1792 against the unfortunate Queen Marie Antoinette. They had their name from a dance song which they sang, and which was composed on the occasion of the taking of Carmagnola, in Piedmont. The word *carmagnole* is also applied to the dress worn by the Carmagnoles; and also, in disparagement, to a soldier of the Republican armies of France.

CARMELITE. A woollen stuff used for dresses, and so named as resembling the garb of the Carmelites, an order of mendicant friars established on Mount Carmel, Syria, in the twelfth century.

CAROLATHINE. A mineral, colour honey-yellow to wine-yellow, resembling mellite, found near Gleiwitz; named after the Prince of Carolath.

CAROLIN or **CAROLIN D'OR.** A gold coin of Bavaria, Hesse-Darmstadt, and Würtemburg, equal to £1 0s. 4¼d., probably named from a ruler, Carlo.

CAROLINEA. A genus of plants, nat. or. *Sterculiaceæ*, the species of which are natives of Guinea, called after Sophia Caroline, Margravine of Baden.

CAROLUS. A broad piece of gold struck in the reign of Charles I., equal to 20s.

CARPET. A covering for the floor, a manufacture of oriental origin. Skinner suggests that the It. *carpetta* may be from *Cairo* and *tapeto;* "q. d. *tapes Cairicus seu Memphiticus*," a carpet of Cairo or Memphis. This agrees with Cotgrave, who renders the O. Fr. *cairin* " Turkie carpet ; such a one as is brought from Caire, in Egypt." Carpets with hair or shag on one side only were called by the ancients *tapetes;* those having shag on both sides were styled *amphitapetes.*

CARP-MEALS. A kind of coarse cloth made in the north of England (*Phillips*); most probably named from some place on the coast. Bailey renders *meales, vales,* " the shelves or banks of sand on the sea-coast of Norway;" but the term is also found in localities on the English coast.

CARRONADE. A short piece of ordnance, so called from the village of Carron, in Stirlingshire, where first made.

CARTESIAN. Pertaining to Descartes, or to his philosophy, which taught the doctrine of vortexes round the sun and planets.

CARUM. A plant from Caria, in Asia Minor, where it was first found. It is now the name of a genus of plants, nat. or. *Umbelliferæ.*

CARYATES, CARYATIDES. In architecture, figures of women dressed in long robes after the Asiatic manner, serving to support entablatures. The Athenians had been long at war with the Caryans; the latter being at length vanquished, and their wives led captive, the Greeks, to perpetuate the event, erected trophies, in which figures of women, dressed in the Caryatic manner, were used to support entablatures. Other female figures were afterwards used in the same manner, but they were called by the same name (*Encyc.*)——They were called *Caryatides* from Carya, a city in the Peloponnesus which sided with the Persians, and on that account was sacked by the other Greeks, its males butchered, and its females reduced to slavery (*Cyc.*)

CASHMERE or CACHEMERE. A peculiar textile fabric first imported from the kingdom of Cashmere, and now well imitated in France and Great Britain. The material of the Cashmere shawls is the downy wool found about the roots of the hair of the Thibet goat.— *Ure.*

CASSANDRA. A name given by several authors to a very elegant sea-shell, of *concha globosa* or *dolium* kind, more usually known under the name of the *lyra* or harp-shell. It is supposed to be called *cassandra* because of its being found on the island of Cassan.—*Chamb. Cyc.*

CASSERIAN. The name given to a semi-lunar ganglion formed by the fifth nerve, and immediately dividing into the ophthalmic, superior maxillary, and inferior maxillary nerves; named after Julius Casserius, of Padua.

CASSIANISM. Sometimes used for *Semi-pelagianism;* the tenets of Cassian, a teacher of Gaul towards the close of the fifth century.

CASSIOPEIA. One of the forty-eight old constellations near Cepheus, not far from the North Pole; so named from Cassiopeia, who, with her husband Cepheus, was fabled by the Greeks as placed among the constellations to witness the punishment inflicted on their daughter Andromeda.

CASSIUS. A purple colour obtained from the chloride of gold by means of tin, much valued for the beautiful colour which it gives to glass or enamel ; named from the discoverer, M. Cassius.

CASTANEA. The chestnut ; a genus of plants, trees, nat. or. *Polyandria* ; so called from Castanea, a town of Thessaly, whence it was brought. See CHESTNUT.

CASTANET. An instrument composed of concave shells of ivory or hard wood ; used by the Spaniards, &c., as an accompaniment to their dances; from Sp. *castañeta*, from *castaña*, a chestnut, from the resemblance to two chestnuts. See CHESTNUT.

CATESBŒA. A genus of plants, the species of which are ornamental shrubs ; called after Mr. Catesby, author of the Natural History of Carolina.—*Crabb.*

CATILINISM. Conspiracy ; the practices of Catiline, the Roman conspirator. See Webster.

CATONIAN. Grave, severe, inflexible ; pertaining to or resembling Cato, the Roman, who was remarkable for his severity of manner. See Bailey and Webster.

CAUDEBEC. A hat made of lamb's wool, down of ostriches, or camel's hair, worn in England about the year 1700 ; named from Caudebec, in Normandy, which, prior to the Protestant emigration after the revocation of the Edict of Nantes, was famed for the manufacture of this kind of hat.

CAULINIA. A genus of endogenous aquatic plants named in honour of Don Filippo Cavolini, a Neapolitan naturalist, author of several botanical works.

CAUZERANITE. A crystallised mineral of a black or dark blue colour, found at Cauzeran, in the Pyrenees.

CAVOLINITE. A variety of nepheline, a mineral occurring in glassy crystals, &c. ; named after Cavolini, a Neapolitan naturalist.

CAYENNE. A very pungent pepper prepared from several species of capsicum, but especially the *capsicum minimum* ; so called because originally imported from Cayenne, capital of French Guiana, on N.E. coast of South America.

CECROPIA. A genus of plants, nat. or. *Urticaceæ*, one species of which is the trumpet-tree or snake-wood, a native of Jamaica ; called after Cecrops, king of Athens, whose legs were fabled to be snakes.

CELLARIUS. A dance introduced by the celebrated French professor of the same name.

CELSIA. A genus of plants, nat. or. *Scrophulariaceæ*, called after Dr. Celsius, professor of Oriental languages in the University of Upsal.

CENTAUREA. A herb named after Chiron, the Centaur, who was healed by it. The name is now applied to a genus of plants, nat. or. *Compositæ*.

• CEPHEUS. A constellation in the northern hemisphere, fabled by the Greeks to represent Cepheus, husband of Cassiopeia, and father of Andromeda.

CEREAL. Pertaining to edible grain, as wheat, rye, &c.; from *Ceres*, goddess of corn.

CEREMONY. Outward rite ; external form in religion ; forms of civility ; rules established by custom for regulating social intercourse ; outward forms of state ; from L. *ceremonia* for *cæremonia* or *cærimonia*, literally sacredness, sanctity, awe, reverence, veneration of the Deity ; then a religious action or usage, a sacred rite, religious ceremony; supposed to be from *Cære* or *Cærete* (anc. Agylla, now Cervetere), a town of Etruria which stood in a very ancient religious connection with Rome ; hence the Romans in their Gallic war carried their sacred relics there. (See Val. Max. I. 1, No. 10 ; Fest. 34. Cf. Nieb. Röm. Gesch. I. 428.) Others derive the Latin word from the goddess *Ceres*, or from *cerus*, which, according to Scaliger, was anciently used for " holy."

CERES. One of the asteroids revolving between the orbits of Mars and Jupiter, discovered by Piazzi at Palermo in 1801 ; named from Ceres.

CERITE. The siliceous oxide of cerium, *q.v.*

CERIUM. A metal of great specific gravity discovered in Sweden, in cerite ; named from the planet Ceres.

CERVANTITE. A mineral ; colour Isabella yellow, sulphur yellow, or nearly white ; found with grey antimony, and resulting from its alteration, at Cervantes, in Galicia, Spain;

Chazelles, in Auvergne ; and Felsobanya, Kremnitz, and else-where in Hungary.

CESARE. In logic, a syllogism in the second figure, consisting of a universal affirmative between two universal negatives ; probably from *Cæsar*.

CESAREAN. The Cesarean operation is the taking of a child from the womb by cutting ; an operation which, it is said, gave birth to Cæsar, the Roman emperor.

CESAREWITCH or CZAREWITCH. The name of a stake run for at Newmarket. It was called in honour of the eldest son of the Czar, whose title is *Czarewitch*, i.e. son of the Czar, in token of his gift of the 500-guinea gold cup called the " Emperor's Cup," run for at Ascot, which, however, since the Crimean War, has been withdrawn.

CEYLANITE. A mineral classed with the ruby family, and called also *pleonaste*. It is the *Scorbus genuinus* of Linnæus, and is chiefly found in the sand of the rivers of Ceylon, from which island it derives its name.

CHABLIS. A celebrated white wine made at Chablis, a town of France (Yonne), in the midst of vineyards.

CHAILLETIA. A genus of shrubs, type of nat. or. *Chailletiaceæ* ; named in honour of M. Chaillet.

CHALCEDONY. An uncrystallised translucent variety of quartz, having a whitish colour, found in a variety of trap rock. The word is derived from *Chalcedon*, a town of Asia Minor, opposite to Byzantium, where it was first found.

CHALLIS. A fine printed soft woollen fabric used for ladies' dresses ; from Chollet, in France, dep. Maine-et-Loire.

CHALYBEATE. Any water or other liquor into which iron enters. As an adjective the word means impregnated with parti-cles of iron; from L. *chalybs*, Gr. χαλυψ, steel; so named from the Chalybes (or, as some say, Chalybs, their city), a people on the Black Sea, near Thermodon, in Pontus, and perhaps partly in Paphlagonia, in whose country very good iron was found, and who are said to have possessed the art of making iron or steel, and also the *fabrica æraria*. (Cf. Plin. H. N. VI. 4, s. 4; and VII. 56 ante med. s. 57; I. 9. med.; Virg. Geo. I. 58.) Chalybs (χαλυψ) was the name of a river of Spain, on which the Chalybes dwelt. (Cf. Just. xliv. 3.)

CHAMBERTIN. A fine red wine from Chambertin, a celebrated côteau in France, dep. Côte-d'Or.

CHAMOISITE. A mineral, considered to be a mixture of magnetic iron and a hydrous silicate of alumina, dug from Mount Chamoisin, in the Valais, Switzerland.

CHAMPAGNE. The wine so called; from Champagne, one of the largest and most important of the former provinces of France. That consumed in England is principally made from gooseberries.

CHAMPAWK. The *Michaelia champaca*, a tree held in great religious veneration by the Hindoos. It is distinguished by large deep-yellow flowers, which during the day are sweet-scented, but have at night an exceedingly disagreeable odour. It has its name from Champaca, a small island of Cochin China, of which it is a native.

CHAMPIGNY. A red wine, from a place of the same name in France.

CHAMPOLLIONIST. A follower of Champollion the Younger in respect to Egyptian hieroglyphics (*Webster*). Jean François Champollion, the celebrated savant, was born at Figeac, Lot, in 1791, and died in 1832.

CHANDELI. A very fine species of cotton fabric of so costly a description as to be used in native courts only (*Elliott*); from *Chandel* or *Chanderi*, properly *Chandhairee*, a town of Malwa, India.

CHANTILLY. A fine rich hand-made lace, which, from its price, can only be worn by the wealthy; from a place of the same name in France.

CHAPTALIA. A species of plants, answering to the Linnæan genus *Perdicium*; named in honour of M. Chaptal.

CHARADE. A sort of riddle, usually in verse, the subject of which is a word of one or more syllables. It is said to have had its name from its inventor. Charadrus (*hodiè* Keyrimios Potamos) is the name of a river, on the left bank of which stood Marathon. The word, however, is not probably of very ancient origin.

CHARLEY. A small patch of hair, sometimes called a door-mat, immediately under the upper lip; named after Charles (I. or II. ?)——A familiar name anciently applied to ward-beadles, street-keepers, and other drowsy functionaries.

CHARLOTTE. In the culinary art, a sweet dish, probably named from the maker. In French cookery the term is of frequent use; as Charlotte de pommes aux confitures; Charlotte de poires à la vanille ; Charlotte d'abricots; Charlotte de pêches ; Charlotte à l'Italienne ; Charlotte Russe.

CHASALIA. A genus of plants, nat. or. *Monogynia*, natives of the Mauritius ; named in honour of D. Chasal.

CHATEAU MARGAUX. One of the four superior sorts of wine called Bordeaux ; produced at the celebrated vineyard of the same name, dep. Gironde, Haut-Medoc. So progressive is the present age that this wine, like that called Lafitte, may be had at nearly all the hotels in Europe, although only 750 hectolitres of the first, and 200 of the second quality, are made annually.

CHATHAM. A moiety of the duty payable by foreign-built ships, and applied to the chest at Chatham. Chatham Chest was established for the relief of English mariners wounded or superannuated in their country's service.—*Crabb*.

CHEDDAR. A celebrated cheese made at Cheddar, Somerset.

CHELMSFORDITE. A siliceous mineral, found usually associated with quartz, mica, and apatite ; occurring at Chelmsford, Mass., U.S.

CHERLERIA. A genus of plants usually growing in moist places near the summits of high mountains ; named in honour of John Henry Cherler, son-in-law and fellow-labourer of the botanist John Bauhin.

CHERRY (anc. *ciris*, L. *cerasus*, Gr. χεζασιον). The fruit of the *Prunus cerasus*. It is said to derive its name from Cerasus, a city of Pontus, near the Euxine, whence it was brought by Lucullus, A.R. 680, after the defeat of Mithridates ; and to have been introduced into England by the Romans about 120 years afterwards, A.D. 55. Pliny, lib. xviii. ch. 23.

"Cerasi, ante victoriam Mithridaticam L. Luculli non fuere in Italiâ. Ad urbis annum MCLXXX is primùm vexit à Ponto: annisque 120 trans oceanum in Britanniam usque pervenire eadem, ut diximus in Ægypto non potuere gigni." According to others the cherry-tree was known to the Greeks long before the time of Lucullus ; and Cerasus (κεραϛους) itself may have had its name from the number of cherry-trees growing there. Ménage says it is not true that this fruit was called from the town of Cerasus, and that it is the reverse, as has been very truly remarked by Casaubon ; and that Theophrastus, a more ancient author than Diphilus, mentions the cherry in his History of Plants, lib. 3, ch. 13. After quoting Servius ("Cerasus civitas est Ponti, quam cum delesset Lucullus, genus hoc pomi inde advexit, et à civitate *cerasum* appellavit. Nam arbor *cerasus* pomum, *cerasum* dicitur. Hoc autem etiam ante Lucullum erat in Italiâ, sed durum, et *cornum* appellabatur : quod postea mixto nomine *cornocerosum* dictum est ") Ménage adds, "Ce qui donne sujet de croire que κερασος a été fait de κερας [a horn], et que les cerises ont été appelées κερασα, de leur ressemblance au fruit du cornuiller ; κερας, κερατος, κεραος, Κερασος."

CHESNEIA. A genus of plants of the papilionaceous family, including only one species ; discovered upon the banks of the Euphrates ; "said to have been named after Lord Chesney."

CHESTERFIELD. A coat named after Lord Chesterfield, a nobleman of the present day.

CHESTERLITE. A mineral found at Chester, in Pennsylvania.

CHESTNUT or CHESNUT (A.S. *cisten-beam*, L. *nux castanea*, or simply *castanea* ; *castanea* sc. *arbor* the tree; Gr. καϛτανον, καϛτανα). The fruit, seed, or nut of a tree belonging to the genus *Castanea* ; nat. or. *Corylaceæ*. Some derive the word from the W. *cast*, envelopment, from its shell or cover ;. but it is more correctly from *Castana*, *Castanæa*, or *Casthanæa*; *Herod.* Κασθαναια, or Κασθαναιη, a town of Magnesia, in Thessaly, which abounded with chestnut trees.

CHIC. A term in very general use in France to express a high degree of perfection in works of art, &c. The Figaro-Programme gives the following account of the origin of the word:—" The celebrated painter David, at the beginning of the present century, gave lessons to young artists, and was paid high prices ; but when a pupil, the son of poor parents, showed proofs of unusual talent, the painter willingly gave his lessons gratis. One of his pupils named Chicque, the son of a fruiterer, displayed so much talent in his studies in oil-painting, that he became a special favourite, and David always expressed his conviction that the lad would become an eminent artist, and do honour to his school. To David's great grief, Chicque died at the age of eighteen. From that time the great painter was in the habit of saying of a bad study, ' Chicque would not have done like that ;' or of a good one, ' This reminds one of Chicque.' The word thus became among his pupils a general term for excellence, and, being constantly used by then in places of public resort, it gradually passed into the popular vocabulary, and was adopted by writers, who suppressed the last syllable, and spelt it *chic*." See Galignani, 15 Aug. 1864.

CHILDRENITE. A mineral, according to Wollaston, consisting of alumina, red oxide of iron, phosphoric acid, and water ; named in honour of Mr. Children.

CHILONIAN, CHILONIC. Brief, compendious, as a Chilonic style ; so called from Chilo, one of the Seven Wise Men of Greece, whose sentences were very short and pithy.—*Bailey*.

CHINA. A species of earthenware originally made in China.

CHINSURAH. A vile cigar made at Chinsurah, near Calcutta.

CHIVIATITE. A mineral, colour lead-grey, resembling bismuth-glance ; from Chiviato, in Peru.

CHOMELIA. A genus of American shrubs, named in honour of Dr. Chomel, physician to Louis XV.

CHRISTEN. To baptise and name ; to initiate into the visible church of Christ by the application of water.

CHRISTIAN. A believer in the religion of Christ.

CHRISTIAN D'OR. A gold coin current in Denmark for 16s. 6d. sterling ; named from a monarch of the country.

CHRISTIANITY. The religion of Christians, or the system of doctrines and precepts taught by Christ, and recorded by the evangelists and apostles.

CHRISTMAS. The festival of the Christian church : so named in memory of the birth of Christ.

CHRIST'S THORN. A thorny plant that flourishes about Christmas. According to some, it is of the same sort as that of which the crown of thorns was made.

CHURRIGUERESQUE. In the style of Joseph Churriguera, who was born at Salamanca about 1660. Mr. Ford says he is the heresiarch of bad taste, and his name is synonymous with absurdity in brick and mortar.

CHUTNEY or CHUTNEE. A condiment or pickle made in India, compounded of sweets and acids, of which there are several local kinds ; Bengal chutney, sweet chutney, green mango chutney, &c. It is much eaten in the East with curries, stews, &c. ; and it may have had its name from Chatna a town of Nepal, or Chatna in Bengal. There is likewise Chutnahulli in Mysore, and the village of Chuttanuttee on the Hoogly, one of the earliest possessions of the British in India.

CICELY. A plant, a species of chœrophyllum : from the Christian name *Cecilia.*

CICERONE. A guide ; one who points out to travellers the curiosities of a place, especially in Italy. " They are said to be so named from their indiscriminately calling every statue or picture *Cicero* when they do not know whom it represents."

CICERONIANISM. Imitation or resemblance of the style or action of Cicero.—*Webster.*

CIMOLITE. A species of clay of a white colour used by the ancients as a remedy for erysipelas and other inflammations. It is now used in removing spots from cloth. One species, of a purple colour, is the steatite or soap-rock ; and from another, found in the Isle of Wight, tobacco-pipes are made. L. *cimolia,* Gr. κιμωλία ; said to be so called from Cimolus (now Argentiera), an isle in the Cretan Sea.—*Pliny,* lib. xxxv. 17.

CINCHONA. A genus of plants, nat. or. *Cinchonaceæ,*

E

growing in the hilly parts of Peru ; so called from the Countess Cinchon, vice-queen of Peru, who was cured of a fever by it, A.D. 1638. See QUININE.

CIRCASSIAN. A kind of woollen cloth from Circassia.

CIRCÆA. A genus of plants called after Circe, the enchantress of the Greeks ; the fruit, which is covered with hooked prickles, laying hold of the clothes of passengers, as Circe is said to have laid hold on persons by her enchantments.—*Crabb.*

CLARENCE. A kind of carriage ; a cross between a common carriage and a britzska, named after the late Duke of Clarence (William IV.)

CLARENCEUX or CLARENCIEUX. In Great Britain, the second king-at-arms, whose office is to marshal the funerals of all knights and esquires on the south of the Trent. He was appointed by Edward IV., and named from the Duke of Clarence.—*Encyc.* and *Bailey.*

CLAUSTHALITE. Native seleniuret of lead, having a lead-grey colour (*Dana*) ; from Klausthal, the chief mining town of the Harz.

CLAYTONIA. A genus of plants, nat. or. *Pontulacaceæ;* called after J. Clayton, a collector of plants in Virginia.

CLEAVELANDITE. A mineral, called also siliceous felspar or albite ; named after Professor Cleaveland.

CLEMENTINES. A portion of the canon law, consisting of decretals or constitutions of Pope Clement V.

CLIFFORTIA. A genus of plants, nat. or. *Rosaceæ;* named in honour of G. Cliffort, of Amsterdam, a patron of Linnæus.—*Crabb.*

CLINTONITE. A mineral ; colour reddish-brown, yellowish, copper-red ; named by Messrs. Fitch, Mather, and Horton in honour of the Hon. de Witt Clinton.

CLIONIDÆ. The Clio tribe, a family of marine mollusca ; the first order of Cuvier's peteropods ; named from Cleio, the muse who presided over history.

CLIQUOT. A celebrated champagne, much patronised by the late King of Prussia ; named from Madame Cliquot, one of the largest producers in France.

CLUSIA. A genus of plants, nat. or. *Guttiferæ*: called after C. de l'Ecluse, a celebrated botanist of Artois.

CLUYTIA. A genus of plants, nat. or. *Euphorbiaceæ*; called after Professor Cluyt, of Leyden.

COACH (Fr. *coche*, Armor. *coich*, It. *cocchio*, Sp. and Port. *coche*, D. *koets*, G. *kutsche*, Pol. *kocz*). The vehicle so named. Ménage derives the word from *vehiculum ;* Tunius from ὀχέω, to carry; Wachter from G. *kutten*, to cover; Lye from Belg. *koetsen*, to lie along, it signifying properly a coach or chair. Webster says the word seems to be radically a couch or bed (Fr. *couche*, *coucher*, a covered bed on wheels for carrying the infirm). Bescherelle says from Fr. *coche*, It. *coccio*, in Turc. *kochi*, char, carrosse. Minshew derives the word from Hungarian *kotczy*, Teut. *kotzen*, *kutzche*, à verbo Hungarico *kotczy*, idem, quòd in Hungariâ hoc curriculi genus (teste historiâ Hungaricâ) primùm inuentum fuerit. Nicolas Berga (Liv. des Grands Chemins, ch. 10, liv. iv.) considers *coche* to be from the Hungarian, the invention having come from Hungary. Rees says some endeavour to prove that the word is of Hungarian origin, and that this carriage was first invented at Kitsee (formerly Kotsee or Cotzo), prov. Weiselburg; and that, however this may be, it is certain that in the sixteenth century, or even at an earlier period, a kind of covered carriages was known under the name of Hungarian carriages. Johnston (*Gaz.*) gives Kitsee as a frontier town of W. Hungary, co. Weiselburg, five miles S.S.W. of Presburg.

COAN. A term frequently applied to Hippocrates, or anything relating to him or his writings; lit. pertaining to, or a native of the isle of Cos, in the Grecian Archipelago, where he was born.

COBÆA. An elegant climber, flowers at first green, a native of Mexico, where it is called *yedra morada*, or violet ivy; named by Cavanilles in memory of Father Barnabas Cobo, a Jesuit, who, after living forty-five years in N. and S. America, composed a natural history of the world, still extant, but never published.

COBALT. A metal found chiefly in combination with arsenic, as arsenical cobalt; or with sulphur and arsenic, as grey cobalt ore ; named from Cobalus, the demon of mines, who is said to have obstructed and destroyed the miners. "The ores of *cobalt*, being at first mysterious and intractable, received their name from this personage." For many years cobalt was found in such abundance in the mines in Saxony that it was neglected and thrown aside as useless. In some of the copper mines (according to Parkes) it was so abundant that "a prayer was offered to God in the German churches that he would preserve the miners from *cobalt-kobolds*, and *other* spirits."

COBURG. A species of cheap twilled stuff, used for making ladies' dresses; named from Coburg, in Germany.——A round loaf of bread.

COCHIN CHINA. A larger sort of fowl brought from Cochin China, in Eastern Asia.

COCKNEY. A native of London, by way of contempt ; in Shakspeare, an effeminate, ignorant, despicable citizen. Ellis derives it from *coquina*, the kitchen. Webster says, "most probably from L. *coquina*, a kitchen, or *coquino*, to cook ; Fr. *coquin*, idle ; *cocagne*, It. *cuccagna*, an imaginary country of idleness and luxury. In some ancient poetry the word seems to signify a cook:

> "And yet I say, by my soul, I have no salt bacon,
> Ne no *cokeney*, by Christe, coloppes to make."

> "At that feast were they served in rich array,
> Every five and five had a *cokeney*."

(See note on Chaucer's Canterbury Tales, line 4206, Edin. 1782.)

Some say the country people gave the Londoners this nickname because they considered them ignorant of everything out of London : that they were as likely to say " a cock neighs " as " a cock crows." According to others, it had its origin in some Londoner having on a certain occasion spoken of a " cock that neighed." Casaubon derives it from Gr. οικογενης, one born and bred at home. Huloet explains " to play the cockney " to play the fool. Barret (in the reign of Elizabeth) defines a cockney " a child tenderly brought up ; a darling." Dicker, a writer contemporary with Barret, derives it from *cocker* or *cock*. The French used *pais de Cocaigne* for a country of dandies. Paris est pour un riche un païs de Cocaigne (*Boileau*). It seems that the word is very ancient, being mentioned in an old Norman-Saxon poem, where it is spelt *Cocayng*. Pegge derives it from old Fr. *coqueliner*, to couple, part. *coqueliné*; whence, by dropping the penultimate, *coqueue*. Cotgrave renders *coquine* "a beggar-woman ; also a cockney, simper-de-cockit, nice thing; dandled, pampered, made a wanton of." Todd says the citation of Camden (*Britannia*)—

> " Were I in my castle of Bungey,
> Upon the river of Waveney,
> I would ne care for the king of *Cockeney* "—

shows that London was known by this name ; hence a cockney may be assumed for a Londoner ; and after all there is most reason to believe that this contemptuous expression originates in that imaginary region of luxury and idleness formerly called *Cocaigne*, or Plenty, as in the poem cited by Hickes—that probably the festival of the *Cocagna* at Naples may have suggested the poem as well as the word (See Keysler's Trav. vol. ii. 309). Hobbes, in allusion to the old poem, has "the land of *Cockany*, where fowls ready roasted cry, 'Come and eat me;' for, among the delicacies of this happy country, ready-roasted geese fly into the house exclaiming ' All hot ! all hot !' "

CODRINGTON. Formerly a coat; named after one of the celebrated family of the same name (admiral ?)

COFFEE. The berry of a tree of the genus *Coffea*, growing in Arabia, Persia, and in other warm climates of Asia and America.——A drink made from the berry of the coffee-tree. It had its name from Káfa, a country of E. Africa, S. of Abyssinia, prov. Narea, and within or on the borders of which are the sources of the Bahr-el-Abiad, or of its chief tributaries ; of which country it is a native, and where it grows spontaneously in great abundance. Indeed, a very large proportion of the coffee now exported from Mocha arrives in that market from the N. frontier of Káfa, and the S. part of Enarea. Miller (*Gard. Dict.*) says it is the wood of the country, produced spontaneously everywhere in great abundance from Caffa (Káfe) to the banks of the Nile. The foot of the mountains, or edge of the marshes nearest Narea, is thick overgrown with coffee-trees, which, if not the only, is the largest tree grown here. (Cf.

Bruce, Abyss. vol. ii. 226, 313). It is said to have been introduced into Aden, in Arabia, from Persia, by Gemaleddin, about the fifteenth century; not long after, it reached Mecca, Medina, &c., and Grand Cairo. Hence it continued its progress to Damascus and Aleppo, and in 1554 became known at Constantinople, being introduced there by two persons of the name of Shems and Hekim, one from Damascus, the other from Aleppo. Each of these men had a public coffee-house in that city. It was known at Marseilles in 1664, was introduced into London in 1652, and at Paris in 1657. Notwithstanding the progressive age in which we live, the berry may still be purchased in England; but as a beverage pure coffee is little known. The Turcic has *kahvet;* also *kahvè,* coffee, wine; the Arabic قهوة *kahwat,* wine, coffee, or a decoction of berries called *bum,* which gives an appetite. The Egyptians call it *eleave.*

COGNAC. The best kind of brandy; named from Cognac, in France, dep. Charente, where, and in the surrounding district, it is made. The quantity produced annually does not exceed 6000 butts, but the number sold under the name of *Les fines Champagnes,* by which the best quality is distinguished, exceeds 15,000 butts. It sometimes finds its way into England, but the mixture usually called cognac is British brandy, first exported to France, and thence returned in Cognac casks.

COHORN or COEHORN (G. *cohörner,* Fr. *mortier à la Coëhorn*). A small mortar or piece of ordnance so called, and used in fortified places; also a particular style of fortification; invented by Cohorn or Coëhorn, a celebrated Dutch engineer, and one of the ablest fortifiers. He was born in 1641, and died at Liége in 1704. At Namur, which was besieged by Vauban and defended by Cohorn, there is still a fort named in honour of the latter.

COLARES. A celebrated wine from Colares, in Portugal.

COLBERTINE or COLBERTEEN. A kind of lace with a square and coarse ground, formerly worn by ladies; much used for ruffles fifty years since. The word is probably derived from the maker, Colbert, or may have been named in honour of Jean Baptiste Colbert, minister of finance under Mazarin.

COLCHICINE. A vegetable alkaloid obtained from colchicum, *q.v.*

COLCHICUM. A medicine used as a remedy for the gout and rheumatism, prepared from the bulbs of the *Colchicum autumnale*. It is supposed to have its name from Colchis, a country of Asia, extending along the eastern shore of the Euxine, where it is said to have grown in great abundance. Cf. Linn. Gen. 457; Schreb. 621; Gœrt. 81; Juss. 47, and Rees's Cyc.

COLDENIA. A genus of plants, the only species of which is the *C. procumbens*, a native of India; named in honour of C. Colden, the American botanist.

COLDSTREAM. The appellation of a regiment of guards, so called from the town of Coldstream, co. Berwick, on the N. side of the Tweed, where it was raised by General Monk. It was with this regiment that Monk marched into England to restore Charles II.

COLIN. A name given by Buffon to the Mexican quail, a bird of the partridge kind found in America and the W. Indies; from the Christian and surname Colin, *i.e.* Nicolin.

COLLINSONIA. A genus of plants, nat. or. *Labiatæ*; called after P. Collinson, F.R.S., a distinguished botanist.

COLMAR. A pear, named from Colmar, in France, dep. Haut-Rhin, where it is raised. It is also called *poire manne, bergamotte tardive*.

COLOPHON. An inscription on the last page of a book, before title-pages were used, containing the place or year, or both, of its publication, the printer's name, &c.; so named from a Greek proverb respecting the people of Colophon, that they always came hindermost.—*Brande, Warton.*

COLOPHONITE. A variety of garnet of a resinous fracture, occurring in small, amorphous granular masses; named from colophony, *q.v.*

COLOPHONY. Black resin; the dark-coloured resin obtained by the distillation of turpentine (*Brande*). The spelling *colophany* given by Ure is erroneous, the substance having been named from Colophon, in Ionia, whence the best was formerly brought. See Pliny, Hist. Nat. xiv. 20.

COLOSSAL or COLOSSEAN. Very large, huge, gigantic, like a Colossus, the name of a statue of gigantic size. The most remarkable colossus of antiquity was one at Rhodes, a statue of Apollo, so high that ships might sail between its legs. It is said to have had its name from Caletus or Coletus, who designed it. According to others, it was both designed and executed by the artists Chares and Laches.

COLT. A celebrated revolving pistol, so named from Colonel Colt, the inventor.

COLUMBIAN. Pertaining to the United States, or to America, which was discovered by Columbus.

COLUMBITE. The ore of columbium, *q.v.*

COLUMBIUM. A metal first discovered in an ore or oxide, found in Connecticut, at New London. The same metal was afterwards discovered in Sweden, and called *tantalum*, and its ore *tantalite* (*Cleaveland*). From *Columbia*, *i.e.* America, discovered by Columbus.

COMMAGENUM. Syrian ointment; named from Commagene, in Syria, whence it was brought.—*Galen.*

COMPLUTENSIAN. The name given to a celebrated polyglot Bible projected by Ximenes, printed in 6 vols. fol. 1514—15, at Alcalá de Henares, anc. called Complutum, quasi confluvium, from the junction of rivers. See Ford's Spain.

COMPTONIA. A genus of plants, or. *Triandria*, the only species of which is the fern-leaved comptonia, native of the United States; named in honour of Henry Compton, Bishop of London.

COMPTONITE. A mineral found in drusy cavities of masses ejected from Vesuvius; identical with thompsonite; called in honour of Lord Compton, who brought it to England in 1818.

CONDURRITE. A mineral substance composed of arsenious acid, oxide of copper, water, sulphur, and arsenic; found in the Condurron, in Cornwall.

CONGREVE. The name formerly given to a sort of lucifer match; so called from the inventor.——A very destructive engine of war invented by Sir William Congreve.

CONISTONITE. A mineral consisting of oxalic acid, lime, soda, magnesia, and water; from the copper mine near Coniston, in Cumberland.

CONNELLITE. A mineral, from trials by Connel, supposed to be a compound of a sulphate and chloride of copper.

CONSTANTIA. A wine produced from the vineyards of the same name near the Cape of Good Hope.——A jelly made of Seville oranges, &c., mixed with Constantia wine.

CONTINENTALS. A name given to bright full-weight sovereigns, very useful to the Continental tourist.

COOPER. The beverage called half-and-half is a mixture of stout and ale; cooper is composed of half stout and half porter, and was probably named from the first mixer.

COPERNICAN. The name of a system of the spheres, proposed by Pythagoras and revived by Copernicus (born at Thorn, in Poland), in which the sun is supposed to be placed in the centre, and all the other planetary bodies to revolve round it in a particular order.

COPIAPITE. A mineral found incrusting coquimbite, *q.v.*

COPPER (L. *cuprum*). The metal; supposed to have been so called from Cyprus, an isle in the Mediterranean, which is probable, it having been called by the Greeks χαλκος Κυπριος, Cyprian brass, brass of Cyprus; and by the Latins *æs Cyprium*.

COPPERAS. A name given to blue, green, and white vitriol, or the factitious sulphate of iron. The Fr. has *couperose;* the D. *koperrood, i.e.* red copper; and *koperroest,* copper rust, verdigris; the Armor. *couperosa, couperos.* Saumaise sur Solin., p. 1160, says, " Germani hodiè appellant chalcanthum aquam cupri; inde nostrum couperose." Ménage derives the word from G. *kupper-vasser (wasser),* copper-water; Labbé from *cuprosa,* for *cuprum;* Bourdelot from *cuprum rosæ;* Skinner from *cuprum rosum, ab uligine, i.e.* from moisture (*rodo, rosum,* to gnaw, eat away, waste away, corrode, consume). He gives also Fr. *rosée de cuivre,* i.e. *ros cupri,* and says, perhaps copper rust. See COPPER.

COPTIC. The language of the Copts or Cophti, the descendants of the ancient Egyptians, as distinct from the

Arabians, and other inhabitants of modern Egypt; from *Coptos*, the metropolis of the Thebaid.

COQUIMBITE. A mineral consisting of sulphuric acid, red oxide of iron, alumina, lime, magnesia, silica, and water, found in the district of Copiapo, in Coquimbo, Chili : hence *copiapite.*

COR CAROLI. An extra-constellated star of the third magnitude, between the Coma Berenices and Ursa Major ; so called by Dr. Halley in honour of King Charles.

CORDIERITE. A mineral, otherwise called *iolite* and *dichroite;* named after M. Cordier, professor of geology at the Museum of Natural History at Paris.

CORDWAIN or **CORDOVAN** (Sp. *cordoban,* Port. *cordovam,* Fr. *cordouan*). Spanish leather, goat-skin tanned and dressed ; so named from Cordova or Cordoba, in Spain.

CORDWAINER (formerly Cordiner). A shoemaker ; from Fr. *cordouanier,* properly a worker in cordwain or Cordovan leather (Fr. *cordonnier,* a shoemaker). See CORDWAIN.

CORINTHIAN. The third and most delicate of the orders of architecture, enriched with a profusion of ornaments ; named from Corinth, where it originated. Vitruvius ascribes it to Callimachus, a Corinthian sculptor.

CORINTHIANS. A term applied by the sporting papers to patrons of the prize-ring ; so named from the Corinthians, who cultivated a good discipline in time of peace and war. Hence, Corinth sent many brave and experienced generals to the other Grecian cities, and it was not uncommon for the latter to prefer a Corinthian general to any of their own.

CORNUTIA. A genus of American trees of two species ; named in honour of James Cornut (according to others Cornus), a French physician, botanist, and Canadian traveller.

CORTUSA. A genus of plants of two species, the one a native of Austria, the other of Siberia ; named by Matthiolus in honour of J. A. Cortusus, a botanist of Padua.

COS. A variety of lettuce, said to have had its name from the island of Cos. This is confirmed by the fact that several varieties of the *lactuca* or lettuce indicate their having come to us from the Greek Archipelago, and the coast of the Levant. (See P. Cyc.) "To Cos (Stanko) we are indebted in England for the Cos lettuce, a vegetable which, among others, is to be had in perfection from the gardens of Tchanak Kalessy" (Knight's Diary of the Dardanelles).

COSSIGNEA. A genus of plants, or. *Trigynia;* named in honour of M. Cossigny, a French naturalist.

CORUNDOPHILITE. A mineral of a dark green colour, related to chloritoid; named by Shepard from the Corundum of North Carolina, on which it is found, and φιλεω, to be attached to.

COSTMARY. A species of tansy, or *Tanacetum;* alecost; from Gr. κοστος, Arab. and Pers. قسط *kost,* L. *costus,* an aromatic herb and the name *Maria.*

CÔTE RÔTIE. A celebrated wine made from grapes grown on a hill of the same name on the Rhone.

COTYTTIA. Festivals celebrated in different cities of Greece in honour of Cotytto, goddess of debauchery. They took place during the night, and were of the most infamous description. The same were observed in Sicily.—*Juv.*

COUZERANITE. A mineral, described in Leonhard's Handbuch as a right rectangular prism, and by Dufresnoy as an oblique rhombic prism; found in the valleys of Seix and Salaix, the Col de la Trappe, and the Picou de Gen, in Les Couzerans, in the Pyrenees.

CRACOVIENNE. A celebrated dance, named from Cracow, in Poland, where it was first introduced.

CRATEVA. The garlic pear; a genus of plants, nat. or. *Capparidaceæ,* a native of Jamaica; named after Cratevas, a botanist mentioned by Hippocrates.

CRAVAT (formerly *crabbat,* Fr. *cravate,* O. Fr. *crabbat,* It. *cravatta,* Sp. *corbata,* Port. *caravata*). A neckcloth; in O. Eng. also handsome, comely (*Bailey*). So called from the Croats, who appeared in Europe at first with some peculiar scarf tied about their necks. "Probably from one Crabbat, a Croatian, who first wore it" (*Bailey*). "So named because this sort of ornament was first worn by the Croats, whom the

French called Cravates. Et ce fut en 1636 que nous primes cette sorte de collet des Cravates, par le commerce que nous usmes en ce tans-là en Allemagne, au sujet de la guerre que nous avions avec l'empereur" (*Ménage*).

CRAWFURDIA. A genus of climbing shrubs, or. *Digynia*; named after John Crawfurd, author of a history of the Indian Archipelago.

CREDNERITE. A mineral consisting of oxide of copper, and oxide of manganese, found at Friedrichrode (Thuringia); analysed by Credner.

CREMONA. A superior kind of violin, made or invented at Cremona, in Italy.——The name is also erroneously given to a stop in the organ voiced like the oboe, but of a different quality, bearing the same relation to the oboe as the stopped diapason to the open; more correctly written *cromorno*, Fr. *cromorne*; from G. *krummhorn*, crooked horn.

CRETA. Chalk ; a genus of earths of the calcareous order ; lit. Cretan earth, *i.e.* earth from the isle of Crete, under which name the ancients included chalk and various kinds of clay.

CRETACEOUS. Chalky; having the qualities of or like chalk; abounding with chalk. See CRETA.

CRETISM (κρητισμος). A falsehood ; a Cretan practice ; from the reputation of the Cretans as liars and deceivers.

CRETIC (κρητικος). A poetic foot of three syllables, one short between two long syllables (*Bentley*); such a foot as the Cretans made use of.

CRICHTONITE. A mineral, colour velvet-black, crystallizing in very acute small rhomboids; called after Dr. Crichton, physician to the Czar.

CRISPIN. A name given to shoemakers, of whom St. Crispin was the patron saint.

CROM-A-BOO! (Crom for ever!) The ancient war-cry of the clan or sept of Fitzgeralds ; from *Crom*, a castle in Limerick, which formerly belonged to this family.

CRONSTEDITE. A mineral accompanying hydrate of iron and calc spar at Przibram, in Bohemia, occurring also at

Wheal Maudlin, in Cornwall; named after Cronsted, the Swedish mineralogist and chemist.

CUBANE. A mineral, consisting of copper, iron, lead, and sulphur; found at Bacaranas, in Cuba, whence its name.

CUFIC or KUFIC. An epithet applied to the older characters of the Arabic language, used at the time of Mohammed, and about three centuries after, when those now in use were invented. They had their name from Cufat (كوفت *Kúfat*), a town of Asiatic Turkey, near Bagdad, on the Euphrates, where they are said to have been invented.

CUMBRIAN. A name given to the slate and grauwacke system which comprises the Bala limestone and the Plynlimmon and Snowdon rocks; so named from its being most reremarkably developed in Cumberland.

CUNONIA. A genus of plants, the only species of which is the *Cunonia Capensis*, a native of the Cape; named in honour of J. C. Cuno, of Amsterdam, a botanist and poet.

CUPANIA. A genus of plants consisting of trees or shrubs; named after Cupani, a Franciscan monk, author of Plantæ Siculæ, &c.

CUPREOUS. Coppery; consisting of or resembling copper, or partaking of its qualities; from L. *cupreus*, from from *cuprum*. See COPPER.

CURAÇOA. A liqueur named from the island of Curaçao, one of the Dutch Antilles, where the best is made.

CURRANT. A shrub of the genus *Ribes;* a small kind of dried grape imported from the Levant, chiefly from Zante and Cephalonia, and the southern shores of the Gulf of Corinth (*e. g.* the monastery of Megalospeleion). They were formerly called *corinthes* or *corinths*, from having been first imported from the neighbourhood of Corinth. "The Fr. name of those coming from the Levant is *raisins de Corinthe*, grapes of Corinth."

CURTISIA. A genus of plants, nat. or. *Aquifoliaceæ*, from the single species of which *C. faginea*, a native of the Cape, the Hottentots and Caffres make their javelins; named after Mr. Curtis, founder of the Botanical Magazine.

CUSSONIA.   A genus of plants, nat. or. *Arabiaceæ*, called after P. Cousson, à French botanist.—*Crabb.*

CYCLOPEAN.   Vast, terrific; a term applied to the remains of a rude and very massive kind of architecture, of the earliest ages, demanding an enormous exertion of physical force.   The stones were irregularly placed, but made to fit each other.   The word is derived from the Cyclops, fabulous giants of antiquity.

CYDONIA.   The quince (*Cydonium malum*); nam d from Cydon, a town of Crete, which abounded in this fruit.

CYPRIAN.   A term applied to a lewd woman; so called from the isle of Cyprus, birthplace of Venus.

CYPRINUS.   A genus of fishes of the *Abdominal* order; named from Cyprus; or from Κυπρις, Venus.

CYPRIS.   A species of fresh-water crustacea, which swarm in stagnant water ; named from Κυπρις, Venus.

CYPRUS.   A celebrated wine brought from Cyprus.—— A thin transparent black stuff.

> Lawn as white as driven snow,
> *Cyprus* black as e'er was crow.
>> *Shak.* W.'s Tale.

> A *cyprus*, not a bosom,
> Hides my poor heart !
>> *Shak.*

CYRILLA.   A handsome plant, of which there is only one species, native of Jamaica : named by L'Heretier after Dominico Cyrillo, professor of medicine at Naples, author of Plantæ Rariores Regni Neapolitani, &c.

D.

DACOITAL.   Robber-like ; lit. after the manner of the Dacoits of India.   Gang-robbery is called dacoity.

DÆDAL.   Various, variegated (*Spenser*) ; skilful (*Webster*); artful, skilful ; fruitful in invention (*Richardson*).

But liuing art may not least part expresse,
  Nor life-resembling pencill it can paint,
All were it Zeuxis or Praxiteles
  His *dædale* hand would fail, and greatly faint,
  And her perfections with his errer taint.
                    Spenser, Fairie Queene, Introd. b. iii.

                    Nor hath
  The *dædal* hand of nature only poured
  Her gifts of outward grace.
                    J. Phillips, b. i.

  Here ancient art her *dædal* fancies play'd
    In the quaint mazes of the crisped roof.
                    Warton, Ode 3.

So called from Dædalus, an ingenious artist, who made the Cretan labyrinth. "Dædalum vocatur quicquid est artificiosè varium et affabrè factum" (*Vossius*).

DÆDALIAN. Formed with art; intricate; maze-like; from *Dædalus.*—See DÆDAL.

DÆDALOUS. Having a margin with various windings and turnings; of a beautiful and delicate texture; a term applied to the leaves of plants; from *Dædalus.*—See DÆDAL.

DAG. A pistol; "perhaps," says Minshew, "because brought into use by the Daci, a people of Germany; and that they were a new fashion of German horsemen appears from the quotation from Knolles, produced by Mr. Nares: 'Neither was anything taken from them but these *dags*, which the German horsemen, after a new fashion, carried at their saddle bows; these the Turks greatly desired, delighted with the noveltie of the invention, to see them shoot off with a firelock without a match: Knolles' Hist. of the Turks, p. 742.' "— *Richardson*.

DAGGER (Fr. *dague;* G. *degen;* Sw. *daggert;* Low L. *dagga, daggerius*). A short weapon, used to stab with. "This word, as well as *dag* (q.v.), Du Cange says, some derive à *Dacis*, as a weapon peculiar to them. Wachter quotes authorities to show that *gladius* was called *degin*, quòd ejus ministerio in defensione utamur; and hence inclines to think it an application of *degen*, viz. fortis, miles; remarking that men and their arms are often designated by the same name."— *Richardson*.

DAGUERREOTYPE. A process for taking views, portraits, &c., by means of reflection from the images themselves in a strong light; named from the discoverer, M. *Daguerre* (a celebrated French dioramic painter, who published it in July, 1839), and Gr. τυπος, a mark, stamp, or impress.

DAHLIA. A genus of plants, perennials, nat. or. *Compositr.* natives of Mexico; introduced into Europe by the Spaniards in 1789; and named by Cavanilles in honour of Andrew Dahl. a Swedish botanist. It is the *Georgina* of Willdenow and other Continental botanists; and was so called in honour of Professor Georgei, the Russian traveller and botanist.

DAHLINE. A vegetable principle discovered in the dahlia, similar to inulin and starch. See DAHLIA.

DALECHAMPIA. A genus of plants, of which there are two species, the one a native of New Granada, the other of the West Indies; named by Plumier in honour of Jacobus Dalechampius, a physician of Lyons, a commentator on Dioscorides and Pliny; and author of Historia Plantarum, 1587.

DALMATICA or DALMATIC. A long white gown, with large open sleeves, worn by deacons in the Roman Catholic church. It was at first used only by bishops, and was called dalmatica because it originated in Dalmatia, now a province of Austria, on the Gulf of Venice.

> Candida ut extensis niteat *Dalmatica* rugis,
> Fimbria neve erret huic sine lege levis.

A tulip was anciently called a Dalmatian.

DAMASCENE. The fruit of the *Prunus Damascena*. See DAMSON.

DAMASCENUM. A genus of plants, nat. or. *Hydrocharaceæ*; named from Damascus.

DAMASK (Fr. *damasquin*). A silk stuff, having some parts raised above the ground, representing flowers and other figures; originally from Damascus; or, as others say, linen or silk woven after a manner invented at Damascus.——To form flowers on stuffs; to variegate; to diversify; as, a bank damasked with flowers.——Red colour, from the damask rose.

To damask wine formerly signified to warm it a little, in order to take off the edge of the cold, and to make it mantle, as Bailey calls it.

DAMASKEENING. A kind of Mosaic work, which consists in ornamenting iron, steel, &c., by making incisions therein, and filling them up with gold or silver wire : used chiefly for adorning sword blades, guards, locks of pistols, &c.; named from Damascus.—See DAMASKIN.

DAMASKIN. Formerly a sabre, so called from the manufacture of Damascus.

DAMASSE or DAMASK. A kind of wrought linen made at Flanders, in imitation of damask silks.—See DAMASK.

DAMASSIN. A kind of damask, with gold and silver flowers woven in the warp and woof.—See DAMASK.

DAMPIERA. A genus of leguminous plants, natives of Australia : named in honour of Captain Dampier.

DAMSON. The fruit of a variety of the *Prunus domestica*, a small black plum; formerly written *damascene*, from Δαμαςκηνος, of Damascus, in whose neighbourhood it first grew.

DANÆA. A very curious genus of tropical plants, named by Dr. Smith, after Professor Dana, of Turin.

DANAIS. A genus of climbing shrubs, natives of the East India islands; named from Danais, one of the Danaides.

DANBURITE. A mineral resembling chondrodite, occurring with oligoclase in dolomite, at Danbury, Connecticut, U.S.

DANEGELT. In England, formerly a tax imposed upon every hide of land, in order to clear the seas of Danish pirates. At a subsequent period, when the Danes became masters, the *danegelt* was a tax levied by the Danish princes on every hide of land owned by the Anglo-Saxons (*P. Cyc.*); from *Dane*, and *gelt*, *geld*, money.

DAPHNE (Δαφνη of Theophrastus and Dioscorides). A genus of plants, whose species are shrubs of no great height; named from the nymph Daphne, whose fabled metamorphosis is well known.

DARIC. A gold coin, supposed to have been equal to 25*s*. sterling; so called from Darius, by whom it was struck.

F

DARWINIA. A genus of plants, drooping shrubs, natives of Australia; named after Dr. Erasmus Darwin.

DASEY. In Ireland, a name for a cloak. A Dublin physician, named Dasey, was in the habit of wearing a cloak to conceal his thefts from the houses which he visited professionally. After he was hanged, for this or some other crime, cloaks were universally discarded in Ireland, and were generally called daseys.—*Anon.*

DAUBENTONIA. A genus of leguminous shrubs, natives of Mexico; named in honour of the French naturalist, Louis Jean Marie Daubenton.

DAVENPORT. A sort of writing desk or escritoire; doubtless named after the maker.

DAVILLA. A genus of climbing shrubs, with yellow flowers, named after H. C. Davilla, an Italian historian.

DAVINA. A new Vesuvian mineral, the same with nepheline; called in honour of Sir H. Davy.

DAVY JONES. A sailor's name for a sea-devil. Hence, " to go to Davy Jones's locker " means " to die," because sailors' dead bodies are buried in the sea.—*S. F. C.*

DELF. Earthenware, covered with enamel or white glazing, in imitation of china ware or porcelain; made at Delft, in Holland; properly, Delft-ware.

DELIA. A festival in honour of Apollo, annually celebrated at Athens, and quintennially at Delos. During its continuance it was illegal to execute any malefactor: thus Xenophon and Plato inform us that Socrates was kept in prison thirty days after his condemnation, on account of the Delian solemnities, whereas they did not scruple to put Phocion to death during a festival dedicated to Jupiter. The origin of the festival is imputed to Theseus.

DELIAC. A kind of sculptured vase; also beautiful bronze and silver (*Elmes*), from *Delos*, an isle in the Grecian Archipelago.

DELIAN. The name of a celebrated problem proposed by the oracle at Delos, and known to geometers as the "duplication of the cube." " The finding the side of a cube which will be

double . . . . . ube is thus named, it is said, because
during . . . . .)elians, on consulting their oracle,
were required . . .ct a cubical altar double the size of
the one which they . .en possessed. This problem is reported
to have puzzled all the school of Plato at Athens."

DELPHIN. An edition of the Latin classics, prepared for
the Dauphin's use (*in usum Delphini*) by order of Louis XIV.

DELTA. Originally applied to the triangle included
between the two main arms of the Nile, and so called from its
resemblance to the Greek letter Δ. Subsequently applied to
any tract of alluvial land at the mouth of a river, though of
different shapes, as the delta of the Mississippi, the delta of the
Ganges.—*S. F. Creswell.*

DELVAUXENE. A mineral of a yellowish brown,
brownish black, or reddish colour; from Berneau, in Belgium ;
analysed by Delvaux.

DENNET. A two-wheeled carriage, named after its
manufacturer.

DENSHIRING. Cutting off the turf of land and burning
it to ashes ; so called because first begun in Devonshire.—
Crabb.

DEODAND. In England (formerly) a personal chattel
which was the immediate occasion of the death of a rational
creature, and for that reason given to God (*Deo dandus*); that
is, forfeited to the king, to be applied to pious uses, and distributed in alms by his high almoner.

DERBY (The). " Since the reign of James I., who founded
the Epsom meeting during his residence at Nonsuch, its immediate locality has been regarded as classic ground by our race-
loving public. In the little parish of Woodmansterne is ' Lambert's Oaks,' formerly an inn, but latterly a place of some interest to the Jockey Club, since it gave name to the famous Oaks
stakes at Epsom races. The house, which stands high and
commands very fine views, was erected by a society called the
Hunters' Club, under a lease from the Lambert family. It
afterwards became the residence of the unfortunate Lieut.-
General Burgoyne, from whom it passed to the eleventh Earl

of Derby, whose grandson Edward Smith Stanley, the twelfth earl, much improved it. Here was given, on the 9th of June, 1774, in anticipation of the marriage of Lord Stanley with Lady Betty Hamilton, the celebrated 'Fête Champêtre,' the first of the kind in England, under the superintendence of Lieut.-General Burgoyne. This rural festival furnished the general with the subject of a dramatic entertainment entitled the 'Maid of the Oaks,' and which, after a few bold touches from Garrick's pen, was performed for the first time at Drury Lane, on Nov. 5, 1774—

> " Whose is this piece ? 'tis all surmise—suggestion—
> Is't *his*, or *hers*, or *yours*, sir ?—that's the question :
> The parent, bashful, whimsical, or poor,
> Left it a puling infant at the door :
> 'Twas laid on flowers, and wrapt in fancied cloaks,
> And on the breast was written ' Maid o' th' Oaks.'
> The actors crowded round ; the girls caress'd it—
> ' Lord, the sweet pretty babe !'—they prais'd and bless'd it ;
> The master peep'd, smil'd, took it, and dress'd it."

On May 14, 1779, Edward Smith Stanley, the twelfth Earl of Derby, originated the famous Oak stakes, so named from his sylvan retreat at Woodmansterne. The first winner of the Oaks stakes at Epsom was Bridget, a bay mare, foaled in 1776, the property of the earl. Bridget was of royal blood, got by King Herod out of Jemima. In the following year (1780) the earl started the Derby stakes, so named out of compliment to its noble founder. The first winner of the Derby stakes was Diomed, a chestnut horse, foaled in 1777, bred by the Hon. Richard Vernon, of Newmarket, and sold to Sir C. Banbury, Bart. Diomed was got by Florizel out of the Spectator mare, dam of Pastorella, Fame, &c. After the death of the Earl of Derby, in 1834, 'The Oaks' estate was sold to Sir Charles Grey, and has since passed to its present proprietor, Joseph Smith, Esq."—*Ed. of N. & Q.*

DERRICK or DERIC. A contrivance for raising heavy weights by means of a pully, and especially for raising ships, and differently constructed according to circumstances ; named after its inventor, Derrick. " It is said to have been named after the Tyburn Jack Ketch, whose namelike instrument it resembled."—Cf. Times, 28 Sep. 1858.

DESCLOÏZITE. A mineral colour, mostly deep black, from South America; analysed by Descloizeaux.

DEUCE or DEUSE. A demon or evil spirit. " What the deuce is the matter ?" " The deuse is in you." "The deuce take you." According to some, the word owes its origin to the name of the Roman general Claudius Drusus, stepson of Augustus. Albert Miræus (Annales Belgici, Bruss. 1624, p. 9) says the name of Drusus, after his German victories, became so dreaded that it was still used in the imprecation common with the Flemings, *Dat den Droes hale*—May Druse take you ; *Drusus te auferat seu evehat;* and Dr. Smith (Dict. Anc. Biog. vol. 1, p. 1086) says, " The misery that Drusus occasioned among the German tribes was undoubtedly excessive. Some antiquaries have imagined that the German imprecation, *Das dich der Drus hol,* may be traced to the traditional dread of this terrible conqueror. Junius gives *Deus take you;* Abi in malam rem, Diobolus te abripiat ; and refers to Dusius, the name of a certain evil spirit. Sharon Turner informs us that Bede, in his Commentary on Luke, mentions demons appearing to men as females, and to women as men, whom he says the Gauls call Dusii (quosdam dæmones quas *dusios* Galli nuncupant), the presumed origin of our word *deuce.* Again, from *Dusius* is said to have been formed the Old Teut. *duyse,* a concubine." See Todd's Johnson; Keysler Antiq. Septentrion. 547 ; Kilian in v. Duyse ; Isidorus, Gloss. 51 ; Augustine de Civ. Dei, lib. xv., c. 23 ; Dr. Whitaker, Cathedral of Cornwall, vol. 1, pp. 345—347, and N. & Q. 2nd S., No. 43, 331. It comes rather from *diaus,* a Celtic corruption of *diabolus,* the devil.

DEVIL. A very wicked person ; named after Satan.——An idol or false god, Lev. xvii., 2 Chron. xi.——In ludicrous language, any great evil ; in profane language, an expletive expressing wonder, vexation, &c.——A printer's errand boy. ——A machine for cutting up rags and cloth for manufacturing purposes.——To pepper excessively; to devil a fowl or a bone.

DEVILISH. Partaking of the qualities of the devil; diabolical; very evil and mischievous; malicious; excessive, enormous, *in a vulgar and ludicrous sense,* as a *devilish* cheat.

DEVIL'S-BIT. The *Scabiosa præmorsa,* so called from having its root, as it were, bitten off at the end.

DEVONIAN. The name given by Professor Sedgwick and Sir R. Murchison to a great portion of the palæozoic strata of N. and S. Devon, and referred to as coeval in formation with the old red sandstone of Herefordshire.

DHOLLERA. A description of Indian cotton, named from Dholarra or Dholera, a town in the British district of Ahmedabad.

DIANA. A name formerly given to silver, from its white shining appearance, like the moon, *i.e.* Diana.——A name given to the arborescent form of the crystallized silver which is disengaged when mercury is put into a solution of nitrate of silver. —— An African species of the monkey, the *Simia Diana* of Linnæus, and Palatine monkey of Pennant; but perhaps better known as the African spotted monkey. It was so called because from the top of its nose is a white line, passing over each eye to the ears in an arched direction, resembling the crescent assigned by the poets to Diana.

DIANELLA. A genus of plants found in woody recesses in warm climates, whence their name from the sylvan Diana.

DIANTHUS. Classical name of the pink, carnation, sweet William, &c.; from Διος ανθος, Jove's flower, or divine flower, from the colour and odour in some species. The genus contains upwards of seventy species.

DIAPER (Fr. *diapré,* diapered). Figured linen cloth; a cloth wove in flowers or figures, much used for towels or napkins : hence, a towel or napkin. The word is derived from *d'Ypres, i.e.* from Ypres, in Flanders, where this article was first manufactured.

DICKEY. A common word for a false shirt-front. The original term still in use at the Dublin University is *tommy,* not from the Christian name, but from Gr. τομη, a section.

DICKSONIA. A genus of plants, nat. or. *Polypodiaceæ;* named after Mr. Dickson, a British botanist.

DICTAMNUS. Dittany ; now applied to a genus of plants, nat. or. *Rutaceæ,* the species of which are perennials ; so called from Dictamnus, in Crete, on whose mountains it grows.

DILLENIA. A genus of very elegant plants, whose species are found in India, New Holland, China, and Brazil ; named in honour of John James Dillenius, born at Darmstadt, in 1607 ; appointed the first botanical professor at Oxford, on Sherrard's foundation ; author of a History of Mosses, and Hortus Eltha-mensis.

DILLNITE. A mineral consisting of silica, alumina, lime, magnesia, and water, found in the Dilln Mine, at Schemnitz, Hungary.

DILLWYNIA. A genus of papilionaceous plants, con-sisting of subshrubs, natives of America ; named in honour of L. W. Dillwyn, F.R.S., a writer on the British *Confervæ.*

DIMITY (found written *dimitty, dimitie,* Fr. *démitte;* also *démitton,* sorte de toile de coton moins large et moins serrée que la démitte ; D. *diemit*). A kind of white cotton cloth, ribbed or figured (*Webster*). It is a cross-barred stuff composed entirely of cotton, and similar in fabric to fustian, from which it differs chiefly in having ornaments woven in it, and in not being dyed. The manufacture of dimities in Europe was first esta-blished at Lyons about 1580, and for a long period our markets were supplied by the French. The works at Manchester have now almost wholly superseded the necessity of importation. Junius derives *dimitie* from διμιτος, wove of a double thread ; hence, says he, μονομιτος, wove of a simple thread ; πολυμιτος, wove of many threads ; λεπτομιτος, wove of a thin thread ; εξαμιτος, samit (samite). The word is more probably derived from *dimyati, i.e.* made at Damietta, in Egypt. " In Tennìs and Dimyát," says Idrísí, who wrote in the middle of the twelfth century, " they manufacture the finest dresses of tanned leather, cotton, and linen ; and the dyed striped clothes of Tennìs, which for price and beauty are unrivalled. A single robe, when embroidered with gold, is sometimes sold for a thousand dínárs or thereabouts (£400). Those that have no gold in them sell for one or two hundred dínárs (£35 or £40). The manufactures of Fú and Damírch and the neighbouring islands, though of a very superior kind, do not at all approach those of Tennís and Dimyát." " This curious passage," says the writer in the Encyc. Metrop., " is entirely omitted in the Epitome of Idrísí's work, translated into Latin under the title of Geographia Nubiensis. The fine manufactures, especially those of cotton, were all imported from the East in the Middle Ages ; hence our calicoes received their name from Cálicút ; our musselines [muslins] from Músul; and, if the conjecture here made be correct, our dimities from Damietta."

DINITE. An aggregation or druse of crystals, having the appearance of ice ; found by Professor Dini, at Lunigiana, in Tuscany.

DIOGENES' CUP. A term applied to the cup-like cavity of the hand, occasioned by bending the metacarpal bone of the little finger.

DIOMEDA. The heron ; a genus of birds ; so called from the Grecian general Diomedes, whose companions are said to have been changed into herons.

DIOPHANTINE. A name applied to problems relating to square and cube numbers, &c., the properties of which were first solved by Diophantus, of Alexandria, who lived in the third century, and was one of the first writers on algebra.

DIOSCOREA. A genus of perennial plants, of which there are several species, mostly tropical plants, chiefly natives of the West Indies ; named in honour of Pedacius Dioscorides, an eminent physician and botanist, who was born at Anazarbus, in Cicilia, and lived in the time of Nero ; he was author of *Materia Medica*, in which from 500 to 600 plants are described ; a work which, till the beginning of the seventeenth century, was considered the most essential to the student of botany.

DIOSCURIA. In classical history, festivals celebrated by the Lacedæmonians with great mirth and festivity in honour of the Dioscuri, or sons of Jupiter, viz., Castor and Pollux.

DITTANY. A plant of the genus *Dictamnus*, q.v.

DODONÆA. A genus of plants, nat. or. *Sapindaceæ*, the species being shrubs; named after Dodonæus, a celebrated botanist.

DOILEY, DOYLY, or DOYLEY. A small napkin, generally coloured, used with fruit and wine (*Smart*); formerly a species of woollen stuff; named from the first maker, Mr. Doyley, "a very respectable warehouseman, whose family had resided in the great old house next to Hodsoll's, the bankers, from the time of Queen Anne." This refers to 346, Strand, east corner of Upper Wellington Street. See Notes and Queries.

DOLLAR (G. *thaler*, D. *daalder*, Dan. and Sw. *daler*, Sp. *dalera*, Russ. *taler*). A silver coin of Spain and of the United States, equal to 100 cents, or about 4s. 4d. sterling (*Webster*). In different parts of Germany the name is given to coins of different values. The Prussian dollar or thaler is equal to about 3s. 4d. sterling. It seems to have originated in Germany. Some derive the name from Dale, the town where they assert it was first coined; but the word *thaler* is more correctly an abbreviation of *Joachimsthaler*, from Joachimsthal, near Carlsbad, in Bohemia, where these pieces were first struck in 1519. The town was formerly of greater importance than at present, owing to its mines of silver and cobalt. With the exception, perhaps, of the mines of Larium, in Attica, opposite Ægina, here is the oldest silver mine in Europe, and the first that was endowed with mining laws. It is 300 fathoms deep, but, instead of 800 miners, only 400 are now employed. "*Joachimsthaler:* on désigne sous ce nom les pièces de monnaie d'argent frappées, vers le fin du XV siècle, dans les mines du Conte de Schlick, à Joachimsthal, en Bohême. C'était une imitation des florins d'empire, et la pureté de leur titre les mit bientôt en telle réputation, que ce type finit par prédominer en même temps que leur nom restait affecté par l'usage aux pièces d'une valeur analogue, sauf que par abbréviation on finit par ne plus dire que *thalers* au lieu de *Joachimsthaler* (sous entendu *munze*), monnaie de Joachimsthal. C'est là l'étymologie du mot *thaler*, que nous traduisons en François par notre mot *écu.* Ces pièces de monnaie sont dites encore *lœwenthaler* (écus du lion), à cause du lion à deux queus de Bohême qu'elles représentent, et quelquefois aussi *Schlickenthaler,* du nom du seigneur qui les fit frapper, en Latin *Slicni,* et aussi *Joachiomici,* ou *Vallones*" (*Dict. de la Conversation*).

DOLLOND. A telescope on the achromatic principle, first introduced by the late Peter Dollond, son of John Dollond, an eminent optician, descended from a French refugee family.

DOLOMITE. A variety of magnesian limestone occurring chiefly massive, and softer than common limestone. Much of the common white marble is dolomite; the Apennines are partly composed of dolomite; it occurs at Iona, and there are dolomite mountains in Tyrol. It was named after the French geologist Doiomieu, born at Grenoble in June, 1750, and who in less than three years published twenty-seven original memoirs, among which were those on the nature of leucite, peridot, anthracite, pyroxene, &c. " See also report, mentioning the two kinds of dolomite, one of which was used in the New Parliament House, London; the sort used decays on exposure."—*S. F. Creswell.*

DOMBEYA. A genus of S. American plants, the only species of which is a tree, native of Chili, called *D. Chilensis ;* named in honour of the French botanist, J. Dombey.

DOMITE. A mineral, having the aspect and gritty feel of a sandy chalk ; from Puy de Dôme, in Auvergne.

DONARIUM. A new metal found at Brevig, in Norway, in the same zircon-syenite that contains wöhlorite and enkolite ; named from the god Donar.

DONATISM. The principles of the Donatists, or followers of Donatus, African schismatics of the fourth century.

DONIA. A genus of beautiful American papilionaceous shrubs, natives of Mexico, &c. ; named after David Don, the Scotch botanist.

DON PEDRO. A low game at cards, probably invented by the mixed English and Irish rabble who fought in Portugal in 1832–3.

DOPPLERITE. A mineral, brownish-black when fresh, found in peat, near Aussee, in Styria ; named after M. Doppler.

DORIC. In architecture, the second order of columns, between the Tuscan and the Ionic, distinguished for simplicity and strength; named from Doris, in Greece.——The dialect of the Dorians, one of the five dialects of the Greek language, differing little from that of Lacedæmon. It is found in the writings of Archimedes and Theocritus.——In music, the first of the authentic modes of the ancients. Its character is to be severe, tempered with gravity and joy.

DORICISM or DORISM. A phrase of the Doric dialect.

DORKING. A peculiar variety of fowl of a large size; distinguished from the common barn-door kind by having five claws on each foot, the hinder claw being double; named from Dorking, Surrey. They are said to have been brought hither by the Romans, and to degenerate in other counties.

DORNIC (found written *dornix*). A species of linen cloth; from *Doornik*, the Flemish form of Tournay, in Belgium. The carpets commonly called Brussels are made at Doornik.

DORNOCK. A kind of figured linen, made at Dornoch, Scotland.

D'ORSAY. Formerly a sort of overcoat; named after the late Count d'Orsay. An article of furniture, and several other things, were called after the same person.

DORSTENIA. A genus of plants, nat. or. *Urticaceæ;* named in honour of Dr. Dorsten, a German botanist.

DOUGLASSIA. A genus of plants, nat. or. *Primulaceæ;* called after Mr. Douglas, an ardent botanist.—*Crabb.*

DOVERCOURT. A term made use of at Dovercourt, near Harwich, in Essex, for a "great noise." "There is a legend that Dovercourt Church once possessed a miraculous cross which spoke; thus noticed in the Collyer of Croyden :—

'And now the rood of *Dovercot*
Confirming his opinions to be true :'

so that it is possible, as Nares suggests, that this church was the scene of confusion alluded to in the proverb, 'Dovercourt—all speakers and no hearers.' Foxe (Martyrology, vol. ii. 302) states that "a rumour was spread that no man could shut the door, which, therefore, stood open night and day ; and that the resort of people to it was much and very great." Others think the proverb may have arisen from the fact that the court held at Dovercourt is composed chiefly of seamen.

DOWLAS. A kind of coarse linen cloth ; probably from the proper name Douglas, which corrupts into Dowlas ; but whether from a surname or local name is doubtful. There is the Forest of Douglas, in Scotland, whose inhabitants are much engaged in cotton weaving and spinning. "From *Dour-lans*, in Picardy " (*Richardson*). " This should be Doulens or Doullens " (*S. F. C.*)

DREELITE. A mineral, found in small unmodified crystals, and in the cavities of a quartzose rock, at Beaujeu, dep. Rhone; and Badenweiler (Baden); named by Dufrénoy after M. de Drée, a liberal patron of science.

DRUGGET. A coarse slight woollen fabric, used as a protection for, and sometimes instead of, a carpet. The Rev. S. F. Creswell derives the name from Drogheda, in Ireland, where it is said to have been first manufactured. Dr. Johnson renders it "a slight kind of woollen stuff;" and there is no doubt that it was anciently used as an article of attire.

> " In *druggets* drest, of thirteen pence a yard.
> See Philip's son amidst his Prussian guard."—*Swift*.

> " Even I, a dunce of more renown than they,
> Was sent before but to prepare thy way ;
> And, coarsely clad in Norwich *drugget*, came
> To teach the nations in thy greater name."
> *Dryden* (Mac Flecknoe).

DRUMMOND LIGHT. A very intense light, produced by turning two streams of gas, one oxygen, the other hydrogen, in a state of ignition, upon a ball of lime ; named from the inventor, Lieut. Drummond.

DRYANDRA. A genus of plants, nat. or. *Proteaceæ*, named after Dryander, a Swedish botanist.

DUBOISIA. A genus of South Australian shrubs ; named in memory of Louis Dubois, a French botanist.

DUCAT. A coin of several countries of Europe. It is of silver or gold. The silver ducat is generally equal to 4s. 6d.

sterling, and the gold ducat is of twice the value. Some assert that Roger II., Duke of Apulia, first (in 1140, or, as others say, in 1240 or 1280) coined the gold ducat bearing the effigy of Christ with the following legend:—" Sit tibi, Christe, datus, quem tu regis, iste ducatus" (Cf. Zachenberg, Diss. de Germ. Med. x. 20, p. 372 ; and Ducange). According to others, the origin of the ducat is referred to one Longinus, governor of Italy, who, revolting against the Emperor Justin the younger, made himself Duke of Ravenna, and called himself Exarcha, *i.e.* without lord or ruler'; and, to show his independence, struck pieces of money of very pure gold, in his own name and with his own stamp, which were called *ducati*, ducats, in the sixth century (Cf. Procopius ; Verg. Polydorus de Invent. Rer. 20).

DUCATELLO. An Egyptian silver coin, current at Alexandria for ten medimni, or measures of capacity ; a diminutive of DUCAT, *q.v.*

DUCATOON. A silver coin ; that of Venice being equal to about 4*s*. 8*d*. sterling ; that of Holland about 5*s*. 6*d*. sterling ; a diminutive of DUCAT, *q.v.*

DUFFEL. A coarse woollen cloth with a thick nap or frieze ; from Duffel, a town of Belgium, prov. Antwerp, having manufactures of linen and flax spinning.

DUFRENITE. A mineral consisting of phosphoric acid, red oxide of iron, oxide of manganese, protoxide, and water ; found at Siegen ; Hirscherg in Reuss ; and Limoges, France ; named after Dufrêne.

DUFRÉNOYSITE. A mineral, composed of lead, silver, copper, iron, arsenic, and sulphur ; found with realgar, blende, and pyrite, in the dolomite of St. Gothard ; named after M. Dufréynoy.

DUMASINE. An empyreumatic oil, obtained by rectifying acetone derived from the acetates ; named from Dumas ; perhaps Charles Louis Dumas, professor of anatomy and physiology to the University of Montpellier, who died in 1806.

DUMDUMMER. In Calcutta, a vehicle familiarly so called, because much used to convey passengers to Dum-Dum, near Calcutta.

DUNCE. A person of weak intellect ; a dolt or thickskull.
Some derive the word from L. *attonitus*, as if thunderstruck, or
struck by lightning ; amazed, astonished, bewildered ; others
from *dumb*, q.d. *dumps*, *i.e.* dumbish. "*Dunce* is said
by Johnson to be a word of unknown etymology Stanihurst
explains it. The term *Duns*, from *Scotus*, 'so famous for his
subtill quiddities,' he says, 'is so trivial and common in all
schools, that whoso surpasseth others either in cavilling, so-
phistrie, or subtill philosophie, is forthwith nicknamed a *Duns*.'
This, he tells us in the margin, is the reason 'why schoolmen
are called *Dunses* ' (Description of Ireland, p. 2). The word
easily passed into a term of scorn, just as a blockhead is
called a Solomon, a bully Hector, and as Moses is the vulgar
name of contempt for a Jew " (Dr. Southey's Omniana, vol. I.
p. 5).—*E. H. B.*

DURANTIA. A genus of plants, nat. or. *Verbenaceæ* ;
named after M. Durantes, a physician and botanist.

E.

EAU-DE-COLOGNE. A spirit principally used as a
perfume ; first made at Cologne by Johann Maria Farina.
There are are at present twenty or thirty persons at Cologne
who claim to be makers of the veritable article.

EDELFORSITE. A mineral ; colour white or grayish ;
found at Aedelfors in Smaoland, Cziklowa in the Bannat, and
Gjelleback in Norway.

EDENIZED. Admitted into Paradise (*Davies*) ; from the
Scripture *Eden*.

EDINGTONITE. A mineral, colour grayish-white, occurring in the Kilpatrick Hills, in Scotland. There are three
places named Edington in England, and Edington Castle
co. Berwick. Edington is also a personal name.

EGERAN. A sub-species of pyramidal garnet, occurring
in felspar and hornblende at Haslau, near Eger, in Bohemia.

EHLITE. A mineral ; colour verdigris-green ; found at
Ehl, on the Rhine, and at Nischne-Tajilsk, in the Ural.

EHRETIA. A genus of plants, nat. or. *Ehretiaceæ ;* called after M. Ehret, a German botanical draughtsman.—*Crabb.*

EKEBERGIA. A genus of plants, the only species of which is a native of the Cape ; named by Sparrman in honour of Sir C. G. Ekeberg, who first brought the tea-plant alive to Europe.

EKEBERGITE. A mineral, a supposed variety of scapolite ; doubtless named after Andrew Gustavus Ekeberg, a chemist, who was born at Stockholm in 1767, became chemical teacher at the University of Upsal, and obtained great celebrity from his analysis of the mineral gadolinite, and many other scientific discoveries.

ELECAMPANE. A plant, named also starwort. The word in Latin is written *Inula* and *Enula campana,* and is derived from *helenium,* Gr. ελενιον, and was so called because it was said to have sprung from the tears of Helen (Ελενη). (See Pliny). *Campana* signifies a bell.

ELIZABETHAN. Pertaining to Queen Elizabeth or her times ; *e.g.* to the styles of architecture, literature, &c., then prevalent.

ELLISIA. A genus of plants, nat. or. *Hydrophyllaceæ ;* so called after M. J. Ellis, an English botanist.—*Crabb.*

ELYSIAN. Pertaining to Elysium ; yielding the highest pleasures ; deliciously soothing ; exceedingly delightful ; as Elysian Fields.

ELZEVIR. A name given to certain editions of the classics, &c., published by the Elzevir family at Amsterdam and Leyden, from about 1595 to 1680, and highly prized for their accuracy and elegance.

ENFIELD. A celebrated rifle, first manufactured at Enfield, Middlesex, but now also at other places. It was adopted for public service in 1853.

ENGLISHERIE. The state or privilege of being an Englishman (not used), "which it was necessary to prove a man to be in the reign of Canute, in case he was murdered, in order that the hundred might be exempt from the amercement which it would otherwise have been liable to."— *Crabb.*

EOLIC. A dialect of the Greek language, which was used by the inhabitants of Eolia, in Asia Minor.

ÉPERNAY. One of the best champagnes, from a place of the same name in France.

ÉPERGNE. (Fr.) An ornamental stand for a large dish in the centre of a table (*Smart*); probably made at Épergne, in France.

EPHESIAN. One of a dissolute life (*Shak.*); so called from Ephesus, in Asia Minor, one of the most splendid cities of antiquity, whose inhabitants are said to have lead a Sybarite life.

EPHESITE. A mineral, placed by Dr. Smith near margarite; found with the emery of Gumuch-dagh, near Ephesus.

EPICTETAN. Pertaining to Epictetus, a Stoic philosopher in the time of the Roman emperor Domitian.—*Arbuthnot.*

EPICURE. One devoted to sensual enjoyments; hence, one who indulges in the luxuries of the table; a follower of Epicurus, the ancient Greek philosopher, who, however, lived chiefly on bread and water, and placed the *summum bonum* in tranquillity of mind; but whose followers disregarded his principles.

EPICUREAN. Pertaining to Epicurus, as the Epicurean philosophy or tenets; a follower of Epicurus; one given to the luxuries of the table.——A sauce made of Indian soy, chili vinegar, walnut catsup, and mushroom catsup.

EPICURIANISM. Attachment to the doctrines of Epicurus.

EPICURISM. Luxury, sensual enjoyments; indulgences in gross pleasure; voluptuousness; the doctrines of Epicurus.

EPSOMITE. A mineral common in mineral waters, as at Epsom, and as an efflorescence on rocks in many other places.

ERASTIANISM. The principles of the Erastians, followers of Thomas Erastus, a German, who maintained that the church is " a mere creature of the state," dependent upon it for its existence, and for all its powers.

ERDMANNITE. A mineral, colour dark brown, found in the isle of Stokö, in the Langesundfiord; named after M. Erdmann.

ESCALLONIA. A genus of S. American plants, inhabiting Alpine regions; named after their discoverer, Escallon, a Spanish botanist.

ESCULAPIAN. Medical; pertaining to the healing art (*Young*); from *Æsculapius*, the celebrated physician.

ESMARKITE. A mineral, a silicate; named after M. Esmark. Two different minerals appear to be confounded under this name.

EUGENIA. A genus of plants, nat. or. *Monogynia;* named by Micheli after Prince Eugene of Savoy, who sent him from Germany nearly all the plants described by Clusius.

EUGÉNIE. A carriage named after the Empress Eugénie.

EUGUBINE. A name given to certain bronze tables having five inscriptions in the Umbrian language, mixed with Etruscan, and two in Latin characters, containing facts relative to the wars of Italy; found at Eugubio or Gubbio, a town of Umbria, in 1444.

EUMACHIA. A genus of plants, or. *Monogynia;* natives of Australia; named after Eumachus, a Greek writer cited by Theophrastus.

EUMENIDIA. Festivals celebrated by the Athenians in honour of the Eumenides, another name for the Furies.

EUPATORINA. An alkaloid obtained from *Eupatorium cannabinum*. See EUPATORIUM.

EUPATORIUM. A genus of plants, nat. or. *Compositæ,* the species of which are known as hemp agrimony; called after its discoverer, Mithridates, surnamed Eupator.

EUSTACHIAN. A term applied to a slender tube, affording a passage for the air from a cavity in the ear to the back part of the mouth and the external air; named after its discoverer, Eustachius, a distinguished Italian physician, who flourished in the sixteenth century at Rome. The Eustachian valve is a fold of the lining membrane of the auricle of the heart.

EUTERPEAN. A term often given to music clubs; from Euterpe, the muse who presides over wind instruments.

EUTYCHIANISM. The doctrines of Eutychius (*Webster*). Eutychius, who lived A.D. 443, held that the divine and human natures of Christ, after their union, became so blended together as to constitute but one nature.

F.

FABIAN. Delaying, dilatory, avoiding battle, in imitation of Quintus Fabius Maximus, a Roman general, who conducted military operations against Hannibal, by declining to risk a battle in the open field, but harassing the enemy by marches, counter-marches, and ambuscades.—*Webster*.

FABRICIA. A genus of Australian shrubs; named in honour of the celebrated entomologist Johann Christian Fabricius, pupil of Linnæus, and author of Systema Entomologiæ, in 1775.

FAGONIA. Herbaceous plants with a woody base, nat. or. *Rutaceœ;* named by Tournefort in compliment to M. Fagon, principal physician to Louis XIV., and a great patron of botany. He was one of the chief promoters of Tournefort's journey to the Levant, which he strongly recommended to the consideration of his sovereign. See Tourn. Inst. 265, t. 141 ; Linn. Gen. 212; and Mart-Mill. Dict. v. 2.

FAHLUNITE. A mineral occurring in opaque, brownish-green, six-side prisms, transversely foliated; from *Fahlun*, in Sweden.

FAHRENHEIT. An arrangement of the thermometrical scale, in which the space between the freezing and the boiling points of water, under a medium pressure of the atmosphere, is divided into 180° ; the freezing point being marked 32°, and the boiling 212° ; invented by Fahrenheit, of Amsterdam, in 1720. See also Philos. Trans. Roy. Soc. vol. xxxiii.

FAÏENCE. Imitation porcelain; a kind of fine pottery embellished with painted designs; from *Faenza* (Faventia), in Italy, where first made.

FALERNIAN. An Italian wine celebrated by Horace, and made at Falernus. According to Mazella, Mount Falernus is now called Rocca di Mondragone ; Baudraud says, Monte Massico. Pliny praises the pears of Falernus.

FALKIA. A genus of plants, nat. or. *Nolanaceœ;* called after Falk, a Swedish botanist.—*Crabb*.

FALLOPIAN. A term applied to two ducts arising from

the womb, usually called *tubes ;* first described by Fallopius, a celebrated anatomist of the sixteenth century, and pupil of Versalius.

FAMAGUSTA. An apple; from *Famagosta*, in the isle of Cyprus.

FANCHONNETTE. In pastry, an *entre-mets* made of fine puff paste and apricot or peach jam; from *Fanchonnette*, a French name formed from *Françoise*.

FARO. A game at cards, in which one plays against the bank kept by the proprietor of the table. The name was formerly written *pharaoh* (Fr. *faron*), the common title of the kings of anc. Egypt. The game is not now played—certainly not in France.

FARSETIA. A genus of cruciferous plants, with purple or light yellow flowers; named after P. Farseti, an Italian botanist.

FASSAITE. A mineral; a variety of pyroxene, found in the Fassa Thal, North Tyrol.

FAUJASITE. A mineral; a hydrous silicate, occurring at Kaiserstuhl, in Baden; named by Damour after Faujas de Saint Fond.

FAUNA. The various kinds of minerals peculiar to a country constitute its Fauna, as the various choice plants constitute its Flora. The term is derived from the Fauni, rural deities in Roman mythology.

FAUNIST. One who attends to rural disquisitions; a naturalist. See FAUNA.

FAYALITE. A mineral found in large nodules and angular pieces on the sea-shore in Fayal, and also in Ireland.

FENUGREEK. A plant allied to clover, whose seeds are used by farriers in cataplasms and fomentations; from L. *fœnum Græcum*, Greek hay.

FERGUSONITE. An ore, consisting of columbic acid, and yttria, with some oxide of cerium and zirconia; brought from Cape Farewell; named after Robert Ferguson, Esq., of Raith.

FERRARA (ANDREA). A celebrated sword named after its maker, who worked either in Spain or the Spanish Netherlands.

FERRARIA. A genus of bulbous plants, natives of the Cape and South America; named after J. B. Ferrari, an Italian botanist.

FESCENNINE. Licentious; a licentious gay song, a nuptial song. Fescennine verses were gay, satirical, rude, or licentious verses sung by young men at weddings and before the nuptial chamber, and were so called from having originated at Fescennium, a town of ancient Etruria, near the present site of Civita Castellana. The same name was applied to pieces of poetry recited by youths at rustic festivals, and sung by country people at harvest time. This is a very ancient custom in Italy, and the practice of making licentious jokes upon each other, and upon strangers passing by, is very prevalent among the vintagers.

FEVILLEA. A genus of plants, the chief species of which are natives of Brazil; called in South America *ghandirhoba*; held in great repute as an antidote to various poisons; named in honour of Louis Feuillée, a French Franciscan monk, Peruvian traveller, and botanist, who died in 1732.

FEZ (Turc. *fèss*). A name by which the red woollen skull-caps or *tarbouch* are known in Turkey and the Levant. They had their name from Fez or Fas, capital of the province of the same name in Morocco, where they were first made. The town has a large commerce with the interior of Africa, and is still famous for its silk stuffs, gauzes, fine figured girdles of gold and silk, moroccoes, arms, saddlery, &c. The fezzes are now principally made at Constantinople. The Turks call the caps of Tunis *fesi tounes*.

FIACRE. A French hackney coach; so named because the first hackney coach set up in Paris customarily started from the Hôtel St. Fiacre. Compare our " Elephants," " Eyre Arms," " Favourites," " Royal Blues," &c. " Le mot *fiacre* vient de ce que les premiers carrosses de cette espèce logeaient à l'image Saint Fiacre, dans la rue Saint Antoine."

FICHTELITE. A resin found in flat acicular crystals, in a bed of turf at Redwitz, near the Fichtelgebirge.

FILBERT. The fruit of the cultivated *Corylus* or hazel. Bailey writes, " *Filberds*, of *full* and *beard*, the skin thereof being covered with a down, like the first appearance of the beard upon the chin;" but the first syllable is rather from the L. *avellana*, id. *Avellana nuces*, filberts; lit. nuts of Abella or Avella, a town of Campania. Conf. Macrob.; also Virg.; and Sil. Minshew says, "filberd or hazel-nut, q. Belg. *wild-beyer*, i. acinus sive fructus sylvestris. Fr. *auelâine*, Port. *auelaū*, It. D. Lat. *auellâna*, primùm dictæ sunt abellinæ, ab Abellino, Campaniæ oppido, quod in Virgilio appellatur Abella, aut Auella, nux est coryli arboris, quæ alio nomine dicitur Nux Pontica quod in Asia Greciamque primum è Ponto venerit; et Prænestina quòd Prænestini his abundant, sive (ut Macrob. placet) quòd Prænestini ab Annibale obsidione cincti, his nucibus famem toleraverint." *Filbert* may have been anciently written *avel-nut*; and afterwards *vel-nut*, *fil-nut*, *fil-but;* whence *filbert*. There are still towns in Naples called Avella and Avellino, and to this day the neighbourhood of the latter abounds in chestnuts and hazel nuts. The latter were much prized by the Romans, and are still celebrated under the name of Avellino nuts. "Hazel-nuts are the fruit of the wild bush of *Corylus Avellana*, unchanged and unimproved by cultivation. They are brought from Spain, the south of France, and Italy. The finest kinds, called Avelines, are brought to Paris from several quarters, as from Toulon, Languedoc, and Piedmont."

FILIPPO. An old silver coin of Milan equal to 4s. 8½d.; doubtless first struck in the reign of Philipp Marie, son of the Duke John Galeacius, who succeeded his brother Johann Marie in 1412.——A money of Modena equal to 6fr. 13c.

FIORITE. A siliceous incrustation; from *Fiora*, in Ischia.

FLACOURTIA. A genus of shrubs, named after M. de Flacourt, a director of the French India Company.

FLEMINGIA. A genus of leguminous plants; named after Dr. John Fleming.

FLORALIA. Festivals held by the Romans in honour of Flora, goddess of flowers. Hence *floral*, pertaining to Flora; as floral games.

FLOREN, FLORENCE. A gold coin of the time of Edward III., equal to 6s. sterling.

FLORENCE.   A kind of wine from Florence.——A kind
of cloth.—*Webster.*

FRIDAY (G. *freitag*, Plat. *freedag*, D. *vrydag*, Fries. *fredi*,
A. S. *frigdæg*).   The sixth day of the week ; Friga's day, the
day on which our ancestors worshipped Friga, Frega, or Frea,
consort of Woden, Wodin, or Odin ; and Venus of the northern
nations.

FLORENTINE.   A kind of silk cloth from Florence.——
A marble (called also landscape marble) in which the figures
of buildings &c. are naturally represented.——A sort of
baked tart or pudding.

FLORIN.   A name given to several coins of gold or
silver, of different values in different countries; the silver
florin varying from 1*s.* to 2*s.* 4*d.* sterling ; the gold florin of
Hanover being valued at 6*s.* 11*d.* sterling.   It is also used as
a money of account (*Kelly*).   The name is said to be derived
from *fiorino*, originally a gold coin first struck at Florence in
1252.   According to others, it was named after Lucius Aquilius
Florus, who impressed it with the head of Augustus on one
side, and on the other with a flower, with these words, " Lucius
Aquilius Florus III., vir."   Ménage says this is ridiculous,
and he asserts that it was named from the *fleur de lis*, the
arms of Florence, which were stamped upon it.   " Fiorino,
monéta d'oro battuta nella città di Firenze ; e così detta dal
giglio fióre, impreso d'essa città, impressovi dentro."

FLOUNCE.   A narrow piece of cloth sewed to a petticoat,
frock, or gown, with the lower border loose and spreading ; perhaps the same as the O. Eng. *florouns* (Fr. *fleuron*), a border of
flower-work or *florences*, a sort of cloth from Florence.

FLUELLEN or FLUELLIN.   The plant speedwell; from
the surname *Fluellyn*, a Celtic corruption of Lewellyn.

FONTANESIA.   A genus of plants, an evergreen shrub,
native of Syria ; named after M. Desfontaines, author of Flora
Atlantica.

FORNACALIA.   Moveable feasts held among the ancient
Romans in honour of the goddess Fornax or Fornix.   They
were first instituted by Numa ; the Quirinalia being instituted
for the sake of those who had not kept the Fornacalia.   They

were solemnized with sacrifices, performed before the mouth of an oven, wherein they dried their corn, baked their bread, &c. The grand curio proclaimed the time of celebration every twelfth of the kalends of March.

FORSKOHLEA. A genus of plants, or. *Pentagynia*, whose species are natives of the Cape and of Teneriffe; named in memory of Forskohl, a Swedish botanist.

FORSTERITE. A crystallized mineral containing silica and magnesia, found at Vesuvius with pleonaste and pyroxene; named after Mr. Foster.

FORSYTHIA. A genus of plants, of which, in the Linnæan system, there is but a single species, a native of Carolina; named in honour of William Forsyth.

FORUM. A tribunal, a court; any assembly empowered to hear and decide causes; also jurisdiction; named from the Forum at Rome, a public place where causes were judicially tried, and orations delivered to the people.

FOSTERA. A genus of plants of but one species, a native of New Zealand; named in memory of J. R. Foster and G. Foster, father and son, who, in a voyage round the world, collected and described many new genera and species of plants.

FOTHERGILLIA. A genus of plants, the species of which is *F. anifolia*, native of Carolina; named after Dr. John Fothergill.

FOURIERISM. The system of Charles Fourier, a Frenchman, who recommends the reorganization of society into small communities living in common.

FOURIERITE. One who favours Fourierism.

FRANC. A French silver coin equal to about 10*d*. sterling, so named from *Francia*, France.

FRANCESCONE. A silver coin in Tuscany, of 10 paoli, equal to 4*s*. 6*d*. sterling; doubtless named from Francesco, one of the Dukes of Tuscany.

FRANGIPANE. A celebrated essence used to perfume the gloves called " gants de Frangipane ;" first made by Mutio Frangipanni, who was both a Roman noble and a noble Roman, he having distributed bread amongst the people in time of famine, whence his name. Near Fiume, in Hungary, is still

to be seen an old castle which formerly belonged to the Frangipanni. Bescherelle doubts this derivation, and thinks the word
may be from "*frangipanier*, arbre odoriférant et laiteux;" or
contracted from two Italian words signifying "pain ou pâte
odoriférante." —— A stomachic made by Frangipanni, and
called by him *rosolis* (*ros solis*, sun-dew).——A sort of pastry
(*tourte de frangipane, tarte à la frangipane*) containing cream
and almonds. —— An extract of milk for preparing arti-
ficial milk, made by evaporating skimmed milk to dryness,
mixed with almonds and sugar.

FRANCOA. A genus of perennial plants, named after
Franco, a Spanish physician and botanist of the sixteenth
century.—*Wright*.

FRANKENIA. Sea heath, a genus of small perennial
plants, named after John Frankenius, a Swedish botanist.

FRANKLINITE. A mineral compound of iron, zinc, and
manganese, found in New Jersey; named from Dr. Franklin.
—*Cleaveland*.

FREDERICK or FREDERICK D'OR. A gold coin of
Prussia, equal to 16s. 3¾d.; named after one of its monarchs
(Frederick the Great?)

FREISLEBEN or FRIESLEBENITE. A mineral of a
blue or bluish-grey colour, occurring in the Himmelsfürst at
Freiberg, in Saxony, and at other places in Europe. *Friesleben*
is a local surname.

FRONTINIAC or FRONTIGNAC. A French wine, so
called from Frontenac, in Languedoc, where it is produced.

FUCHSIA. A genus of plants, whose species are very
numerous; all natives of America, chiefly of Mexico and
Chili; named in honour of Leonard Fuchs or Fuchsius,
physician and botanist, born at Wembdingen, in Bavaria, in
1501.

FUCHSIASINE. A kind of purple produced chemically
from the refuse matter of our gas-works. See FUCHSIA.

FUDGE. A made-up story; stuff; nonsense; an exclama-
tion of contempt (*Goldsmith*). "Todd does not trace it beyond
Goldsmith (Vicar of Wakefield), but it is no invention of his.
In a pamphlet entitled. 'Remarks upon the Navy. 1700,' the

term is declared to have been the name of a nautical personage who lived in the lifetime of the writer. 'There was in our time one Captain Fudge, commander of a merchantman, who upon a return from a voyage, however ill fraught soever his ship was, always brought home his owners a good stock of lies, so much so that now aboard ship the sailors, when they hear a great lie told, cry out, You *fudge* it.'" (Disraeli's Curiosities of Literature, article "Neology.")

FUIRENA. A genus of plants of only one species, *F. paniculata;* native of Surinam; named after Fuiren, a Danish botanist.

FUSTIAN. A coarse twilled cotton stuff, embracing pillow, corduroy, velveteen, &c. Some derive the word from *fustanum,* used by corrupt Latin writers in the same sense; supposed from L. *fustis,* because a sort of fustian is made from a wood which bears cotton. Bochart (with whom Ménage agrees) derives the word from *Fustát,* the Arabic name of Memphis or Misr, in Egypt, where it was first made, and where cotton was produced in great abundance. Ménage also informs us that in Arabic they call *alfusta* "a house whose walls are hung with fustian" (*fustát,* tentorium pec. ex pilis caprinis). Cf. Elmain, Hist. Saras. liv. 1, chap. 3; Voss de Vit. Serm. liv. 2; Du Cange, Gloss.——An inflated style of writing; a kind of writing in which high-sounding words are used, above the dignity of the thoughts or subject; a swelling style; bombast. Indeed the stuff may, like that called bombast, have been used to swell out garments. Bailey seems to think that *fustian* in the second sense of the word may also be from Gr. φυσητος, blown up.

FUSTIANIST. One who writes bombast.—*Milton.*

G.

GADOLINITE. A mineral; colour blackish, having the appearance of vitreous lava; called after Professor Gadolin. It contains the earth called ittria.

GAHNITE. A mineral containing oxide of zinc in combination with alumina and oxide of iron; named after Gahn, its discoverer.

GALATEA. A name given by M. Tempel to the secondary planet discovered by him at Marseilles on the 29th Aug. 1862; from Galatea, daughter of Nereus and Doris.

GALENIC. The appellation given to certain remedies, consisting of preparations of herbs and roots by infusion, decoction, &c., conformable to the rules of the celebrated physician Galen.

GALENISM. The doctrines of Galen.

GALIGNANI. A daily newspaper in English published in Paris; named from the publishers, Galignani & Co., Rue de Rivoli.

GALILEAN. The name of a refracting telescope, in which the eyeglass is a concave instead of a convex lens; so named because originally adopted by Galileo, the celebrated astronomer.

GALILEE. A large portico, porch, or chapel, usually situated at or near the west end of great abbey churches, although the word has also been frequently, but improperly, used to designate the nave of the church. The term is supposed by some to have arisen from the fact that in ancient times, when any female applied at the abbey gate for leave to see her relative, who was a monk, she was directed to the western porch of the church, and told in the words of Scripture, "He goeth before you into Galilee; there shall you see him." One writer, speaking of the galilee at Durham, says, " As this building was erected expressly for the use of females, and as, according to Gervase, all interviews between the males and their female relatives took place in these porches or chapels, the name may have been given to denote that the monks, in their occasional interviews with women, were to be as cautious and guarded as the Jews, who dwelt in Judea in the south, and in Samaria, in the centre of Palestine, were, in their communications with the people of Galilee, termed Galilee of the Gentiles, because it was peopled chiefly by Phœnicians, Syrians, and Arabians." Another writer says, "The galilee porch or chapel was always considered as somewhat less sacred than the other portions of the sacred edifice" (*Bloxam*). "Comparatively speaking, it was 'looked down upon;' it was the despised portion of the sacred building; it was the farthest distance (either literally or figuratively) from the altar or holy place. And this is the reason why, as it seems to me, this ¡porch or chapel was called 'the Galilee,' that is to say, 'the despised place.' For what was the geographical Galilee but the despised place? Not only locally, but figuratively, it was considered to be far off from the Holy City."

GALLICISM. A mode of speech peculiar to the French nation; an idiomatic manner of using words in the French or Gallic language.

GALLIGASKINS. Large open hose; used only in ludicrous language (*Philips*); said to be from *caligæ Vasconum*, Gascon hose. Bailey says, "Galligaskins (q.d. *caligæ Gallo-Vasconicæ*, so called because the Vascones used such instead of splatterdashes), a sort of wide slops or breeches used by the inhabitants of Gascoign, in France."

GALLIO. One indifferent in matters of opinion. "Then all the Greeks took Sosthenes, the chief ruler of the synagogue, and beat him before the judgment-seat. And Gallio cared for none of those things (Acts xviii. 17).—*S. F. Creswell*.

GALLITZINITE. Rutile, an ore of titanium; named after one of the Gallitzins, a princely Russian family; probably from Demetrius de Gallitzin, the celebrated mineralogist and naturalist; author of several works, and president of the mineralogical society of Yena.

GALLOWAY. A horse of a small size, first bred in Galloway, Scotland.

GALOSH or GOLOSH (Fr. *galoche*, Sp. *galocha*, a clog or wooden shoe). A patten, clog, or wooden shoe, or a shoe to be worn over another shoe to keep the foot dry; said to be from the L. *gallicæ*, wooden pattens, lit. Gaulish shoes. It is now made generally of India rubber and gutta percha.

GALVANISM. A method in which electricity is developed without the aid of friction, and in which chemical action takes place between certain bodies; named from Galvani, of Bologna, the discoverer.

GALVANIZED. Affected with galvanism. Galvanized iron is a name given to sheets of iron which are first dipped into melted zinc, and then into melted tin, and are thus prepared, by the supposed galvanic action of these metals, to resist oxidation.

GAMBOGE. A resinous juice, produce of a tree, the *Gambogia gutta*, or *Garcina Gambogia*, used as a pigment, and in medicine as a drastic purge; brought from Cambodia, Cambodja, or Cambogia, an extensive country without the Ganges.

GAMBROON. A kind of twilled linen cloth for linings; perhaps originally from Gombroon, a seaport of Persia, convenient for Kerman, which has a trade in carpets.

GARCINIA. A genus of Asiatic trees, among the chief species of which are *Mangostan* or *Mangosteen*, common in Java and the Molucca Islands, whose fruit is esteemed the most delicious and salubrious of all Oriental fruits; named in honour of Dr. Laurence Garcin, the Oriental traveller, who accurately described it.

GARDENIA. A genus of plants, containing about fifty species of trees and shrubs, chiefly natives of the East Indies and the Cape; named in honour of the eminent Scottish botanist and zoologist Alexander Garden, who died in 1791.

GARDNERIA. A genus of East India climbing shrubs; named in honour of the Hon. Edward Gardner.

GARIBALDI. A dress or jacket worn by ladies; made after the fashion of a garment worn by Garibaldi and his soldiers, the Garibaldini.

GARIDELLA. A genus of small, slender, erect herbs; named in honour of Pierre Garidel, M.D.

GASCONADE (Fr. *gasconade*). A boasting; a vaunt; a bravado; a bragging; so called from the people of Gascony, who are noted for boasting :—

> " Voila Philis; quant aux *Gascons*,
> Il était *Gascon*, c'est tout dire;
> Je laisse à penser si le sire
> Importuna la veuve, et s'il fit des serments."

> " Ceux des *Gascons* et des Normands
> Passent peu pour mots d'Evangile."
>
> " Sans être *Gascon*, je puis dire
> Que je suis un merveilleux sire."
>
> *La Fontaine.*

GAULTHERIA. A genus of plants, nat. or. *Ericaceæ ;* called after Gaulthier, a botanist of Canada.—*Crabb.*

GAUZE (Fr. *gaze,* Amor. *gazen,* Sp. *gasa).* A very thin, slight, transparent stuff of silk or linen. The word is said to have had its name from Gaza, in Palestine, where it was first manufactured. It may, however, be from the L. *gossipium* or *gossipion,* the cotton tree ; or *gausape, gausapa, gausapum, gausapes,* a kind of thick woollen cloth; a frieze or rough garment which soldiers used ; a furred coat, a hair mantle; Gr. γαυσαπης.

GAVOT (Fr. *gavotte,* formerly *gavote;* Sp. *gavóta).* A kind of dance or tune, the air of which has two brisk and lively strains in common time, each of which is played twice over *(Encyc.)* The word is said to be derived from the Gavots, a people inhabiting the mountainous region called Gap, in France. Lamartinière mentions Gavot as the name of a little district of Savoy, in the Chablais, the principal places in which are Evian and St. Gigo.

GAY-LUSSITE. A crystalline mineral substance, found in South America ; named after the French chemist, Gay-Lussac.

GEHLENITE. A mineral of a greyish colour, consisting chiefly of silica, alumina, and lime ; found principally at Mount Monzoni, in the Fassa Thal, Tyrol ; named by Fuchs after his colleague Gehlen, the celebrated chemist, member of the Royal Academy of Munich, born in 1775.

GELDER-ROSE or GUELDER ROSE. A plant, a species of *Viburnum.* This singular variety is probably from Gelderland, in Holland, as the Dutch call it *Gheldersche roose.* From the extreme whiteness of the flowers, and swelling out into a globular form, some country people have given it the name of snowball-tree, which Miller seems to think preferable to the common appellation of Guelder-rose, and which is conformable to the *Schneeball* of the Germans. Gerarde calls it Elder-rose and Rose-elder.

GENAPPE. A worsted yarn or cord used in the manufacture of braids, fringes, &c., its smoothness enabling it to be well combined with silk; from *Genappe*, in Belgium.

GENEVANISM. Calvinism, Calvin having resided at Geneva.

GENOVINA. A coin of Genova, *i.e.* Genoa, both in gold and silver. The assay value of the genovina of 100 lire was £3 9s. 9d. sterling; that of the genovina of 1790, £3 3s. 4d.

GENTIAN (Fr. *gentiane*, L. *gentiana*, *Gentiana lutea*; Gr. γεντιανη). The popular name of a genus of plants of many species, whose root, sometimes called felwort, is used as an ingredient in stomachic bitters. The officinal gentian is a native of the mountainous parts of Germany. The gentian is also found in other parts of Europe, under the Sub-Alpine mountains; also in Auvergne; upon the most elevated summits of the Vosges, and in the plain near Dijon. Pliny derives the Latin word from Gentius, king of Illyria, who is said to have discovered the properties of this plant.

GENTIATINE. An alkali discovered in *Gentiana lutea* by MM. Henri and Caventori. See GENTIAN.

GEOCRONITE. A lead-grey ore of antimony and lead (*Dana*); from Gr. γη earth, Κρονος Saturn, the alchemistic name of lead.

GEOFFROYA. A genus of plants, trees, natives of the tropical parts of America; of two species, one of which, *G. inermis*, yields a bark having emetic, drastic, purgative, and narcotic properties, and much valued as a powerful anthelmintic; named after Geoffroy, Memb. Acad. Paris, author of Materia Medica, who died in 1731.

GEORGE. A figure of St. George on horseback, worn by knights of the Garter. (*Shak.*)——A brown loaf.

GEORGE THE FOURTH. Name of a peach tree.

GEORGIA. The bark of the *Pinckneya pubens*, used as a substitute for cinchona; from Georgia, U.S.

GEORGIA. The moss called by Linnæus *Mnium pellucidum*,

which Ehrhart established as a new genus, and named after George III. of Great Britain.

GEORGIAD. A poem in honour of one of the Georges.

GEORGIUM SIDUS. (L.) The name first given, in honour of George III., to the planet Uranus.

GERARDIA. A genus of plants consisting of herbs or undershrubs; named after John Gerarde, author of the Herbal.

GERMANISM. An idiom of the German language.

GERVILLIA. A genus of fossil bivalves, placed by Cuvier under *Les Pernes*, between *Crenatula* and *Inoceramus*; named after M. de Gerville, by whom the species, on which the genus was established, was found in the Baculite limestone of Normandy.

GESNERA or GESNERIA. A genus of plants, named after Conrad Gesner, of Zürich, the celebrated naturalist, who died in 1788.

GHIBELINES, GHIBELLINES, or GIBBELINES (Fr. *Gibelins*). A faction in Italy in the twelfth, thirteenth, and fourteenth centuries, which favoured the German emperors, and opposed the Guelfs or adherents of the Popes. They are said to have had their name from Waiblingen (anc. *Wibelingen*), a small town of Würtemberg, near Stuttgart. At the battle of Wemsberg (1140), between Conrad III. of Waiblingen and Duke Welf (Guelf), the battle-cry of the former was "Hie Waiblingen!" Some assert that the Guelfs or Guelphs derived their name from G. *wolf*, a wolf, on account of the grievous evils committed by this faction. According to others, they were called from a German family named *Guelfe*, who lived at Pistoia, and they assert that his brother *Gibel* gave the appellation to the Ghibelines. According to others, the Emperor Conrad III. having taken the duchy of Bavaria from Welfe III., brother of Henry, duke of Bavaria, Welfe, assisted by the forces of Roger, king of Sicily, made war on Conrad, and thus gave birth to the faction of the Guelphs. Guelph, Guelf, Welfe, Welfo would seem to be merely different orthographies of the same name.

GIBBERISH (found written *geberish*). Rapid and in-

articulate tattle ; unintelligible language; unmeaning words.
Webster derives the word from *gibber* (*obs.*), to speak rapidly
and inarticulately ; probably allied to *gabble* and to *jabber*.
Bailey gives also the O. Fr. *gaber*, to banter ; It. *gabbare*, to
put a trick on. Mr. Ford says the language of the Iberians
was the Basque, which was superseded by the Romance, a
corrupt idiom formed from the fusion of the Roman and Gothic
languages ; that this hybrid underwent a further change from
its admixture with the Arabic at the Moorish invasion, when
two new dialects were formed—the *Aljamia* or Spanish, as
spoken by the Moors, and the *Algarabia* or Arabic, as spoken
by the Spaniards ; that the latter was so bad that the term in
its secondary sense is applied to any *gibberish* (*garabia*)—a
word which, strictly speaking, means *logat-al-árabra*, the
Arabic language. Dr. Johnson supposes that the term *gibberish* was originally applied to the language of Geber, the Arabian
alchemist ; and, as a learned writer observes, many of the
quotations given by Dr. Salmon (Clavis Alchymiæ, 1692)
would certainly justify the etymology.

GIBBSITE. A mineral, colour dirty white, greenish white,
and greyish ; occurring in irregular stalactical masses at Rich-
mond in Massachusetts; named after George Gibbs, Esq.,
president of the American Geological Society.

GIBUS. A celebrated spring hat (a sort of *chapeau bras*) ;
named from the inventor, M. Gibus.

GIESECKITE. A mineral occurring in six-sided prisms;
considered identical with elaolite ; named after Sir C.
Giesecke.

GILBERTIA. A genus of plants, consisting of small
trees or shrubs ; named after J. E. Gilibert, the French
botanist.

GILBERTITE. A mineral, colour yellowish-white, consisting of alumina, silica, lime, magnesia, protoxide of iron,
and water ; from Stonagwyn, St. Just, Cornwall; named by
Dr. Thomson, in honour of Davies Gilbert, president of the
Royal Society.

GILIA. A genus of plants, or. *Monogynia* ; named in
honour of Philippe Salvador Gilio, a Spanish botanist.

GILLIESIA. A genus of plants; named in honour of Dr. Gillies. of Concepcion, in Chili.

GINGER (Fr. *gingembre*, It. *gengivo*. Sp. *gengibre*. Port. *gengivre*, G. *ingber*. D. *gember*, Sw. *ingefära*. Dan. *ingefer*. Arab. Pers. and Turc. *zingibil* or *zinjibil*. Syr. and Ch. nearly the same). A plant, or the root of *Zingiber officinale*, a native of China and the East Indies, but extensively cultivated in the West Indies and America. The word, which in L. is *zingiber*, in Gr. ζιγγεβερις, is said to derive its name from the town of Gengi in China, in the neighbourhood of which it was first found. I find no such place, but Gingee is the name of a town of British India.

GINGERLY. Nicely, cautiously; from *ginger*, q.v.

GINGHAM. A kind of striped cotton cloth: so named from Guingamp, France, Côtes du Nord, where its manufacture, as well as that of cotton and linen goods in general, is largely carried on (*S. F. Creswell*).——An umbrella made of gingham.

GIPSY (L. *Ægypti*, Hun. *Pharas huerpek*. race of Pharaoh; It. *cingani*, *cingari*, *zingani*, *zingari*. Sp. *gitános*, bandits; G. *ziguener*, *zigeni*, and *zigeuni*, Fr. *Bohémiens*, Dan. and Sw. *Tartares*; Arab. *arami*, thieves; D. *heidenen*, idolators; Hind. *suders*; by others *Saracens*, and in 22 Hen. VIII. cap. 10 (1530), *Ægyptians*). One of a race of vagabonds who infest Europe, Africa, and Asia, strolling about, and subsisting mostly by theft, robbery, and fortune-telling. Pope Pius II. calls them *Zigari*, and supposes them to have migrated from the country of the Zigri, which nearly answers to the modern Circassia. The word *gipsy* is without doubt derived from *Ægyptii*, from the supposition that the gipsies were from Egypt, although their language indicates that they originated in Hindustan. Cf. Munster, Geog. lib. iii. cap. 5; Pasquier, Recherch. liv. iv. chap. 19; Ralph Volaterranus: Grellman, Germ. Disser. on Gipsies, trans. by Matt. Raper, 1787; Sir Wm. Jones, Asiat. Res. V. iii. p. 7; Miscell. Bolognese, in 18 vol. Rer. Italic.; Krantz, Hist. Sax.; and Muratori, Antich. Ital.——A reproachful name for a dark complexion. (*Shak.*)——A name of slight reproach to a woman, some-

H

times implying artifice or cunning.——The language of the gipsies.

GIPSYISM. The state of a gipsy; the arts and practices of gipsies; deception; cheating; flattery.

GIRARDIN. A kind of graft, after the manner of Girardin, a French gardener.

GIRONDE. In French political history, the name of a celebrated Republican party, which, during the first years of the Revolution of 1789, formed a powerful section of the second National Assembly, called the Legislative, in contradistinction to the first, or Constituante, which framed the constitution of 1791. It was so named from the department of La Gironde, which had returned Vergniaud, Gensonné, Guadet, &c., the leaders of the party; and it consisted chiefly of the members of the departments of the west and south.

GIRONDIN, GIRONDIST. One of the Gironde, *q.v.*

GISEKIA. A genus of plants, consisting of one species, the trailing gisekia, a native of the East Indies; named in honour of P. D. Giseke, a Dutch botanist.

GISMONDINE. A mineral consisting chiefly of silica and lime, with traces of magnesia, oxide of iron, and oxide of manganese; found at Capo de Bove, near Rome; named in honour of the mineralogist Gismondi.

GIULIO or JULIO. A small coin of base silver, at Leghorn and Florence, equal to about 6*d*. sterling; doubtless named after one of the Popes of Rome.

GLEDITSCHIA. A genus of plants, trees, which attain a height of fifty to eighty feet, natives of the Carolinas and Virginia; named after Gottlieb Gleditsch, of Leipsic.

GLOXINIA. A genus of plants, nat. or. *Gesneriaceæ*; called after M. Gloxin, a German botanist.— *Crabb.*

GMELINA. A tree, one species of which is a native of Java, Amboina, and other parts of the East Indies. It received its name from John George Gmelin, native of Tübingen, professor of chemistry and natural history at Petersburg, who spent ten years in travelling through Siberia at the expense of the Russian government, and whose Flora Sibirica is a work of great reputation and merit. This genus also serves to commemorate four or five other botanists of the same family, especially Samuel Theophilus Gmelin, nephew of the former.

GMELINITE. A mineral, a hydrous silicate, occurring at Montecchio Maggiore; at Castel, in the Vicentine; at Glenarm; and in the island of Magee; named after Professor C Gmelin, of Tübingen.

GOBELINS. A term applied in France to a species of rich tapestry; derived from Gilles Gobelins, a celebrated dyer in the reign of Francis I. (*Dict. de l'Acad.*) "Gobelins, a celebrated manufactory established in Paris in the Faubourg St. Marcel, for the making of tapestry and other furniture for the use of the crown. The house where this manufactory is carried on was built by two brothers, Giles and John Gobelins, both excellent dyers, and the first that brought to Paris, in the reign of Francis I., the secret of dyeing that beautiful scarlet colour still known by their name, as well as the little river Bièvre, on whose banks they fixed their dye-house, and which is now known by no other name than that of the Gobelins. It was in 1667 that this place, till then called Gobelins' Folly, changed its name into that of the Hôtel Royal des Gobelins, in consequence of an edict of Louis XIV. M. Colbert, having re-established, and with new magnificence enriched and completed, the king's palaces, particularly the Louvre and Tuilleries, began to think of making furniture suitable to the grandeur of those buildings. With this view he called together all the ablest workmen in the divers arts and manufactures, particularly painters, tapestry makers, sculptors, goldsmiths, ebonists, &c., and by splendid offers, pensions, privileges, &c., called others from foreign nations. And to render the intended establishment firm and lasting, he besought the king to purchase the Gobelins for them to work in, and draw up a system of laws or policy in seventeen articles. By these it is provided that the new manufactory shall be under the administration of the superintendent of the king's buildings, arts, &c.; that the ordinary masters thereof shall take cognizance of all actions and processes brought against any of the persons in the said manufactory, their servants and dependants; that no other tapestry work shall be imported from any other country, &c. The Gobelins has since then remained the first manufactory of the kind in the world. The quantity and noble works that have been produced by it, and the number of the best workmen bred up therein, are incredible ; and the present flourishing condition of the arts and manufactures of France is in a great measure owing thereto. Tapestry work in particular is their glory. During the superintendence of M. Colbert and his successor M. de Louvois the working of tapestry is said to have been practised to a degree of perfection scarce inferior to what was before done by the English and French. The Battles of Alexander, the Four Seasons, the Four Elements, the King's Palaces, and a series of the principal actions of the life of Louis XIV. from the time of his marriage to the first conquest of Franche Comté, done from the designs of M. le Brun, director of the manufactory of the Gobelins, are masterpieces in their kind (*Chamb. Cyc.* 1788).

GODOYA. A genus of plants, trees ; named in honour of Emanuel Godoy, duke of Arcadia.

GOETHEA. A genus of plants, consisting of trees and shrubs ; named in honour of the poet Goethe.

GOETHITE. A rare German mineral, colour brownish-red, by reflection yellowish ; named in honour of the poet Goethe.

GOLDFUSSIA. A genus of plants, or. *Angiospermia;* named after Dr. Goldfuss.

GOLGOTHA. The elevated pew or gallery in which the heads of houses till lately sat at Great St. Mary's, Cambridge ; so called because it was the place of skulls. Cf. John xix. 17. —*S. F. Creswell.*

GOLIATH. A name given by Lambert to a genus of insects remarkable for their size and beauty, whose species inhabit Africa, the East Indies, and the tropical parts of America ; named from Goliath, the giant leader of the Philistines.——A synonym for *giant.*

GOMARA. A genus of plants, or. *Angiospermia ;* natives of Peru; named in honour of Lopez de Gomara, a Spanish botanist.

GOMESA. A genus of orchidaceous plants; named in honour of Señor Gomez, a Spanish physician.

GONGORISM. A term used for bombastic writing; so called from Luis Gongora y Argote, a poet who tortured the Spanish language without mercy, called his new phraseology *estilo culto*, and answered with intemperate abuse the judicious censure of his eminent contemporaries, the two brothers Argensolas, Lope de Vega, and Quevedo. Gongora was born at Cordova in 1561. A *romancero* entitled "Delicias del Parnasso," contains all his romances and *letrillas*. The *cultorista* Alonso Castillo Solorzano extended Gongorism even to America, where he published his own works in Mexico in 1625. See P. Cyc.

GOODENIA. A genus of herbaceous perennial plants, or. *Monogynia;* named in honour of Dr. Goodenough, bishop of Carlisle.

GOODYERA. A genus of plants, one species of which, *G. repens*, is found in Scotland; named after Mr. John Goodyer.

GORDIAN KNOT. An inextricable difficulty; hence, *to cut the Gordian knot* is to remove a difficulty by bold or unusual measures. The Gordian knot was a knot in the leather or harness of Gordius, a king of Phrygia, so very intricate that there was no finding where it began or ended. An oracle declared that he who should untie this knot should be master of Asia. Alexander, fearing that his inability to untie it should prove an ill augury, cut it asunder with his sword.

GORGONA. A name given to the anchovy from the isle of Gorgona, in the Gulf of Genoa, noted for its anchovy fisheries, in which the inhabitants are chiefly engaged.

GORGONEIA. In architectural sculpture, masks carved in imitation of the head of Medusa, who was one of the three Gorgons; used generally as key-stones. The Gorgons by a mere look killed men, and even petrified them; they were destroyed by Perseus because they had polluted the temple of Minerva. Perseus gave the head of Medusa to Minerva, who fixed it on her ægis or shield, which thenceforth had the power of turning the beholders into stone.

GORGONEUM. A mask used in Greek and Roman

theatres to represent hideous figures, in imitation of the Gorgons.

GORTERIA. A genus of composite plants, mostly shrubs, named after Professor Gorter, physician to Elizabeth, empress of Russia.

GOSLARITE. A mineral, colour white, reddish, bluish; found in the Rammelsberg Mine near Goslar in the Harz, and at other places in Europe.

GOSSAMER (found written *gossamore*, *gossamour*, and *gossomer*). A fine filmy substance, like cobwebs, floating in the air in calm clear weather, especially in autumn. It is seen in stubble fields, and on furze or low bushes, and is probably formed by a species of spider. Some derive the word from L. *gossipium*, cotton. A contributor to N. & Q. 3rd S. 11, 16, says, " The hold which the fable of the origin of these webs had on the minds of the vulgar is shown by the persistent use of the name *Mary* in *Marien-Fäden*, *Mariengern*, and *Marien-sommer*." (Nativ. V. M., 8th Sep.) The French name also is *Fil de la Bonne Vierge*. Hence, and as all these religious fables were necessarily widely known, it appears to me that *gaze à Marie* (Mr. T. Keightley says *gase-Marie*), Eng. *gauze o' Mary*, is a more likely derivation of *gossamer* than any yet proposed. The old spellings of *gossamour* and *gossamore* perhaps show the tendency to emphasize the last syllable, and as equivalent to *love-down* (Fr. *amour*, It. *amore*). They are worth notice as exemplifying the fanciful and euphuistic etymologies of Holofernes and others of his day."

GOTH. A rude, ignorant, or uncivilized person : *lit.* one of the tribe or nation that anciently inhabited Scandinavia, now Sweden and Norway.

GOTHAMIST. A wiseacre; a person deficient in wisdom; so called from Gotham, in Nottinghamshire, noted for some pleasant blunders (*Bp. Morton*). Old " Drunken Barnaby " seems to have visited Gotham in one of his poetical journies to the North, for he sings—

> " Thence to Gotham, where sure am I,
> Though all not fools, I saw many ;

Here a she-gull found I prancing,
And in moonshine nimbly dancing;
There another wanton madling,
Who her hog was set a sadling."

Throsby, however, seems to be of a different opinion, for he
says he now thinks the inhabitants of this village as wise as
their neighbours. A variety of opinions, indeed, have gone
abroad respecting this place. Warton, speaking of " the idle
pranks of the men of Gotham," says, " that such pranks bore
a reference to some customary law tenures belonging to that
place or its neighbourhood, now grown obsolete, and that
Blount might have enriched his book of ancient tenures with
those ludicrous stories." Hearne also says, " nor is there more
reason to esteem the Merry Tales of the Mad Men of Gotham
(which was much valued and cried up in Henry VIII.'s
time, though now sold at ballad-singers' stalls) as altogether a romance, a certain skilful person having told me more
than once that they formerly held lands there by such sports
and customs as are touched upon in this book." But Fuller
says, that the proverb, "As wise as a man of Gotham," " passeth
publicly for the periphrasis of a fool; and a hundred fopperies
are forged and fathered on the townsfolk of Gotham." Still,
he thinks it no more remarkable than the customs of other
nations, for it has been well observed that a custom seems to
have prevailed, even among the earliest nations, of stigmatizing
some particular spot as remarkable for stupidity. Amongst the
Asiatics Phrygia was considered as the Gotham of that day,
Abdera amongst the Thracians, and Bœotia amongst the Greeks.
Fuller, however, adds, " but, to return to Gotham, it doth
breed as wise people as any which causelessly laugh at their
simplicity. Sure I am Mr. William de Gotham, fifth master
of Michael House, Cambridge, anno 1339, and twice chancellor
of the university, was as grave a governor as that age did
afford; and Gotham is a goodly large lordship, where the
ancient and respected family of St. Andrew have flourished
some hundreds of years, till of late the name is extinct, and
lands divided betwixt female co-heirs matched unto very
worshipful persons." From these various protests in favour
of the men of Gotham, it is evident that considerable publicity

had been given to the many ridiculous fables traditionally
told; particularly of their having heard the cuckoo, but never
having seen her, and therefore hedged in a bush from whence
her note seemed to proceed, that being confined within so small
a compass, they might at length catch her, and satisfy their
curiosity. It has been observed by several writers in the last
century that what gave rise to the story is not now remembered;
but they all mention that there is at a place called Courthill in
the parish, a bush still designated by the name of the Cuckoo-
bush. Cf. Beauties of England and Wales, Lond. 1813, vol.
xii. part. 1, Nottinghamshire, where may be found several
anecdotes concerning the Wise Men of Gotham.

GOTHAMITE. A term sportively applied to New York;
so called from *Gotham*. See GOTHAMIST.

GOTHIC. The language of, or pertaining to, the Goths; as
Gothic customs, Gothic barbarity; rude, ancient, barbarous.
——A style of architecture with high and sharply-pointed
arches, clustered columns, &c.; a term first used by Sir
Christopher Wren (by way of derision, it is said) to denote the
architecture of the Middle Ages, in contradistinction to
Classic architecture. According to Torré, the term *Gothic*
was first applied as a designation by Cesare Cesariano, trans-
lator of Vitruvius, in his commentary, 1521. Cesariano was
one of the architects of the Cathedral of Milan in 1491, and
author of "Saggio sopra l'Architettura Gotica con più proposito,
Germanica dinominata."

GOUANIA. A genus of plants of one species, native of
St. Domingo; named by Jacquin after Antoine Gouan, M.D.,
author of Flora Monspeliaca, Hortus Monspeliensis, &c.

GRACE-CARD. The six of hearts, so termed in Ireland.
A Kilkenny gentleman, named Grace, solicited, with promises
of royal favour, to espouse the cause of William III., gave the
following answer, written on the back of the six of hearts, to
an emissary of Marshal Schomberg, who had been commis-
sioned to make the proposal to him:—"Tell your master I
despise his offer, and that honour and conscience are dearer
to a gentleman than all the wealth and titles a prince can
bestow."—*J. C. H.*

GRECISM. An idiom of the Greek language.

GREEK. On the Continent, a name given to a gambler who cheats. Towards the end of the reign of Louis XVI., a chevalier of Greek origin named Apoulos, having obtained admission to the court circle, played with great success. One day, however, he was taken *flagrante delicto*, and, having been convicted, was condemned to the galleys for twenty years. The circumstance caused a great noise at the time, and ever since similar rogues have been termed Greeks.——A jocular term for an Irishman; the Irish, as they assert, being the founders of the Greek nation.

GREENGAGE. A species of plum. It has been asserted that it was brought into England by a member of the Gage family some time in the last century. A writer in N. & Q. thinks it was a Sir Thomas Gage of Hengrave, in Suffolk; that his own family were intimate with the Gage family, and he is almost certain he had heard them allude to the circumstance. In Macintosh's Book of the Garden (ed. 1855, ii. 531) occurs the following respecting the greengage :—" Of early origin, introduced by Lord Gage from the Chartreux monastery near Paris." Macintosh, however, enumerates several other sorts of gage, as the imperial gage, Lawson's golden gage, the purple gage, the red gage, the Woolston black gage, and the yellow gage; and the most probable derivation of the word is from the vernacular G. *quetsche* or *qvetsche*, Low G. *kwets*, a plum. Cf. N. & Q. 3rd S. iii. 493.

GREENOCKITE. A native sulphuret of cadmium, colour honey-yellow ; found at Bishopstown (Renfrew) and Cockneyburn (Dumbarton); named in honour of Lord Greenock, afterwards Earl Cathcart.

GREENOVITE. A mineral, colour deep rose-red, consisting of silica, oxide of titanium, lime, and protoxide of manganese ; found at St. Marcel, Piedmont; named in honour of Mr. Greenough.

GREGORIARA. In Spain, the scientific name of the *espinillera* or right-hand grieve of iron and leather, worn by the *picadores* in the bull-fights ; named from its inventor, Don Gregorio Gallo.

GROBYA. A genus of orchidaceous plants; named in honour of Lord Grey of Groby.

GROG. A mixture of spirit and water not sweetened. Old Admiral Vernon first introduced rum and water as a beverage on board ship. The veteran used to wear a grogram cloak (*i.e.* a cloak made of stuff composed of silk and mohair) in foul weather, which gained him the appellation of Old Grog. From himself the sailors transferred the name to the liquor.— *Œconomist*, 1824.

GROGGY. In vulgar language, tipsy, intoxicated; from *grog*, q.v. A groggy horse is one that bears wholly on his heels in trotting ; a grog-blossom, a rum-bud, a redness on the nose or face of those who drink ardent spirits to excess, a deformity that marks the vice of intemperance.

GROPPITE. A mineral, colour rose-red to brownish-red ; found in the limestone quarry of Gropptorp in Södermanland, Sweden.

GROS DE NAPLES. A kind of stout silk so called because made at Naples (Fr. *gros*, thick). Gros de Tours is a silk made at Tours in imitation of gros de Naples.

GRUB-STREET. A term applied to low writing, as a *Grub-street* poem ; from the name of a street (now Milton Street) near Moorfields, London, formerly much inhabited by low writers.

GRUNAUITE. A mineral found with quartz and copper pyrites. It was named grunauite from Grünau, and saynite from Sayn Altenkerchen, where it is respectively found.

GRUYÈRE. A celebrated cheese to be met with in most parts of the Continent; from *Gruyère*, in Switzerland.

GUELFS. See GHIBELINES.

GUERNSEY. A woollen waistcoat first made at Guernsey.

GUETTARDA. A genus of plants, natives of South America; named after J. S. Guettard, M.D., author of a local French Flora; Observations sur les Plantes, 1747; and other botanical works.

GUICHENOTIA. A genus of New Holland shrubs; named after Antony Guichenot, who sailed round the world with Captain Baudin.

GUILANDINA. The Bonduc or nicker-tree, a genus of plants consisting of trees or shrubs; named by Linnæus in honour of Melchior Guilandinus, a Prussian, who filled the botanical chair at Padua about 1583 or 1589.

GUILLEMOT. A waterfowl of the genus *Uria*, allied to the penguins, auks, and divers; found in the northern parts of Europe, Asia, and America. (*P. Cyc.*) Webster derives the word from W. *çwilawg*, whirling about; but it is more probably from the name of the discoverer, Guillemot, a French diminutive of Guillaume, *i.e.* William.

GUILLOTINE. (Fr.) An instrument for the infliction of capital punishment, proposed to the National Assembly of France by Joseph Ignace Guillotin, a physician, native of Xaintes, and a member of the Assembly; and which from him took its name. It was adopted by decree of 20th March, 1792. The guillotine under other names had existed as a means of public execution long before in Germany, Bohemia, Italy, Scotland, and England. Crusius, in his Annales Suevici, fol. 1595—6, tom. ii. 296, says, "Antiquis autem temporibus, in Germaniâ etiam decollatio non gladio fiebat, sed querno ligno habente scindens acutissimè ferrum. Addit Widermannus, se vidisse tale instrumentum Halæ in vetere Nosodocheo (Siechaus) priusquam id destrueretur, et hodiernum ibi ædificaretur. Efferebatur inde illa machina, si quis plectendus esset : supplicioque peracto eodem referebatur."—"Postea usus gladii successit." In German this instrument was called *der planke der deil*, the plank of wood; and in olden language *falbiel*, the falling hatchet. In Bohemia it was called *hagec*, something akin to the plank. In Italy it was known by the name of *manaia*. An engraving of it may be seen in Achillis Bocchii Bonon. Symbolicarum Quæstionum, lib. v. 8vo, Bonon. 1555, p. 36. There is a very beautiful engraving of the German instrument in a representation of the beheading of the son of Titus Manlius, by Henry Aldegrevers, dated 1553. Evelyn, in his Memoirs, vol. i. 170, states that he saw a similar instrument at Naples. Its use at Halifax is traced as far back as the time of Edward III. In England what has been since called the guillotine was used only at Halifax, and confined even there to the punishment of felonies committed within the forest of Hardwick. It was in 1650 that the last malefactors there suffered by it (Watson's Hist. of Halifax, 214, 239). Joseph Ignace Guillotin, who revived the use of this instrument in France, is supposed by many to have perished at a later period of the Revolution, like the Regent Morton, by his own invention; but this is not correct, as Dr. Guillotin died a natural death, 26th May, 1814, at the age of seventy-six. See Biog. Universelle; P. Cyc.; Galignani, 4 Feb. 1857; and Memoirs of Empress Josephine, Lond. 1828.

GUINEA. Formerly a gold coin of Great Britain, at first equal to 20s. sterling, but afterwards raised to 21s. sterling. The appellation of *guinea* was given to it because great quantities of them were first struck by Charles II., in 1663, from gold brought from the Guinea coast by the Royal African Company. They were distinguished, some by an elephant under the head, some a castle, others without, which was continued under each reign until George I.

GUINEA-FOWL or GUINEA-HEN. A fowl of the gallinaceous order, larger than the common domestic hen; originally from Guinea, where they are found in flocks of 200 or 300, perching on trees, and feeding on worms and grasshoppers.

GUNDELIA. A genus of perennial composite plants; named in honour of Andrew Gundelsheimer, a German botanist.

GUNNERA. A genus of plants of but one species, *G. perpensa*, native of the Cape; named by Linnæus in honour of John Ernest Gunner, bishop of Drontheim, founder of the Royal Norwegian Society, to the "Transactions" of which he contributed several valuable treatises on natural history; author of Flora Norwegica; born at Christiania in 1718.

GURHOFITE. A sub-variety of magnesian carbonate of lime, colour snow-white; found near Gurhof, in Lower Austria.

GURRAH. A kind of coarse India muslin; doubtless from Gurrah, in the British territory of Saugur and Nerbudda.

GUSTAVIA. A genus of plants of only one species; named in honour of Gustavus III. of Sweden, patron of Linnæus.

GUTTA PERCHA (erroneously pronounced *perka*). A gum which exudes from a forest tree growing in Singapore, Borneo, and other of the Eastern islands, and which was first imported into England in 1843. There are three varieties, viz., *Gutta Girek*, *Gutta Tuban*, and *Gutta Percha*. According to some, *Percha* is the Malayan name for the tree which yields this particular gum. It was, however, originally called *Gutta pulo Perecha*, i.e. "gum of the island Percha;" which, nevertheless, may have been so named from abounding in these trees. Marsden, indeed, calls the island of Sumatra Púlan Percha. The Malay *gatah*, *guttah*, is gum, balsam.

GUYAQUILLITE. A resin, consisting of carbon, hydrogen, and oxygen, found at Guyaquil, in South America; allied to " bog-butter," found in Irish bogs.

GUZMANNIA. A genus of plants, one species of which grows on the branches of trees in Peru; dedicated to Guzman·

GUY. A fright, a dowdy, an ill-dressed person; so called from the effigy of Guy Fawkes, carried about by boys on the 5th of November.

H.

HACKNEY. The carriage so named. This word is inserted on account of the very general belief that this vehicle had its name from the suburb of Hackney. Mr. Pulleyn says, " Hackney coaches, as well as hackney horses, derive their name from the village of Hackney, which was, at a former period, of such great resort that numbers of coaches and horses were in constant employ in carrying the citizens thither. It was in the year 1634 that Captain Bayley first introduced these coaches, when a tolerable long ride might then be procured for the small sum of 4*d*." Singularly enough, in another part of the same work, Mr. Pulleyn says, " This village [Hackney] was anciently celebrated for the numerous seats of the nobility and gentry, ' which occasioned,' says Maitland, ' a mighty resort thither of persons of all conditions from the city of London ; whereby so great a number of horses were

hired in the city on that account, that they were called
hackney or hack horses, and, from the number of them employed to go to this neighbourhood, in process of time gave a
name to this locality." I am disposed to think that neither of
these statements is correct. It is admitted that the hackney
coach was not introduced into England until 1634, whereas in
the most ancient record, dated in 1253, Hackney is called
Hakeneye (Cl. 37, Hen. III., m. 14, de quâdam viâ obstructâ
apud Hakeneye). It is most probable that the place was
named either from an early owner, one *Hacon;* or from *Aken-ey,*
which might be rendered " the isle or place near water,
abounding with oaks ;" and that the carriage had its name
from the horse by which it was drawn. Roquefort (1808) has
haquenée, hacquenée, jument de prix, cheval de parade pour les
dames ; d'*equus; haquet, hacquet,* petit cheval, et sorte de
voiture pour conduire des vins, des ballots—

> Sus, sus, allez-vous en Jaquet,
> Et pensez le petit *hacquet,*
> Et luy faictes bien sa litière.
> *Coquillart, Monol. du Pays.*

haquetier, conducteur de haquet ; *haque,* cheval hongre,
d'*equus.* The Dicc. de la Acad. Españ. (1734) has *hacanea,*
caballo algo mayor que las hacas, y menor que las caballos.
Covarr. dice que es voz Italiana, que este género de caballos
vienen de Inglaterra y de Polonia ; Lat. *equus Britannicus,* vel
Polonus ; haca, caballo pequeño, que de sa naturaleza y casta
no tiene la estatura de los demás caballos. Ménage (1694)
renders the Fr. *haquenée,* L. *equus gradarius;* and he derives
the Eng. *hacney* (sic), Flem. *hackney,* through the Fr. word
from the Barb. L. *hakinea,* from L. *equus,* thus *equus, akus,
akinus, akineus, akinea,* haquenée. He says further that
akinea, by aphœresis, became *kinea,* whence the It. *chinea ;*
and that from *akus* came the diminutive *akettus* whence
haquet. Cotgrave (1650) gives *hacquenée,* commonly an am-
bling horse, gelding, or mare ; *haquet,* a dray or low and
open cart, such as London brewers use ; *haquetier,* a drayman.
Minshew (1617) gives *hackney horse,* Fr. *haquenée,* com. g.
haquenart, It. *acchinéa, acchenia, chinea,* Sp. *hacanéa, háca,*

Belg. *hakeneys*, dictus à pedibus alternatìm eleuatis ac sonitum reddentibus, *hacke*, *hacke*, *hacke*, &c. &c. Dufresne gives the Med. L. *hakeneius* et *hakenettus*, equus tolutarius, graduarius, Gallice *haquenée*. Mandatum Eduardi III., Regis Angliæ, ann. 1373, apud Rymer, tom. 7, 27. Et vobis Hakeneios cariagia, et alia necessaria pro ductione filiorum prædictorum, in hac parte, pro denariis nostris, inde solvendis habere faciant. Charta ann. 1413, ibid. p. 124. Et quatuor equorum, et unius hakenetti ; haqueneya, equus tolutarius, Gall. *haquenée*. Comput. ann. 1402, inter Probat. tom. 3. Hist. Nem. p. 169, col. 1: A Johanne Arraudi, pro una haqueneya morella, xxxvij francos valentes, xxxij libras Turon. Un haubby d'Irlande, apud Math. de Couciaco in Carolo VII. 593.

HADLEY. An excellent quadrant used at sea ; so called from its inventor, John Hadley, Esq.

HAGLOE. A crab apple, raised by Mr. Bellamy, of Hagloe, co. Gloucester.

HAIDINGERITE. A very rare mineral; an arseniate of lime and water ; supposed to have been found at Joachimsthal, in Bohemia ; named from its discoverer or analyser, Haidinger.

HAMITIC. A term applied to languages considered to be intermediate between the Semitic and African languages. The word has been replaced by the term African, and is probably derived from Χημι, the Coptic name of Egypt.

HANDY-PADDY. An instrument to economise the labour of Irishmen in lifting building materials to a great height. It consists of a wheel and axle, a long rope and a basket, and can be seen at work any day in London, except on Sunday.— *S. F. Creswell*.

HANK. Two or more skeins of silk, cotton, &c., tied together. Webster gives the Dan. *hank*, a handle, a hook, a tack, a clasp ; Sw. *hank*, a band. A correspondent of N. & Q., (3rd S. ii. 478) says, Hanks, a Brabant manufacturer, invited over to England by Edward III., circa 1331, gave his name to the skein of worsted.

HANSARD. A merchant of one of the Hanse towns, in the north of Germany.

HANSARD. The name of the books containing the official

printed records of the proceedings in Parliament; so called from the name of the printer.

HANSOM. A superior kind of light two-wheeled street cab, in which the driver is perched on an elevated seat behind; named from the inventor or manufacturer.

HARBONG KÁ RÁJ. In Hindustan, civil disorders, maladministration : *lit.* the rule of Harbong, a rajah so named, said to have ruled at a place opposite Allahabad, on the Ganges; thence termed *Harbong-pur*, and of whose silliness and unfitness for government many traditional anecdotes and proverbial phrases bear record. — *Elliot.*

HARDAUR, HARDOUR. A name given to oblong mounds raised in villages in Upper India, and studded with flags to avert epidemic diseases, and especially cholera; so named in honour of Hardaul Lálá, a Bundelkhand chief, who, the natives of Hindustan believe, visited the camp of Lord Hastings with cholera, in punishment of the profanation committed by the Europeans in having once slaughtered cows in the grove where Hardaul's ashes repose.— *Wilson. Gloss.*

HARLEQUIN (Fr. *id.* a buffoon; It. *arlecchino,* Sp. *arlequin,* Armor. *harliqin, furluqin,* a juggler). A buffoon, dressed in party-coloured clothes, who plays tricks, like a merry Andrew, to divert the populace. This character was first introduced into the Italian comedy, but is now a standing character in English pantomime entertainments. It has been suggested that the last part of the word is from the Goth. and Sw. *leca,* to play. Ménage derives the word from the name of a celebrated comedian, who so much frequented the house of M. de Harley that his friends and acquaintances used to call him Harlequino, "little Harley." This derivation is not satisfactory. But see PANTALOON.

HARLEIAN. A name given to a most valuable collection of MSS. now in the British Museum ; made by Robert Harley, Earl of Oxford and Mortimer ; born 1661, died 1724.

HARLOT. A prostitute, a common woman. Webster gives W. *herlawd,* a stripling ; *herlodes,* a hoiden, from *her* to push or challenge, *llawd* a lad ; and he says that the word originally signified a *bold stripling,* or a *hoiden,* and was formerly applied to males as well as females. Bailey says, q.d. *whorelet*, a little whore. The modern It. *arlotta* is a glutton, devourer. Dr. Johnson says the mother of William I. of England, a furrier's daughter of Falaise, and whose name was Arlotta (others write Arletta), was of so infamous a character that our term *harlot* is derived from her. Camden also derives the word from one *Arlotha*, concubine to William the Conqueror.——In Scripture, one who forsakes the true God and worships idols (Is. i. 3).——A servant, a rogue, a cheat (obs.); wanton, lewd, low, base (*Shak.*); and, as a verb, to practise lewdness (*Milton*).

HARPY. Any rapacious or ravenous animal; an extortioner; a plunderer (*Webster*) : so named from the fabulous winged monsters, having the face of a woman and the body of a vulture, with their feet and fingers armed with sharp claws, of which Virgil gives a description.——The largest of the eagle tribe, the *Harpyia destructor*, inhabiting Mexico and Brazil.

HARLINGTONITE. A mineral, colour snow-white; of a compact texture, much like an almond, occurring in the north of Ireland; named after one of the Harrington family.

HARTITE. A resin found in clefts in brown coal and fossil wood at Oberhart, near *Gloggnitz*, in Austria.

HARTOGIA. A genus of plants, trees, from which the natives of Africa make their arrows; named after Hartog, a Dutch naturalist.

HARVEY. An apple; named after the celebrated Dr. Gabriel Harvey.

HARVEY. A sauce invented by a Mr. Harvey.

HASSELQUISTIA. A genus of plants, or. *Digynia*; named in honour of Fred. Hasselquist, a Swedish naturalist, one of the most distinguished pupils of Linnæus.

HASSELTIA. A genus of South American trees, or. *Monogynia*; named in honour of the Dutch botanist Van Hasselt.

HATCHETINE. A wax-like substance occurring in the nodules of ironstone in South Wales; named after Mr. Hatchett.

I

HAUSMANNITE. One of the ores of manganese, colour brownish-black, named after M. Hausmann.

HAUYNE. A mineral of a blue colour of various shades, found imbedded in volcanic rocks, basalt, clinkstone, &c.; named after the French mineralogist Haüy.

HAVANNAH. A celebrated tobacco, of which cigars are made; named from Havannah, capital city of the island of Cuba, whence it is brought.

HAVETIA. A genus of plants, trees, natives of the Andes; named in honour of the French botanist, M. Havet.

HAWKESBURY. Name of a duck (the *Anas jubata*) inhabiting New South Wales, especially Hawkesbury River there.

HAYDENITE. A mineral resembling chabasite, and perhaps identical with it; occurring near Baltimore, where it was discovered by Dr. Hayden.—*Webster*.

HAYESINE. A mineral, a borate, occurring over the dry plains near Iquique, in Southern Peru; named after Hayes. The native name is *tiza*.

HAYLOCKIA. A genus of plants, or. *Monogynia*; named in honour of Mr. M. Haylocke.

HEBENSTREITIA. A genus of plants, or. *Angiospermia*; natives of the Cape; named after Ernst Hebenstreit, a professor at Upsal.

HECTOR. To threaten; to bully; to treat with insolence (*Dryden*). To tease; to vex; to torment by words; from *Hector*, son of Priam, and the most valiant of all the Trojans. The sense seems to have been greatly changed. ("The epithet of a *hectoring fellow* is a more familiar instance of a participle similarly formed, though strangely distorted in its use to express a meaning almost the opposite of its original. The *Hector* of Homer unites, we know,

'The mildest manners with the bravest mind.'

The sole bulwark of Troy, he reveres the opinion of her citizens; armed and hastening to the battle, he stops to caress his infant and to soothe the afflictions of its mother; to his brother's faults he is indulgent; and Helen herself witnesses over his grave that she had never heard from him one accent of unkindness, or ceased to be protected from the reproach of others by his mild speech and kindly dispositions :—

'Σῇ τ᾽ ἀγανοφροσύνῃ, καὶ τοῖς ἀγανοῖς ἐπέεσσι.' "

Nugæ Metricæ, an unpublished work by Lord Grenville, 1824, p. 86. *E. H. B.*)

HEDENBERGITE. A dark or nearly black cleavable variety of augite, semi-metallic in appearance, containing a large proportion of oxide of iron (*Dana*) ; from Hedenberg, who first analysed it.

HEISTERIA. A genus of plants, nat. or *Olacaceæ*, called after M. Heister, professor of botany at Helmstadt.—*Crabb.*

HELILAH-KABULEE or CABULI. A purgative Indian plum, the myrobalan of the Arabs. D'Herbelot thinks the name to be from *Cabul*, from having been first brought thence to Arabia.

HELLENISM. A phrase in the idiom, genius, or construction of the Greek language, *i.e.* the language spoken by the Hellenes, who were so called from Hellas, in Greece, or, as some say, from Hellen.

HELLENIST. A Grecian Jew; a Jew who used the Greek language; one skilled in the Greek language. See HELLENISM.

HELLENISTIC. Pertaining to the Hellenists; as the Hellenistic language, *i.e.* the Greek spoken or used by the Jews who lived in Egypt and other countries where the Greek language prevailed.

HELOT. A slave in ancient Sparta; so named from Helos (Ελος), a city of Laconia, which was taken and destroyed by the Lacedæmonians, under Agis III., who reduced the Ειλωται to the lowest and most miserable slavery.

HELOTISM. The condition of the Helots, *q.v.*

HERACLEA. Water horehound ; from *Heraclea*, near which it grows.—*Forsyth.*

HERCULEAN. Very great, difficult, or dangerous; such

as it would require the strength and courage of Hercules to encounter or accomplish; as Herculean labour or task.—— Having extraordinary strength and size; as Herculean limbs.

HERCULES. A constellation in the northern hemisphere, near Lyra; named from Hercules. It has also been called *Hercules cum Ramo et Cerbero.*

HERDERITE. A mineral occurring in Saxony, in crystals imbedded in fluor (*Brande*); named from Herder, who discovered it.

HERITIERA. Looking-glass plant, a genus, nat. or. *Sterculariaceæ;* called after L'Heritier de Bautelle, a French botanist.—*Crabb.*

HERMANNIA. A genus of plants, nat. or. *Sterculariaceæ;* called after Hermann, a botanist and traveller in Ceylon.

HERMAPHRODITE. An animal partaking of the nature of the two sexes. The word is said to be derived from Hermaphroditus, son of Hermes and Venus. The poets feign that Salmacis fell in love with him, and begged of the gods that their bodies might be always united, and make but one. The word is derived from Ερμης Mercury, Αφροδιτη Venus; *i.e.* partaking of both sexes.——A flower that contains both the stamen and the pistil, or the male and female organs of generation within the same calyx, or on the same receptacle. ——A plant that has only hermaphrodite flowers.——A brig that is square-rigged forward, and schooner-rigged aft.

HERMENEUTIC, HERMENEUTICAL. Interpreting, explaining, unfolding the signification, as hermeneutic theology, the art of expounding the Scriptures; from ερμηνευς an interpreter, from Ερμης Mercury.

HERMENEUTICS. The science of interpretation, or of finding the meaning of an author's words and phrases, and of explaining it to others; particularly applied to the interpretation of the Scriptures. See HERMENEUTIC.

HERMES. A name given to rough quadrangular stones or pillars, having a head sculptured on the top, without arms or body. Such stones were placed by the Greeks in front of buildings, and used by the Romans as boundaries or land-marks. As they originally bore the head of Hermes, or

Mercury, they have been called by this name, even when sur
mounted by the heads of other deities, &c.

HERMETIC, HERMETICAL. Designating chemistry;
chemical; as the hermetic art; so named from Hermes,
Mercury, fabled inventor of chemistry; others say from
Hermes Trismegistus, an Egyptian priest and philosopher, who,
according to Diodorus, was the friend and counsellor of the
great Osiris.——Designating that species of philosophy which
pretends to solve and explain all the phenomena of nature
from the three chemical principles, salt, sulphur, and mercury;
as the hermetic philosophy.——Designating the system which
explains the causes of diseases, and the operations of medicine,
on the principles of the hermetic philosophy, and particularly
on the system of an alkali and acid; as hermetical physic or
medicine.——Perfectly close, so that no air, gas, or spirit can
escape; as a hermetic seal. Hence, hermetic books; books of
the Egyptians, which treat of astrology; books which treat of
universal principles, of the nature and orders of celestial
beings, of medicine, and other topics.

HERMITAGE. A fine, high-flavoured, red wine, grown
on the slope of a hill near L'Hermitage, Tain, in the valley of
the Rhone.——A white wine. The grape is called Ceras, and
is said to have been brought from Shiraz, in Persia, by one of
the hermits of the mountain, on whose summit are ruins of
what is supposed to have been a hermit's cell.

HERMODACTYL. In the *materia medica*, a root from
Turkey, in the shape of a heart flattened, anciently in great
repute as a cathartic; but that which is now furnished having
little or no cathartic quality. Some derive the word from
Εϱμης Mercury, δακτυλος a finger; Mercury's finger. Forsyth, however, thinks it was more probably named from *Her-
mius*, a river of Asia, upon whose banks it grew; and δακτυλος,
a date, which, he says, it resembles.

HERNANDIA. A genus of plants, the only species of
which are *H. sonora*, Whistling Hernandia, or jack-in-a-box,
a tall erect tree, native of various parts of the East and West
Indies; named from the noise made by the wind in whistling
through its persistent involucels; and the *H. ovigera* or *Ino-*

carpus, egg-pointed Hernandia, native of North America. The genus derives its name from Francisco Hernandez, a naturalist sent out to Mexico by Philip II. of Spain.

HERSCHEL. A planet discovered by Dr. Herschel in 1781, first called *Georgium Sidus,* and now *Uranus.*

HERSCHELIAN. Designating a reflecting telescope of the form invented by Sir William Herschel. In this telescope only one speculum is employed, by means of which an image of the object is formed near one side of the open end of the tube, to which the eyeglass is applied directly.

HERSCHELITE. A mineral found in olivine, *i.e.* an olive-coloured silicate of lime and magnesia, along with Phillipsite, at Aci Castello, Etna, Sicily, by one of the Herschels.

HESSIAN. A boot formerly much worn in England; so named either from being introduced from Hesse, in Germany, or from being first worn by Hessian troops.——A small two-winged fly or midge, nearly black, very destructive to young wheat; so called from having been brought into America by the Hessian troops during the revolution.

HESYCHIUS. A valuable Greek lexicon extant, bearing the name of the author, who is supposed to have lived about the fifth or sixth century after the Christian era.

HEULANDITE. A mineral, colour of various shades of white passing into red, grey, and brown; occurring principally in amygdaloidal rocks, also in gneiss, &c.; named after the English mineralogist Heuland.

HIBBERTIA. A genus of plants, natives of Australia; named in honour of George Hibbert, F.R.S.

HIBERNICISM. An idiom or mode of speech peculiar to the Irish, *i.e.* the natives of Hibernia.

HILARY TERM. The term of courts, &c, beginning about the festival of St. Hilary, or near the middle of January.

HINDOOISM or HINDUISM. The doctrines and rites of the Hindoos or Hindús; the system of religious principles among the Hindoos, or natives of Hindustan.

HINDOOSTANEE or HINDÚSTÁNÍ. The language of the Hindoos or Hindús.

HIPPOCRAS or IPOCRAS. A medicinal drink, composed of wine with an infusion of spices and other ingredients; used as a cordial.——A name given to a kind of hot spiced wine, much in use in the Middle Ages, and drank at all great entertainments between the courses, or at the conclusion of the repast. It appears to have been indifferently made of red or white wine. Some assert that it was first made by Hippocrates or Hippocras. Webster says "*quasi* wine of Hippocrates." According to others it had its name from a peculiar sort of cloth bag called *Hippocrates' sleeve*, through which it was strained. Ménage derives the Fr. *hypocras* (formerly written *ipocras*) from ιπος, which he says in Hippocrates signifies a drink, and κρατιον, a word used by the modern Greeks for wine; although it evidently comes from κρατις, signifying a mixture, and everything made of wine with water. See also Quar. Rev. June, 1825, 245. Gent. Mag. vol. 98, part ii. 304, 1828; and Pegge.

HIPPOCRATEA. A genus of plants, nat. or. *Hippocrateaceæ*; called after Hippocrates, a Greek physician, considered the father of botany.

HIPPOCRATISM. The philosophy of Hippocrates, as it regards medicine.

HISINGERITE. A mineral found in the cavities of calcareous spar, in Sudermannland; doubtless named after Hisinger. *Hisingen* is the appellation of an island upon which Gottenburg was originally built.

HOBBISM. The principles of the sceptical Thomas Hobbes.—*Skelton*.

HOBSON'S CHOICE. A vulgar proverbial expression denoting a choice without an alternative; the thing offered or nothing. It is said to have had its origin in a person at Cambridge named Hobson, who let horses, and obliged every customer to take in his turn that horse which stood next the stable door.—*Encyc. Am.*

HOCK. A highly esteemed Rhenish wine, properly called Hochheimer; from *Hochheim*, in Nassau, where it is produced.

HOCUS-POCUS. A juggler, a juggler's trick, a cheat used

by jugglers; and, as a verb, to cheat. Webster suggests that this word may be from W. *hocced*, a cheat or trick, and *bwg* or *pwca*, a hobgoblin. According to others, this familiar phrase originated in derision of the words *Hoc est corpus meum,* slovenly pronounced by the mumbling priest in delivering the emblem as a reality (Cf. D'Israeli. Amen. Lit., and Athen. Sept. 18, 1841). Tillotson is of the same opinion. He says, " In all probability these common juggling words are nothing but a corruption of *Hoc est corpus,* by way of ridiculous imitation of the priests of the Church of Rome in their trick of Transubstantiation. Sharon Turner (Hist. Anglo-Saxons, Append. to b. ii. c. 3), however, derives the word from Ochus-Bochus, a magician and demon much feared in the north of Europe. Further he derives the term *Old Nick* from Nechus, a malign deity who frequented the waters.

HOFFMANSEGGIA.   A family of leguminous plants, shrubs, named in honour of J. C. Hoffmansegg, a German botanist.

HOLLAND.   Fine linen first manufactured in Holland. It is called in French *toile d'Hollande.* In like manner the Spaniards call a sort of fine linen *bretaña,* from being brought from Bretagne.

HOLLANDS (*Schiedam*).   A spirit made in Holland.   It resembles gin, except in the impurity of the latter.

HOLMITE.   A variety of carbonate of lime, analysed by Holme.

HOMERIC.   Pertaining to Homer or his poetry; resembling his verse.

HONITON.   A pillow or cushion lace remarkable for the beauty of its figures and sprigs, which are sewed on to a net ; made at Honiton, in Devonshire.

HOO SZE.   Raw silk ; so called from Hoo-kwang, a province of China, where it is produced.

HOTTENTOT.   A savage brutal man ; lit. one belonging to a South African tribe, formerly considered the most degraded of the human race.

HOTTENTOTISM.   Amman distinguishes two species of stammering ; the first he calls Hottentotism, which consists in modifying the sounds in such a manner that they become unintelligible; so called from the Hottentots of South Africa.

HOTTONIA. The water-violet, a genus of plants; named in honour of Professor Hotton, of Leyden.

HOUSTONIA. A vernal plant, native of Virginia; named after Wm. Houston, F.R.S., an English physician and botanist. He died in the West Indies in 1733, leaving a MS. catalogue of plants, the publication of which was undertaken by Sir Joseph Banks.

HOUTTUYNIA. A plant, root annual, discovered by Thunberg in Japan; named in honour of Mart. Houttuyn, M.D., of Holland, author of Natuurlyke Historie, Amst. 1773-83.

HOVENIA. A genus of Asiatic plants, or. *Monogynia*; named in honour of Dr. Hoven, of Amsterdam.

HUDIBRASTIC. A term applied to doggerel verse, like that in which Butler's Hudibras is composed. "Its author is known as the immortal Samuel Butler, and every specimen of later satirical verse remotely approaching his in measure or style is christened Hudibrastic." . . . "From the general level of broad humour and pungent wit which has given a name to the Hudibrastic manner, he sometimes rises by a touch of imagination into a pure poetical beauty which would not be generally called Hudibrastic." Sat. Rev. July 16, 1864.

HUDSONIA. A genus of plants, shrubs; or. *Monogynia*; named after William Hudson, F.R.S.

HUERNIA. A genus of plants, or. *Digynia*; named in honour of the botanist Justus Huernius.

HUGONIA. A plant, a tree, of only one species, native of the East Indies; named by Linnæus in memory of Augustus Johannes de Hugo, who travelled in Switzerland with Haller in 1732, and assisted him with his Herbarium.

HUGUENOT. A name formerly given to a Protestant by the Catholics of France. Numerous derivations have been suggested, many of which will be found in Ménage. Among others are G. *eidgenossen*, confederates, from *eid* oath, *genoss* consort; les *guenots* de *Husse,* John Huss's imps; *huc nos venimus,* the beginning of the first protestation of the

Apologetical Oration made before Cardinal Lotharingus, temp. Francis II. of France; but the most reasonable suggestion is from Hugon, a gate in Tours, where they first assembled; or from Hugo, Hugon, or Hugues, their leader. The author of *Mémoires et Recherches de la France*, attributed to Jan de la Haye, p. 261, speaking of the ravages made by the Huguenots against the Ecclesiastics, says, "De là furent appellez *Huguenots*, parce que les François se souvinrent de la grande persécution que leur ayeux avoient receu tant des Gots, Visigots, et Ostrogots, et nommèrent ces derniers persécuteurs *Huguenots*, acause d'un nommé *Hugues*, lequel avoit esté Sacramentaire du temps du Roy Charles VI." Again. J. Le Frere de Laval, *La Vraye et entiere Histoire des Troubles*, p. 103, says "Un certain historien Espagnol, qui a écrit l'Histoire des Papes en sa langue, a inventé un homme de sa façon, appellé *Hugo*, Hérésiarque Sacramentaire; Hugo, Hæresiarcha Sacramentarius; de qui les Hérétiques de France ont esté appellez Huguenots."

——Bailey gives also "Huguenote (Fr.), a kind of kettle for a stove, or an earthen stove for a pot to boil on; hence, *A la huguenote*, in cookery, a particular way of dressing eggs with gravy."

HUMBOLDTINE.   A native oxalate of iron; named after Humboldt.

HUMBOLDTITE.   A rare mineral, consisting of a borosilicate of iron, found in trap rocks in the Tyrol; named after Humboldt.

HUMBUG.   An imposition under pretences; one who thus imposes.   According to some, the word is derived from *Hamburg*, or rather, "news from Hamburg," because in war times news from that city, being frequently false, was generally looked upon with distrust.   The word has also been derived from Homberg, the distinguished chemist of the court of the Duke of Orleans, who, according to a passage from Bishop Berkeley's *Siris*, was an ardent and successful seeker after the philosopher's stone !   "The derivation of this word, now in such common use, is not generally known; but it is of Scotch origin.   There was in former years residing in the neighbourhood of the Mearns. in Scotland, a gentleman of landed property whose name was Hume or Home; and his estate was known as the Bogue. From the great falsehoods that Hume of the Bogue was in the habit of relating about himself, his family, and everything connected with him, it soon became customary, when persons heard anything that was remarkably extravagant or absurd, to say, 'That is a Hume o' the Bogue.' The expression spread like wildfire over the whole country, and those who did not understand the origin of the phrase, and applied it only to any extravagant action or saying, contracted it into one word, and corrupted it to *hum-bug*. We must define *humbug*. It is not naked untruth. A draper's assistant who tells a lady that a dress will wash when it will not does not humbug her—he merely cheats her; but if he persuades her to buy a good-for-nothing muslin by telling her that he has sold such another to a duchess he humbugs her, whether he speaks truly or not; he imposes an inference in favour of his commodity, through her large vanity upon her small mind. Humbug thus consists in making people deceive themselves, by supplying them with premises, true or false, from which, by reason of their ignorance, weakness, or prejudice, they draw wrong conclusion."—*Pulleyn*. See also *Hotten's* Slang Dict.

HUMITE. A reddish-brown mineral, found near Naples in a rock of granular topaz; named after Sir Abraham Hume.

HUNGARY GREEN or MOUNTAIN GREEN. A sort of greenish powder found in little grains, like sand, among the mountains of Kernausent in Hungary, and those of Moldavia.

HUNTERIA. A genus of plants, trees, named in honour of Dr. William Hunter, of Bengal.

HUNTLEYA. A genus of orchidaceous plants; named after the Rev. J. T. Huntley.

HUREAULITE. A mineral of a reddish-yellow hue, occurring in very small crystals, found in the granite of Hureau or Hureault, near Limoges, in France.

HURLY-BURLY. Tumult, bustle, confusion (*Shak.*); "said to owe its origin to Hurleigh and Burleigh, two neighbouring families that filled the country around them with contest and violence " (*Pulleyn*).

HURONIA. The generic name assigned by Mr. C. Stokes to certain radiated corallines found by Dr. Bigsby in the transition limestone of Lake Huron, Upper Canada.

HURONITE. A mineral, colour yellowish-green ; found in boulder stones in the neighbourhood of Lake Huron.

HURRAH. A shout of joy or exultation. The origin of this word belongs to the primitive idea that all men who die for their country go to heaven; *hur-raj* in Slavonic meaning Paradise.—*Dalmatian Observer.*

HUYGHENIAN. An eye-piece for diminishing the spherical aberration by producing the refractions at two glasses instead of one, and increasing the field of view; invented by Huyghens, the eminent mathematician and astronomer.

HYACINTH (L. *hyacinthus*, Gr. ὑακινθος). Popular name of some species of a genus of plants, said by the poets to have been called after the youth Hyacinthus, who, having been accidentally killed, was changed by his friend Apollo into this flower.——A red variety of zircon, sometimes used as a gem. ——The colour of " tenne " or orange.

HYACINTHINE. Made of, consisting of, or resembling hyacinth.—*Milton.*

HYGIEINA, HYGIEINE, or **HYGIENE.** Health, or the art or science of preserving health ; that department of medicine which treats of the preservation of health ; said to be so named from Hygeia, goddess of health. The Greek has ὑγιαινω, to be well.

HYGIENIC. Pertaining to health. See HYGIEINA.

HYMEN (Gr. ὑμην). The virginal membrane; said to have been so called from Hymen, son of Bacchus and Venus, who presided over marriages, because this membrane is supposed to be entire before marriage.——The fine pellicle which encloses a flower in the bud.

HYMENEAL, HYMENEAN. Pertaining to marriage (*Pope*).——A marriage song (*Milton*). See HYMEN.

HYSON. A species of green tea from China ; named after the merchant who first imported (exported ?) it.—*Encyc. Brit.*

I.

IBERIS. A genus of plants, nat. or. *Cruciferæ;* so called from Iberia, in Spain, where it was first found.

ICARIAN. Adventurous in flight; soaring too high for safety, like Icarus, son of Dædalus, who fled on wings to escape the resentment of Minos, but whose flight being too high, he fell into the sea and was drowned, the sun having melted the wax that cemented his wings.

IDRIALIN. A substance consisting of carbon and hydrogen; from the quicksilver mines at Idria, in Carniola.

ILIAD. An epic poem in twenty-four books, composed by Homer. The subject of this poem is the wrath of Achilles, in describing which the poet exhibits the miserable effects of disunion and public dissensions; hence the phrase *Ilias malorum,* an Iliad of woes or calamities; a world of disasters (*Cicero*); named from Ilium, Ilion, Troy.

ILMENITE (another name for Mengite). A black metallic mineral, consisting of titanic acid and oxide of iron; said to occur in granite veins in the Ilmen mountains; but qu. where? Ilmen is the name of a lake of Russia, gov. Novgorod, which discharges its surplus waters into Lake Ladoga; and Ilmenau is the appellation of a town and of a river of Germany. Brooke's name *Ilmenite* being preoccupied, it was changed by Rose to *Mengite.*

INDIA or INDIAN RUBBER. A substance produced by incision from several trees of different genera; from India.

INDIAMAN. A large ship employed in the India trade.

INDIAN or INDIA INK. A substance said to consist of lampblack and animal glue, brought chiefly from China, and used in water colours.

INDIANITE. A doubtful mineral of the feldspar family; from India.

INDICOLITE. A variety of shorl or tourmalin of an indigo-blue colour, sometimes with a tinge of azure or green; from *indicum,* indigo, and λιθος, a stone.

INDIGO. A drug of a fine colour, prepared from the leaves and branches of the *Indigofera tinctoria*. The word was formerly written *indico*, and is derived from *Indicum lignum*, being brought from India.

INDIGOGEN. White or reduced indigo, produced by the action upon blue indigo of any deoxidating body.

INDIGOMETER. An instrument for ascertaining the strength of indigo.

INNISHEOWN. A celebrated whisky distilled at Innisheown, near Derry, Ireland.

INULA. See ELECAMPANE.

INULIN. A peculiar vegetable principle extracted from the *Inula helenium*, or elecampane. See ELECAMPANE.

INVERNESS. A sort of woollen cape worn by men; from *Inverness*, in Scotland.

IONIC. An order in architecture characterised by a species of column, simple and majestic, more slender than the Doric and the Tuscan, but less slender and less ornamented than the Corinthian and Composite, and whose distinguishing feature is the volute of its capital; named from Ionia, in Asia Minor, where it originated.——A dialect of the Greek language used in Ionia.——In poetry, a foot consisting of four syllables, either two short and two long, or two long and two short.—— Among the ancients a light and airy kind of music.

IRANEE. A horse well limbed, and very powerful in the quarters; brought from Iran, the ancient name of Persia.

IRISHISM. A mode of speaking peculiar to the Irish.

IRVINISM. The *ism* of the Rev. Edward Irving, who associated himself with the so-called "prophets," who pretended to be inspired with the gift of prophecy, encouraged manifestations of the "unknown tongues," and committed other offences against ecclesiastical discipline. In 1830 he was convicted by the Scotch presbytery in London, and dismissed from his incumbency in Regent Square. A vacant picture gallery in Newman Street, Oxford Street, was, however, afterwards converted into a chapel for him by his admirers, and here he was permitted to indulge unrestrained the prophetic messages with which he believed himself to be charged. He was born in 1792 at Annan, in Scotland, and died 6th December, 1834.

ISABEL (Fr. *isabelle, couleur Isabelle*). A brownish-yellow colour with a shade of brownish-red; named after Isabelle of Austria, daughter of Philip II. of Spain and Elizabeth of France. Isabelle (born 1566, died 1633), having married Albert, son of the Emperor Maximilian, and received as a dowry the sovereignty of the Low Countries, declared war against Holland, was present and assisted at the famous siege of Ostend, and frustrated the attempts of the Prince of Orange to draw over to his side the Roman Catholic provinces. Despairing at the long resistance of the siege, Isabelle, it is said, swore she would not change her linen until she was mistress of the place. Ostend having resisted nearly three years, the linen worn by the princess became of a tawny colour; hence, it is said, the name *Isabelle* for this colour. The French biographer says, " The epoch at which the infanta made this strange vow is not fixed, but, inasmuch as the siege lasted three years, three months, and three days, it is not at all astonishing that the linen which the princess wore should have become of the fawn colour, which, after her name, is still called *couleur Isabelle*." It is possible, however, that the colour may have been named from the complexion of the princess. After speaking of the vain attempts to place the princess on the throne of France, the biographer says, " C'est ainsi que des années entières d'efforts et de combinaisons politiques se terminèrent par une scène de comédie. Ce ridicule ne pouvait échapper aux auteurs de la fameuse *Satire Ménippée*. Dans la caricature des états de Paris, c'est le portrait de *l'Epousée de la Ligue*, c'est-à-dire de l'infante elle-même, qui est suspendu sur la tête du président. Au-dessous du portrait sont écrits ces vers, qui contiennent une double épigramme—

> ' Pourtant si je suis brunette,
> Amy, n'en prenez émoy ;
> Car autant aimer souhaitte
> Qu'une plus blanche que moy.'

Le teint basané de la princesse, et son âge, qui n'était cepen-
dant que de vingt-huit à trente ans, ne sont jamais oubliés dans
les satires ni même dans les discours dont elle était l'objet."
The French word is also used in Entomology, Ichthyology,
Ornithology, &c.

ISABELLINO. A new gold coin of Spain equal to 100
reals; named from Queen Isabel.

ITALICS. Italic letters or characters; letters which
stand inclining; *the letters in which this clause is printed*. So
called because first used in Italy.

ITALIANATE. To render Italian, or conformable to
Italian customs (*obs.*)

ITALIANIZE. To play the Italian; to speak Italian.

IOXIA. A genus of bulbous plants, or. *Monogynia*. Some
derive the word from Gr. ιξος, glue, from its viscous juice.
According to others, it was so called because its flower when
open resembles the wheel of Ixion.

J.

JACK. A general term of contempt for any saucy or
paltry fellow; from *Jack*, nickname for *John*.——An instrument that supplies the place of a boy; an instrument to pull
off boots. —— An engine to turn a spit; as a kitchen
jack, a smoke jack, a bottle jack.——A young pike. ——
A pitcher of waxed leather.——A small bowl thrown out
for a mark to the bowlers.——Part of a musical instrument
called a virginal.——The male of certain animals, as of the
ass.——A horse or wooden frame on which wood or timber
is sawn.——In archæology, a kind of defensive coat-armour
formerly worn by horsemen. —— In sea language, a flag,
ensign, or colours, displayed from a staff on the end of a bowsprit.——A quarter of a pint; in Yorkshire half-a-pint.——
In mechanics, a machine for raising heavy weights. ——In
botany, a species of the bread-fruit tree.——A term often

applied to seafaring men.——A large wooden male screw turning in a female one.

JACK KETCH. In England, a public executioner or hangman, a most useful officer. Macaulay (Hist. Eng. vol. I. 627), describing the execution of the Duke of Monmouth on Tower Hill, July 15, 1685, says, "Monmouth mounted the scaffold, then accosted John Ketch, the executioner, a wretch who had butchered many brave and noble victims, and whose name has, during a century and a half, been vulgarly given to all who have succeeded him in his odious office. 'Here,' said the duke, 'are six guineas for you. Do not hack me as you did my Lord Russell. I have heard that you struck him three or four times: my servant will give you some more gold if you do the work well.' He then undressed, felt the edge of the axe, expressed some fear that it was not sharp enough, and laid his head on the block. The hangman addressed himself to his office, but he had been disconcerted by what the duke had said. The first blow only made a slight wound. The duke struggled, rose from the block, and looked reproachfully at the executioner. The head sank once more, the stroke was repeated again and again, but still the neck was not severed, and the body continued to move. Yells of rage and horror rose from the crowd. Ketch flung down the axe with a curse: 'I cannot do it,' he said, 'my heart fails me.' 'Take up the axe, man,' said the sheriff. 'Fling him over the rails,' roared the mob. At last the axe was taken up. Two more blows extinguished the last remains of life, but a knife was used to separate the head from the shoulders. In the year which followed Monmouth's execution Ketch was turned out of his office for insulting one of the sheriffs, and was succeeded by a butcher named Rose ; but in four months Rose himself was hanged at Tyburn, and Ketch was reinstated."

JACKET (Fr. *jaquette*, Bas. *jacaya*, O. Sp. *xaquéta*, now *jaquéta*, a jacket, a short loose coat; *xaco*, now *jáco*, a short jacket; *xaquetilla*, now *jacquetilla*, a small jacket). The garment so named, said to be of German origin. The word is probably a diminutive of the name Jacques, or, as some say, of Jack. Froissart says Henry, duke of Lancaster, on his

K

return to England, entered London in a "courte jacques of cloth of gold, à la fachon d'Almayne" (see Planché). Mr. Boys thinks *jacket* is "Little John," or "Little Jacky," the term being transferred from the wearer to his coat; and he instances the Portuguese *josezinho*, i.e. Little Joseph or Little Joey, which is often used for the dress of the schoolboy.

JACOB. A ladder; from Jacob's dream.—*Grose.*

JACOBÆA. St. James's wort; ragwort; "so named because it was dedicated to St. James, or because it was directed to be gathered about the feast of that saint."— *Forsyth.*

JACOBINISM. Unreasonable or violent opposition to legitimate government; an attempt to overthrow or change government by secret cabals or irregular means; popular turbulence; the principles of the Jacobins, a society of violent revolutionists, who, during the French Revolution of 1789, held secret meetings, in which measures were concerted to direct the proceedings of the National Assembly, and who had their name from the place of meeting, the monastery of the Jacobine monks.

JACOBITISM. The principles of the partisans or adherents of James II. of England after he abdicated the throne, and of his descendants of course; opposers of the Revolution in 1688 in favour of William and Mary. From *Jacobus,* James.

JACOB'S LADDER. In naval affairs, a rope ladder with wooden steps or spokes for going aloft; so named from Jacob's ladder (Gen. xxviii. 12).——A plant of the genus *Smilax.*

JACOB'S MEMBRANE. The thin external membrane of the retina, considered by Dr. Jacob to be a serous membrane.

JACOBSON'S NERVE. Another name for the tympanic branch, described by Jacobson.

JACOB'S STAFF. An instrument (called also *cross-staff* and *bore-staff*) formerly used for taking the meridian altitude of the sun or stars; said to be so named because the divisions marked upon it resembled the steps of Jacob's ladder (Gen. xxviii. 12). "On l'appelait, dit-on, bâton de Jacob, parceque

les divisions marquées sur le montant ressemblaient aux degrés de l'échelle mystérieuse de Jacob (See Encyc. Cathol. "Baton").
——A pilgrim's staff, concealing a dagger, formerly used by pilgrims in Spain.

JACOBUS. Gold coins of the value of 20s., 23s., and 25s., struck in the reign of James I.

JACONET. A light soft muslin, of an open texture, used for dresses, necklocks, &c.; probably from the name of the first manufacturer, Jaconet, a double diminutive of *Jacques*.

JACQUARD. An appendage to a loom, consisting of a set of perforated cards and droppers for weaving figured goods, both silk and cotton; named from the inventor, Jacquard, who was born at Leyden 7th July, 1752, and who caused so great a revolution in the industry of weaving. The term has also been applied to carpets.

JAQUEMONTIA. A genus of South American plants, herbs or sub-shrubs; named in honour of Victor Jacquemont.

JACQUERIE. In French history, the name given to the revolt of the French peasantry against the nobility in 1356; so called from their leader Jacques, or Jacques Bonhomme. Roquefort gives "*Jacquerie*, révolte qui eut lieu en 1356; elle fut ainsi nommée de son chef, qui s'appeloit Jacques; d'où *Jacquiers*, les séditieux qui participèrent à cette révolte; en bas Bret. *jacquer*, persécuteur; *Jaquerie, Jaques;* soldats, faction de séditieux et de voleurs. Ce nom fut donné à une troupe de paysans qui se révoltèrent en 1318 (suivant Borel) contre leur seigneurs, à cause des exactions qu'ils exerçoient contr'eux. Comme le Roi Jean, qui régnoit alors, étoit prisonnier en Angleterre (ce qui n'est arrivé qu'en 1356), les seigneurs, par dérision, appelèrent cette sédition la *Jaquerie*, du nom de leur chef *Jaques Bonhomme*, et les factieux *Jacquiers:* elle commença dans le Beauvoisis. Froissart parle de cette sédition." The Encyc. des Gens du Monde says, "*Jacquerie:* en France, vers le milieu du XIV⁰ siècle, les nobles appelaient par dérision le peuple *Jacques Bonhomme*, et quand leur excès eurent fait soulever ce dernier, la sédition populaire s'appela *Jacquerie*. La Jacquerie appartient au règne du Roi Jean, l'un des plus malheureux que l'histoire nous ait fait connaître ; guerre étrangère, guerre civile, peste, famine, tout sembla se réunir alors pour livrer la France à la plus horrible misère."

JACQUINIA. A genus of plants, the species of which are shrubs, natives of South America and other warm climates ; named by Linnæus in honour of the celebrated Nicholas Joseph Von Jacquin, professor of botany at Vienna, born at Leyden in 1727, who published a history of American plants, &c.

JALAP (Sp. and Port, *jalápa*, Fr. *jalap*). The root of a plant having little or no taste or smell, much used in powder as a cathartic ; from *Xalapa* or *Jalapá*, in Mexico, whence it is imported.

JALAPIN. A vegetable proximate principle of the officinal jalap.

JAMACINA or JAMAICIN. An alkaloid obtained from the *Andira inermis*, or cabbage bark tree, of the West Indies ; named from Jamaica.

JAMESONITE. A steel-grey ore of antimony and lead ; named after Professor Jameson.

JANSENISM. The doctrine of Cornelius Jansen, a Roman Catholic bishop of Ypres, in Flanders, who was asserted to have denied free will, and to have held to irresistible grace and atonement, in his book called Augustinus.—*S. F. Cresswell.*

JANUARY (L. *Januarius*). The first month of the year according to the present computation. At the foundation of Rome March was considered the first month. January and February were introduced by Numa Pompilius (*Encyc.*). The Latin word is said to be derived from the Roman god Janus (Dor. Ζαν, Ζανος, Jupiter), to whom this month was supposed to be sacred. He had two faces, and the doors of his temple were shut in time of peace, and open in time of war. Hall says January was so called from being the gate or opening (*janua*) of the year.

JAPAN. Work varnished and figured in the manner practised by the Japanese. Hence, to cover with a thick coat of hard brilliant varnish, an art derived from the Japanese ;

hence, to black and gloss, as in blacking shoes or boots.——
To ordain (*University*).

JAPHETIC. A term formerly applied to the nations inhabiting the north of Asia and all Europe, and to the languages spoken by them; so called from Japhet, eldest son of
Noah.

JASEY. A contemptuous name for a wig, and even for a
head of bushy hair; as if composed of *Jersey* yarn, of which
jazy is a corrupt pronunciation.—*Forby*.

JEAN. A twilled cotton, usually striped, used for stays,
&c.; probably from the first maker, Jean (John). Satin jean
is woven smooth and glossy, after the manner of satin.

JEFFERSONIA. A genus of North American herbaceous plants; named in honour of Jefferson, president of the
United States.

JEFFERSONITE. A variety of augite, colour dark
olive green, passing into brown; found embedded in franklinite
and garnet, in New Jersey, North America; named in honour
of Jefferson, president of the United States.

JEHU. A name for a coachman; said to be so called from
Jehu, son of Nimshi, who rode in a chariot. " And the driving
is like the driving of Jehu, the son of Nimshi, for he driveth
furiously." 2 Kings, ix. 20.—*S. F. Creswell*.

JEMMY. In thieves' language, a short and stout crowbar
for opening doors; from the nickname for *James*.

**JENNETING, JUNEATING, JUNETING, or GINET-
TING.** A species of early apple; "said to be corrupted from
juneating, an apple ripe in June, or at St. Jean, the name of a
place in France.—*Webster*.

JENNY. A machine for spinning, moved by water or
steam, and used in manufactories. " It was originally invented by Hargreaves in 1767, but ultimately improved by
Richard Arkwright, a barber, but who afterwards became an
eminent manufacturer, ultimately Sir Richard Arkwright, Bart.
The term *jenny* was derived from his wife, whose name was
Jane, but whom he used to address by the familiar name of
Jenny; thinking, no doubt, that, as the latter had been very
prolific, his new invention would be equally so under a simi-

lar appellation. The result justified such a conclusion."—
Pulleyn.

JEREMIADE. Lamentation; a tale of grief, sorrow, or
complaint; from the Lamentations of Jeremiah, the prophet,
over Jerusalem.

JERKIN. A jacket; a short coat; a close waistcoat.
Bailey derives the word from A. S. *cyrtelkin*, diminutive of
cyrtel, a coat. The Rev. Mr. Boys thinks *jerkin* may be a
diminutive of *Jerry*, i.e. Little Jerry, and he instances the
dress of the schoolboy in Portugal, often called *josezinho*, i.e.
Little Joseph or Little Joey, the term being facetiously transferred from the wearer to his coat."

JERSEY. A fine yarn of wool; named from the island so
called. —— A woollen over-jacket all in a piece, used in
rowing, &c.

JESSE. A branch, or large candlestick of brass branched
into several sconces, hanging down in the middle of a church
or choir, in order to spread the light to all parts; so called as
resembling the branch or genealogical tree of Jesse (arbor
Jessæ; stirps *Jessæ*), of which a picture was formerly hung
up in churches. It was first brought over into England by
Hugh de Flory, abbot of St. Austin's in Canterbury, about
1100, as thus recorded by the historian of the abbey :—" Pul-
pitum etiam in ecclesia fecit, candelabrum etiam magnum in
choro æreum, quod *Jesse* vocatur, in partibus emit transma-
rinis." Chron. Will. Thorn., p. 1796 ; and Cowel, Interpreter.

JESUITIC, JESUITICAL. Designing; cunning; deceitful; prevaricating; lit. pertaining to the Jesuits or their
principles and arts. The Jesuits were members of the Society
of Jesus, founded by Ignatius Loyola in 1534, a society remarkable for their cunning in propagating their principles.

JET (D. *git*, Fr. *jayet*, L. *gagates*). A mineral, of a velvet-
black colour, found in unconnected heaps; wrought into toys,
buttons, mourning jewels, &c. ; the same word as *agate*, q.v.

JEW. A cheat; to cheat; overreaching being by all nations supposed to be the peculiar function of a Jew.—*S. F.
Creswell.*

JEWISHNESS. The rights of the Jews.—*Martin.*

JEW'S EAR. Popular name of a species of fungus bearing some resemblance to the human ear.

JEZEBEL. Formerly employed to denote a forward impertinent woman, and perhaps not yet wholly disused (*Johnson*); an impertinent, daring, vicious woman (*Spectator*); so called from Jezebel, who displayed her pernicious charms at her window (*Ibid*). Jezebel (whose name, by the bye, in Hebrew signifies *chaste*) was such an impious woman that she is regarded in the Scriptures as the symbol of fornication and wickedness. After Jehu had slain her son Jehoram he came to Jezreel, and "Jezebel heard of it; and she painted her face and tired her head, and looked out at a window" (2 Kings. ix. 30).

JINGO. "By Jingo." A common form of oath, said to be a corruption of St. Gingoulph. See Halliwell.

JOBATION. A scolding; a long tedious reproof (*Grose*); a lecture, reprimand; from *Job*, his friends having remonstrated much with him. "Probably corrupted from *jawbation*, a jawing" (*S. F. Creswell*).

JOB'S TEARS. A grass-like plant of the genus *Coix*, with shining pearly fruit, resembling falling tears.

JOCKEY. A man who rides horses in a race; primarily a boy that rides horses; from *Jackey*, a diminutive of *Jack*. ——A dealer in horses; one who makes it his business to buy and sell horses for gain.——A cheat; one who deceives or takes undue advantage in trade.——To cheat; to trick; to deceive in trade.——To jostle by riding against one.

JOE. A too marvellous tale, a lie, a stale joke; from *Joe Miller*. The full name is occasionally used, as in the phrase, "I don't see the *Joe Miller* of it," *i.e.* I don't perceive the wit you intend.—*J. C. Hotten.*

JOE or JOEY. A fourpenny piece, a supply of which was kept by the late Joseph Hume for paying cabmen (*S. F. Creswell*). "These pieces are said to have owed their existence to the pressing instance of Mr. Hume, from whence they for some time bore the nickname of *Joeys*. As they were very convenient to pay short cab fares, the Hon. M.P. was extremely unpopular with the drivers, who frequently received only " a groat" where otherwise they would have received a sixpence without any demand for change" (Hawkins's Hist. Silver Coinage of England).

JOHANNES. A Portuguese coin equal to 8 dollars; often contracted into *joe;* as a *joe, half-joe;* named from the figure of King John, which it bears.

JOHANNITE. A mineral consisting of sulphate of copper, sulphate of oxide of uranium, and water, in unknown proportions; found in crystals and reniform masses at Joachimsthal and *Johann*-Georgenstadt, in Bohemia.

JOHANNISBERG. The most famous of the Rhenish wines; named from the Château of Johannisberg, the property of Prince Metternich, near Rüdesheim, on the right bank of the Rhine, situated in the midst of the vineyards themselves. The first owners of the vineyard were the monks, it having been originally attached to the abbey and convent of St. John, afterwards secularized. The best grapes grow close under the castle, and, indeed, partly over the cellars. So precious are they that those which fall are picked off the ground with a kind of fork made for the purpose.

JOHN. A pear used in Worcestershire for making perry; probably named from the gardener.

JOHN APPLE (*Deux Ans*). An apple good for spring use, when other fruit is spent; perhaps named from the gardener. It is probably the same with the Apple John mentioned by Shakspeare.

JOHN BULL. The well-known collective name of the English nation, first used in Arbuthnot's satire, the History of John Bull, usually published in Swift's works.

JOHNSONISM. A peculiar word or manner of Dr. Johnson; the literary style introduced by him.

JONATHAN. The origin of this term, as applied to the United States, is as follows :—" When General Washington, after being appointed commander of the army of the revolutionary war, went to Massachusetts to organize it, he found a great want of ammunition and other means for its defence, and on one occasion it seemed that no means could be devised for the necessary supply. Jonathan Trumbull the elder was then governor of the State of Connecticut, and the general, placing the greatest reliance on his excellency's judgment, remarked, 'We must consult Brother Jonathan on the subject.' The general did so, and the governor was successful in supplying many of the wants of the army; and thenceforth, when difficulties arose, and the army was spread over the country, it became a bye-phrase, 'We must consult Brother Jonathan,' and the name has now become a designation for the whole country, as 'John Bull' has for England."—*Bartlett.*

JONCQUETIA. A genus of plants of only one species, native of Guiana, where it is called *Tapiriri*; named in memory of Denis Joncquet, who published a catalogue of his own garden, entitled Hortus, seu Index Plantarum, quas colebat a 1658 & 1659.

JONESIA. A genus of leguminous plants, trees, whose species are few, and indigenous to the islands of the Malayan Archipelago; named in honour of Sir Wm. Jones, the cele-brated scholar; born 1743, died at Calcutta 1794.

JOSEPH. A woman's riding dress, formerly much in use (*Grose*). See JACKET.

JOSEPHINIA. A genus of Australian herbaceous plants; named by Ventetat in honour of his munificent patroness, the Empress Josephine.

JOSEPHISM. The Emperor Maximilian belonged to a family which, although it boasts of its orthodoxy, has given a name to the heresy which under the name of *Josephism* is more distasteful than Jansenism or Protestantism to the Court of Rome.—*Sat. Rev.* 16th July, 1864.

JOSSINIA. A genus of plants, trees and shrubs, indige-nous to the Mauritius; named after Jossin.

JOVE. The planet Jupiter; from *Jove*, the supreme deity among the Romans.——The air or atmosphere, or the god of the air.——In alchemy, a name for tin.

JOVELLANA. A genus of South American plants, or. *Angiospermia;* named in honour of Don Gaspar Melchior de Jovellanos, one of the most distinguished Spaniards of modern times.

JOVIAL. Gay, merry, airy, joyous, jolly, as a jovial youth,

a jovial throng; from L. *jovialis*, lit. belonging to Jupiter; or, as others say, "Merry as Jove;" or *q.d.* one born *Jove læto*, under the influence of the planet Jove or Jupiter. See JOVE.

JUDAIC, JUDAICAL. Pertaining to the Jews; from *Judah*.

JUDAISM. The religious doctrines and rites of the Jews, as enjoined in the laws of Moses; from *Judah*.——Conformity to the Jewish rites and ceremonies.

JUDAIZE. To conform to the religious doctrines and rites of the Jews.

JUDAS. A deceitful person; so named from Judas Iscariot. *Judas-haired :* red haired, deceitful.

JUDAS-TREE. A leguminous flowering tree, of the genus *Cercis*, common in the East, on one of which Judas is said to have hung himself.

JUGLANS. A genus of plants of eight species, one of which is the common walnut-tree; from *Jovis glans*, the nut or acorn of Jupiter, to whom the oak was sacred. "Quasi *Jovis glans*, the royal fruit, from its magnitude."—*Forsyth*.

JULIAN. In chronology, the designation of a period of 7980 years, a number produced by multiplying 28, the years of the solar cycle, by 19, the years of the lunar cycle, and their product by 15, the years of the Roman indiction; named in honour of Julius Scaliger, who invented it.——The old account of the year, as regulated by Julius Cæsar, which continued to be used in England till 1752, when the Gregorian year, or new style, was adopted.——Among the Romans, a law which made adultery punishable by death; also a law made by Julius Cæsar to regulate the office and duties of a judge. Cf. Aulus Gellius, Attic Nights, c. ii.; Heineccius, p. 646; and Gibbon.——In cookery, a pottage made of a leg of mutton roasted, and put into a pot with beef, a fillet of veal, &c.

JULIENNE (*soupe à la Julienne*). A soup made of several sorts of herbs and vegetables; perhaps named after a French cook.——The name of a French plant.

JULY (L. *Julius*). The seventh month of the year. It was at first called by the Romans *Quintilis*, or the fifth month, according to the old calendar, in which March was the first month of the year. The name was afterwards changed to *Julius*, in honour of Julius Cæsar, who was born in this month.

JUNE (L. *Junius, Junius mensis*). The sixth month of the year; from the surname of a Roman family, the most noted of whom was L. Junius Brutus, who abolished regal power at Rome.

JUNGERMANNIA. A genus of cryptogamic plants; named after Louis Jungermann, a German botanist, who died in 1653.

JUNO. A small telescopic planet, which revolves round the sun between the orbits of Mars and Jupiter; discovered in 1804 by Harding of Bremen; named after Juno, sister and wife of Jupiter.

JURA. A term applied to the limestones belonging to the oolitic group, and constituting the chief part of the mountains of the Jura, between France and Switzerland.

JURANÇON. A white wine, perhaps the best in the Pyrenees; named from the village of Jurançon, where it grows.

JURASSIC. A system, with Continental writers, synonymous with our oolitic system; named from the mountains of the Jura. *q.v.*

JUSSIEUA or JUSSLÆA. A genus of plants, of eleven species, mostly annuals, natives of Jamaica, Java, Japan, South America, and India; named by Linnæus in honour of Antoine de Jussieu (uncle of the celebrated Antoine Laurent de Jussieu), demonstrator of plants in the royal garden at Paris, who edited Tournefort's Institutes in 1719, and described plants in the Paris Memoirs for 1709.

JUSTICIA. A genus of tropical plants, whose species are very numerous, mostly shrubby or herbaceous annuals; named after James Justice, F.R.S.

JUSTINIAN. The appellation of a code or general compilation of the best and most useful laws or constitutions, promulgated by the emperors previous to the reign of Justinian, beginning from Hadrian's perpetual edict down to his own time; made by order of Justinian. The code was first published in April, A.D. 529, and the revised code, under the title of Codex Justinianeus, repetitæ prælectionis, in December, 534.

K.

KALLABIZE. To open letters surreptitiously. " The trial of Kallab, the post official, who in three years opened and destroyed above 60,000 letters, is now going on at Vienna. The fellow lies so impudently that he severely tries the patience of his judges and of the public. The Viennese have formed a verb from the man's name, and letters surreptitiously opened are said to be *kallabized*."—*Times*, 1 Oct., 1862, p. 10.

KANEITE. A mineral, consisting of manganese, arsenic, and a trace of iron; supposed to be from Saxony; so named from being first observed attached to a mass of galena by Mr. R. J. Kane, of Dublin.

KANTISM. The doctrines or theory of Emanuel Kant, the celebrated German metaphysician.

KAOLIN (Fr. *terre à porcelaine*; G. *porzellanerde*). The name given by the Chinese to fine white clay with which they fabricate the biscuit of their porcelains. "A variety of clay used for making porcelain, proceeding from the decomposition of the mineral feldspar; it is also called petunse" (*Dana*). In Chinese the word is written kaou-ling (*kaou lin*), and was so called from a hill on the east side of the village of King-tih-chin, where it is found. The earth of this hill (says Morrison), when first taken to form the *tun* (or petuntsze), belonged to four people, whose names were Wang, Ho, Fung, Fang, and these names are still stamped on the kaouling clods. From the Kaouling Hill there were superior, middling, and inferior earths taken. The best sort was known by breaking and examining the porcelain, *i.e.* if the breaking was smooth and even, and without veins or granular coarseness; but if it appeared as cut with a knife, the porcelain was of a weak brittle nature. Speaking of *petuntze* (var. *petuntse*, *petunse*), Morrison says the *tun* or stone is divided into red, yellow, and white tun (*petuntsze*); the red and white tun are used for the fine wares; the yellow only for the coarse wares. Morrison does not, however, render *tun*, stone; it is therefore possible that *petuntsze*, i.e. white *tuntsze* (*pih tuntsze*), may have been so called as coming from Tuntsze, the name of a place on the Grand Canal. I note, however, that *pĭh tung* signifies white copper (*tung*, copper or brass). " Kaolin is found in Devon and Cornwall " (*S. F. Creswell*).

KEITHIA. A genus of labiate plants; named in honour of the Rev. Patrick Keith.

KENDAL-GREEN. A species of green cloth formerly made at Kendal or Kirby-Kendal, county Westmoreland.

KENNEDY. A poker; also to strike or kill with a poker; a St. Giles's term, so given from a man of the name being killed with a poker; frequently shortened to neddy.—*J. C. H.*

KEPLER'S LAWS. In astronomy, laws established by Johann Kepler, who was born in 1571 near Weil, in Würtemburg; called to the chair of astronomy at Gratz in 1593, and died in 1630. These laws are three: 1. That every planet moves so that the line drawn from it to the sun describes about the sun areas proportional to the times. 2. That the planets all move in elliptic orbits, of which the sun occupies one of the foci. 3. That the squares of the times of the revolutions of the planets are as the cubes of their mean distances from the sun.

KERSEY (D. *kerzaai*; O. D. and Teut. *karsaye, kerseye*; Sp. *carisea*; Fr. *cariset, carisée, carize*). A species of coarse woollen cloth; a coarse stuff made chiefly in Kent and Devonshire. Kerseymere, more commonly cassimere (found *cassimer* and *casimer*, Sp. *casimero*), is a twilled cotton cloth. According to some, *kersey* is a corruption of " coarse say " (*say*, a kind of serge used for linings, &c.; Fr. *sayette*, a sort of woollen stuff made at Amiens). If so, *kerseymere* would seem to be compounded of *kersey* and *mere*, which anciently signified " entire;" or of Fr. *mère*, " principal, first," whence *mère-laine*, " choice wool." Skinner queries *kersey* as being derived from *Cesarea*, or *Jersey*. The Encyc. Metrop. says, " *Kersey* is either *coarse* and *say* (a stuff), or from the island of *Jersey* (Gersey), formerly, perhaps, famous for this kind of cloth; kerseymere is a thin stuff, generally woven plain from the finest wools, and in England manufactured chiefly in the Western districts; but that *kersey*, on the other hand, is a very coarse stuff, usually ribbed and woven from long wool, and the principal manufactures of it are in the North of England. It is plain that these two words signifying such distinct things cannot have a common origin; whatever may be the source of *kersey*, *kerseymere* is probably a corruption of *Cashmir*, a country in which the finest wool is produced, and which consequently is most celebrated for the works of its looms."

KERSEYMERE. See KERSEY.

KEVENHULLER. A large triangular cocked hat worn in England about the end of the reign of George II., imported from Germany (See Planché's Hist. Brit. Cost.); probably named after the ancient and illustrious German family of Kevenhuller.

KIDDERMINSTER. An ingrain carpeting, named from Kidderminster, in Worcestershire, where it was originally made. The largest quantity is now manufactured in Scotland.

KIEFEKIL or **KEFFEKIL.** A species of clay used chiefly in forming the bowls of tobacco pipes; and by the Tatars in place of soap. According to some, it is another name for meerschaum, and signifies "earth of Kaffa" (Turc. ݢﻞ *ghil*, clay); but qu. from Kaffa, a country of Eastern Africa, south of Abyssinia; or from Kaffa (Theodosia), a town of Russia on the south-east coast of the Crimea; or Kaiffa, a seaport of Palestine. This clay is also found in Canada, in Flanders, and in other places.

KILLINEY. A mineral resembling spodumene, discovered in granite veins at Killiney, near Dublin.

KILLINGIA or **KYLLINGIA.** A genus of plants of seven species, natives of the East and West Indies, Japan, the Society Isles, and the Levant; named by Rottböll in memory of Petrus Kylling, a Dane, who in 1688 published a botanical work entitled Viridarium Danicum.

KIMMERIDGE. A thick bed of clay, constituting a member of the oolitic group, occurring well developed at Kimmeridge, in the isle of Purbeck, Dorsetshire.

KINATE (D. *kina*). A salt formed by the union of kinic acid with a base. See KINIC ACID and CINCHONA.

KINIC ACID. An acid procured from the *Cinchona* or Peruvian bark. See CINCHONA and QUININE.

KIRSCH or KIRSCHWASSER. A distilled liquor obtained by fermenting the small black cherry ; from G. *kirsche*, a cherry, *q.v.*

KIRWANITE. A mineral, colour dark olive-green ; found in cavities of basalt on the north-east coast of Ireland ; named in honour of Mr. Richard Kirwan, an eminent mineralogist, who died in 1812.

KITAIBELIA. A genus of herbaceous plants ; named in honour of Professor Robert Kitaibel, of Hungary, one of the authors of Plantæ Rariores Hungariæ.

KIT-KAT. A name given to a particular size or dimension of portrait-painting, viz., three feet by two feet four inches of canvas ; so called from a club of gentlemen in the reign of Queen Anne, whose portraits were taken on canvas of that dimension. The club held their meetings at a house kept by one *Christopher Kat* or *Kit Kat*, and consisted of forty-two members, whose portraits were painted by Sir Godfrey Kneller in 1710. The apartment not being sufficiently large for half-lengths, a shorter canvas was adopted ; hence the technical term *Kit-Kat* size.——" A term applied to a club in London to which Addison and Steele belonged ; so called from Christopher Cat, a pastrycook, who served the club with mutton pies ; applied also to portraits a little less than a half-length, because such were placed in the club-room."—*Chalmers.*

KLAPROTHIA. A genus of plants or twining shrubs ; named in honour of M. H. Klaproth, distinguished for his chemical and mineralogical researches, and professor of chemistry at Berlin ; born at Wernigerode, Upper Saxony, in 1743, died in 1817.

KLEINHOVIA. A genus of plants of only one species, the *K. hospita*, a tree, native of Java, Amboina, and the Philippine Islands ; named by Linnæus in honour of M. Kleinhoff, formerly director of the Botanic Gardens in Batavia.

KLEINIA. A genus of plants, or. *Polygamia æqualis ;* named in honour of the German zoologist, James Theodore Klein, who flourished in the early part of the eighteenth century.

KLUGIA. A genus of plants, or. *Angiospermia;* named in honour of Dr. F. A. Klug.

KNAUTIA. A genus of herbaceous plants; named in honour of two distinguished German botanists, Christopher Knaut the father, and Christian Knaut the son.

KNEBELITE. A mineral; colour gray, spotted dirty-white, red, brown, and green; locality unknown; named by Dobereiner after Major Von Knebel.

KNICKERBOCKERS or **NICKERBOCKERS.** Long loose breeches, generally worn without braces, and buckled or buttoned round the waist and knee (See *Times,* 23 May, 1859, p. 12, c. 3); of American origin, but whether derived from a proper name is doubtful. Washington Irving published his Sketch Book and his History of New York under the name of Diedrich Knickerbocker. Mr. J. A. Bartlett renders the word *Knickerbocker,* " a descendant of one of the old Dutch families of New York City."

KNOXIA. A genus of plants of only two species, *K. Zeylanica,* native of Ceylon, and *K. corymbosa,* native of the East Indies; named by Linnæus in honour of **Robert Knox,** an Englishman, who spent many years in examining the natural productions of Ceylon, and who published an historical relation of that island in 1681.

KOBELLITE. A mineral resembling grey antimony, but brighter in lustre; from the cobalt mine of Hvena, in Sweden; named after Von Kobell.

KOELPINIA. A genus of plants, formerly established by several eminent botanists under the name of *Rhagadiolus,* and by Linnæus under that of *Lapsana;* named by Pallas in honour of **Alexander Bernard Koelpin,** professor of physic at Stettin, and author of several botanical tracts.

KŒNIGIA. A genus of plants of but one species, an annual, native of Iceland; named by Linnæus in honour of his friend and disciple, **Dr. John Gerard Kœnig,** M.D., of Courland, who first found the plant in Iceland, in 1765, and who made several valuable botanical contributions to Linnæus from his observations in India.

KOHAUTIA. A genus of erect herbaceous plants; named in honour of **Francis Kohaut.**

KÖLREUTERIA. A genus of plants, natives of China; named in honour of John Theophilus Kölreuter, M.D., professor of natural history at Carlsruhe, and author of several botanical dissertations.

KÖNIGA. A genus of cruciform plants; named in honour of Charles König, F.R.S., of the British Museum.

KRAMERIA. A genus of plants, shrubs, nat. or. *Polygalaceæ*; natives of South America; named in honour of the German botanists, J. G. H. and W. H. Kramer, father and son.

KREMNITZ. A pure variety of white lead, from Kremnitz, in Hungary.

KRUBERA. A genus of herbaceous plants; named in honour of John Julius Kruber.

KÜHNIA. A genus of North American plants, trees; named by Linnæus in honour of his pupil, Adam Kühn, of Pennsylvania, who first brought this plant to Europe.

KUMAON. A celebrated tea from Kumaon, a province of North Hindustan, at the foot of the Himalayas.

KUTCHIN-KUTCHING. A child's amusement which consists in jumping about with the legs bent in a sitting posture. A correspondent of Notes and Queries, speaking of the expedition of Sir John Richardson to the Arctic shores, refers to his picture of the Kutchin-Kutcha Indians dancing, in which the principal performer is actually figuring in the midst of the wild circle in the way described; and he thinks the nursery term may be something more than a mere coincidence. See N. & Q. 1st S. ix. 304.

KYANIZE. To prevent the rotting of wood by immersing it in a solution of corrosive sublimate or other substances (*Silliman*); from *Kyan*, the inventor of the process (*Webster*).

L.

LABATIA. A genus of plants, evergreen trees, natives of Guiana and Hispaniola; named by Professor Schwartz in honour of Jean Baptiste Labat, a Dominican friar, who, between 1700 and 1713, investigated the plants of Africa and the West Indies.

LABRADORÌTE. A variety of opalescent felspar from Labrador. It is also called opaline, or Labrador spar.

LABYRINTH (L. *labyrinthus*, Gr. λαβυρινθος). A maze, an inexplicable difficulty; so called from the Egyptian or Cretan Labyrinths, places formed with winding passages, which rendered it difficult to find the way from the interior to the entrance.——In anatomy, that part of the internal ear behind the cavity of the tympanum. ——In metallurgy, a series of troughs in a stamping-mill through which water passes for washing pulverized ore.

LACHENALIA. A genus of bulbous plants, almost exclusively natives of the Cape; named by Jacquin jun. in honour of Werner de Lachenal, formerly professor of botany and anatomy at Basle, a distinguished pupil of Haller, and friend of Linnæus.

LACONIC, LACONICAL. Short, brief, pithy, sententious, expressing much in few words, as a *laconic* phrase; so named from the Laconians or Spartans, who spoke in this style.

LACONICUM. A stove or sweating-room; so called because they were much used by the natives of Laconia.

LACONISM or **LACONICISM.** A concise style; a brief sententious phrase or expression.— See LACONIC.

LACRIMA CRISTI (*Lachryma Christi*). "The tears of Christ;" a celebrated wine made from a grape growing at the foot of Vesuvius.

LAFAYETTE FISH (*Leiostomus obliquus*). A delicious sea-fish, which appears in the summer in great abundance at Cape Island, on the Jersey coast, and is hence called the Cape May-Goody. The name *Lafayette Fish*, by which it is known at New York and its vicinity, was given it on account of its appearance one summer coinciding with the last visit of General Lafayette to America.—Professor *S. F. Baird.*

LAFITTE (CHÂTEAU). One of the four famous red Bordeaux wines, called *Clarets* by the English; so named from the extensive vineyard of Château Lafitte in the Haut-Médoc, which produces annually about 943 hectolitres of the first quality, and 200 of the second quality.

LAGERSTROEMIA. A genus of plants, nat. or. *Lythraceæ*, whose species are natives of the East Indies; called after M. Lagerstroem.

LALLA ROOKH. A mantle of pale grey cloth, trimmed with black velvet, and forming a plain circular in front; so called from Moore's Lalla Rookh.

LAMIUM. A genus of plants, nat. or. *Labiatæ* (archangel or dead nettle); so named from Lamium, a mountain of Ionia, where it grew; or from *lama*, a ditch, because it usually grew about ditches and neglected places.— *Forsyth*.

LANARKITE. A mineral, a sulpho-carbonate of lead, found at Leadhill, in Lanarkshire, Scotland; also in Siberia, the Harz, and the Tyrol.

LANDAU. A carriage whose top may be opened and thrown back; called from Landau, in Germany, where first made.

LANDAULET. A chariot opening at the top like a landau, of which word it is a diminutive.

LAODICEAN. Lukewarm in religion, like the Christians of Laodicea (now Latakia), in Asia Minor.

LAODICEANISM. Lukewarmness in religion. Revelation of St. John, iii. 16.

LAPUTAN. Impossible, absurd, ridiculous; a term derived from Laputa, the flying island mentioned in Gulliver's Travels, whose inhabitants (or rather those of Lagudo, metropolis of the underlying island) were engaged in all sorts of absurdities. "It is plain from the context that the late Archbishop of Dublin meant to include his friend's project among those which are taken for Laputan before they are realized, and taken for granted after, as if neither in conception nor execution they had ever involved any theoretical or practical difficulty."—The *Globe*, on Babbage, Sep. 1864.

LARDIZABALA. A genus of South American plants, a twining shrub, found in the woods of Chili and Peru; named in honour of Michael Lardizabala, a Spanish naturalist.

LATAKIA. A tobacco famed both in the East and

throughout Europe; brought from Latikía (the anc. Laodicea), in Syria, near which it is largely cultivated.

LATERAN. Certain ecclesiastical councils, so called from having been held at the Lateran, one of the churches at Rome, with a palace and other buildings annexed to it. The church is said to have been named from a man who owned the ground in the time of Nero. See Burgon's Letters from Rome, and Wordsworth's Italy.

LATINISM. A Latin idiom, a mode of speech peculiar to the Latins, or people of Latium, in Italy.

LATOUR. A celebrated Bordeaux wine from Château Latour, between Julien and Pauillac.

LATROBITE. A mineral, colour pink or rose red, allied to the felspars; from the island of Latrobe, near the Labrador coast.

LAUBENHEIMER. A wine from Laubenheim, in Germany.

LAUGERIA. An upright branching shrub ten feet high, native of Carthagena, Havannah, &c.; named by Jacquin after Robert Laugier, professor of chemistry and botany at the University of Vienna when the botanic garden was first established there.

LAUMONITE. A mineral found in groups of prismatic crystals or prismatic distinct concretions; called from Gillet Laumont, who first observed it, in 1785, in the lead mines of Hulgoet, in Bretagne.

LAURENTIAN. A vast series of stratified and crystalline rocks of gneiss, mica-schist, quartzite, and limestone, about 40,000 feet in thickness, discovered by Sir W. E. Logan northward of the St. Lawrence, in Canada.

LAUROSIS. The spodium of silver; so called from Mount Laurus, where there were silver mines.—*Forsyth.*

LAVATERA. A genus of plants, nat. or. *Malvaceæ;* named by Tournefort in honour of Lavater, physician and botanist of Zurich, and father of the celebrated physiognomist.

LAVOISERA. A genus of showy Brazilian shrubs, or. *Monogynia;* named in honour of M. Lavoisier.

LAWSONIA. A genus of plants, nat. or. *Lythraceæ;* native of India, Egypt, &c., whose leaves are much used by the Egyptian women to colour their nails yellow, which they esteem an ornament; dedicated by Linnæus to John (Miller says Isaac) Lawson, M.D., of North Britain, author of a Voyage to Carolina, containing much information on the plants of that country, Lond. 1709. The Arabian plant alcanna or henna is a species of *Lawsonia*.

LAXMANNIA. A name originally given by Forster (Genera, t. 47) to a syngenesious tree of St. Helena, which Solander considered as a *Bidens*, but which George Forster (Plantæ Atlanticæ, 56) subsequently referred to *Spilanthus*. The name was given in honour of the Rev. Ericus Laxmann, native of Finland (professor of the Academy at Petersburg), who made many botanical discoveries in Siberia, and who died in 1796.

LAZAR (Sp. *lazaro*). A person infected with nauseous and pestilential disease (*Shaks. Dryden*); named from Lazarus.

LAZARET or LAZARETTO (Sp. *lazereto;* It. *lazzeretto;* Fr. *lazaret*). Sometimes called a lazar-house; a public building, hospital, or pest-house for the reception of diseased persons, especially those affected with contagious distempers; so named from Lazarus. For a good account of a Lazaret see Dict. de la Convers. Par. 1837.

LAZZARONI (It.). In Naples, the poor who live by begging, or have no permanent habitation; so called from the hospital of St. Lazarus, which serves as their refuge.—*Brande.*

LEADHILLITE. A mineral related to aragonite, found principally at Leadhills, in Lanarkshire, Scotland, associated with other ores of lead. The island of Grenada, and that of Serpho in the Grecian Archipelago, are also stated to be localities for it.

LEBECKIA. A genus of leguminous plants, natives of the Cape; named in honour of M. Lebeck.

LEBRETONIA. A genus of plants, or. *Polyandria;* named in honour of Manuel le Breton, a French botanist.

LECCA GUM. The gum of the olive tree, which is abundantly collected at Lecca, in Calabria.

LECHEA. A genus of North American plants, or. *Ori-*

gynia; named by Linnæus in honour of Professor John Leche, of Abo, Finland, member of the Stockholm Academy, and author of several papers on zoology, botany, and rural economy.

LECHENAULTIA. A genus of plants, or. *Monogynia,* natives of the tropical parts of New Holland; named after M. Lechenault, a distinguished French botanist and traveller.

LEDEBURIA. A genus of umbelliferous plants; named in honour of M. Ledebure.

LEDERERITE. A mineral; a hydrous silicate; found in bright, transparent, six-sided prisms at Cape Blomidon, in Nova Scotia, supposed to be chabasie; named after Baron Lederer, formerly Austrian consul at New York.

LEEA. A genus of shrubby plants, natives of the East Indies; named by Linnæus in honour of Mr. James Lee, author of An Introduction to Botany.

LEEDSITE. A mineral regarded as a mechanical mixture of sulphates of lime and baryta; from near Leeds, Yorkshire.

LEELITE. A mineral; colour deep flesh-red; consisting of silica, alumina, protoxide of iron, and potash; called after Dr. Lee, of St. John's College, Cambridge.

LEHUNTITE. A compact zeolite found in Antrim by Captain Lehunt.

LEMANEA. A genus of *Fuci,* in which the frond is hollow, and converted into a recepticle; named in honour of M. Leman, a French botanist.

LEMANITE. A synonym of felspar; named from Lac Leman (Lake of Geneva), where it is found.

LEMNIAS (Lemnian earth). A kind of astringent medicinal earth used in the same cases as bole; from the isle of *Lemnos,* in the Ægean Sea, whence it is brought.

LEMONIA. A genus of West Indian plants, or. *Monogynia;* named after Sir C. Lemon.

LENZINITE. A mineral of two kinds, the opaline and argillaceous; a variety of clay found at Eifeld, in Prussia; named after Lenzius, a German mineralogist.

LEONHARDITE. A mineral, consisting chiefly of silica, alumina, and lime; found in Hungary and Bavaria; also at

Copper Falls and in Lake Superior region; doubtless named after its discoverer Leonhard.

LEOPOLD. A gold coin of Belgium, equal to 24fr. 20c.; named after the present King of Belgium.

LEOPOLDONE. A silver coin of Tuscany, similar to the francescone; that of 1790 being of the assay value of 4s. 5¾d.; named after Leopoldo, a Duke of Tuscany.

LERBACHITE. A mineral composed of lead, mercury, and selenium; found under the same circumstances as clausthalite at Lerbach and Tilkerode, in the Harz.

LERCHEA. An irregular-growing shrub; named by Linnæus in honour of John James Lerche, principal physician to the Russian armies, who was born at Potsdam in 1703, and died at Petersburg in 1780.

LESPEDEZA. A genus of North American leguminous plants; named after Lespedez, formerly Governor of Florida.

LESSERTIA. A genus of leguminous plants, natives of the Cape; named after M. B. Lessert, of Paris.

LESTIBUDESIA. A genus of plants, the best known species of which is the *L. arborescens*, found in New Holland; named in honour of Lestiboudois, a French naturalist.

LETHEAN. Inducing forgetfulness or oblivion. "Time will show how far the Prince (Napoleon) is superior to the Lethean and somniferous effects of the atmosphere of the official circle" (*Standard*). Shakspeare uses *lethe'd* in the same sense. From *Lethe*, a river of the infernal regions, whose waters were said to cause forgetfulness of the past (Gr. λήθη, forgetfulness, oblivion).

LETTSOMIA. A genus of plants, or. *Monogynia*; named after Dr. John C. Lettsom, F.R.S.

LEUCHTENBERGITE. A mineral, composed of silica, alumina, magnesia, peroxide of iron, lime, and water; named after the Duke of Leuchtenberg, or from Leuchtenberg in Bavaria.

LEUISIA. A genus of plants; named after Captain M. Lewis, who accompanied Captain Clerke to North America.

LEUSEA. A genus of composite plants; named by Candolle after his friend M. Leleuse.

LEUTHRITE or LEUTTRITE. A greyish-white mineral; a decomposed rock, analogous to the sandy varieties of dolomite; found at Leuthra or Leuttra, near Jena, in Saxony.

LEVANTER. A strong easterly wind in the Mediterranean, so called because it comes from the Levant.——The cant name for one who bets at a horse-race, and runs away without paying the wager lost; any one who runs away disgracefully. It was no doubt formerly considered fashionable to travel in the East; when, therefore, any one was in pecuniary difficulties, and it was convenient for him to keep out of the way, it was perhaps given out that he was gone to the Levant; hence doubtless the term *levanter.*

LEVANTIN. A name still given not only to all the traffickers and ships of the maritime towns of the Levant, but also to those of the States of Barbary. The sailors of Provence and Languedoc were called Levantins, when the French marine was divided into Ocean marine or of the West, and marine of the Mediterranean or of the Levant or East.

LEVANTINE. A kind of silk cloth from the Levant.

LEVITICAL. Priestly (*Milton*); from the Levites, officers in the Jewish church.

LEVITICUS. A canonical book of the Old Testament, containing the laws and regulations relating to the priests and Levites among the Jews, or the body of the ceremonial law.

LEVYNE. A mineral, supposed to be identical with chabasite; found in Scotland, Farol, Greenland, Iceland, &c.; named after the English mineralogist Levy.

LEYDEN JAR. A glass jar or bottle used to accumulate electricity; invented at Leyden, in Holland.

LHERZOLITE. A mineral, a variety of pyroxene; from Lherz, in the Pyrenees.

LIBANUS. The frankincense tree; from *Lebanon* (or Libanus), a mountain in Syria, where it grows.—*Forsyth.*

LIBETHENITE. A mineral, consisting of phosphoric acid, oxide of copper, and water; found in cavities in mica slate at Libethen in Hungary, at Ehl near Linz on the Rhine, at Gunnis Lake in Cornwall, and at Nischnii-Tagilsk in the Ural.

LICHTENBERG'S FIGURES. When the knob of a charged Leyden phial is drawn over a flat surface of lac or resin, as, for instance, the plate of an electro-phosphorus, it leaves a charge in its track, positive or negative, as we choose ; and if after this a mixture of certain powders be sifted upon the plate, as, for instance, of powdered sulphur and red lead, the sulphur will adhere to the one, and the red lead to the other electrified surface, and, with a little management, groups of figures resembling flowers may be thus brought out as Lichtenberg first observed.—*Brande.*

LIEBERKÜHNIAN GLANDS. In anatomy, simple secerning cavities, thickly distributed over the whole surface of the large and smaller intestines ; so called after Lieberkühnn, who observed them in the small intestines, where they are visible only with the aid of a lens, their orifices appearing as minute dots scattered between the villi.

LIEBIGIA. A genus of plants, nat. or. *Gesneraceæ;* named in honour of Professor Liebig.

LIEBIGITE. A mineral of a green colour, found with pechuran at Adrianople ; named after Liebig.

LIEVRITE. A mineral first discovered in 1802 on the Rio la Marina, in the isle of Elba, by M. Leliévre. It has also been found in Norway, Siberia, the Harz, and in Tyrol and Saxony. It was named lievrite after its discoverer ; ilvaite from Elba ; and yenite or jenite by the French, in commemoration of the battle of Jena, in 1806.

LIGURITE. A mineral ; colour apple-green, occasionally speckled ; named from Liguria, in ancient geography a division of Italy.

LILLIPUTIAN. A person of very small size (sometimes used as an adjective) ; *lit.* one belonging to a diminutive race described in Swift's Kingdom of Lilliput (Gulliver's Travels). " Cette fable est une imitation assez ingénieuse de celle des pygmées dont il est tant de fois question dans les anciens poëtes."

LINARITE. The cupreous sulphate of lead, a mineral so named from occurring at Linares, in Andalusia ; but also found at Leadhills in Scotland, Roughten Gill in Cumberland, and near Ems in Germany.

LINCOLN GREEN. A colour of cloth formerly made in Lincoln (*Spenser*). "And worn by foresters and rovers" (*S. F. C.*)

LINCOLNIA. A genus of plants, shrubs, natives of the Cape; named by Linnæus in honour of a botanist named Lincoln.

LINDACKERITE. A mineral, vitreous; verdigris to apple-green; analysed by Lindacker.

LINDERA. A genus of plants, the only species of which is a tree, *L. umbella*, native of Japan; named by Thunberg in memory of John Linder, a celebrated Swedish botanist, author of Flora Wiksbergensis.

LINDERNIA. A genus of plants, or. *Angiospermia*, whose species are herbaceous annuals; named by Alboni in honour of Francis Balthazar von Lindern, a physician of Strasbourg.

LINNÆA. A genus of plants, or. *Angiospermia*; named by Gronovius in honour of his friend Linnæus.

LINNÆAN SYSTEM. The mode of classification for distinguishing plants, animals, and minerals adopted by Linnæus or Von Linné, the celebrated botanist, who was born at Rashult, province Smaland, in Sweden, 13 May, 1707, O.S.

LINSEY-WOOLSEY. Stuff made of linen and wool (mixed), originally manufactured at Lindsey, near Hadleigh, in Suffolk.——Vile; mean; of different and unsuitable parts (*Johnson*).

LISBON. A sweet light-coloured wine from Lisbon.

LIVONICA-TERRA. A species of fine bole found in Livonia, a government of Russia.

LIVORNINA. An old silver coin current at Livorno (Leghorn), equal to 4s. 5½d.

LLOYD'S. A part of the Royal Exchange, in London, appropriated to the use of underwriters and insurance brokers; so named from Lloyd's Coffee-house, where there were formerly rooms for the same purpose.

LOBELIA. An extensive genus of plants; named after M. Lobel, a French physican to King James I. The *L. inflata*, or Indian tobacco, is an annual plant of North America, and has been often used as an emetic and expectorant, &c.

LOCHABER AXE. A formidable war weapon formerly used by the Scotch Highlanders; so named from Lochaber, a district of Invernessshire, domain of Banquo, Thane of Lochaber, and ancestor of the royal house of Stewart. It was upon one of the wildest mountains in this wild country that the Pretender erected his standard in 1745.

> " Farewell to *Lochaber*, and farewell my Jean,
> Where heartsome with thee I have many days been."
>
> *Ramsay.*

LOLLARDY. The doctrines of the Lollards (*Webster*), a sect in Germany who dissented from the church before she renounced popery. They sprang from William Lollard, who began to propagate his opinions in 1315, and was burned at Cologne in 1351. After his death the term was used reproachfully to designate the disciples of Wickliffe. They were proscribed by Parliament in 1406, and many of them were executed about 1414.

LOMBARD. A money-lender or banker; a profession first exercised in London by the Lombards.—*Smart.*

LOMBARD-HOUSE or LOMBARD. A public institution for lending money to the poor at a moderate interest upon articles deposited and pledged; called also *Mont de Piété.* See LOMBARD.

LOMBARDIC. An epithet applied to one of the ancient alphabets derived from the Roman, and relating to the manuscripts of Italy (*Astle*); so named from the Lombards.

LONDON CLAY. An extensive deposit of a bluish clay, except near the surface, abounding in Middlesex, Essex, Suffolk, and part of Norfolk. It occasionally includes beds of sandstone, and of a coarse argillaceous limestone, from which Parker's Roman cement is made.

LONDON PRIDE. A flower; the *Saxifraga umbrosa.*

LONDONISM. A mode of speaking peculiar to London. —*Pegge.*

LONDONIZE. To give a manner or character which distinguishes the people of London.—*Smart.*

LORCHA. A Chinese ship; Mr. Cobden (H. of C. 26

Feb. 1857) says, " a vessel called a *lorcha*, a name derived from the Portuguese settlement at Macao, at the mouth of the Canton River, opposite Hong Kong, and which merely means that it is built after the European model, but not that it is built in Europe." This word may however be from the Chinese *low chuen*, a sort of fighting ships ; from *chuen*, a ship, or any vessel that navigates the water ; or from the Portuguese *lanchu*, a launch, pinnace, or small ship.

LORETTE.   A modern French term designating a class of women of light and easy manners, and given to pleasure.   The *lorette* has much analogy with the *grisette*, from whom, however, she distinguishes herself by habits of luxury, ordinarily ignored by the latter.   " The *Lorettes* are said to have received their name from formerly frequenting the Church of Notre Dame de Lorette at Paris " (*S. F. Creswell*).

LOTHARIO.   A gay deceiver.   A correspondent of Notes and Queries says, " This expression doubtless takes its name from Don Quixote, where, in the ' Impertinent Curiosity ' (a story inserted in the second part of that romance), Lothario is the name of one of the characters, who seduces his friend's wife;" but the term is more probably derived from the following line in Rowe's tragedy of the Fair Penitent, act v. sc. 1:—

> " Is this that haughty gallant, gay Lothario ?"

Another correspondent of N. & Q. says, " ' The gallant, gay Lothario!' the ' dear Perfidious!' is a character in one of the early tragedies of the poet Nicholas Rowe, the Fair Penitent, which is somewhat upon the model of *Le Festin de Pierre* of Molière : the hero of each being a *libertin effréné;* and perhaps I may more delicately explain the characters of both by quoting the *monologue* of the valet of Molière's hero (*Sganarelle*), upon the dénouement ; or I might say, *la catastrophe*, did not Molière call it a *comedy:*—' Voilà par sa mort, un chacun satisfait.   Ciel offensé, lois violées, filles séduites, familles déshonorées, parens outragés, femmes mises à mal, maris poussés à bout, tout le monde est content.' "   See also Notes and Queries, 2nd S. 102, 479.

LOUDONIA. A Swan River shrub discovered by Drummond in 1843. "The genus was named by Dr. Lindley in compliment to Mr. Loudon."—*Mrs. Loudon.*

LOUIS D'OR. A gold coin of France, first struck in 1640, in the reign of Louis XIII.; value 20*s.* sterling.

LUBAN-MATTEE. A gum olibanum, possessing a strong agreeable citron-like odour, and but little taste; named from Bunder Mattee, the port whence it is brought.

LUCERN, LUCERNE, or LUZERNE (Port. *luzerna* and *medicagem dos pastos*). A leguminous plant of the genus *Mendicago*, cultivated for fodder. "Qu. W. *llysau*, plants; *llysieuyn*, a plant; Corn. *lyzuan;* or from *Lucerne*, in Switzerland."—*Webster.*

LUCULLITE. A sub-species of rhomboidal limestone, the *nero antico* of the Italians. The Consul Lucullus so much admired its compact variety as to honour it with his name.

LUDLOW ROCKS. A name given by Murchison to the upper portion of the Silurian system, as developed near Ludlow, in Shropshire.

LUDWIGIA. A genus of plants, natives of India; named by Linnæus in honour of C. T. Ludwig, author of Definitiones Plantarum.

LUHEA. A genus of plants, trees, natives of Brazil; named by Willdenow in honour of Charles Van der Luhe, a German botanist.

LULLABY. A song to soothe babes; that which quiets (*Locke*). "As is a nurse's song of lullaby, to bring her babe to sleep" (*Shak.*) From *lull* and *by.* "Lullaby, or L'Elaby, from a supposed fairy called Ellaby Gathon, whom nurses invited to watch the sleeping babes, that they might not be changed for others. Hence changeling, or infant changed" (*Pulleyn*).

LUNANEA. A genus of plants, nat. or. *Terebinthaceæ;* named after John Lunan, author of Hortus Jamaicensis.

LUSH. Intoxicating drinks of all kinds, but generally used for beer. "Lush and its derivatives claim Lushington, the brewer, as sponsor."—*Globe*, 8 Sep. 1859.

LUSHINGTON. A drunkard, or one who continually

soaks himself with drams and pints of beer. " Some years since there was a Lushington Club in Bow Street, Covent Garden " (*J. C. H.*) See LUSH.

LUSIAD. The celebrated epic poem written by Camoens on the establishment of the Portuguese government in India. The Portuguese title which he gave it, *Os Lusiados,* " The Lusitanians," denotes the true motive of its subject. Don Luis de Camoens, called the Homer and Virgil of Portugal, was born at Lisbon, although Coimbra and Santarem have disputed this honour. According to some, he was born in 1517; but most biographers say 1524.

LUTHERANISM. The doctrines of religion as taught by Martin Luther, who was born in 1483 at Eisleben, in Lower Saxony, and died there 18 Feb. 1546.

LYCEUM (Fr. *Lycée*). A house or apartment appropriated to instruction by lectures or disquisitions ; named from Lyceum (Λυκειον), a place near the River Ilissus, in Attica, where Aristotle taught philosophy.——An association of men for literary purposes.

LYDIAN. Soft, effeminate ; a kind of soft slow music anciently in vogue ; so called from Lydia, in Asia Minor.

LYDIAN STONE. A flint slate used by the ancients to try gold and silver ; a touchstone ; named from Lydia, in Asia Minor, where it was doubtless found.

LYNCH (an American word). To inflict pain or punish summarily without the forms of law, as by a mob, or by unauthorized persons. See LYNCH LAW.

LYNCH LAW. The practice of punishing men for crimes or offences by private unauthorized persons without a legal trial. " A name given in America to an irregular and summary administration of justice by the populace, and which originated from the difficulty of adhering to the usual forms of law in the newly-formed states. The name is derived from a Virginian farmer of the name of Lynch, who was the first to flog a thief without any judiciary appeal." (*T. Wright, M.A.*) Lynch law originated in what is now known as the Piedmont country of Virginia, which was at the time the western frontier. The nearest court of criminal jurisdiction held its sessions at Williamsburg, which is but seven miles from Jamestown, where the first settlement was made. When the condition of the country at that time is duly considered, it will be seen that practically the inhabitants of the Piedmont country had no law, and were actually forced to be a law unto themselves. Misdemeanours and crimes of every sort were of frequent occurrence; and yet the apprehension and delivery of a criminal involved an arduous journey of hundreds of miles, mostly through a wilderness, which not only occupied weeks, but months. Now in every district there were men of sound judgment and high character, to whom controversies were constantly referred, and whose decisions were regarded as final. Prominent among these was a man named Lynch, whose awards exhibited so much justice, judgment, and impartiality that he was known throughout the country as Judge Lynch. In the course of time criminals were brought before him, and he awarded such punishments as he considered just and proper. There were other persons, in different districts, who acted as arbitrators, and who awarded punishments; but Judge Lynch was the most conspicuous, and consequently the system took his name, and was called Lynch law. This was a compliment to his integrity and high character. But of late years the term has been regarded as a reproach, because violent and unprincipled men, such men as Lynch was wont to punish, have set the laws at defiance, and, while inflamed with passion, or maddened by a thirst for revenge, have usurped the prerogatives of the courts of justice.—*Washington Sentinel.*

LYSANDRIA. A Samian festival, celebrated with sacrifices and games, in honour of Lysander a Spartan general, very celebrated about the close of the Peloponnesian War.

LYSIARCH. An ancient magistrate, being the pontiff of Lycia, or superintendent of the sacred games of that province.

LYSIMACHIA. A genus of herbaceous plants, of four British species, one of which (money-wort) is very common in marshes in the north of England; named after Lysimachus of Sicily, who is said to have discovered its styptic and astringent qualities.

M.

MAASTRICHT ROCKS.   An upper calcareous formation about ten feet thick, reposing on ordinary white chalk with flints, at Maastricht, on the banks of the Meuse.

MACABRE or MACABER.   Antiquaries are not decided as to the origin and meaning of the name of the Macaber Dances, commonly called Dance of Death.   The general opinion seems to be that they received their name from Macaber, a German, who first headed this whimsical subject in some verses, in 1460, translated by P. Desrey of Troyes into Latin.   The most ancient known representation of these dances is in the cloisters of a convent at Minden, in Westphalia, bearing date in 1383.   In the fifteenth century they were painted on the walls of cloisters, cemeteries, and churches; on covered bridges, as on the bridge at Lucerne, in Switzerland; in castles, as at the Castle of Blois, built by Louis XII. in 1502 (See Université Catholique, vol. ii. 376).   "Macaber: an early German poet, author of a work entitled the Dance of Death, or the Dance of Macaber, consisting of a series of dialogues between Death and a number of personages belonging to various ranks of society.   An English translation of this work was published by Dugdale and Dodsworth, in the third volume of the Monasticon Anglicanum; and French and Latin versions have been repeatedly printed.   The Dance of the Dead painted by Holbein, in the cloister of the Augustinian convent at Basle, has contributed much to the fame of Macaber." (*Rose Biog. Dict.*)   Macaber, poëte allemand, serait tout à fait inconnu sans l'ouvrage qu'on a sous son nom: c'est un recueil de dialogues entre la Mort et des personnages choisis dans les divers états de la société; idée rajeunie et développée par Jacques Jacques, chanoine d'Embrun, dans le *Faut mourir.*   Cet ouvrage, indiqué par Fabricius (*Bibl. med. et infin. latinitat*) sous ce titre, *Speculum morticini,* ou *Speculum choreæ mortuorum* (le Miroir de la mort, ou le Miroir de la danse des morts), paraît avoir été écrit originairement en allemand, et a passé de cet langage en latin, en français, et même en anglais. La 1re édition française, restée longtemps inconnue aux plus savants bibliographes, a été découverte par Champollion-Figeac, dans les manuscrits de la bibliothèque de Grenoble; et il a donné une *Notice* de ce livre singulier dans le *Magasin Encyclopédique*, année 1811, t. 6, 355 et suiv. Cette édition, composée de deux cahiers formant dix feuillets et vingt pages petit in-fol., contient dix-sept dialogues et autant de petites estampes gravées sur bois; elle a été imprimée à Paris, par Guy ou Guyot Marchant, *demorant au grant hostel de Nauarre*, le 28 Septembre, 1485. Le même imprimeur en publia une 2e édition, augmentée de plusieurs nouveaux personnages, avec cet intitulé, *Ce présent livre est appelé Miroir salutaire pour toutes gens, et de tous estats, et est de grande utilité et récréation*, etc. Paris, 1846, le 7 juin. Debure en a donné la description dans la *Bibliographie instructive*, no. 3109; mais il n'en a pas copié le titre, et il a réuni sous le même article deux ouvrages distincts; la *Danse Macabre des hommes*, et la *Danse Macabre des femmes*. D'après le catalogue de la bibliothèque de Paris, Debure attribue la version française de cet ouvrage à Michel Marot; mais c'est une distraction un peu forte, puisque Clément, père de Michel Marot, n'était pas encore né. Les biographes indiquent une 3e édition de la *Danse Macabre*, sortie des presses de Guy Marchant, sous ce titre—*Chorea ab eximio Macabro versibus alemanicis edita*, etc., Paris, pour Godefroi de Marnef, Octobre, 1490, in-fol., fig.; elle avait été revue et corrigée par Pierre Desrey de Troyes. Champollion, qui a donné la note chronologique des éditions de la *Danse Macabre*, n'a pas cité celle de Desrey; et M. Brunet, trompé par le double titre latin et français, a supposé qu'il avait paru deux éditions différentes de cet ouvrage, en 1490, chez le même imprimeur (*voy.* le *Manuel du Libraire*, t. 1^{er,} 385 et 386). La *Danse Macabre* des hommes et celle des femmes ont été réunies pour la première fois, suivant Champollion, dans l'édition de Troyes, Nicolas Lerouge, in-fol., fig. goth. sous ce titre—*la Grant Danse Macabre des hommes et des femmes*, historiée et augmentée de personnages et beaux dits en latin, en vers, sans date, mais avant l'an 1500;

et ce savant n'a connu que deux éditions postérieures—Genève, 1503, in-4°, et Paris, 1589, in 8°, citées toutes deux dans la *Bibliographie* de Debure. M. Brunet en indique trois autres : Lyon, 1499, in-fol. goth.; Rouen, Guill. de la Mare, sans date, in-4°, fig., lettres rondes; et Paris, Groulleau, 1550, petit in-12, fig. La traduction anglaise de la *Danse Macabre* est due à Jean Porcy, poëte resté inconnu même à ses compatriotes; elle a été insérée dans le *Monasticon anglicanum* de Rog. Dodsworth et Guill. Dugdale (Londres, 1673), t. 3, 368—374, précédée d'une seule gravure de W. Hollar. La *Danse des morts* a été souvent reproduite par les artistes du 15e et du 16e siècle; on en retrouve les différents sujets dans les encadrements des livres de prières, réimprimés si fréquemment en caractères semi-gothiques, de 1490 à 1550. La *Danse des morts*, que le fameux peintre Holbein avait exécutée dans le cloître du couvent des augustins de Bâle, a joui longtemps d'une grande célébrité (*voy.* Holbein et *Mathias* Merian). Paul Chrétien Hilscher, pasteur à Dresde, mort le 3 août, 1730, a publié en allemand une notice des *Danses des morts*, à l'occasion des dessins et des tableaux de ce genre conservés dans la galerie de Dresde : *Beschreibung des Todten Tantzes wie solcher zu Dressden auf den Schloss gemahlet*, Budissen, Richter, 1721, in-8° Biog. Univ. vol. 25, Par. in voce Macaber. The writer of the article, in a note, says:—Est-ce bien là le nom d'un écrivain ? " Et n'est ce pas plutôt, suivant l'ingénieuse conjecture de M. Van Praet, l'altération du mot arabe *Magbarah*, qui signifie cimitière ? C'est ce qu'on ne peut deviner; et on a dû suivre l'opinion commune, ne fût-ce que pour pouvoir donner une idée d'un livre singulier et recherché des curieux."

MACADAMIZE. To cover, as a road, way, or path, with small broken stones, so as to form a smooth, hard surface ; so called from the inventor, McAdam.

MACASSAR OIL. An oil which is said to beautify and promote the growth of the hair ; so called from Macassar, a Dutch settlement on the south-west peninsula of the island Celebes, whence it is *said* to be brought. Hence *antimacassar*, a coverlet for chairs, sofas, &c., originally used to protect from oil and dirt, but now chiefly as an ornament.

MACCABEES. Name of certain apocryphal books of the Old Testament, which give an account of Jewish affairs in the time of the Maccabean princes.—*Murdock*.

MACHIAVEL. An epithet for a knave. See *post*.

MACHIAVELISM. The principles of Machiavel, or practice in conformity with them; political cunning and artifice. intended to favour arbitrary power.—*Cyc*.

> " Am I politick ? am I subtle ? am I a Machiavel ?"
>
> *Merry W. of W.*
>
> " Alençon, that notorious Machiavel."
>
> 1 *Hen. VI.*
>
> " And set the murd'rous Machiavel to school."
>
> 3 *Hen. VI.*

From Niccolo Machiavelli, the celebrated political writer and historian, secretary and historiographer to the Republic of Florence, author of Del Principe, who was born at Florence in 1469, and who died in 1530. The intention of the writer of Del Principe has been matter of great controversy, some holding him up as a promoter of tyranny, others maintaining that he was its concealed but decided enemy, and that he meant to put the people on their guard against its machinations. It has nevertheless affixed to his name a lasting stigma, and machiavelism has become a received appellation for perfidious and infamous politics. The present age had better pass no judgment upon the matter.

MACKINTOSH. A term applied to waterproof garments, particularly overcoats, made so by the use of India rubber; named from the inventor.

MACLEAYA. A genus of plants, natives of China; named in honour of A. Mac Leay, F.R.S.

MACLURITE. A mineral, colour brilliant pale green, consisting of magnesia with other matters; occurring in New Jersey, in Orange County, New York, and at Pargas, in Finland; named in honour of Dr. Maclure, the mineralogist.

MAÇON. A celebrated red wine made from grapes grown in the neighbourhood of Maçon, on the Saône.

MACQUARIA (Fr. *Macquarie*; L. *Macquaria*). A genus

M 2

of fishes established by Cuvier and Valenciennes (Hist. de Poiss. t. 2, 377), the only species of which is the *Macquaria Australasica*, whose flesh is said to be very delicate ; named from the River Macquarie, in Eastern Australia; also the name of a river of Tasmania.

MACQUER'S SALT (*Sel arsenical de Macquer*). Neutral arsenical salt ; super-arseniate of potass ; so named from Pierre Joseph Macquer, who first discovered the combinations of arsenic acid. Macquer was born in Paris in 1718, of a noble family, originally from Scotland ; was a skilful chemist, physician, and professor of pharmacy; made many discoveries in natural philosophy, and was author of several works on chemistry, &c. He died in 1784.

MADAPOLLAM. A sort of long cloth sufficiently fine to be fit for the Indian market ; named from Madapollam or Maddapollum, a maritime town of Hindustan, prov. Madras, in whose vicinity it is manufactured.

MADEIRA. A rich sherry formerly made on the Isle of Madeira. I have drank very good at Christiania within the last ten years, and it might even be had in England within the last twenty years.

MADELINE (*Poire de la Madelaine*). A pear, called, among other names, poire de St. Jean.

MADONNA. Artistic name for any picture representing Our Lady.

MADONNINA. A silver coin of Genoa of twenty soldi ; probably struck in honour of the Madonna.

MADRAS. A handkerchief made at Madras.——A rice.

MADRIGAL (Sp. and Port. *id.*; It. *madrigale*). A little amorous poem, sometimes called a *pastoral poem*, containing a certain number of free, unequal verses, not confined to the scrupulous regularity of a sonnet, or the subtilty of the epigram, but containing some tender and delicate, though simple, thought, suitably expressed (*Cyc.*)——An elaborate vocal composition in five or six parts. There is a diversity of opinion as to the origin of the word. Some derive it from Gr. μανδρα, a fold, stable, enclosure. Covarruvias (Trésor de la langage Castillane), under *mandra*, says, " y de aqui se dixo *madrigal*, cancion de pastores, quando se recogen a festear en las madras o cavernas ; quasi *mandrigal ;*" and hence *madrigal*, song of the shepherds, when they assemble together to feast in the *madras* or caverns ; as though *mandrigal*. And at the word madrigal : " Madrigal, villa famosa por el buen vino; madrigal, quasi mandrigal ; cancion de las que los pastores cantan sesteando en las cavernas ;" *Madrigal*, famous place for good wine ; *madrigal*, as though *mandrigal*, song sung by shepherds when feasting in the caverns. Of the same opinion are Bembo, Dolce, and Ménage. Ménage, citing the above passages from Covarruvias, says, " The Italians have dropped the *n* in *madriale*, from *mandriale*, as in *sposo* from *sponsus*, *misura* from *mensura*, *preso* from *prehensus*, &c.;" and that in French the word was anciently *madrigale*, not *madrigal*. Ménage, however, admits — from the passage in Covarruvias, and from the following, from Papirius Masso, in the life of Pope Eugenius IV., "Alfonsum Tostatum, Hispania, excellentium ingeniorum parens, in Madrigale tenui vico, genuit "—that there was a place in Spain called Madrigal ; and he adds, "N'auroit-on point appelé de ce lieu les Madrigaux ? de la mesme façon que de la vallée de Vire, on a appelé Vaudevilles, les Vaudevilles." There can be little doubt that the word is derived from some locality in Spain. There is Madrigal, a town, province Avila, memorable as the birthplace of Isabella of Castile; Madrigal, in Guadalajara ; Madrigal, a small village, province Caceres ; Madrigal, a pasture ground and a house, province Toledo ; and Madrigal del Monte, province Burgos. Of Madrigal in Avila, Madoz says, " Destruida esta poblacion en las guerras entre cristianos y musulmanes, la repoblaron estos, quienes la dieron el nombre de Madrigal." Huet (Traité des Romans, 124, last ed.) thinks Martegales and Madrigaux the same thing, and that both words had their origin from the Martegaux, montagnards of Provence; and he says in like manner the Gavots, montagnards of the country of Gap, gave name to the dance called Gavotte.

MAGDEBURG HEMISPHERES. A hollow sphere composed of two hemispheres which fit air-tight; intended to show the amount of the air's pressure, by the amount of force with which they are so held together after the interior air has been removed by the air-pump. It was first suggested by Otto Von Guericke, an eminent philosopher, who was born in 1602, settled at Magdeburg, and died in 1686.

MAGELLANIC CLOUDS. Three conspicuous nebulæ situated near the South Pole, resembling thin white clouds; so called from Magellan or Magalhaens, the Portuguese navigator, who also discovered the Straits of Magellan, at the extremity of South America.

MAGENTA. A brilliant red colour (discovered by Hoffman?); so called in honour of Napoleon III.'s victory at Magenta, in North Italy.—*S. F. Creswell.*

MAGIANISM. The doctrines of the Magi, a sect of philosophers, who held that there are two principles, one the cause of good, the other of evil. See MAGIC.

MAGIC. The production of wonderful effects by the supposed aid of superhuman beings, or of departed spirits; sorcery; enchantment; L. *magia*, G. μαγεια; so called, according to some, from Μαγος, a Persian philosopher.

MAGNESIA. A soft white powder without taste or smell, seldom found pure, but mixed with other minerals; so named from Magnesia, in Asia Minor, now Manisa or Manser, a city in the pashalic of Anadolia, where it was found. Others derive the word from μαγνης, the loadstone, because it sticks to the tongue as iron does to the magnet.

MAGNESITE. A silicate of magnesia, containing a large quantity of water; a name also given to a carbonate of magnesia, *q.v.*

MAGNET. The loadstone; a term applied to certain specimens of iron ore, having the property of attracting iron and some of its ores, and, when freely suspended, of pointing to the Pole; a bar of steel to which the peculiar properties of the loadstone have been imparted, either by contact or by other means. L. *magnes, tis,* Gr. μαγνης, the loadstone; so called from the mountains of Magnesia, in Asia Minor, which were famous for the production of the loadstone. According to Pliny (i. 5, c. 30 and 36, and i. 36, c. 16), the loadstone was found on Ida, in Phrygia, by one Magnes. Lempriere says " Magnes was a young man who found himself detained by the iron nails which were under his shoes as he walked over a stone mine. This was no other than the magnet, which received its name from the person who had been first sensible of its power." Some make Magnes a slave of Medea, whom that enchantress changed into a magnet.

MAGNETIC. A term applied to any metal, as iron, nickel, cobalt, &c., which may receive, by any means, the properties of the loadstone, and lie when suspended in the direction of a magnetic meridian.

MAGNETISM. The properties of the magnet, *q.v.*

MAGNOLIA (Fr. *magnolier*). A genus of plants, trees or shrubs, all natives of North America and Asia; named by Plumier in honour of Professor Magnole, of Montpellier.

MAJOLICA (It. *maiólica, maiórica*). A name given to a kind of earth used for making dishes, vases, &c.; afterwards applied to the ware itself, which resembles porcelain; so called from Maiolica or Maiorica, *i.e.* Majorca, where it was first made. A similar ware was also anciently made at Faenza, in the Romagna.

MAJORANA (*Origana majorana*). Systematic name of sweet marjoram; so called from flowering in May (*quod mense Maio floreat*).

MAHERNIA. A genus of plants, natives of the Cape; named, according to Professor Martyn, as anagrammatic of *Hermannia* (q.v.), a genus to which it is very nearly allied.

MAHMOUDI or MAMOUDI. A silver coin of Persia, equal to about 50 centimes French money; also a silver piece of 5 piasters, equal to 4fr. 14c.; struck by Sultan Mahmoud in 1811.

MAHOUND. A term which was popularly applied to any idol, and thence given to the devil, and sometimes to any savage character; mediæval corruption of the name Mahommed.—*T. Wright, M.A.*

MAID MARIAN. Originally the lady of the May games, in a morris dance; afterwards a character personated by a man in woman's clothes; also the name of a dance.—*Toone. Smart.*

MAINTENON (cotelettes à la). A manner of dressing cutlets; so called after Madame de Maintenon, mistress of Louis XIV.

MALABATHRUM (μαλαβαθρον). The leaf of the tree whose bark is called Cassia; named from Malabar, whence it is brought, and Hind. *betre*, a leaf.

MALAGA. A sweet wine from Malaga, in Spain.

MALAPROPISM. An ignorant vulgar misapplication of language; so named from Mrs. Malaprop, a character in Sheridan's comedy of *The Rivals*. Mrs. Partington has lately succeeded to the mantle of Mrs. Malaprop, but the phrase Partingtonism is as yet uncoined.—*J. C. Hotten.*

MALAYAN. A great variety of the human family, supposed to have originated in the Malay peninsula, and which are distributed over the Western Oceania.——The language of the Malay peninsula.

MAL DE SIAM. In India, a name for yellow fever; supposed to have been originally brought from Siam.

MALLAM-TODDALI. A tree in Malabar, whose root, bark, leaves, and fruit are esteemed as a specific in epilepsy; so called from Malayalam, native name of the province of Malabar.

MALKIN. A mop; hence, a dirty drab (*Webster*). A kind of mop, made of clouts, for sweeping ovens; hence a frightful figure of clouts dressed up; hence a dirty wench (*Hanmer*)—

> " The kitchin *malkin* pinnes
> Her richest lockram 'bout her reechie necke,
> Clamb'ring the walls to eye him."—*Shaks.*

> " Put on the shape of order and humanity,
> Or you must marry *malkin* the May lady."
> *Beaum.* and *F.*   Mons. Thomas.

> " He went, and ere *malkin* could well lick her ear
> (For it but the next door was, forsooth), we were there."—
> *Cotton.* Voyage to Ireland, c. 2.

——A diminutive of *Mal, Moll*, the nickname of **Mary.**

MALLIGO. Malaga wine. Corruption of **Malaga.**

> " And *Malligo* glasses fox thee."—*Sp. Gipsy*, iii. 1.

MALMSEY (Fr. *malvoisie*, formerly *malvaise*, It. *malvosio*, Sp. *marvisia*). A sort of grape; also a strong and sweet wine.

" And then throw him into the *malmsey-butt* in the next room."—*Shaks.*

" I'll drown you in the *malmsey-butt* within."—*Ibid.*

" That arrant *malmsey-nose* knave, Bardolph."—*Ibid.*

The word is derived from Malvasia (hodie *Monemvasia*), a town near Argos, in the Morea, in whose territory the grape grew. This wine is now principally made at Madeira, and if not manufactured in London, it is simply because it is not in demand.

MALPIGHIA. A genus of plants, trees or shrubs; called after Malpighi, a naturalist of Pisa.

MALTHUSIAN. The political doctrines of the Rev. Thomas Robert Malthus, F.R.S., as laid down in his essay on the Principles of Population. In this work the learned author advocates the anti-connubial system ; a system founded on the supposition that population increases in a geometrical, while food only increases in an arithmetrical, degree. Malthus was born at Albury, in Surrey, in 1766, and died at Bath in 1835.

MAMERTINES (Fr. *Mamertins*). A band of mercenaries, who, uniting with the Sicilians, seized upon Messana (Messina) B.C. 270. Pressed by the Carthaginians, they sought the aid of the Romans (B.C. 264-265), and thus originated the first Punic war. Some assert that the Mamertines were so called from Mamers or Mars ; but according to the best authority, these people derived their name from Mamerte, in ancient geography a town of Sicily, near Messina. Mamers is the name of a place in France (Sarthe).

MAMMET. A doll, or dollish person ; probably so called from Mahomet, to whom the black dolls hanging over rag-shops bear a distant resemblance. *Mammet* and *poppet* were old names for what is now called a Marionette (*S. F. Creswell*). Webster renders *mammet*, a puppet ; a figure dressed. Johnson derives *mammet* from *mam* or *mamma.* Richardson renders *mawmet*, *mammot*, *mammet*, anything set up as an object of adoration: a popet or puppet, a fondling; generally an idol, a graven image; from Mahomet; and *mawmetry*, the religion of Mahomet; idolatory; the worship of graven images.

> " This no is world to play with *mammets*, and to tilt with lips."—
> 1 Hen. iv.

> " And then to haue a wretched puling foole,
> A whining mammet, in her fortune's tender,
> To answer, Ile not wed, I cannot loue."—R. & J.

> " There you shall find in every corner a *maumet*; at every door a beggar; and in every dish a priest."—*Bp. Hall.* Ep. i. Dec. 1.

> " In destruction of *maumetrie*,
> And in encrese of Cristes lawe dere,
> They ben accorded so as ye may here."
> *Chaucer.* The Man of Lawes Tale, v. 4656.

> " An idolastre peraventure ne hath not but o *maumet* or two, and the avaricious man hath many; for certes, every florene in his coffre is a *maumet*. And certes, the sinne of *maumetrie* is the first that God defended in the ten commandments, as bereth witnesse Exod. c. xx. Thou shalt have no false gods before me, ne thou shalt make to thee no graven thing."—*Id.* The Persones Tale.

> " We charge the prelatical clergy with popery, to make them odious, tho' we know they are guilty of no such things: just as heretofore they call'd images *mammets*, and the adoration of images *mammetry*; that is, Mahomet and Mahometry; odious names, when all the world knows the Turks are forbidden images by their religion." — *Selden.* Table Talk. Popery.

See also Notes and Queries, July 6, 1864, p. 28; and Promp. Parv. under " Mawmet," *et seq.*

MAMMON (Syr.). Riches, wealth.

> " *Mammon* is riches or aboundance of goods."
> *Tyndall.* Works, p. 233.

> " Ye cannot serve God and *mammon*."—Matt. vi.

> " And of *mammonaes* money mad hym many frendes."
> *Piers Ploughman*, p. 170.

So called from Mammon, god of riches, the god chiefly worshipped by Christians in the present age of progress.

MAMMONIST. One devoted to the acquisition of wealth;

one whose affections are placed supremely on riches; a world-ling (*Hammond*). So called from Mammon, god of riches.

> " When I'd arrive the very top of all,
> That the mistaken *mammonists* miscall,
> And think their chiefest blessings, health and wit."
>   *Brome.* A Paraphrase upon Ecclesiastes, c. i.

> " The great *mammonist* would say, he is rich that can maintain an army."
> —*Bp. Hall.* The Righteous Mammon.

MANCINITE. A mineral, colour brown; from Mancino, near Leghorn.

MANDILLIAN. A kind of garment worn temp. Elizabeth: *i.q.* Mandeville, which Randal Holmes describes as "a loose hanging garment," and much like to our jacket or jumps, but without sleeves, only having holes to put the arms through; yet some were made with sleeves, but for no other use than to hang on the back (*Planché*). The word is doubtless derived from either a local name or a local surname.

MANDOZY. A term of endearment; probably named from the valiant fighter Mendoza.—*J. C. Hotten.*

MANGABEY. The precarious name of a monkey found in the territory of Mangabey, near Madagascar. See Buffon.

MANGANATE, MANGANESATE. A compound of manganesic acid, with a base. See MANGANESE.

MANGANESE (at first called by Gahn *magnesium*). A greyish-white metal, found in the ashes of plants, the bones of animals, and in many minerals; very hard and difficult to fuse; from Magnesia, *q.v.*

MANGANITE. One of the ores of manganese (*q.v.*); called also manganese ore.

MANICHEISM. The doctrines or system of principles of the Manichees or Manicheans, followers of Manes, a Persian, who tried to combine the Oriental philosophy with Christianity, and maintained that there are two supreme principles, the one good, the other evil, which produce all the happiness and calamities of the world. They held the first principle, or *light*, to be the author of all good; the second, or *darkness*, the author of all evil.

MANILLA. A cigar from Manila, capital of Luzon, and of all the Philippine Isles.

MANNHEIM GOLD. Another name for Dutch gold or orsedew, an inferior sort of gold-leaf, made of copper and zinc, sometimes called *leaf-brass*; so named from being principally manufactured at Mannheim, on the Rhine.

MANSARD. In *architecture*, a roof with a double slope on each side; a gambrel roof (Fr. *mansarde*, a garret; garret-window); so called from its inventor, Mansard, a French architect, who died in 1666.

MANTON. A celebrated gun manufactured by the late Joseph Manton.

MANUS CHRISTI. Refined sugar, so boiled as to make a cordial for weak persons.—*Crabb.*

MANX. A term applied to the ancient language of the Isle of Man; whence its name.

MAPPIA. A genus of plants, the only species of which is the *M. guianensis*, a shrub, native of Guiana; named after Marcus Mappus, professor of medicine at Strasburg, author of Catal. Plantarum Horti Acad. Argentinensis, 1691; Hist. Plant. Alsaticarum, a posthumous work by Ehrmann, 1742.

MARANTA. A genus of perennial tropical plants, from the roots of one species of which (*M. arundinacea*) is principally obtained the arrowroot of commerce, which species is much cultivated in the gardens and provision grounds of the West Indies; named by Plumier in memory of Bartholomeo Maranta, a Venetian physician, who lived towards the middle of the sixteenth century, and was one of the chief Italian botanists of his time.

MARAUDER. A rover in quest of booty or plunder; a plunderer; usually applied to small parties of soldiers. To go in a *marauding* party is to go in search of pillage or plunder.

> " Some place decoys, nor will they not avail,
> Replete with roasted crabs; in every grove
> These fell *marauders* gnaw."
>   *Grainger.* Sugar Cane, b. ii.

Some derive the word from the Fr. *maraud*, a rascal; from Gr. μιαρος, stained, contaminated, infamous. Webster gives the

Fr. *maraud*, the Ethiopic *marada*, to hurry, to run; the Heb. ברד (*marad*), to rebel; the Dan. *maroder*, a robber in war, a corsair. The Heb. *marad* signifies to be disobedient, perverse, rebel, fall away from one's allegiance; the Arab. *marada*, to be obstinate, stubborn, contumacious, wilful. Richardson seems to think the word may be from the verb to mar. Ménage notices the derivation from a Count Merodes, who commanded in the armies of Ferdinand II., but Duchat shows that the word existed long before. A correspondent of Notes and Queries says, "On the old carriage road from Achen to Cologne, not many miles from Achen, is an extensive wood, in which is a fine old chateau called Merode. It was formerly quite concealed from the road by the thick wood, or perhaps, more correctly speaking, *forest*. It had the reputation of possessing a brigand for its owner. The persons who made expeditions with the owner from this chateau were called *Meroders*, and were marauders."

MARAVEDI. In Spain, a small copper coin less than a farthing sterling. It is now a fictitious money, of which 2 form an ochavo, and 34 a real. The word is derived from the Arab. *marábateen*, literally money of the tyrants Almoravides, a family of Mussulman princes (five in number, of whom Abubekr, son of Omar, was the first) who reigned in Africa and Spain in the eleventh, twelfth, and thirteenth centuries, and who were so called from Arab. *almorabeth*, signifying "champion of religion." "Mot par lequel les Espagnols désignaient une petite monnaie de cuivre qui vaut un centime et demi. C'est aujourd'hui une monnaie fictive dont deux forment un ochavo, et 34 un réal. La plus ancienne mention qui soit faite des maravédis dans l'histoire d'Espagne est sous Alphonse, lors de la bataille de Las Navas. On trouve dans les lois Espagnoles des maravédis de différentes espéces (de Almoravide)."

MARCELINE. A mineral, colour greenish-black; so named from being found near Saint Marcel, in Piedmont.

MARCELLIANISM. The doctrines and opinions of the Marcellians, a sect towards the close of the second century; so called from Marcellus of Ancyra, their leader, who was accused of reviving the errors of Sabellius. Some, however, are of opinion that Marcellus was orthodox, and that it was his enemies, the Arians, who fathered their errors upon him.— *Chambers's Cyc.*

MARCETIA. A genus of Brazilian shrubs; named in honour of M. Marcet, a friend of De Candolle.

MARCH (L. *Martius*). The third month of the year, according to modern computation. The Roman year originally began with this month. Romulus named it Martius in honour of his father, Mars, god of war. "*March* is drawn in tawny, with a fierce aspect, and a helmet upon his head, to show this month was dedicated to Mars" (*Peacham*).

MARCHIONESS. A maid of all work; a title now in regular use, but derived from the nickname of a character in Charles Dickens's Old Curiosity Shop.—*J. C. Hotten.*

MARCOBRUNNER. A celebrated Rhine wine, possessing much body and aroma, from Markobrunn.

MARE (A. S. *mara*, G. *mar*, D. *maere*, Sw. *mara*, incubus, D. *nacht-merrie*, G. *nachtmar*). The morbid oppression in sleep otherwise called incubus. "The word is now only used in the compound *nightmare*, which ought to be written *nightmar*" (*Webster*). "Mushrooms cause the incubus, or the *mare* in the stomach" (Bacon's Nat Hist.). The word is said to be derived from *Mara*, in Northern mythology, a spirit that oppressed persons in sleep. "*Mara*, from whence our *nightmare* is derived, was, in the Runic theology, a spirit or spectre of the night, which seized men in their sleep, and suddenly deprived them of speech and motion" (Warton, Hist. Eng. Poetry, vol. i. diss. 1).

> " Mab, his merry queen. by night
> Bestrides young folks that be upright,
> In elder times the *mare* that hight,
> Which plagues them out of measure."—*Drayton.*

MARENGO. In Piedmont, an appellation for the twenty franc gold piece; doubtless named from Marengo, province Alessandria.

MARGARET or **MAGDALEN.** An apple so named.

MARGARET (QUEEN) or **CHINESE STAR.** A plant (*Reine Marguerite*).

MARIBOUS. In a deed of John Arundell, Esq., of Lan-
herne, Cornwall, dated 25 January, 1632, appointing John
Dale, his bayliff for the Manor of Connerton and Hundred of
Penwith, Cornwall, said John Dale is ordered to collect "Ale
Silver, Smoke Silver, Tything-money, Maribous-money, and
Maribous of themselves." In a deputation (10 April, 1648)
the word is written Mariboues or Maribones, the letters *u* and
n in all old deeds being commonly written exactly alike. This
word may be the same with *maraboutin*, of which Bescherelle
says, "Monnaie d'or qui eut cours dans le moyen âge en
Espagne, en Portugal, en Languedoc. De graves discussions
s'élevèrent au commencement du XVIIIᵉ siècle au sujet de
ce mot; mais aucun d'eux ne paraît avoir deviné la véritable
étymologie du nom de cette monnaie, qui doit avoir été intro-
duite ou frappée dans la Péninsule, sous la dénomination des
Morabethoun ou Almoravides."

MARIENGROSCHE. A coin of Hamburg, equal to
about a penny; so named from *Marie*, and G. *groschen*.

MARIGOLD (*Mary* and *gold; Caltha*, Lat.) A yellow
flower, devoted, I suppose, to the Virgin (*Johnson*); "q.d.
aurum *Mariæ*, a colore floris luteo; from the yellow colour of
the flower" (*Skinner*).

> "Absence hath robb'd thee of thy wealth and pleasure,
> And I remain, like *marigold*, of sun
> Depriv'd, that dies by shadow of some mountain."
>
> *Drummond.* Son. 54, pt. i.

MARIOLA. In ancient writers, a shrine or image of the
Virgin Mary (*Bailey*). *Hic quoque fere perficit pulchram* Mario-
lam *cum pertinentiis.* Mat. Paris in Vitis Abbatum S. Albani.
In australi ecclesiæ parte, juxta nobilem Mariolam, ibid (*Cowel*).

MARIOLATRY. A term used to denote the worship of
the Virgin Mary by Roman Catholics (λατρευω, to worship).

MARIONETTES. Puppets moved by springs. Ménage
renders the word "*petites filles;* en prenant l'éspéce pour le
genre: comme qui diroit, *petites Marions*" (*Marion* being itself
a diminutive of *Marie*). Bouillet (Dict. des Sciences, &c.,
Paris, 1854) derives the name from Marion, an Italian, who

introduced the marionettes into France under Charles IX.   The
Greeks knew marionettes under the name of *neurospasta*, and
the Romans under that of *imagunculæ, simulacra, oscilla.*   The
Italians, who are very great amateurs in marionettes, call them
puppi and *fantoccini.*   M. Ch. Magnin published in 1852 a
curious " Histoire des Marionnettes."

MARMATITE.   A black mineral, consisting of the sul-
phurets of zinc and iron; so named from being found at
Candado and Salto, near Marmato, in New Granada.

MARONEAN (*Vinum Maroneum*).   Among the Greeks, a
wine said to have been grown on the side of Ismarus, a hill or
promontory of Thrace; doubtless near the town of Maronea;
probably so named from Maro or Maron, a king of Thrace and
priest of Apollo, who gave Ulysses the excellent wine that
would bear twenty times as much water, and with which he
intoxicated Polyphemus.   See Hom. Od. i. 197, seq.; Pliny,
H. N. x. iv. 4.

MARRIOTTE'S LAW.   In pneumatics, a general pro-
perty of elastic fluids, that the pressure is directly proportional
to the density; discovered by Marriotte, an eminent French
philosopher, native of Burgundy, who flourished about the
middle of the seventeenth century, and was author of several
important works.

MARRUBIUM.   Horehound, a genus of plants.   Some
derive the word from the Heb. *marrob*, a bitter juice, on
account of its taste.   According to others, it was so called by
the ancients from having been originally found near *Marrubium*,
a town of the Marsyans in Italy, eastward of Lake Fucinus.

MARRY (properly *Mary*).   A vulgar oath.

> " Ye ? quod the preest, ye, sire, and wol ye so?
>   *Mary* thereof I pray you hertily."—*Chauc.*

A corruption of *By Mary* (*Tyrwhitt*) or *By Holy Mary*—

> " *By Holy Mary* (Butts), there's knavery,
>   Let 'em alone, and draw the curtaine close."—*Shaks.*

MARS.   One of the seven primary planets, remarkable for
the red colour of his light; named after Mars, god of war.

——In heraldry, another name for gules or red.——An old mythological designation of several preparations of iron.

MARSALA. A wine made at Marsala, a seaport of Sicily. The Marsala wines only came into repute since 1802, when Lord Nelson introduced them for the use of the British fleet. The district is estimated to yield annually about 30,000 pipes of wine, of which two-thirds are exported. There are at Marsala six establishments, four British and two Sicilian. Three of the British are on a large scale.

MARSDENIA. A genus of plants, natives of New Holland; named in honour of William Marsden, Esq., F.R.S., late secretary to the Admiralty, author of a History of Sumatra, and of a Dictionary of the Malayan Language.

MARSEILLAISE. A patriotic and warlike hymn, the words and music of which were composed at Strasbourg, in 1792, by Rouget de Lisle, an officer in the army. It had been written for the army of the Rhine, and on that account received from its author the title of "Le chant de guerre de l'armée du Rhin," but shortly afterwards, the Marseillais, who in 1792 came to Paris to demand the abolition of royalty, and who took part in the attack on the Tuileries, made it known in the capital, when it was baptised by the name of the *Marseillaise*, or *Hymne des Marseillais*, the only appellation by which it is now known.

MARSELLA. A twilled linen, probably from Marseilles, which is also noted, amongst other articles, for its elegant quilts.

MARTELLO. A sort of tower or fortification adapted to the defence of sea-coasts; so named from Martello, a Corsican engineer, the first inventor. Hence our Martello towers, circular buildings of masonry erected along parts of the British coasts as a defence against the meditated invasion of Bonaparte.

MARTEN or MARTERNE. A carnivorous animal allied to the weasel, whose fur is used in making hats and muffs. "L. *martes*, a name that seems to come *a Marte*, because it destroys poultry and other birds; *Vi martia* (Vossius and Gesner)."—*Richardson*.

MARTIAL. Pertaining to war, united to war, as *martial* equipage, *martial* music, *martial* appearance; so called from Mars (gen. Martis), god of war.——Warlike, brave, given to war, as a *martial* nation or people.——Suited to battle, as a *martial* array.——Belonging to war, or to an army and navy; opposed to *civil*, as *martial* law; a court-martial.——Pertaining to Mars, or borrowing the properties of that planet. ——Pertaining to iron, called by the old alchemists Mars.

MARTIAL. A pear; in some parts called Angelic Pear (*Poire Angelique*), and in the South of France *Poire Douce*.

MARTIALISM. Bravery; martial exercises. See MARTIAL. (*obs.*)

MARTIN, MARTINET, or **MARTLET** (Fr. *martinet*, Sp. *martinete*). A bird of the swallow kind, which forms its nest in buildings. The Germans call it *mauer-schwalbe*, wall swallow, and Webster seems to think, therefore, that the word may have been formed from the root of L. *murus* (W. *mur*), a wall:

> " But, like the *martlet*,
> Builds in the weather on the outward wall,
> Euen in the force and rode of casualtie."—*Shaks.*

Minshew thinks—with more ingenuity than truth, says Skinner—"that these birds are so called because they come here about the end of March, and leave us about the feast of St. Martin."

MARTIN. The Lord Martin (Martin Sire); a pear so named; called also Hocrenaille and Ronoille.

MARTINET. In military language, a strict disciplinarian, or rather one who is stupidly fussy about trifles, derived from Col. Martinet, an officer of the French infantry.

MARTINGAL, MARTINGALE (Fr. *martingale*, It. and Sp. *martingala*). A strap or thong fastened to the girth under a horse's belly, and at the other end of the musrole, passing between the fore legs.

> " Lord what a hunting head she carries; sure she has been ridden with a *martingale.—Beaum. & F.*

According to Berenger (Hist. and Art of Horsemanship, c.

10), it was invented by Evangelista, an eminent horseman of Milan. The primary signification of the French word is rendered " Culottes dont le pont était placé par derrière." The martingale breeches are said to have been so called from the Martegaux, a people of Provence, who first wore them. They were still in fashion at the French court in 1579. See Beza, H. Stephens, Ménage Dict. Nat.; Dial. du Nouv. Lang. Fr. Ital. p. 210; and Rabelais, liv. i. ch. 20.——In ships a short perpendicular spar, under the bowsprit end, used for reeving the stays.——Technical name of a system employed by gamblers, as they imagine, to make success certain. It consists in doubling the stake every time you lose.

MARTINMAS. The mass or feast of St. Martin, the 11th of November.

MARTYNIA. A genus of plants, nat. or. *Pedaliaceæ*; named after Professor Martyn.

MARYLAND. One of the principal kinds of tobacco imported into England; from Maryland, in the United States.

MASCAGNIN (*mas-kan'-yin*). Native sulphate of ammonia, found in volcanic districts; named after Mascagni, who first discovered it.

MASDEU. A red wine, doubtless from Masdeu, France, dep. Pyrénees-Orientales (Roussillon). Mas-dieu is the name of a village, dep. Gard (Languedoc).

MASONITE. A mineral, colour blackish-green, found near Katharinenburg, in Siberia, and in Rhode Island; named after Mason.

MASORETIC, MASORETICAL. Relating to the Masorites, inventors of the Hebrew vowel points and accents. They adhered to the traditionary readings of the Scriptures, and were authors of the *Masora*, a Jewish critical work on the text of the Hebrew Scriptures, written in the eighth and ninth centuries. The word *masora* signifies tradition, from מסר, to deliver.

MASSONIA. A genus of plants of four species, natives of the Cape; named by Thunberg after Francis Masson, author of Stapeliæ Novæ, who, in company with Thunberg, found these plants.

MATARO. A wine from Mataro, in Catalonia.

MATLOCKITE. A mineral of a yellowish colour, with sometimes a greenish tinge, found in the Cromford Level, near Matlock, county Derby.

MATTHIOLA. A tree, a species of Guettarda, a native of America; named by Plumier after Pietro Andrea Matthiolus, the celebrated botanist and commentator on Dioscorides.

MATUSCHKÆA. A genus of plants of only one species, a native of Guiana; named after Count Matuschka, author of Flora Silesiaca.

MAUD. A grey woollen shepherd's plaid, something between a shawl and a railway rug. The word occurs in Guy Mannering. It was probably named after one of the royal family of England or Scotland, perhaps Matilda or Maud, daughter of Malcolm, King of Scots, and first wife of Henry I.; or Henry's daughter, the Empress Matilda; or Matilda, who married Stephen, grandson of William the Conqueror.

MAUDLIN. Sentimental; drunk; fuddled; approaching to intoxication; stupid.

> " And the *maudlin* crowd melts in her praise."—*Southern.*

> "She largely, what she wants in words, supplies
>   With *maudlin* eloquence of trickling eyes."—*Roscommon.*

The word is corrupted from Magdalen, from a ludicrous resemblance to the picture of St. Mary Magdalene, who is drawn by painters with eyes swelled and red with weeping.——A reformed prostitute.——(Sweet) A plant of the genus *Achillea*, allied to milfoil.

MAUMETRY. See **Mammet.**

MAURANDIA. A genus of plants, evergreen climbing herbs; named by Dr. Ortega in honour of the wife of Dr. Maurandy, professor of botany at Carthagena.

MAURIA. A genus of plants, trees, nat. or. *Terebinthaceæ;* natives of Peru; named in honour of Antonio Mauri.

MAURITIA. A genus of plants, or. *Hexandria;* natives of Surinam; named in honour of Prince Maurice of Nassau.

MAUSOLEUM. A magnificent tomb, or stately sepulchral monument; so called from Mausolus, king of Caria, a
province of Asia Minor, to whom Artemisia, his widow,
raised a superb monument. This building, erected B.C. 352,
was esteemed one of the seven wonders of the world. According to Pliny, it was 111 feet in circumference, and 140
feet high, and it is said to have been encompassed by thirty-
six columns, and greatly enriched with sculpture. " Artemisia was renowned in history for her extraordinary grief
at the death of her husband Mausolus. She is said to have
mixed his ashes in her daily drink, and to have gradually
died away in grief during the two years that she survived
him. She induced the most eminent Greek rhetoricians
to proclaim his praise in their oratory, and to perpetuate
his memory she built at Halicarnassus the celebrated monument Mausoleum, which was regarded as one of the seven
wonders of the world, and whose name subsequently became
the generic term for any splendid sepulchral monument " (Cic.
Tusc. iii. 31 ; Strabo xiv. p. 656; Gellius x. 18 ; Plin. H. N.
xxv. 36, xxxvi. 4, 9; Val. Max. iv. 6, ext. 1 ; Suid. Harpocr,
s. vv. Αρτεμισια and Μαυσωλος). Another celebrated monument was erected by her in the island of Rhodes, to commemorate her success in making herself mistress of the
island. The Rhodians, after recovering their liberty, made it
inaccessible, whence it was called in later times the Αβατον
(Vitruv. ii. 8). See Dr. W. Smith's Dict.

> " Some (great princes) have amused the dull, sad years of life,
> (Life spent in indolence, and therefore sad)
> With schemes of monumental fame ; and sought
> By pyramids and *mausolean* pomp,
> Short liv'd themselves, t' immortalise their bones."
>
> *Cowper.* Task, b. 5.

" The whole chapel called by his (Henry VII.) name, is properly
but his *mausoleum*, he building it solely for the burial-place of
himself and the royal family, and accordingly ordering by his
will that no person should be interred there." Dart. Antiq.
Westm. Abbey, vol. I. p. 32. See also Holland, Plinie, b.
xxxvi. c. 5.

MAWMETRY or MAUMETRY. See MAMMET.

MAWWORM. A hypocrite ; so named from a character in Cibber's play of the Hypocrite.

"Ah, do despise me ; I'm the prouder for it ; I likes to be despised."

MAX D'OR or MAXIMILIAN. A gold coin of Bavaria, equal to 13s. 7½d. ; doubtless named after the Emperor Maximilian.

MAY (L. *Maius*, Fr. *Mai*, It. *Maggio*, Sp. *Mayo*). The fifth month of the year beginning with January, but the third beginning with March, as was the ancient practice of the Romans. Some derive " Maius à *majoribus*, like Junius à junioribus." Bailey says, " Maius from *majores*, so called by Romulus in respect of the senators." Festus derives the word from *Maia*, mother of Mercury, to whom this month was made sacred.——To celebrate the 1st of May with rural sports.

MAY-DUKE. The popular and most universally cultivated cherry, thriving well in nearly all countries, situations, and soils. The name is said to be a corruption of Médoc, a district in the south of France, where this variety (the type of all the class now called dukes) is said to have originated. Charles McIntosh's Book of the Garden, ii. 542.

MAZARINE. Formerly a hood made after the fashion of that worn by the Duchess of Mazarin.—*Bailey*.

MAZARINE. A deep blue colour ; probably named after Cardinal Mazarin, regent of France during the minority of Louis XIV.——A particular way of dressing fowls (in Fr. *à la Mazarine*).——Formerly a little dish to be set in the middle of a large one.——Formerly a sort of small tart filled with sweetmeats.

MEANDER. A winding course ; a winding or turning in a passage, as the *meanders* of the veins and arteries (*Hale*).

" While lingering rivers in *meanders* glide."—*Blackmore*.

So named from Meander, a tortuous river of Phrygia.—— A maze ; a labyrinth ; perplexity, as the *meanders* of the law (*Arbuthnot*).——To wind, to turn, to flow round ; to make flexuous; to wind or turn in a course or passage; to be intricate.——A fretwork in arched roofs (found *mœander*).

MEANDRINA. A genus of corals with meandering cells, as the brain-stone coral.—*Mantell.* See MEANDER.

MECÆNATIANUM. In ancient Italy, a rare wine, of exquisite flavour, introduced at his table by Mecænas, the friend of Augustus, Virgil, and Horace.

MECHLIN. A species of beautiful and durable lace made at Mechlin (Malines), in Belgium. It is now nearly superseded by the manufacture of tulles, and only a very small quantity is made.

MECHOACAN (*mechoacanna*). White jalap, the root of an American species of convolvulus, from Mechoacan, in Mexico; a purgative of slow operation, but safe.—*Encyc.*

MEDICA. A sort of trefoil; from Media, its native soil. —*Forsyth.* But see MEDICAGO.

MEDICAGO. A genus of plants, nat. or. *Leguminosæ;* from Medike, the name given by Discorides to a Median grass.

MEDIN, MEDINO. A coin and money of account in Egypt. According to Kelly, at Cairo forty Medini are equal to 1*s.* 7¼*d.* It was probably first coined at Medina.

MEDINENSIS VENA. The muscular worm, which in some countries inhabits the cellular membrane between the skin and muscles; the guinea worm. " So called because it is frequent in Medina, and improperly called *vena* for *vermis;* and sometimes *nervus Medinensis.*" Hooper, Lex. Med.

MEDJIDITE. A mineral, a hydrous sulphate, occurring near Adrianople, Turkey; also at Joachimsthal, in Germany; named in honour of Sultan Abdul Medjid.

MÉDOC. A celebrated red wine produced at Médoc, an ancient district of France, prov. Guienne, now comprised in dep. Gironde.——A kind of shining pebble.

MEDUSA. A tree from Cochin China. See MEDUSÆ.

MEDUSÆ. A genus of gelatinous radiate animals called sea-nettles; so named because their organs of motion spread out like the snaky hair of Medusa.

MEDUSIDANS. Gelatinous radiate animals, which float or swim in the sea, of which Medusæ is the genus. See MEDUSÆ.

MEIBOMIAN or MEIBOMIUS'S GLANDS (*ciliary follicles*). The small glands lying under the inner membrane of the eyelid, first described by Henry Meibomius, an eminent professor of medicine, who was born at Lübeck in 1638. Hooper, Lex. Med.

MELAMPODIUM. Black hellibore; from Melampus, the shepherd who first used it (*Forsyth*). But qy. from Gr. μελαμποδιον, blackfoot.

MELEAGRIS. The guinea-fowl, a genus of birds of the or. *Gallinæ;* so called fiom Meleager, whose sisters were turned into this bird.——A bulbous plant, a species of fritillaria or crown imperial; so called because its flowers are spotted like a guinea-fowl.

MEMBRANA RUYSCHIANA. " Ruysch discovered that the choroid membrane of the eye was composed of two laminæ. He gave the name of *Membrana Ruyschiana* to the internal lamina, leaving the old name of choroides to the external."—*Forsyth.*

MEMPHIAN. Pertaining to Memphis; very dark; a sense borrowed from the darkness of Egypt in the time of Moses; from Memphis, the ancient metropolis of Egypt. " Qy. from some oracle, or covered labyrinth at Memphis" (*S. F. C.*).

MENACHANITE. One of the ores of titanium, a metal, colour deep blue, discovered by Gregor in 1791 in the bed of a rivulet which flows into the valley of Menacan, in Cornwall. Other ores of this metal are called Iserine, from the river Iser, in Silesia; Nigrine, from its black colour; Spene, Rutile, and Octahedrite.

MENDIPITE. A mineral; yellowish-white, straw-yellow, pale red, pale blue; found with ores of lead, calcite, and earthy black manganese, at Churchill, in the Mendip Hills, in Somersetshire, and at Brilon, in Westphalia.

MENEGHINITE. A mineral in compact fibrous forms; from Bottino, in Tuscany, where it was obtained, along with Boulangerite and Jamesonite, by Professor Meneghini.

MENILITE. A brown impure opal, occurring in flattened nodular concretions at *Menil* Montant, near Paris.—*Dana.*

MENTOR. A wise and faithful counsellor or monitor; so called from Mentor, counsellor of Telemachus.

MENTZELIA. A genus of annual plants, natives of South America; named by Plumier in honour of Dr. Christian Mentzel, a German botanical writer, and councillor and physician to the Elector of Brandenburg.

MEMNON. A celebrated statue (of which there is a copy in the British Museum) which stood near Thebes in Egypt, and which was said to have the property of emitting a sound like the snapping asunder of a musical string, as the first beams of sunrise fell upon it; named, as Mannert thinks, after Memnon, a celebrated architect of Syene; but according to Champollion, after Memnon, whom he identifies with Amenophis II. Champollion, indeed, makes the inscription on the base of the statue equivalent to Amenoph ($A\mu\varepsilon\nu\omega\phi$). But see Lempriere.

MEMNONIDES or MEMNONIANS. Certain birds which are said to have arisen from the ashes of Memnon (a king of Ethiopia, son of Tithonus and Aurora), who was killed at the siege of Troy, and which birds came every year to visit his tomb upon the banks of the Hellespont. But see Lempriere, under "Memnon."

MENZIESIA. A genus of plants, shrubs, mostly natives of North America; named in honour of Archibald Menzies, F.L.S., who made a voyage round the world with Vancouver, and collected many rare plants in New Holland and North America.

MEPHISTOPHELIAN. Diabolical, sardonic, like to Mephistopheles, one of the principal characters in Goethe's Faust, the subject of which was suggested by the tale of Dr. Faustus, where, however, the name under which the devil appears is *Mephostopheles*, supposed to be for *Nephostopheles*, from $\nu\varepsilon\phi o\varsigma$ a cloud, $\phi\iota\lambda\varepsilon\omega$ to love.

MERCATOR'S CHART. A chart constructed on the principle projected by Mercator, a Flemish geographer. In this chart the degrees upon the meridian increase towards the poles in the same proportion as the parallel circles decrease towards them.

MERCURIAL. Formed under the influence of the god Mercury; active, sprightly, full of fire or vigour; as, a *mercurial* youth, a *mercurial* nation.——Pertaining to Mercury, as god of trade; hence money-making, crafty.——Pertaining to or containing quicksilver, or consisting of mercury; as, *mercurial* preparations or medicines.

MERCURIALIS. A genus of plants, nat. or. *Euphorbiaceæ;* called after Mercury, its fabled discoverer.

MERCURIALIST. One under the influence of the god Mercury, or one resembling him in variety of character.

MERCURY. The smallest of the inferior planets; named after Mercury, messenger and interpreter of the gods.—— Quicksilver, a metal used in barometers.

> " Sol gold is, and Luna silver we threpe;
> Mars iren, *Mercurie* quicksilver we clepe."—*Chaucer.*

——Heat of constitutional temperament, spirit, sprightly qualities.——The name of a newspaper or periodical publication.——A messenger, a news-carrier; "from the office of the god Mercury" (*Webster*).——In *heraldry*, the tincture *purpure* in blazoning.

MEROVINGIAN. A term applied to the written character of certain MSS. still extant in the French libraries; so called from Mérovée, first king of France of a race which reigned 333 years, viz., from Pharamond to Charles Martel.

MERRY-ANDREW. A buffoon, a zany, one whose business is to make sport for others; particularly one who attends a mountebank or quack doctor. " He would be a statesman, because he is a buffoon; as if there went no more to the making of a counsellor than the faculties of a *Merry-Andrew* or tumbler " (*L'Estrange*). " The first who made the experiment was a *Merry-Andrew* " (*Spectator*). " This term is said to have originated from one Andrew Borde, a physician in the time of Henry VIII., who attracted attention and gained patients by facetious speeches to the multitude " (*Smart*). " 'Twas from the doctor's method of using such speeches at markets and fairs that in after-times those that imitated the like humorous jocose language were styled Merry-Andrews, a term much in vogue on our stages" (Wharton, English Poetry).

MESMERISM. Animal magnetism; the art of communicating a sort of sleep which is supposed to affect the body while the mind, *i.e.* the brain, is active and intelligent; first introduced in 1778 by Frederic Anton Mesmer, a physician, born at Mersburg, in Swabia, about 1734. Now-a-days phrenology and spirit-rapping are more in vogue.

METONIC. The cycle of the moon, or period of nineteen years, in which the lunations of the moon return to the same days of the month; so called from its discoverer Meton, the Athenian. See Aelian, Var. Hist. x. 7; Censorinus, c. 18; Diodorus, xii. 36; Ptol. Synt. iii. 2; and Dr. W. Smith's Dict., under "Meton."

MEXICANUM. A name of the balsam of Peru; so called from Mexico, whence it is brought.

MIASCITE. A columnar variety of bitterspar, inter nixed with asbestos; from Miaska, in Siberia.

MICHAELITE. A sub-variety of siliceous sinter, found in the isle of St. Michael.—*J. W. Webster.*

MICHAELMAS. The feast of St. Michael, a festival of the Roman Catholic church celebrated September 29th.——In colloquial language, autumn.

MIDAS. The generic name of a small monkey of which there are seven species, among which are *Midas rosalia* and *Marikina* or *Silky Tamarin*; probably called Midas from the large size and breadth of its ears, like to those of *Midas*, which were changed by Apollo into ass's ears.

MIDDLETONITE. A resin found in small rounded masses, or thin seams between layers of coal, at Middleton, near Leeds, and also at Newcastle.

MIEMITE. A variety of magnesian limestone, colour light green or greenish-white; first found at Miemo, in Tuscany.

MIKE. To loiter; or, as a costermonger defined it, to "lazy about." The term probably originated at St. Giles's, which used to be thronged with Irish labourers (Mike being so common a term with them as to become a generic appellation for Irishmen with the vulgar), who used to loiter about the Pound, and lean against the public-houses in the "Dials" waiting for hire.—*J. C. Hotten.*

MILESIAN. A term sometimes applied to the Irish; so called from Milesius, whose eight sons are said to have made an expedition from Spain, and to have obtained possession of Ireland. The term Milesian fables is given to certain tales or novels composed by Aristides of Miletus (the Boccaccio of his time), much praised for the grace and naïveté of the style and the gaiety of the narration. They were translated into Latin by the historian Sisenna, friend of Atticus, and had a great success at Rome. Plutarch, in his life of Crassus, tells us that after the defeat of Carhes (Carrhæ ?) some Milesiacs were found in the baggage of the Roman prisoners. The Greek text and the translation have been long lost. The only fable of this sort that we have left is that of Psyche, which Apuleius calls *Milesius sermo*, a work which gives a very good idea of the Milesian fables, and which makes one much regret their loss.

MILLEA. A genus of Mexican plants; named after Julian Milla, chief gardener of Royal Botanical Gardens at Madrid.

MILLER. A word frequently called out when a person relates a stale joke; for Joe Miller.—*J. C. H.*

MILLERIA. A genus of plants, nat. or. *Compositæ;* called after Mr. Miller, author of the Gardener's Dictionary.—*Crabb.*

MILLINER. A woman who makes and sells headdresses, bonnets, &c., for females.

" He hath songs for man or woman, of all sizes; no *milliner* can so fit his customers with gloues."—*Shaks.*

Richardson says, " one who deals in a *mixed* variety of articles." Bailey renders *milliner* a seller of ribbons, gloves, &c., of L. *mille*, a thousand (*i. e.*, one who sells a thousand sorts of things). Richardson says, " so called from *Milaner*, one from *Milan;* or *Malineer*, from *Maline* (*Malines*); or *millenarius*, because he deals in a thousand articles. It is perhaps *mistlener*, from *mistlen* or *mestlin*, a medley or mixture."

MILTONIA. A genus of Orchidaceous plants, said to have been named in honour of the poet Milton.

MINERVALIA. Festivals at Rome in honour of Minerva. During these solemnities scholars obtained some relaxation from their studies, and it was customary for them to offer to their masters a present called *minerval*, in allusion to the goddess being the patroness of literature.

MINIÉ. A celebrated rifle invented by Captain (now Colonel) Minié, a Frenchman.

MINOTAUR (L. *minotaurus*). A monster invented by the poets, half man and half bull, kept in Dædalus's labyrinth.

> " Thou may'st not wander in that labyrinth,
>   There *minotaurs* and ugly treasons lurk."—*Shaks.*

> " Here I, enclosed from all the world asunder,
>   The *minotaur* of shame. kept for disgrace;
>   The monster of fortune, and the world's wonder,
>   Liv'd cloist'red in so desolate a cave."
>   *Daniel.* The Complaint of Rosamond.

> " And by his banner borne in his penon
>   Of gold full riche, in which ther was ybete
>   The *minotaure* which that he slew in Crete."
>   *Chaucer.* The Knightes Tale, v. 981.

The word is derived from *Minois taurus,* bull of Minos.

MIQUELETS. A species of partisan troops raised in the north of Spain (*T. Wright*). They were found principally in the Pyrenees, upon the borders of Catalonia and Arragon, and received their name from their leader Miguel. Napoleon in 1808 created a corps called Miquelets Français, to oppose the Spanish guerillas. Louis XIV. had previously formed a corps in 1689, Louis XV. another in 1744, and the Republic had done the same in 1789.

MIRBELIA. A genus of Australian subshrubs; named in honour of M. Mirbel, a French botanist, formerly superintendent of the botanic garden at Malmaison, author of several excellent works on the anatomy and physiology of vegetables.

MITCHELLS. Among builders, Purbeck stones, from fifteen inches square to two feet, squared and hewn ready for building; probably from a surname.

MITHRIDATE. An antidote against poison, or a composition in form of an electuary, supposed to serve either as a

remedy or a preservative against poison. " Were it not strange
a physician should decline exhibiting of *mithridate*, because it
was a known medicine, and famous for its cures many ages
since ?" (Boyle, Works, vol. ii., p. 288.)

> " But as in *mithridate*, or just perfumes,
>   Where all good things being met, no one presumes
>   To govern, or to triumph on the rest."
>
> *Donne.* Progress of the Soul.

It is said to take its name from Mithridates, king of Pontus,
its supposed inventor. " Cratevas hath ascribed the invention
of one hearbe to King Mithridates himselfe, called after his
name *Mithridation* " (Holland, Plinie, b. xxv. c. 6). " Mithridates experiencing the virtues of the simples separately,
afterwards combined them; but then this composition consisted
of but few ingredients, viz., twenty leaves of rue, two walnuts,
two figs, and a little salt: of this he took a dose every morning,
to guard himself against the effects of poison, &c." (*Forsyth*).

MOAB. An university term applied to the turban-shaped
hat fashionable among ladies, and ladylike swells of the other
sex, in 1858-9; from the Scripture phrase, "Moab is my
washpot" (Ps. lx. 8), which article the hat in question is
supposed to resemble.—*J. C. Hotten.*

MOCHA. A celebrated coffee which still maintains its
superiority over the coffee produced in the European colonies.
It is brought from Mocha, in Arabia; or rather, it is grown at
Bulgosa, near Bait-al-Fakih, and exported from Mocha.——A
term applied to a cat of a black colour, intermixed with brown ;
from the Mocha pebble. (Prov.)—*Halliwell.*

MOCHA STONE. A mineral, in the interior of which
appear brown, reddish-brown, blackish, or green delineations of
shrubs destitute of leaves; from Mocha, in Arabia.

MOCO. A monkey so called, as coming from Moco, in the
Persian Gulf. See Buffon.

MODENA. A crimson-like colour ; from Modena, in Italy.

MOEHRINGIA. A genus of plants, nat. or. *Caryophylleæ ;*
named after P. H. G. Moehring, a German physician, author
of Hortus Proprius, and other works.

MOENCHIA. A genus of plants, nat. or. *Caryophylleæ ;*

named after Conrad Moench, professor of botany at Marburg, author of Enumeratio Plantarum Indigenarum Hassiæ, præsertim inferioris, and a work on the cultivation of North American forest trees in Germany, &c.

MOGADORE. A bees'-wax from Mogador, a seaport of Morocco.

MOHAMMEDANISM. The religion or doctrines and precepts of Mohammad or Mahomet, as contained in the Koran.

MOHAWK or MOHOCK. The appellation given to certain ruffians who infested the streets of London early in the eighteenth century; so called from Mohawk or Mohock, native name of one of the Iroquois tribes of Indians. Cf. Amer. Journ. Sciences, conducted by Prof. Silliman, vol. 41, p. 28.

MOLINÆA. A genus of plants (by some treated as a species of *Cupania*); named by Commerson in honour of Johannes Molinæus (Jean des Moulins), to whose assistance Dalechamp had recourse in the composition of his work.

MOLINISM. The doctrines of the Molinists or followers of the opinions of Molina, a Spanish Jesuit, which doctrines somewhat resemble the tenets of the Arminians.

MOLL. A girl; nickname for Mary.—*J. C. H.*

MOLMUTIN LAWS. The laws of Dunwallo Molmutius, sixteenth king of the Britains. They were famous here till the time of William the Conqueror.—*Bailey.*

MOLUCCELLA (Molucca balm). A genus of plants, nat. or. *Labiatæ;* said to be natives of the Moluccas.—*Crabb.*

MONARDA. A genus of North American herbaceous perennial plants; named after Nicholas Monardes, a Spanish physician and botanist, who lived at Seville about the end of the sixteenth century; author of the Materia Medica of the New World, and other works.

MONETIA. A genus of plants; named by M. L'Heritier in honour of J. B. de Monet, Chevalier de Lamarck, a celebrated French botanical writer.

MONEY. A stamped piece of metal; from L. *moneta,* the Roman name for money or coins; so called, it is said, because the Romans kept their silver money in the Temple of Juno Moneta, mother of the Muses, on which account the latter is commonly represented on medals as a female with a pair of scales, and is symbolical of justice, liberality, &c. See Liv. vi. 20; Cic. Phil. vii. 1; Cic. Att. viii. 7; Suet.; Cæs. 76.

MONMOUTH CAP. A kind of flat cap formerly worn by the common people.—*Halliwell.*

MONONGAHELA. Rye whiskey; so called in America because large quantities of it were produced in the neighbour-hood of the Monongahela, a river of Pennsylvania (*Bartlett*). ——American whiskey in general, as distinguished from usquebaugh and innishowen, the Scotch and Irish sorts.

MONRADITE. A mineral, a hydrous silicate, from Bergen, in Norway; named after M. Monrad.

MONROLITE. A mineral consisting of silica, alumina, magnesia, and water; found at Monroe, Orange Co., New York.

MONS MENELAUS. A modern northern constellation of eleven stars; named after Menelaus, husband of Helen.

MONTANISM. See Montanize.

MONTANIZE. To think as Montanus thought; to adopt, to follow, the doctrine of Montanus (*Ency. Met.*) "Tertullian, together with such as were his followers, beganne to *montanize*, and pretending to perfect the seueritie of Christian discipline, brought in sundrie unaccustomed dayes of fasting, continued their fasts a great deale longer, and made them more rigorous than the vse of the church had been" (Hooker, Eccles. Pol. b, v. s. 72, fol. 392). "Whereupon Tertullian, proclaiming euen open warre to the church, maintained *Montanisme*, wrote a booke in defence of the new fast, intituled the same, a Treatise of Fasting, against the opinion of the carnall sort" (*Id. ib.*)

MONTEFIASCO. A rich wine made at Montefiascone, in Italy.

MONTEPULCIANO. A celebrated wine made at Monte-pulciano, a town of Tuscany, prov. Florence.

MONTETH. A vessel in which glasses are washed; named after the inventor.

> " New things produce new words, and thus *Monteth*
>   Has by one vessel sav'd his name from death."—*King.*

MONTGOLFIER (Fr. *montgolfière*). A name given to

balloons which receive their buoyancy from the burning of combustible materials; so called from their originator, Jacques Etienne Montgolfier, celebrated for his inventions.

MONTMARTRITE. A mineral, colour yellowish; found at Montmartre, Paris.

MONTMORILLONITE. A mineral, a hydrous silicate, colour rose-red; from Montmorillon, in France; also found at Confolens (Charente), and near St. Jean de Colle (Dordogne).

MOORCROFTIA. A genus of East Indian plants; named in honour of William Moorcroft.

MORAVIANISM. The religious system of the Moravians, a congregation of Christians who sprung up in Moravia and Bohemia at the dawn of the Reformation, and are otherwise called United Brethren, and on the Continent Herrn Hüters. They generally adhere to the Augsburg Confession, and are distinguished by their Christian virtues and great simplicity of dress and manners. They have settlements in Germany, Switzerland, England, and America, and are noted for the energy they display in directing missions for the conversion of what are termed "the heathen" to the remotest parts of the globe.

MOREA. A genus of plants whose species are bulbs, natives of the Cape; named by Miller after Robert More, of Shrewsbury, a celebrated botanist and naturalist.

MORESQUE or MORESCO (It. *moresco*). A kind of painting or carving done after the Moorish manner, consisting of grotesque pieces and compartments promiscuously interspersed; arabesque.

MORETTIA. A genus of cruciferous plants; named in honour of J. L. Moretti, an Italian botanist.

MORGANIA. A genus of herbaceous plants, natives of the tropical parts of Australia; named by Mr. R. Brown in honour of Hugh Morgan, an English horticulturist, who flourished temp. Queen Elizabeth, and whose garden is often mentioned by Lobel and Gerarde.

MORION (found *morrion*, *morian*, and *murrion*; Fr. *morion*, It. *morione*, Sp. *morrion*). A kind of open helmet, without visor or beaver, somewhat resembling a hat.

" Philopoemen reformed all this, perswading them to use the pike and shield instead of the little target, spear, or bore-staff, and to put good *morians* or burganets on their heads."—*Sir Thomas North.* Plutarch, fol. 309.

" Their beef they often in their *murrions* stewed."
King. Art of Cookery.

" Then to herselfe she gives her Ægide shield,
And steel-hed speare, and *morion* on her hedd,
Such as she oft is seene in warlike field."
Spenser. Muiopotmos.

Some derive the word from L. *morus*, dark-coloured, black ; and Ménage tells us that the Low Latin writers call a cuirass *brunia*, on account of its brown colour. According to others, it was so called because introduced into Europe by the Moors. Bochart says " from *Maurus*, a *Maurorum* usu (because used by the Moors): ut Moresque, *saltationis genus*." " C'était autrefois la coiffure spéciale des arquebusiers et des mousquetaires. C'était aussi le nom d'une sorte de châtiment militaire qui consistait à frapper sur le derrière le soldat coupable avec la hampe d'une hallebarde ou la crosse d'un mousquet " (Bouillet, Dict. des Sciences).

MORISCO or MORISK. A term variously applied by old writers to the work called *moresque;* to the *Moorish* language ; and also to a dance, or a dancer of *morris* or *Moorish* dances.—*Webster.*

MORMONISM. The doctrines of the Mormonites, followers of the factitious prophet Mormon, usually called Mormons.

MORNA. A genus of composite plants ; so named after a heroine of Northern romance.—*T. Wright, M.A.*

MOROCCO (found *marroquin*, Fr. *maroquin*). A fine kind of leather, prepared commonly from goatskin (though an inferior kind is made of sheepskin), and tanned with sumach ; from Morocco, or rather Marocco, where first manufactured.

——A strong ale brewed with beef or some other sort of meat at Levens Hall, in Cumberland. " Morocco is the name of the drink ; it is brewed at Levens, near Milnthorp, from a recipe found wrapped up in lead near an evergreen in the old garden. Flesh is certainly introduced, as I believe it to be in the Durham University strong beer. The exact recipe for brewing morocco is kept strictly secret. There is a legend that the secret was brought by a Crusader, Howard, and during the Civil Wars buried where it was found, as above, some years ago. Helpless, truly, is the state of that man who stoops to drink inferior liquor after imbibing the mighty morocco. It is almost dark, pours like oil, and tastes mild as milk in its treachery." See N. & Q. 3rd S. vii. 74.

MORPHIA, MORPHINA, or MORPHINE. A vegetable alkaloid extracted from opium, of which it constitutes one of the narcotic principles ; so called from Morpheus, god of sleep.

MORRIS or MORRICE (Fr. *moresque*). A Moorish dance ; a dance in the Middle Ages, in imitation of the Moors, as sarabands, chacons, &c., usually performed with castanets, tambours, &c., by young men in their shirts, with bells at their feet, and ribbons of various colours tied round their arms and flung across their shoulders. It was common in Spain. The Spanish fandango, danced to the present day, is the old Moorish or morris dance.——A kind of game sometimes played in the field with nine holes in the ground, and called *nine-men's morris;* sometimes played on a board (*Shak. Torby*). The morris or morrice (found *moriske*) is said to have been introduced into England by John of Gaunt, who supposed the Galician Spanish dance to be of Moorish origin.

MOSAIC, MOSAICAL. Pertaining to Moses ; as the *Mosaic* law, rites, or institutions.

MOSAIC (Fr. *mosaique;* It. *mosaico;* Sp. *mosayco;* L. *musivus, musivum opus*). An assemblage of little pieces of glass, marble, precious stones, &c., of various colours, cut square, and cemented on a ground of stucco, in such a manner as to imitate the colours and granulations of painting ; from μουσειον, relating to the Muses, on account of its elegance. Hence mosaic gold (*aurum musivum*), the alchemical name of the bi-sulphuret of tin, produced in fine flakes of a beautiful gold colour, and used as a pigment. See also MUSEUM.

MOSASAURUS. A saurian reptile, related to the crocodile, whose remains are found in beds of clay near Maestricht, in

Holland; from *Mosa*, Latin name of the Meuse, and Gr. σαυρος, a lizard. [N.B.—Maestricht was called *Pons Mosæ.* —*S. F. C.*]

MOSELLE. A sparkling wine made, or supposed to be made, on the banks of the Moselle, which falls into the Rhine, at Coblenz. The Moselle wines, however, like the Rhine wines, are usually denominated from the particular locality where they are made.

MOUCHARD. "In the vocabulary of the secret police the terms *mouchard* and *mouton* are the two which are most familiar to those who are uninitiated in its mysteries. The word *mouchard* is not of modern origin. A certain Antoine de Mouchy, otherwise Democharis, a Doctor of the Sorbonne and Canon of Noyon, in 1574 acquired an unenviable notoriety among his contemporaries by his zeal against the Reformers, and was appointed 'Inquisitor of the Faith.' The Reformers who were persecuted by, and who naturally hated him, gave the name of *mouchards* to those whom he employed as spies to hunt out dissenters. In his History of the Parliament of Paris, Voltaire says, 'The famous Mouchy was in reality an informer, a spy of the Cardinal de Lorraine, and it was for him that the nickname of *mouchard* was invented, and which designated all spies. The term has become an insult.' Other authorities will have it that it comes from *mouche,* a fly, because the *mouchard,* like the fly, is ever buzzing about the ears of people. '*Mouton*' is applied to an agent who, a prisoner himself, is employed to lead the conversation of his fellows in plots and conspiracies, and to gradually tempt them to disclose their plots with the same apparent frankness that he reveals his own. They follow him as a flock of sheep follow their leader. Agents of this kind are employed in most political conspiracies, and when all is ready they either disappear, or may be included among the arrested as a matter of form, and when brought to trial inform against their accomplices or those who confide their secrets to them."—*Times,* 26 Feb., 1864.

MUHLENBERGIA. A genus of American grasses; named by Schrœber in honour of Henry Muhlenberg, D.D., of Lancaster, in Pennsylvania, who discovered this genus, and wrote several valuable botanical treatises.

MÜLLERIZE. To cut down a hat, after the manner of the late Franz Müller ; a term now used by some hatters.

MULLINGAR HEIFER. A girl with thick ankles (*Irish*). " The story goes that a traveller passing through Mullingar was so struck with this local peculiarity in the women that he determined to accost the first he next met. ' May I ask,' said he, ' if you wear hay in your shoes ?' ' Faith ! an' I do,' said the girl, ' and what then ?' ' Because,' says the traveller, ' that accounts for the calves of your legs coming down to feed on it.' "—*J. C. Hotten*.

MUM (G. *mumme*, D. *momme*). A malt liquor, made of malt of wheat, oatmeal, and ground beans, brewed with water, much used in Germany, and called sometimes Brunswick mum; sometimes Hamburg mum.

> " See how the Belgæ, sedulous and stout,
>   With bowls of fattening *mum* or blissful cups
>   Of kernel-relish'd fluids, the fair star
>   Of early phosphorus salute."—*J. Philips*. Cider, b. ii.

> " The clamorous crowd is hush'd with mugs of *mum*,
>   Till all, tun'd equal, send a general hum."
>   *Pope*. The Dunciad, b. ii.

" Skinner," says Richardson, " calls the G. *mumme* a strong kind of beer introduced by us from Brunswick, and derived either from G. *mummeln*, to mumble, or from *mum* (silentii index), *i.e.* either drink that will (ut nos dicimus) make a cat speak, or drink that will take away the power of speech." The German word is with more probability derived from Christiern Mumme, a brewer of Braunschweig (Brunswick) Wolfenbüttel, who first made it in 1492, and who, in 1498, lived in the house No. 846, which is still standing, with his sign, viz., the backbone of a fish (Cf. Itin. d'Allemagne, Richard). For a Catch in Praise of Mum, see Playford's Second Book of the Musical Companion, W. Pearson, 1715. Cf. also Notes and Queries, 3rd S. vi. 434, 503; and vii. 41.

MUMMERS. Performers at a travelling theatre (*anc.*)

Rustic performers at Christmas in the West of England (*J. C. Hotten*). See MUMMERY.

MUMMERY (Fr. *momerie*; O. Fr. *mommerie*; Sp. *momeria*). Masking, sport, diversion, frolicking in masks, low contemptible amusement, buffoonery, farcical show, hypocritical disguise and parade to delude vulgar minds.

> " Curse not (this mad-man sayd), but sweare
>   That women be vutrew,
>   Their loue is but a *mummerie*,
>   Or as an April's dew."—*Warner*. Albion's England.

> " This same truth is a naked and open day-light, that doth not shew the masques, and *mummeries*, and triumphs of the world, half so stately, and daintily, as candle-lights."—*Bacon*. Ess. of Truth.

> " The temple and its holy rites profan'd,
>   By *mu. ('ries* he that dwelt in it disdain'd."
>   *Cowper*. Expostulation.

Ducange derives this word from Mahomeria, the temple of the Mahometans. Cowel says, " Mahomeria, the temple of *Mahomet*, so called by Matt. Paris; and because the gestures, noise, and songs there used were ridiculous to the Christians, therefore they called antic dancing, and every ridiculous thing a *mommerie*." Ménage derives *mommerie* from Momus, god of ridicule and raillery: thus *Momus*, *momarius*, *momaria*, *mommerie*. We have, however, the word *mummer*, one who masks himself, and makes diversion in disguise; originally, says Webster, one who made sport by gestures, without speaking; and Webster gives also the word *mumm*, to mask, to sport or make diversion in a mask or disguise, Dan. *mumme*, a mask; D. *mommen*, to mask; G. *mumme* a mask or muffle, *mummeln* to mask, to mumble; Sw. *förmumma*, to personate; which he thinks may be allied to the god Momus. (Μωμος, the make-game even of his brother gods, transmitting his name and characteristics to all the modern European languages, says Richardson). Others, again, derive the word from Gr. μορμω. *terriculum* (what we call a bugbear).

MUNTZ'S METAL. A brass composed of forty parts of zinc to sixty of copper. The proportions may be somewhat varied, but the above are commonly regarded as the most favourable for rolling into sheets ; manufactured by Mr. Muntz.

MURCHISONITE. A variety of felspar ; named after Sir Roderick Murchison, the geologist.

MURPHY. A vulgar name for a potato ; probably so called from the common Irish surname.

MURRAYA. A genus of plants, nat. or. *Aurantiaceæ.* whose species are natives of the East Indies ; called after Mr. Murray, professor of botany at Göttingen.

MUSA. A genus of plants of three species, natives of the East Indies, and other parts of the Asiatic continent, the Molucca Islands, and probably of Africa. The Egyptian name was Mauz, which was changed into Musa by Plumier, in memory of Antonius Musa, freedman of Augustus.

MUSEIA. Grecian festivals in honour of the Muses.

MUSEUM. A repository of natural, scientific, and literary curiosities, or of works of art ; from Μουσειον, originally the name of places in Alexandria and Athens ; so called as being destined and set apart to the Muses and the sciences.

MUSLIN (found *musselin ;* Fr. *mousseline ;* It. *mussolina, mussolino, mússolo ;* Sp. *muselina*). A sort of cotton cloth. Some derive the Fr. word from *mousse,* moss, because all the cloths of fine cotton brought from the Indies have a down which they compare to *mousse.* Webster says, "If this is a compound word, it is formed from *mousse,* moss, or its root, on account of its soft nap, and *lin,* flax." The most reasonable etymology is that from Moussoul (Músul), a town of Asiatic Turkey (Mesopotamia), whence this cloth was first brought. According to others, however, it was imported from the East Indies circa 1670 ; and if so, the name may be derived from Masulipatam, cap. district same name, pres. Madras. A sort of Indian calico is called by the French masulipatan. Bailey says muslin is a fine sort of cotton linen cloth brought from India, &c. The towns of Alençon, Tarare, and St. Quentin, in France, now produce very first-rate muslins ; indeed, with the exception of Switzerland, they may be said to have the monopoly of this industry.

MUSLINET.   A sort of coarse cotton cloth; diminutive of *muslin*, q.v.

MUSSCHIA.   A genus of plants, nat. or. *Campanulaceæ*; named in honour of J. M. Mussche.

MUSSITE.   A variety of pyroxene of a greenish-white colour; otherwise called diopside; from *Mussa*, a valley in Piedmont.

MUSTARD VILLARS.   Formerly a colour so named. "Of olden times," says Stow, "I read that the officers of this city wore gowns of party-colours, as the right side of one colour and the left side of another.   As for example, I read in books of accounts in Guildhall that in the nineteenth year of King Henry VI. there was bought for an officer's gown two yards of cloth coloured *mustard villars*, a colour now out of use, and two yards of cloth coloured blew, price two shillings the yard, in all eight shillings more, paid to John Pope, draper, for two gown-cloths, eight yards, of two colours, *eux ombo deyx de rouge* or red medley, brune and porre (or purple) colour.   Price the yard two shillings.   These gowns were for Piers Rider and John Buckle, clerks of the chamber."   "*Mustard villars* has been said to be a corruption of *moitié velours*, and consequently to signify the species of stuff, and not the colour; but Stow speaks of it here as a colour distinctly.   A town called *Moustiers de Villiers*, near Harfleur, is mentioned by the historians of the preceding reign in their accounts of Henry's expedition, and most probably gave its name to the dye or the stuff there manufactured" (*Planché*).

MUTISIA.   A climbing plant, like clematis, of only one species; named in memory of Joseph Cœlestine Mutis, an American botanist, who designed a History of American Plants, especially of palms, and communicated many new plants to the younger Linnæus and others.   Joseph de Jussieu had before given this genus the Peruvian name *Guariruma*.

MUTSCHEN DIAMONDS.   A kind of crystals found near Mutschen, in Saxony.

MYATT'S PINE.   A celebrated strawberry; named after its cultivator.

MYGINDA.   A genus of plants, shrubs, natives of the

West Indies; named by Jacquin in honour of Francis von Mygind, a German nobleman, who largely patronised the botanic garden at Vienna, and was himself a practical scientific botanist.

MYRMIDON. A soldier of a rough character, a desperate soldier or ruffian under some daring leader: hence the "myrmidons of the law," &c.

> "The mass of the people will not endure to be governed by Clodius and Curio, at the head of their *myrmidons*, though these be ever so numerous, and composed of their own representatives."—*Swift*.

So called from the Myrmidons, a people on the borders of Thessaly, who accompanied Achilles to the war against Troy. The Myrmidons were probably named either from their numbers or their industry; from Gr. μυρμηδων, an ant-hill.

MYSORIN or MYSORINE. A mineral of a blackish-brown colour when pure; usually green or red, from mixture with malachite and red oxide of iron; found at Mysore, in Hindustan.

N.

NABONASSAR. A computation of time from the reign of Nabonassar, on that account called the Era of Nabonassar, which was the era followed by Ptolemy the astronomer.

NABOTH'S GLANDS (*Ovula Nabothi*). Small semi-transparent vesicles situated within and around the cervix uteri; mistaken by Naboth for ovula.

NAJAS. A water plant of only one species, native of the sea-coast of Europe; in the canal between Pisa and Leghorn, and in the Rhine near Bâle; named after Najas or Naias, nymph of the springs.

NAMBY-PAMBY. Particular; over-nice; effeminate. "A term applied to that which is contemptible for affected prettiness" (*Smart*). Sir John Stoddart, in his article "Grammar" (Encyc. Met., vol. 1, p. 118), remarks that the word *namby-pamby* seems to be of modern fabrication, and is particularly intended to describe that style of poetry which affects the infantine simplicity of the nursery, and that it would perhaps be difficult to trace any part of it to a significant origin. It is asserted that Henry Carey, author of " Chrononhotonthologos," and of " The Dragoness of Wantley," wrote a work called *Namby-Pamby*, in burlesque of Ambrose Phillips's style of poetry, and the title of it was probably intended to trifle with that poet's name. Macaulay, in his essay on Addison and his Writings, speaks of Ambrose Phillips, who was a great adulator of Addison, as " a middling poet, whose verses introduced a species of composition which has been called after his name, *namby-pamby*." Johnson, in his life of Ambrose Phillips, says, " The pieces that please best are those for which Pope and Pope's adherents procured him the name of *Namby-Pamby*, the poems of short lines, by which he paid his court to all ages and characters—from Walpole, ' the steerer of the realm,' to Miss Pulteney in the nursery. The numbers are smooth and sprightly, and the diction is seldom faulty. They are not loaded with much thought ; yet if they had been written by Addison they would have had admirers. Little things are not valued but when they are done by those who can do greater." Another writer says, " *Namby-pamby* belongs to a tolerable numerous class of words in our language, all formed on the same rhyming principle. They are all familiar, and some of them childish, which last circumstance probably suggested to Pope the invention of *namby-pamby*, to designate the infantine style which Ambrose Phillips had introduced. Many of them, however, are used by old and approved writers, and the principle upon which they are formed must be of great antiquity in our language " (Cf. N. & Q., 1st Series). *Pamby* is doubtless an illiteration of *Namby*, for *Amby*, a nickname for *Ambrose*. Among many other words of the *namby-pamby* school have been given the following : bow-wow, chit-chat, fiddle-faddle, flim-flam, hab or nab, handy-dandy, harum-scarum, helter-skelter, &c. See also Hotten's Slang Dictionary.

NANCEIC ACID. An acid procured from sour rice and other acescent vegetable substances ; named by Braconnot in honour of his native town, Nancy, in France.

NANKEEN. A species of cloth made of cotton, naturally of a kind of permanent yellow colour; first manufactured at Nankin, in China. It is now also made in Georgia, United States, and is imitated by the manufacturers of Great Britain, though with far less permanency of colour than the Chinese fabric.——A dye made by boiling anatto and carbonate of potash in water.

NAPIER'S BONES. A set of rods made of bone, ivory, horn, or the like, contrived by Lord Napier for facilitating the arithmetical operations of multiplication and division. They have, however, been completely superseded by the use of logarithms, which were also invented by the same eminent mathematician.

NAPLES YELLOW. A fine yellow pigment used in oil painting, also for porcelain and enamel; long prepared in Italy by a secret process. Its proper name is *giallolino*, a diminutive of It. *giallo*, yellow.

NAPOLEON. A gold coin of France, a piece of twenty francs bearing the effigy of the Emperor Napoleon. The word is also applied to twenty-franc pieces with the effigy of the kings who have succeeded Napoleon. There were formerly napoleons of the value of forty francs, and the name is also applied to certain French copper pieces of the value of ten centimes, marked with the letter N.——A fine plant from Africa.——In the United States, a sort of cannon.

NAPOLEONISM. The ism of Napoleon III.; sphinx-ism.

NAPOLITE. A blue mineral from Vesuvius; doubtless derived from Napoli, *i.e.* Naples.

NATRON or NATRUM (anc. called *Nitrum*). Native carbonate of soda; so called from being found crystallised in great abundance in Lake Natron, in Judea. It is, however, also found in other hot countries, in sands surrounding lakes of salt water.——Name formerly given by the College of Physicians to the alkali now called soda.——An impure sub-carbonate of soda, obtained by burning various marine plants.

NAUMANNITE. A mineral consisting of silver, lead, and selenium; found at Tilkerode, in the Harz; probably named after Dr. Carl Friedrich Naumann, prof. of the University of Leipzig, author of Lehrbuch der Geognosie.

NAUPACTUS. A genus of insects found abundantly upon the leaves of vegetables, of which there are 140 species, natives of America; so called from Naupactus, a town of Etolia. The genus was formed by Mégerle, and adopted by Dejean and Schœnherr.

NAZARITISM. The vow and practice of the Nazarites, Jews who bound themselves to extraordinary purity of life and devotion; lit. inhabitants of Nazareth.

NEAPOLITANUS MORBUS. The venereal disease; so called because it was said to have been first discovered at Naples (Neapolis), when in possession of the French.—*Forsyth.*

NECKERA. A genus of cryptogamic plants; named in honour of Dr. Natalis Joseph de Necker, a German botanist to the Elector Palatine; born 1730, died 1793.

NEDDY. A life preserver; contraction of Kennedy, name of the first man, it is said, in St. Giles's, who had his head broken by a poker. *Vide* Mornings at Bow Street.—*J. C. H.*

NEEDHAMIA. A genus of Australian plants; named in honour of John Tuberville Needham, who, in his work, " An Account of Some New Microscopical Discoveries," gave the earliest account of the structure and economy of the pollen in plants.

NEGRO (Sp. and It. *id.*) A native or descendant of the black race of men in Africa. The word is never applied to the tawny or olive-coloured inhabitants of the northern coast of Africa, but to the more southern race of men, who are quite black; doubtless so called from dwelling in the country watered by the Niger. Hence *Nigritia* (Soudan), and perhaps the Latin word *niger*, black. Pliny calls the Negros *Nigritæ;* and their chief city, Guber or Cano, is called by Ptolemy *Nigira.*

NEGUS. A liquor made of wine, water, sugar, nutmeg, and lemon-juice; said to have been named after its first maker, Colonel Negus. Mr. Pulleyn says, " Wine and water first received this name from Francis Negus, Esq., in the reign of George I. Party spirit ran high at that period between whigs and tories, and wine-bibbing was resorted to as an excitement. On one occasion some leading whigs and tories having, *par accident*, got over their cups together, and Mr. Negus being present, and high words ensuing, he recommended them in future to dilute their wine as he did, which suggestion fortunately directed their attention from an argument which probably would have ended seriously, to one on the merits of wine and water, which concluded by their nicknaming it ' Negus.' "

NEILLIA. A genus of plants, nat. or. *Homaliaceæ ;* named after Patrick Neill, a Scotch botanist, secretary to the Wernerian and Caledonian Horticultural Societies of Edinburgh.

NEMESIA. In antiquity, a religious solemnity in memory of deceased persons ; so called from the goddess Nemesis, who was supposed to defend the relics and the memory of the dead from all insult.——A genus of herbaceous plants, nat. or. *Scrophulariaceæ.*

NEPTUNE. A large planet beyond Uranus, discovered in consequence of the computations of Le Verrier, of Paris, by Galle, of Berlin, Sep. 23, 1846 ; named after Neptune, god of the ocean. "Discovered theoretically in 1845 by Mr. Adams, of St. John's College, Cambridge " (*S. F. C.*)

NEPTUNIAN. Pertaining to the ocean or aqueous solution ; as *Neptunian* rocks, *Neptunian* theory ; the theory of Werner, which refers the formation of all rocks and strata to the agency of water ; opposed to the Plutonic theory ; so called from Neptune, god of the ocean.——One who adopts the theory that the substances of the globe were formed from aqueous solution.—*Pinkerton.*

NEUFCHATEL. A celebrated cream cheese, not, as the *Times* once asserted, made at Neufchatel in Switzerland, but Neufchatel-en-Bray in France, dep. Seine-Inférieure, also noted for its excellent butter.

NEWMARKET. In the sporting world, the ordinary methods of tossing are styled " two and three," and " five and nine," *i.e.* best out of three, best out of nine. Newmarket is first call, equivalent to "sudden death." Mr. J. C. Hotten makes it best two out of three, but I am told there never were any heats at Newmarket.

NEWTONIAN. A follower of or pertaining to Sir Isaac Newton, or formed or discovered by him, as the Newtonian philosophy or system.——A reflecting telescope of the form invented by Newton, in which, by means of a plane mirror, the image is reflected to the eye through one side of the tube, where it is viewed by the eyeglass.

NICARAGUA WOOD. The wood of a tree growing in Nicaragua, in Central America, used in dyeing red.

NICENE CREED. A summary of Christian faith, drawn up by the Council of Nice against Arianism, A.D. 325, altered and confirmed by the Council of Constantinople, A.D. 381. This was the first and most important general council ever held by the Christian Church. From Nice (now called by the Turks Isnik), a town of Asia Minor.

NICKEL (*Niccolum*). A metal, colour white or reddish-white, of great hardness, difficult to be purified, always magnetic, and, when perfectly pure, malleable and ductile. It doubtless had its name from its discoverer, a German. Nickel is found as a German surname, and in composition of local names, as Nickelhajen. Nickelsdorf (Prussia), Nickelstadt (Silesia).

NICOTIAN. Pertaining to or denoting tobacco; and, as a noun, tobacco. See NICOTIN.

NICOTIANA. A genus of plants, nat. or. *Solanaceæ;* called after M. Nicot, ambassador from the King of France to Portugal, who first introduced it into France in 1560.

NICOTIANINA or NICOTIANINE. A concrete or solid oil obtained from tobacco, and one of its active principles. See NICOTIN.

NICOTIN. An alkaloid obtained from tobacco, and one of its active principles. See NICOTIANINA.

NIERSTEINER. A good second-class wine, produced in the vineyards surrounding Nierstein, near Mayence, on the Rhine.

NILOMETER. A graduated column for measuring the increase and decrease of the Nile (Gr. μετρον, a measure).

NIOBIUM. A metal recently discovered in tantalite in Bavaria ; so named from Niobe, daughter of Tantalus.

NISSOLIA. A genus of South American plants ; named by Jacquin and Linnæus in memory of William Nissolle, M.D., of Montpellier, author of several botanical essays, and mentioned as an excellent naturalist by Tournefort, who dedicated a supposed genus to him.

NIVERNOIS. A hat much worn in 1770. " It was exceedingly small, and the flaps fastened up to the shallow crown, which was seen above them, by hooks and eyes. The corner worn in front was of the old spout or shovel shape, and stiffened out by a wire " (*Planché*). Doubtless so called from Le Nivernois or Nivernais, an old province of France, now composing dep. Nièvre; or from Nièvre, or its capital, Nevers, where they were first worn.

NIZZARD. A native of Nizza or Nice, in France ; formerly a division of the continental portion of Sardinia.

NOACHIAN. Pertaining to Noah, or to his time, as the Noachian flood.

NOBILI'S FIGURES. The name given to an electro-chemical phenomenon discovered by Nobili.

NONTRONITE. A mineral consisting of silica, peroxide of iron, alumina, magnesia, clay, and water, occurring in an ore of manganese, in the arrondissement of Nontron, France, dep. Dordogne.

NOOTH'S APPARATUS. A series of three glass vessels, placed vertically, for the purpose of impregnating water with carbonic acid gas (*Brande*) ; invented by Nooth.

NORFOLK CRAG (better known as Norwich Crag). In geology, an English tertiary formation, consisting of irregular, ferruginous, sandy clay, mixed with marine shells.

NORMAN. In seaman's language, a short wooden bar, to be thrust into a hole of the windlass, on which to fasten the cable ; probably named from the inventor.

NORTHAMPTON TABLES. Life assurance tables based upon the calculation of the average mortality in Northampton.

NORWICHER. More than one's share ; said of a person who leaves less than half the contents of a tankard for his companion. In what the term originated, or why Norwich was selected, before any other city, I have not been able to discover.—*J. C. H.*

NORY.　Mathematical tables comprising logarithms, numbers, sines, tangents, quo-sines, and quo-tangents, with minor tables of lunar phases and equations of time, calculated and published by the late Mr. Nory.

NUITS (*vin de Nuits*).　A fine Burgundy wine ; named from Nuits, dep. Côte-d'Or, situated in a fine wine country.

NUREMBERG EGGS.　The name given to watches, or pocket clocks, originally of an oval form, and generally believed to have been first invented at Nuremberg.　Cf. Proc. Soc. Antiq. Lond. May, 1848, p. 267, and Beckman, Orig. Invent.

NUSSIERITE.　A mineral containing phosphoric acid, arsenic acid, oxide of lead, lime, protoxide of iron, chloride of lead, and silica ; found at La Nussière, near Beaujeu, dep. Rhône, France.

NUTTALLITE.　A mineral occurring in prismatic crystals at Boston, in Massachusetts ; by some considered as identical with seapolite ; the wernerite of Haüy ; named after Professor Nuttall.

O.

OAKS.　See DERBY.

OBRINE (KNIGHTS OF).　A military order, instituted in the thirteenth century by Conrad, Duke of Mazovia and Cujavia, whom some authors call also Duke of Poland.　Conrad I. styled it the Order of Jesus Christ ; but he having put the knights in possession of Fort Obrine, in the county of Cedeliz, in Cujavia, they hence took the name of *Knights of Obrine*.　The principal object of the order was to oppose the incursions of the Prussians in Poland, but the Prussians blocking up the fort, so that none of the knights could get out, the order became useless, and was soon suppressed by Conrad, who called to his assistance the Teutonic Knights. — *T. Wright, M.A.*

OBSIDIANUM (*Vitrum obsidianum*, Plin.) A species of glass which resembled the obsidian stone (the *obsidianus lapis* of Pliny, in Isid. *obsius lapis*). Another name for the Chian marble. Some derive the word from οψις, seeing, being called by Greek writers οψιανος, and not οψιδιανος ; others from one Obsidius, who discovered it in Ethiopia. The stone was quite black and transparent, and therefore used for mirrors (Plin. H. N. xxxvi. 26); also images and various other things were made from it: hence, *Obsidiana imago ; Obsidianos elephantos*, Plin. *ib.*——A sort of colour with which vessels were glazed (*Plin.*)——Glass of antimony (*Labavius*). The terms obsidional crown, obsidional coins, are from a different root.

OBSIDIAN. Glossy lava, a mineral of two kinds, translucent and transparent, consisting chiefly of silica and alumina, with slight admixtures of potash, lime, soda, and the oxide of iron and manganese ; from obsidianum, *q.v.*

ŒDERA. A genus of plants, nat. or. *Compositæ ;* called after Œder, a Danish botanist.—*Crabb.*

OGYGIAN. Of great and dark antiquity (*Lempriere*) ; lit. pertaining to Ogyges, the most ancient monarch in Greece, and to a great deluge in Attica in his days. His death is fixed in Blair's Chronological Tables at B.C. 1764.

OHM'S LAW. An important law which refers to all the causes that tend to impede the action of the voltaic battery. It is, that "the intensity of an electric current, when a battery is in action, is directly as the whole electromotive force in operation, and inversely as the sum of all the impediments to conduction ;" named after Ohm, who discovered it.

OÏDIUM TUCKERI. The term *oïdium* (from Gr. ωον an egg, ειδος form), for the vine disease, was given it from the circumstance of the abnormal condition of the vine being attributed to a fungus propagated by sporules excessively minute, which are contained in an oval or egg-shaped seed-pod. Edward Tucker, a gardener in Margate, was the first to observe and notice it in England (in 1845) ; and hence it is to this day known under the name of *Oïdium Tuckeri.*

OISANITE or OYSANITE. A pyramidical ore of titanium, occurring abundantly near Oysans, in Dauphiné. It is the same with anatase and octahedrite, which are found in France, Norway, Spain, and some parts of South America.

OLBERS. A name given to the planet Pallas, after Dr. Olbers, by whom it was discovered in 1802.

OLDBUCK. An antiquary ; from the name of a character in Sir W. Scott's Antiquary.—*J. C. H.*

OLD NICK. The evil one ; from *Nick*, in the Northern mythology, an evil spirit of the waters. Knicker was one of the names of Odin, as the destroying or evil spirit. According to others, the term was derived from *Nicolo* Macchiavelli, the celebrated political writer. "Out of his surname they have coined an epithet for a knave, and out of his Christian name a synonyme for the devil" (*Ed. Rev.*, March, 1827).

> " Nick Machiavel had ne'er a trick,
> Tho' he gave his name to our old Nick."
> Hudibras, Part iii., Canto 1.

OLÉRON LAWS. The laws, constituencies, or judgments of Oléron are a capitulary of ancient maritime customs, written in old French, and bearing the name of Oléron for several centuries, because tradition points to the island so called, in the French department of Charente-Inférieure, as the place of their original promulgation. It has been commonly held that these laws were made by Richard I. of England, at Oléron, on his return from the Holy Land, but there is no ground for the statement, and there are strong reasons for assigning them to an earlier date than that of Richard I.

OLIVER. A dogcart, or wheel carriage, on the American plan, lately built by Mr. Mulliner, of Northampton, of imported hickory ; named after Captain Oliver, of Sholebooke Lodge, Towcester, for whom it was first made.——The moon. "Oliver don't whiddle," *i.e.*, The moon does not shine (Bulwer's P. Clifford).

OLYMPIAD. A period of four years, reckoned from one celebration of the Olympic games to another, and constituting an important epoch in history and chronology. The first Olympiad commenced 776 years B.C., and 23 years before the foundation of Rome. The computation by Olympiads ceased at the 364th Olympiad, in the year 440 of the Christian era. See next.

OLYMPIC GAMES, or OLYMPICS. Solemn games among the ancient Greeks, dedicated to Olympian Jupiter, celebrated once in four years at Olympia.

ONANISM. The crime of the Scripture Onan.

ONOFRITE. A mineral composed of mercury, sulphur, and selenium ; occurring at San Onofre, in Mexico ; also near Clausthal, in the Harz.

OPUNTIA. The same with Cactus Opuntia ; "ab opunte, from the city Opus, near which it flourished" (*Forsyth*). A name given by botanists to those cactaceous plants which gardeners call Indian figs. On one of them, Opuntia co-chenillifera, the cochineal insect is fed, and others yield a pleasant subacid fruit, which is eaten in hot countries.

ORENBURGH GUM (*Gummi Orenburgense*). A gum which issues from the pinus larix, whence the larch forests in Russia take fire ; so called from Orenburg, an extensive government of the Russian empire, where it is found.

ORGEIS. A fish, called also organ-ling ; supposed to be from the Orkneys, on whose coast it is taken.—*Johnson*.

ORICIA. A species of fir or turpentine tree ; from Oricus, a city of Epirus, near which it grows.—*Forsyth*.

ORIGENISM. The doctrines or tenets of Origen of Alexandria, one of the earliest and most learned of the Greek Fathers, who flourished in the third century. He united Platonism with Christianity ; supposed that human souls existed before their union with bodies ; that they were origi-nally holy, but became sinful in the pre-existent state ; that all men probably will at last be saved, and that Christ is again to die for the salvation of devils.—*Murdock*.

ORLEANS. A cloth made of worsted and cotton, used for dresses, &c. ; from Orleans, in France.——Orleans (vulg. *arline*) plum, a large and common variety of plum.

ORONOCO or ORONOKO. One of the principal kinds of tobacco imported into England from Orinoco, one of the great divisions of the republic of Venezuela, South America.

ORONTIACEÆ. A genus of herbaceous plants; named from *Orontum*, the principal genus, of which there are only two species—*Aquatic O.*, native of rivers and pools in North America, and *Japan O.*, both perennials, and cultivated at Kew. The genus is said to have been so called from growing on the banks of the Orontes, in Syria.

ORPHEAN or ORPHIC. Pertaining to Orpheus, a poet who had the power of moving inanimate bodies by the music of his lyre; as, *Orphic* hymns.

ORPHICA. Certain works falsely ascribed to Orpheus, which embodied the opinions of a class of persons described by Müller. Fabricius's Bibliotheca Græca contains a list of the writings ascribed to Orpheus. But see Tiedemann's Initia Philos. Græc., p. 1-100; Fabric., Bib. Græc. I., p. 140; Clinton's Fasti; Funke's Real. Schullexicon; P. Cyc., " Orphica."

ORRERY. An astronomical machine for exhibiting the several motions of the heavenly bodies. It was invented by George Graham, but Rowley, a workman, borrowed one from him, and made a copy for the Earl of Orrery, after whom it was named by Sir Richard Steele. Similar machines are called also planetariums (*Barlow*). The origin of the term " orrery " is thus given by Mr. Desaguliers, in his Course of Experimental Philosophy, 4to, London, 1734, I. p. 431. After stating his belief that Mr. George Graham, about 1700, first invented a movement for exhibiting the motion of the earth about the sun at the same time that the moon revolved round the earth, he remarks, " This machine being in the hands of an instrument maker, to be sent with some of his own instruments to Prince Eugene, he copied it, and made the first for the late Earl of Orrery, and then several others, with additions of his own. Sir Richard Steele, who knew nothing of Mr. Graham's machine, in one of his lucubrations, thinking to do justice to the first encourager, as well as to the inventor, of such a curious instrument, called it an *orrery*, and gave Mr. J. Rowley the praise due to Mr. Graham" (*P. Cyc.*)

ORVIETAN (Fr. *orviétan*). An antidote or counter poison; also a charlatan, an empiric; It. *orvietano*; so called from a charlatan of Orvieto, who first made it. "From a mountebank of Orvieta (Orvieto?), in Italy, who first made himself famous by taking such things upon the stage, after doses of pretended poisons. Though some say its inventor was one H. F. Orvietanus, and that it is named after him" (*Forsyth*). Ménage (writing in 1694) says the charlatan in question was not long since living in Paris.

OSBECKIA. A plant of two species, the one, native of the East Indies and China, called by the Chinese *komm-hyong-loaa*, "feather of gold roses;" the other, native of Ceylon, where it was found by Kœnig ; named by Linnæus in honour of Peter Osbeck, rector of Hasloef and Woxtorp, in Sweden ; member of the Academy of Stockholm, &c. ; author of a Voyage to China and the East Indies in 1751.

OSMANLI. The language of the Osman or Ottoman Turks, who form the ruling portion of the Turkish empire. "It is spoken by persons of rank and education, and by all government authorities in Syria, in Egypt, at Tunis, and at Tripoli. In the southern provinces of Asiatic Russia, along the borders of the Caspian, and through the whole of Turkestan it is the language of the people. It is heard even at the Court of Teheran, and is understood by official personages in Persia" (*Max Müller*). The word originated in Othman or Osman, a sultan who assumed the government about 1300, and whose descendants were called Osmanli or Ottomans.

OSMUND. A plant of the genus *Osmunda*, whose most remarkable species is the Osmund royal, or flowering fern, which is used in stiffening linen. "According to Gerarde (herbal), it is a type or memorial of one Osmund, a waterman, whose history had not come down even to that old writer, but whose heart, he says, was commemorated in the core of the root." "Osmunda, from Osmund, who first used it" (*Forsyth*).

OSNABURG. A species of coarse linen, of which there are two kinds, the one white, the other brown ; imported from Osnaburg (Osnabrück), Hanover.

OTAHEITE SALEP. Another name for Tacca starch, or Tahiti arrowroot; from Tahiti, or Otaheite, the principal of the Society Islands.

OTTOA. A genus of umbelliferous plants; named in honour of Frederick Otta, a Prussian botanist.

OTTOMAN. A sort of thick-stuffed mat used by the Turks or Ottomans.——In England, a stool with a stuffed seat.

OTTRELITE. A mineral, colour blackish-grey, greenish-grey, black; found in clay slate at Ottrez, near Stavelot, on the frontier of Luxemburg.

OUT-HEROD. To overact the character of Herod, which in the old plays was always a violent one.—*Smart.*

> " It out-herod's Herod."—Hamlet.

OXFORD CLAY. Clunch clay; a great argillaceous bed interposed between the lower and the middle oolite. In its lower part are beds of limestone called Kelloway rock.

OZARKITE. A mineral occurring with elœolite at the Ozark Mountains, Arkansas.

P.

PACCHIONIAN GLANDS. The small round whi ι.h granulations found in the superior longitudinal sinus of the membranes of the brain, which Pacchioni incorrectly described as *conglobate glands.*

PACTOLIAN. Pertaining to Pactolus, a river of Lydia, famous for its golden sands.—*Webster.*

PACTOLUS. A genus of brachyurous crustacea, of only one species, locality unknown (*Encyc. Met.*); named from the River Pactolus.

PADDY, PAT, or PADDY WHACK. An Irishman.

> " I'm Paddy Whack, from Ballyhack,
>   Not long ago turn'd soldier ;
> In storm and sack, in front attack,
>   None other can be boulder."—Irish Song.

From Paddy, nickname for Patricius. "The meanest subjects of the Roman empire assumed the *illustrious* name of *Patricius*, which, by the conversion of Ireland, has been communicated to a whole nation " (Gibbon, vol. 6, c. xxxvi.)

PADRA. A kind of black tea of superior quality; perhaps from Padra, a town of Guzerat.

PADUAN COINS. A modern coin, closely imitating the antique; or a new medal struck with all the marks and characters of antiquity. The name is derived from Paduan or Paduanus, who succeeded so well in this kind of forgery that the best judges are at a loss to distinguish his medals from genuine ones. Paduan, who flourished in the seventeenth century, was called, from his birthplace, Padua; his proper name was Giovanni Cavino (others say Lewis Lee). Gotlieb Rink says he had an associate in his forgery named Alexander Bassianus. His son Octavian, though born at Rome, was also called the Paduan. Properly, those medals only are called *Paduan* that are struck on the matrices of the elder *Paduan*, which are still preserved. The term, however, is commonly applied to medals generally that closely imitate the ancient, and are of masterly execution. Joubert observes that there have been a *Paduan* and a *Parmesan* in Italy, and a *Carteron* in Holland, who had the knack of imitating the antique in perfection. The Parmesan was Laurentius Parmesanus. We may also add another Italian who excelled in this way, viz., Valerius Bellus Vicentinus.

PADUASOY. A kind of silk stuff from Padua (Fr. *soie*, silk). "By tailors called Paddaway, a mispronunciation of Padua" (*S. F. C.*)

PÆAN or PEAN (Gr. παιάν). Among the ancients, a song of rejoicing in honour of Παιών, Apollo: hence a loud and joyous song; a song of triumph.

PÆON (Gr. παιών; written also, though less correctly, pæan). In ancient poetry, a foot of four syllables, of which there were four kinds; so called from Παιών, Apollo.

PÆONY (παιωνία). A plant and flower of the genus *Pæonia*, nat. or. *Ranunculaceæ*; so called from Παιων, Apollo, who is said to have first applied it to medicinal purposes.

PAISBERGITE. A mineral allied to Rhodonite; from Paisberg's iron mine, in Phillipstadt, Sweden.

PAISLEY. A shawl made at Paisley, co. Renfrew (Scotland); celebrated also for its manufactures of silk and other shawls, muslin, cotton thread, and ornamental fancy goods.

PAIXHAN. A howitzer of great weight and strength, used by the Americans for throwing shells of a very large size, first adopted in France about 1824; named after the inventor, Henri Joseph Paixhans, general of artillery in the French army, author of many military works; born in 1783 at Metz, in France.

PALACE. A magnificent house in which an emperor, king, or other distinguished person resides; from the **Fr.** *palais*, L. *palatium*; so named from the first imperial residence on the Palatium or Palatine Hill, one of the seven hills of Rome, the first that was built upon. The emperor Augustus dwelt on this hill, and many fine palaces were consequently built there.

PALADIN (anc. *palatin*, i.e. man of the palace, of the court). A knight-errant. In the old romances the name was given to certain knights whose whole occupation was to seek adventures, and to find out occasions to exercise their valour and to prove their gallantry. At the close of their adventures they retired in the palaces of the princes, where they were received with courtesy, and notably in the palace of King Arthur, at whose court, it is said, commenced the mania of knight-errantry. See PALACE.

PALAGONITE. A mineral found as an ingredient of the volcanic tufa near Palagonia, in the Val di Noto, in Sicily, and also in Iceland.

PALAMPO. A quilt or bed-cover; probably from Palanpore, a town of India, renowned for its manufacture of chintz counterpanes.—*J. C. Hotten.*

PALAVIA. A genus of South American plants, of two species; named by Linnæus in honour of Dr. Antonio Palau y Verdera, professor of botany in the royal garden at Madrid.

PALEMPUREZ. A kind of carpet brought from the East Indies. "Palemporez, a species of Indian dimity, of elegant patterns, used for bed coverlets. They are sometimes flowered with gold, made of silk, and worked in shawl and other patterns of coloured woven cotton" (*Simmonds*); doubtless from Pahlunpore, pres. Bombay; or Pahlunpore in Guzerat.

PALLADIUM (Gr. παλλαδιον). Something that affords effectual defence, protection, and safety; as when we say the trial by jury is the *palladium* of our civil rights; primarily, a statue of Pallas, which represented her as sitting with a pike in her right hand, and in her left a distaff and spindle. On the preservation of this statue depended the safety of Troy. "The Romans, imagining that Æneas brought the true Palladium to Rome, preserved the image with the utmost care as their safeguard" (*Crabb*).——A metal drawn from crude platina, discovered by Wollaston in 1803.

PALLAS. A new planet discovered by Dr. Olbers, of Bremen, in 1802; named after Pallas, goddess of wisdom.

PALLASIA. A genus of North American plants, nat. or. *Corymbiferæ*; named by Linnæus in honour of Dr. Peter Simon Pallas, the celebrated Prussian naturalist.

PALMERSTONISM. The ism of Lord Palmerston; old-soldierism; soft-soap; lip-salve for the million; rhodomontade.

PANDEAN PIPES. An ancient wind instrument made of reeds; named after Pan, god of shepherds, &c., who invented the flute with seven reeds, which he called Syrinx, in honour of a beautiful nymph of the same name.

PANDER, prop. PANDAR. A pimp, a procurer.

> "To whom you should have been a pandar."
>
> M. W. of Windsor.

> "Troilus the first employer of pandars."
>
> M. Ado about Nothing.

> "Camillo was his help in this, his pandar."—W.'s Tale.

> "Let all pitiful goers-between be call'd to the world's end after my name; call them all pandars."—Troilus and Cress.

Pandarus is the name of one of the characters in Shakespeare's Troilus and Cressida. "From Pandarus (says Skinner), who procured the love and good graces of Chryseis; which imputation, it may be added, depends upon no better authority than the fabulous histories of Dictys Cretensis and Dares Phrygius."

PANIC (Sp. and It. *panico;* Fr. *panique;* Gr. πανικοσ). Sudden fright ; particularly a sudden fright without real cause, or terror inspired by a trifling cause or misapprehension of danger ; as, *panic* fear, *i.e.* extreme or sudden fear; the troops were seized with a panic ; they fled in a panic ; *lit.* agitated by Pan, the frightful deity of the woods or shepherds, also god of huntsmen, and all (παν) the people of the country. "Poly-næus fetches the origin of the phrase (panic fear) from *Pan,* one of the captains of Bacchus, who, with a few men, put a numerous army to rout, by a noise which his soldiers raised in a rocky valley, favoured with a great number of echoes. This stratagem making their number appear much greater than it really was, the enemy quitted a very commodious encampment and fled. Hence all ill-grounded fears have been called *panics* or *panic fears;* and it was this that gave occasion to the fable of the nymph Echo being beloved by the god Pan. Others derive the origin of the expression hence ; that, in the wars of the Titans against the gods, Pan was the first who struck terror into the hearts of the giants. Theon on Aratus says he did it by means of a sea-shell, which served him for a trumpet, whereof he was the inventor" (*Chambers's Cyc.*)

PANSLAVONIC. A term used to express a union of all the Slavonic nations (παν, all).

PANTALOON (Fr. *pantalon*). A garment for males, in which breeches and stockings are in a piece (*obs.*); in the plural, *pantaloons,* a sort of close long trowsers. —— A character in the Italian comedy.——A character in panto-mimes.

> " And as the French we conquer'd once
> Now give us laws for *pantaloons,*
> The length of breeches."—Hudib. pt. 1, c. 3.

" The next age shifts into the leane and slipper'd *pantaloone.*"—As You Like it.

Webster queries the W. *pannu,* to involve, or *panu,* to cover, and Fr. *talon,* the heel. Addison says the pantaloon in Italian comedies was so called from his close dress. Meyrick says, " From the circumstance of the *standard-bearers* of the Venetian army wearing tight hose, that kind of dress came to be called *pantaloons*, a corruption of *pianta leone*, i.e. ' plant of Leon,' the *standard* of the Republic being the ' Lion of St. Mark.' " ! ! ! Charpentier (Origines) says the name and the usage of the pantalon was derived from the Venetians, who first introduced this habit, which they called *pantaloni*, from St. Pantaléon, their patron ; that according to others, *Pantalon* was the name of a buffoon in the Italian theatre, clothed ordinarily in this manner, which gave the name of *pantalon* first to those who wore this sort of chaussure, and finally to the chaussure itself. **J. B. J.** Breton (Voyage en Piémont, 8º, 1803, vol. 1, p. 167, and note 12 at end), alluding to the origin of the characters of harlequin, pantaloon, punch, &c., says each of these masked personages was originally destined to characterise the principal towns of Italy. " Pantaleone étoit un marchand Vénitien ; Dottore, un médecin de Bologne ; Spaviento, un tirailleur ou spadassin de Naples ; Pulhcinella, un goguenard de la Pouille (Apulia), province du même royaume de Naples, dont on prétendoit que la plupart des habitans étaient bossus ou contrefaits ; Giangvrla et Coviello, des paysans de la Calabre ; Gelsomino, un petit maître de Rome ; Beltrame, un niais de Milan ; Brighella, un intrigant de Ferrara ; et enfin Arlechino, un valet de Bergamo." There is a town in Italy called Pantaleone, and Pantaleone is also a surname. Charpentier says also that *pantalon* is the appellation of a vertical harpsicord, having a body straighter than the ordinary harpsicord, and that it was named after its inventor, Pantaléon Hebenstreit, who made it known at the court of Dresden in 1718.

PAOLO (Paul). A Roman coin. See **PAUL.**

PAPHIAN. Pertaining to the rights of Venus, who was worshipped at Paphos (hod. Baffa), a city of Cyprus.

PAPIRIA (LEX). The Jus Papirianum was a collection of ancient Roman laws, containing those made by the kings of Rome, and compiled immediately after their expulsion. It is supposed to have been collected by Sextus or Publius Papirius, and is sometimes called the Lex Papiria.

PAPIST (Fr. *papiste*, It. *papista*). A Roman Catholic ;

one that adheres to the Church of Rome and the authority of the *Papa* or Pope.

PARACELSIAN. A follower of Paracelsus, a celebrated Swiss physician, who lived at the close of the fifteenth century. ——The medical practice of Paracelsus.

PARADISE. French slang for the gallery of a theatre, "up amongst the gods."—*J. C. Hotten.*

PARADISEA. Bird of Paradise, a genus of birds, or. *Picæ*, which chiefly inhabit New Guinea.

PARADISUS (*Granum Paradisi*, grain of Paradise). A pungent seed resembling cardamom ; named on account of its virtues.

PARAMATTA. A soft woollen fabric used for dresses, &c.; named from Paramatta, a town of New South Wales, where it is manufactured.

PARCHMENT (L. *pergamēna;* Fr. *parchemin;* Norm. *pargam, pargemin,* a MS. on parchment; Armor. *parich, parichemin;* It. *pargameno;* Sp. *pargamino;* G. *pergament;* D. *parkement*). The skin of a sheep or goat prepared and rendered fit for writing on. It was invented B.C. 198 by Eumenes II., king of Pergamos, in Asia, in consequence of the prohibition of the export of papyrus from Egypt by Ptolemy Epiphanes. Pliny says, "Eumenes having established a rival library to that of Ptolemy Epiphanes, the Egyptian monarch, in a fit of jealousy, forbade the exportation of papyrus from his dominions, and that the invention of parchment (*Charta Pergamēna*), or perhaps the improvement of this material, was the consequence."

PARGASITE. A mineral, a variety of hornblende, colour greyish or bluish green ; from Isle Pargas, in Finland.

PARIAN. A superior kind of white marble; named from Paros, an isle in the Ægæan Sea, where it was found.——A chronicle of the city of Athers, which was engraved on marble in capital letters in the Isle of Paros. It contained a chronological account of events from Cecrops, 1582 B.C., to the archonship of Diognetus, 264 B.C. ; but the chronicle o the last ninety years is lost. This marble was procured from Asia Minor in 1627 by the Earl of Arundel, and, being broken, the pieces are called *Arundelian marbles*. They are now deposited in the University of Oxford. The antiquity of the inscription has been disputed.—*P. Cyc. Edin. Encyc.*

PARIS. A genus of plants, nat. or. *Melanthaceæ*, of two species, natives of most parts of Europe, particularly the northern parts, and also of Japan. The juice of *P. quadrifolia*, Herb Paris, True-Love, or One-Berry, has been considered useful in inflammations of the eyes. Ambrosinus derives the word *a paritate foliorum*, from the uniformity or equality of the four leaves, which make, as it were, two pairs, equally situated; but it was more probably named after Paris, who adjudged the golden apple to Venus.

PARKINSONIA. A plant, a small tree, called in Jamaica Jerusalem thorn; named by Plumier in memory of John Parkinson, apothecary of London, author of Paradisus Terrestris, 1629, and Theatrum Botanicum, 1640.

PARMESAN. A delicate kind of cheese made at Parma, in Italy.

PARNASSIA. A genus of plants, nat. or. *Saxifragaceæ*; said to be called from Mount Parnassus, on which, according to Dioscorides, a plant called *gramen Parnassi* grew. The name was altered by Tournefort to Parnassia.

PARNASSIAN. Pertaining to Parnassus, a celebrated mountain in Greece, sacred to Apollo and the Muses.

PARNEL. A wanton immodest girl; a slut; doubtless named from a character in one of the old plays; probably corrupted from *Petronilla*, a feminine diminutive of *Peter*.

PARSEEISM. The religion of the Parsees or fire-worshippers of India; substantially the religion of the ancient Persians. In Persia they are called by the Mohammedans, Guebers, infidels, and their sacred book is the *Zend-Avesta*. The Parsees, who reside near Surat and Bombay, are an honest thrifty people, and number about 700,000.

PARTSCHIN. A mineral found in sand from Olahpian, in Hungary, with rutil, ilmenite, zircon, and kyanite; named after P. Partsch, of the Vienna Museum.

PASCALIN. A mathematical instrument invented by the celebrated French mathematician Pascal.

PASQUINADE (found *pasquin* and *pasquil*). A lampoon, a satirical writing.

"He never valued any *pasquils* that were dropped up and down, to think them worthy of his revenge."—*Howel.*

"The *pasquils*, lampoons, and libels we meet with now-a-days are a sort of playing with the four and twenty letters, without sense, truth, or wit."—*Tatler.*

Pasquino was the name of a Roman cobbler who was remarkable for his sneers and gibes. Near his shop, in a corner of the palace of the Orsini, was dug up a mutilated statue, which was called Pasquin. From it having been customary, in later times, to paste satiric papers upon this statue, is said to have originated the word pasquinade. "Pasquin, the name given to a mutilated ancient statue which stood at the corner of the Palace Santobuono, in a small open place in the city of Rome, near the Piazza Navona. It represents a warrior in the attitude of defence. The subject of the statue is not known. Pasquino was the name of a tailor who lived in that neighbourhood 'many years since,' says Parisio in his Antiquities of Rome, published A.D. 1600. The shop of Pasquino was a sort of place of meeting for the people of the district, who came there to tell or hear the news of the day, as is still the custom in the apothecaries' shops in the provincial towns of Italy. The tailor was a facetious man, and his witty sayings were styled 'Pasquinate,' which afterwards became a common appellation for humourous epigrams and sarcastic lampoons, a kind of composition for which the modern Romans are noted. These lampoons, which often attacked people in high stations, and the government itself, were fixed in the night on or near the statue already mentioned; and thus the statue itself came to be called Pasquino, as being the representative of the witty tailor of that name. Collections of these epigrams have been made, and some of them are very witty, though often scurrilous and coarse" (*P. Cyc.*) The writer in the Encyc. des Gens du Monde concludes: "Le muet Pasquin recevait sur son piédestal les satires et les épigrammes adressées à la cour du souverain pontife, et il entretenait à cet égard un échange incessant de bons mots avec un confrère du nom de Marforio. Cet usage durait encore à l'entrée des troupes françaises dans les États pontificaux. Par extension, on a nommé *pasquinade* toute raillerie satirique lancée contre le public ou contre les gens en place. Mais en général, une *pasquinade* est un bon mot de bas étage." For a full account of Pasquino, see Ménage, quoting Castelvetto, in his work entitled *Ragioni d'alcune cose segnate nella Canzone di Messer' Annibal Caro*.

PATAGONULA. A genus of plants, nat. or. *Cordiaceæ ;* natives of Patagonia, in South America.

PATAVINITY. The use of local words, or the peculiar style or diction of Livy, the Roman historian ; so called from Patavium (Padua), in Italy, where he was born.

PAUL (It. *Paolo*). A silver coin of Tuscany and the States of the Church, with its double, half, and quarter. In the former forty-six, and in the latter forty-five pauls are equal to an English sovereign ; named after one of the Popes of Rome.

PAUL PRY. An inquisitive person ; so named from a character in the well-known play of the same name, in which the late Mr. Liston gained much celebrity.——" An infamous newspaper so called, now extinct " (*S. F. C.*)

PAULLINIA. A climbing shrub, some species of which are natives of the East Indies, and others of the West Indies, Jamaica, Mexico, the Caribees, Curaçao, South America, &c.; named by Linnæus after Simon Paulli, professor of botany at Copenhagen, author of Botanicum Quadripartitum, 1640, and Flora Danica, 1648.

PAUSANIA. A Spartan festival in honour of Pausanias, under whose conduct the Greeks defeated Mardonius at Platææ. At this feast there were public games, in which free-born Spartans only were allowed to contend. An oration was always spoken in praise of Pausanias.

PAVAN or PAVIN (Fr. *pavane*, It. and Sp. *pavana*). A grave dance among the Spaniards.

> " Your Spanish *pavin* [is] the best dance."
> *B. Jonson.* The Alchymist, Act iv. sc. 2.

"And with that turning up of his mustachoes, and marching as if he would begin a *paven*, he went toward Zelmane."—*Sidney*. Arcadia, b. iii.

"Then he's a rogue, and a passy-measure *pavin*; I hate a drunken rogue."—*Shaks*. Tw. N.

"Spanish pavan—The 'Engelsche indraeyende Dans Londesteyn' (the turning dance of London) in Friesche Lust-Hof, 1634, is another version of this tune. The two first bars are identical. *I love my love for love again*, in the Skene MS., is the same after the first eight bars. 'Pavan. Instrumental players play the pavan faster,' says Thoinot Arbeau, 'and call it the passamezzo'—*Anglicé*, the passing measures' pavan. Puttenham says, 'Songs, for secret recreation and pastime in chambers, with company or alone, were the ordinary musickes amorous; such as might be sung with voice, or to the lute, cithern, or harpe; or daunced by measures—as the Italian pavan and gulliard are at these daies in princes' courts, and other places of honourable or civil assembly'" (Art of Poesie, p. 37, reprint). See also Chappell's Popular Music, 157, 242; 772, 776. "In this dance the performers make a kind of wheel before each other, the gentlemen dancing with cap and sword, princes with long robes, and the ladies with long trails, the motions resembling the stately steps of the peacock (*pavo*)" (*Encyc.; Sp. Dict.*) Hawkins likewise derives the word from *pavo*, a peacock; but according to the Italian writers, *pavan* is derived from *Paduana*, i.e. a Paduan dance, a dance from Padua.

PAVIN. See PAVAN.

PEA (A. S. *pisa*, Fr. *pois*, It. *pisello*, L. *pisum*, Gr. πισον). A plant of the genus Pisum, *q.v.*

PEACH (It. *pesca*, Fr. *pêche*, G. *pfirsiche*, Arab. *firsic*). A tree, and its fruit of many varieties. The word is derived from *pessicum*, for *Persicum malum*, a peach; *persica*, a peach-tree; literally a tree and fruit from Persia.

PECKSNIFF. A hypocritical rascal; from a character in Dickens's Martin Chuzzlewit (*J. C. Hotten*); a character said to be founded on that of a late shifty minister, whose memory is still much revered by the present age of hypocrisy and humbug.

PEDRO XIMENES. A sweet Spanish wine of the sherry grape ; named after the grower.

PEELER. A vulgar appellation given to a policeman ; so called after the late Sir Robert Peel, who brought in the Police Act. " Properly applied to the Irish constabulary rather than the City police, the former force having been established by Sir Robert Peel " (*J. C. Hotten*).

PEEPING TOM. A nickname for a curious prying fellow, derived from an old legendary tale told of a tailor of Coventry, who, when Godiva, Countess of Chester, rode at noon quite naked through that town, in order to procure certain immunities for the inhabitants (notwithstanding the rest of the people shut up their houses), slily peeped out of a hole in his house, for which he was miraculously struck blind. His figure, peeping out of a window, is still kept up in remembrance of the transaction, and an annual procession is still held at Coventry, in which the feat of Lady Godiva is attempted to be represented without violating the principles of public decency. See Halliwell.

PEGASUS. One of the forty-eight old northern constellations, figured in the form of a winged horse ; so called from Pegasus, Πηγασος, a winged horse, generated from the blood of Medusa, when Perseus cut off her head.——A genus of fishes with large pectoral fins, by means of which they take short flights or leaps through the air.

PELAGIANISM. The doctrines of Pelagius, a monk of Bangor, in Wales, who lived in the fourth century. He denied original sin, and asserted the doctrine of free will and the merit of good works.

PENÆA. A genus of plants, natives of the Cape ; named by Linnæus in honour of Peter Pena, a learned Frenchman, who afforded great assistance to Lobel in the composition of his Adversaria Botanica, published in 1570.

PENTELIC. The appellation of a marble resembling the Parian, but somewhat denser and finer grained, with occasional greenish zones, produced by greenish talc, whence it is called by the Italians *cipilino statuario*. The Parthenon, Propyleum, the Hippodrome, and other monuments at Athens were made of this marble, of which fine specimens may be seen among the Elgin collection in the British Museum. It was named from Mount Penteles, near Athens, where it was found.

PENTZIA. A genus of plants, natives of the Cape; named by Thunberg after his pupil J. C. Pentz.

PEPYSIAN. A valuable collection of MSS. of naval memoirs, prints, ancient English poetry, &c., bequeathed to Magdalen College, Cambridge, by Samuel Pepys, secretary to the Admiralty, temp. Charles II. and James II., is called the *Pepysian* Library, in honour of the donor.

PERALTIA. A genus of leguminous plants, subor. *Cæsalpiniæ*, subshrubs, natives of Mexico; named in honour of Joseph Peralt, a Spanish botanist, who assisted Humboldt in collecting several botanical specimens in South America.

PERCYLITE. A mineral, colour sky-blue, found in minute crystals, accompanied by gold, in a matrix of quartz and red oxide of iron; said to have come from La Sonora, in Mexico; analysed by Dr. Percy.

PERESKIA. A genus of plants, nat. or. *Cactaceæ*, shrubs and trees; named by Plumier in honour of Nicholas Fabricius Peiresk, a senator of Aix, in Provence, celebrated for his botanical learning.

PERKINISM. A mode of treatment introduced by Perkins, of America, consisting in the application, to diseased parts, of the extremities of two needles made of different metals, called by him *metallic tractors*.

PERKINS. Beer; dandy or affected shortening of the more widely-known slang phrase, "Barclay and Perkins."— *J. C. Hotten.*

PERMIAN. A geological term applied to magnesian limestone by Sir R. Murchison; from Perm, a province of Russia, where this is a prominent characteristic.—*S. F. Creswell.*

PEROWSKITE. A mineral, consisting of titanic acid, lime, magnesia, and protoxide of iron; found at Vogsburg, on the Kaiserstuhl, and at Achmatowsk, near Slatoust, in the

Ural; named in honour of Von Perowski, of St. Petersburg. The mineral tetraphyline is called perowskine.

PERROQUET or PARRAKEET (Fr. *perroquet*). A small species of parrot. Some derive the French word from *Perrot*, diminutive of *Pierre* (Peter), the man's name given to the bird. Ménage says, "Nous avons donné des noms d'homme aux animaux. C'est ainsi que nous avons appelé un merle, *Sansonnet*; un pie, *Margot*; un corbeau, *Colas*; un geay, *Richard*; un asne, *Martin*; un singe, *Robert*; un écureuil, Fouquet; une chèvre, Guionne; et en Basse Normandie, *Janne*." According to others, *perroquet* is a diminutive of *parrot*; from L. *parra*, a bird whose cry was esteemed an ill omen, perhaps a jay; but *parrot* itself may have even been corrupted from *perroquet*. "Probably *parrot* is a contracted form of some Spanish or Portuguese word derived from *parra*" (*S. F. C.*)

PERRYAN. A celebrated steel pen invented by the late Mr. James Perry, of London.

PERSEPOLITAN. Pertaining to Persepolis, or its architecture; in ancient geography, the cap. of Persis Proper and of the Persian Empire.

PERSEUS. A northern constellation of fifty-nine stars, the principal of which is Algenib; named after Perseus, son of Jupiter by Danaë.

PERSIAN FIRE (*Persicus ignis*). A term applied by Avicenna to a carbuncle attended with pustules and vesications.

PERSIAN WHEEL. A contrivance for raising water to some height above the level of a stream, by means of a wheel with buckets on its rim.—*Brande.*

PERSICA. A genus of plants, nat. or. *Rosaceæ*, the fruit of which is known by the English name of *peach* and *nectarine*; so called from Persia, of which it is a native.

PERSICARIA, POLYGONUM PERSICARIA. A plant; so called because its blossoms are like those of the *persica* or peach.

PESTALOZZIAN. Pertaining to the system of education founded by Pestalozzi, a philosopher and philanthropist, who was born at Zurich in 1745, and died in 1827. Pestalozzi's method turns on the idea of communicating all instruction by immediate address to the sensations or conceptions, and effecting the education of the child by constantly calling all his powers into exercise. He composed some works illustrative of his plans, and, among other productions of a moral tendency, wrote the romance of " Leinhard and Gertrude."

PETAGNA. A genus of herbs, natives of Sicily ; named in honour of Vincent Petagna, a Neapolitan botanist, author of Institutiones Botanicæ, 1787.

PETER. A very common oath or imprecation in the early English writers ; "by St. Peter." Cowslips. Arch. xxx. 411. ——A portmanteau or cloak bag (a bundle or valise, Bulwer's Paul Clifford).——A cash-box.——Formerly a familiar epithet applied to the watermen, fishermen, and mariners of the Thames (*Giff.*)——A wine, one of the richest and most delicate of the Malaga wines, generally termed *Peter-see-me*, q.v.

PETER-BOAT. A fishing-boat ; a small boat formed alike at stem and stern, and which may be rowed with either foremost at pleasure ; or, as Fosbrooke has described it, " precisely the Roman *amphiprora*." See PETER-MAN.

PETER-MAN. " A familiar term for a fisherman ; from the occupation of St. Peter " (*T. Wright, M.A.*) "Peterer or Peterman, one who follows hackney and stage coaches, and cuts off the portmanteaus and trunks from behind. *Nearly obsolete. Ancient* term for a fisherman, still used at Gravesend " (*J. C. Hotten*). Cowel, however, renders Peter-men, " those who used unlawful arts or engines for catching fish on the River Thames." See also Stow's Survey of London, p. 19. May not the word, therefore, have been originally *peder-men*, i.e. men who unlawfully used baskets or *peds* to catch fish with ? The word Peterman seems also to have had another meaning. John Aubrey, in one of his MSS., says of Kington Langley, near Chippenham, " Here was a chapel dedicated to *St. Peter*. The *Revel* is still kept (1670) the Sunday after *St. Peter's* Day: it is one of the eminentest feastes in these partes. Old John Wastefield told me that he had been *Peterman* in the beginning of Her Majesty's reign." A correspondent of N. & Q., referring to the above, asks, " Is it probable that the *Peter-*

man was a sort of master of the ceremonies at the revel ?"
See N. & Q., vol. vi., No. 149, Sep. 4, 1852, p. 223.

PETER-PENCE. An annual tax or tribute formerly paid
by the English to the Pope ; being a penny for every house,
payable at Lammas Day ; so called from St. Peter. It was
called also *Romescot.—Hall.*

PETER - SEE - ME, PETER-SA - MEENE, PETER-
SEMINE, or PETER. A rich Malaga wine.

> " Peter-see-me shall wash thy nowl,
> And Malligo glasses fox thee."
>
> *Middl.* Span. Gipsy, iii. 7.

Said to be corrupted from *Pedro Ximenes* (q.v.), name of a
Spanish wine.

PETER'S FISH. The haddock. It has spots on either
side, which are said to be marks of St. Peter's fingers, when
he caught that fish for the tribute.—*T. Wright, M.A.*

PETERER. See PETER-MAN.

PETERSHAM. Formerly, a great-coat made of a sort of
rough cloth ; named after Lord Petersham, who probably set
the fashion.——" A large hat with curly brims, now worn by
old dandies " (*S. F. C.*)

PETERWORT or SAINT PETER'S WORT. A plant
of the genus *Ascyrum*, another of the genus *Hypericum*.

PETIVERIA. A genus of plants, nat. or. *Petiveriaceæ*,
whose species are called in English *henweed ;* named in
honour of James Petiver, F.R.S., an eminent English botanist
in the beginning of the eighteenth century, author of several
works on history, but principally celebrated for his extensive
collection of rare and various plants, animals, and insects,
for which, after his death, Sir Hans Sloane gave £4000,
and which now form part of the collection in the British
Museum.

PETREA. A genus of South American plants, or. *Angiospermia ;* named in honour of Lord Petre, a patron of botany.

PETUNTSE. See KAOLIN.

PETWORTH MARBLE (*Sussex marble*). A variously-
coloured limestone, occurring in the Weald clay, composed of

the remains of fresh-water shells; named from the town of Petworth.

PEUTINGERIAN TABLE. An epithet applied to a rude chart drawn on parchment by an unknown hand during the reign of Theodosius the Great, and marking the Roman military roads throughout the greatest part of the Western empire. It was found in the fifteenth century, in the library of a monastery at Speyer, by Conrad Celtes, who presented it to Conrad Peutinger, a learned German writer, born at Augsburg in 1465. He intended to publish it, but it did not appear for several years after his death. At length fragments of it were found and published at Venice in 1591, under the title of Fragmenta Tabulæ Antiquæ ex Peutingerarum Bibliotheca. The original map remained at Augsburg in the possession of Peutinger's descendants till 1714, when it was purchased by Prince Eugene, who gave it to the imperial library of Vienna. An exact copy of it was made by F. C. von Scheyb at Vienna in 1753, with notes and dissertations, and dedicated to the Empress Maria Theresa. See T. Wright.

PEYER'S GLANDS (*Plexus intestinales*). The small glands under the villous coat of the intestines; first discovered by Peyer, of Schaffhausen, who described them in a work entitled Exercitatio Anatomico-Medica de Glandulis Intestinorum, published in 1677. Von Brun compared them collectively to a second pancreas, and after him they have been also named Brunner's Glands.

PHÆBE. "A dance mentioned in an old nursery rhyme. A correspondent gives me the following lines of a very old song, the only ones he can recollect :—

> ' Cannot you dance the *Phœbe?*
> Don't you see what pains I take?
> Don't you see how my shoulders shake?
> Cannot you dance the *Phœbe?*' "—*Halliwell.*

Probably so called from *Phœbe*, a name of Diana, or the moon.

PHAETON. An open carriage like a chaise, on four wheels, and drawn by two horses; so called from Phaëton (son of Phœbus), driver of the chariot of the sun. Phaëton, to prove his paternity, begged of Phœbus to permit him to guide his chariot of the sun, in doing which he manifested want of skill, and, being struck with a thunderbolt by Jupiter, was hurled headlong into the River Po.

"Such a waggoner as Phaëton would whip you to the West."—Rom. & J.

"Down, down I come, like glistering Phaëton, wanting the manage of unruly jades."—Rich. II.

"Now Phaëton hath tumbled from his car, and made an evening at the noon-tide pride."—3 Hen VI.

——Tropic-bird, a genus of birds, or. *Anseres*.

PHALECIAN. A term applied to verses of eleven syllables; so called from Phalecus (*Bailey*). Phalœcus was an old Grecian poet mentioned by Ausonius. His verse was called Carmen Phalœcium, Phalœcum, or Phaleucium. Cf. Scheller's Grammar; Auson. E. iv., 85; and Scheller's Lex.

PHANARIOTS. A portion of the Greek people, who in the days of bondage peopled the famous quarter of Constantinople called the Phanar.

PHARAON, PHARO, or FARO. Name of a game of chance; Fr. *pharaon*, a game at cards; probably from Pharaon (the Fr. form of Pharaoh), but why is doubtful.

PHARICUM. A violent kind of poison; from Pharos, the island whence it was brought.—*Forsyth*.

PHARISAIC, PHARISAICAL. Addicted to external forms and ceremonies; making show of religion without the spirit of it; as *pharisaic* holiness; lit. pertaining to or resembling the Pharisees, a Jewish sect distinguished by their zeal for the traditions of the elders, and by their exact observance of these traditions and the ritual law, and whose pretended holiness led them to separate themselves as a sect, considering themselves more righteous than other Jews.

PHARISAISM. The notions, doctrines, and conduct of the Pharisees, as a sect; rigid observance of external forms of religion without genuine piety; hypocrisy in religion.

PHAROAH. A strong ale. "Old Pharoh" is mentioned in the Praise of Yorkshire Ale, 1697, p. 3 (*Halliwell*).

PHAROS (Fr. *phare*, It. *faro*). Any lighthouse for the

direction of seamen ; a watch-tower ; a beacon ; so called from
Pharos, a lighthouse or tower erected by Ptolemy Philadelphus·
on a small isle of the same name near one of the mouths of the
Nile.   It consisted of seven stories and galleries, with a
lantern on the top, which was kept burning at night as a guide
to seamen, the coasts being full of sands and shelves.   It was
considered by the ancients as one of the seven wonders of the
world.   There are still several faros, as Faro di Messina, &c.

PHASIANUS.   A genus of birds, or. *Gallinœ.*   See
PHEASANT.

PHEASANT   (Fr. *faisan,* Sp. *faysan,* It. *fagiano,* D.
faizant, G. *fasan,* Russ. *phazan,* L. *phasianus, gallus phasianus,* Gr. φασιανος).   A name common to several species of
gallinaceous birds, all the known species of which are natives
of Asia.   This bird is said to have been called φασιανος from
having been originally brought from the banks of the Phasis,
a river of Colchis, flowing into the Black Sea.   It is the
Rhion of modern geography, a river of Asiatic Russia, Trans-
caucasia.   It is said, indeed, that the bird still frequents an
island at the mouth of this river.   The word *phasid* in Syriac
signifies a river.

PHELYPŒA.   A genus of plants of three species, natives
of the Levant, the district of Mount Caucasus, Portugal, Barbary, Arabia, Algiers, &c. ; named in honour of the family of
Phelipeaux, two of whom are mentioned by Tournefort as the
Mæcenates of his time.

PHEREPHATTIA.   A festival kept at Cyricum in honour
of Proserpine, who was also called Pherephatta.   The sacrifice
was a black heifer.

PHIGALIAN.   An epithet applied to certain marbles
discovered near the site of the ancient Phigalia, a town of
Arcadia, in Greece, and which have been brought to England,
and deposited in the British Museum among the collection
known by the name of the Elgin marbles.   The Phigalian
marbles form a series of sculpture in alto-relievo.—*T. Wright.*

PHILADELPHIA LAWYER.   This Transatlantic limb
of the law is considered to be the very acme of acuteness.
Sailors relate many stories of his artful abilities.—*J. C. Hotten.*

PHILADELPHIAN. Pertaining to Ptolemy Philadelphus.

PHILADELPHUS. The common or white syringa or mock orange, a shrub, mentioned by Athenæus, that sends up a great number of slender stalks from the root, seven or eight feet in height; probably a native of the south of Europe. It is the φιλαδελφος of Aristotle; and Linnæus supposes it was designed to commemorate Ptolemy Philadelphus, King of Egypt; but, says Rees, it is much more probable that the plant of Athenæus was of the twining or clasping kind, something like *Periploca Græca*, and that the word, by a poetical fancy, was intended to express its brotherly love for those near it (φιλος-αδελφος).

PHILANDERING. Making love; from Philander, name of a character in one of the old ballads, garlands, or operas. Under the head "Philander" and "Philandering" I find the following in the Library of the British Museum:—1. A Strange Apparition; or, the Second Meeting of Two Self-Murthering Lovers, Phillis and Phillander; Lond. fo. 1680? (a very curious old ballad). 2. Philander's Garland, composed of five delightful new songs, Newc. 12⁰, 1780. 3. Philandering; or the Rose Queen. A comic opera in three acts, performed at the New Theatre Royal Drury Lane on Tuesday, January 13, 1824. The music by Mr. C. E. Horn. [By S. Beazley]. Lond. 8⁰, 1824 (in prose). 4. Songs, duets, and concerted pieces in the comic opera of Philander; or the Rose Queen, &c. Lond. 8⁰, 1824. No. 1 is headed—

> " Mistaken Phillis kill'd herself, thinking Philander slain;
> Philander quickly followed her, and now they are met again."
>> To the tune of " Oh, Cruel Bloody Fate."

In No. 2 the first song is entitled " Philander's Complaint to his Beautiful Phillis;" the second, " Beautiful Phillis' Answer to Philander's Complaint." No. 3 commences with an essay on the Art of Philandering. The chorus to the finale runs—

> " All *Philanders* must expect
> To give their lovers pain. sir,
> Nor should they certainly object
> If { men should / maidens } flirt again."

The title page has the following :—

> " To be paddling palms, and pinching fingers,
>   And making practis'd smiles, as in a looking-glass ;
>   And then to sigh, as 'twere the mort of the deer ;
>   O that is *Philandering!*
>
>   Is whispering nothing ?
>   Is leaning cheek—stopping the career
>   Of laughter with a sigh—wishing clock more swift—
>   Hours minutes—minutes hours—noon midnight—
>   Is this nothing ? 'Tis *Philandering!*
>
>   This weak impress of love is as a figure
>   Trench'd in ice, which, with an hour's heat,
>   Dissolves to water, and doth lose its form."
>
>   *Shakspeare* (mutilated).

PHILIP. A Macedonian coin, value unknown ; named after Philip the Great.

PHILIPPEI or **PHILIPPI.** Pieces coined in the reign of Philip of Macedon, and with his image. Horat. Ep. 2, 1, 284 ; Liv. 34, 52 ; 37, 59 ; 39, 5, 7 ; and Lempriere.

PHILIPPIC. Discourse or declamation full of acrimonious invective ; so called from an oration of Demosthenes against Philip of Macedon, in which the orator aroused the Athenians from their indolence. The fourteen orations of Cicero against Mark Antony are also called Philippics.

PHILIPPIZE. To write or utter invective ; to declaim against (*Burke*). To side with Philip ; to support or advocate Philip (*Swift*). See PHILIPPIC.

PHILIPSIA. A genus of trilobites found in the mountain limestone of England and Ireland ; doubtless named from the discoverer, Philips.

PHILISTINE. A cant term applied to bailiffs, sheriffs' officers, and drunkards (*Halliwell*). "A policeman. The German students call all townspeople not of their body *Philister*, as ours say *cads*. The departing student says, mournfully, in one of the Burschenlieder, ' Muss selber nun *Philister* seyn !' ' I must now myself *Philistine* be !' ". (Slang. *J. C. Hotten*).

PHILISTINISM. Manners of the Philistines.—*Carlyle.*

PHILLIPSITE. A mineral consisting chiefly of silica and aluminia ; allied to harmotone, *i.e.* cross-stone or staurolite ; named after W. Phillips.

PHILLYREA. Mock-privet. A genus of plants, or. *De-candria;* name of the daughter of Chiron, who first applied it medicinally.—*Forsyth.*

PHILOMEL or **PHILOMELA.** The nightingale; said to be so called from Philomela, daughter of Pandion, king of Athens, who was changed into a nightingale.

> " For worse than Philomel you us'd my daughter."—Tit. Andron.

> " Wer't thou thus surpris'd, sweet girl, ravish'd and wrong'd as Philomela was."—*Ibid.*

PHILONIUM. A warm opiate; from Philo, its inventor. —*Forsyth.*

PHRYGIAN. An epithet applied to a sprightly, animated kind of music; so called from the Phrygians, in Asia Minor. ——A warlike kind of music, fit for trumpets, hautboys, &c.

PHRYGIAN STONE. A stone described by the ancients, used in dyeing; a light spongy stone, resembling a pumice, said to be drying and astringent; so called from Phrygia.

PIAST. As history goes, the Poles, in 700, gave the command, under the title of Duke, to Cracus, founder of Cracow. His posterity failing, a peasant, in the year 830, named Piastus, was elected. He lived to the age of 120, and from the length and prosperity of his reign every native Pole who was subsequently elected king was called *Piast.* The Polish dictionary says the term *Piast* was used to denote a Polish nobleman, who stood candidate for the crown elective of Poland, in competition with a foreign prince. *Jedni cheieli Piasta drudzy cudzoziemca;* some have wished to have a Pole, others a foreigner, for a king.

PIAUZITE. An earthy resin, colour brownish-black; found in a bed of brown coal in the vicinity of Piauze, near Neustadt, in Carniola.

PICCADEL or **PICCADILLY.** Formerly a game so called.

> " And their lands to coyn they distil ye,
> And then with the money
> You see how they run ye
> To loose it at *piccadilly.*"—*Flecknoe.* Epigrams.

Doubtless so called from Piccadilly, London, where it was played.

PICKERINGITE. A mineral found in white fibrous masses; from Iquique, in South America; found also in some parts of Africa and Europe; named after Pickering.

PICKLE (D. *pekel*, G. *pökel*, O. G. *bökel*). Brine; a solution of salt and water or of vinegar, sometimes impregnated with spices, in which flesh, fish, or other substance is preserved: hence, a vegetable or fruit preserved in pickle. Several derivations have been suggested; but the general opinion seems to be that the O. G. *bökel* is derived from Beukelzoon (who was born and died at Biervliet, a small town on an island in the West Scheldt), who invented the art of salting and barrelling herrings. Authors differ as to the date of the invention, some making it in 1337, others 1347, 1397, and 1414; and the name of the inventor is found written Böckel, Bückel, Beukels, Bökel, Bökelszoon, Beukelzoon. See N. & Q. 2nd S. vii., No. 4, p. 78; also Zedler "Bieruliet."——"A pickle, a young pickle, a boy who cannot be kept in order without repeated punishment. So called from the birch-rod, which used to lie in brine till wanted" (*S. F. Creswell*).—— A state or condition of difficulty or disorder; *a word used in ridicule or contempt*. You are in a fine *pickle*. *Pickle* is also a local name in England for a parcel of land enclosed with a hedge; but is derived from a different root.

PIGMEAN. Anything little; dwarfish; pertaining to a pigmy or dwarf; so called from the *Pigmæi*, among the ancients, a race of beings not exceeding a cubit in height, who inhabited Thrace, and who waged war with the cranes and were destroyed.

PINCHBECK. An alloy of copper and zinc, resembling gold in its appearance, said to have been first brought into notice by a person of the same name. Pinchbeck is also the appellation of a parish, co. Lincoln. " It was very fashionable in the last century, and derived its name from a Mr. Pinchbeck, a well-known London tradesman, who manufactured watches, buckles, and other articles out of it. Pinchbeck first obtained his notoriety by the invention of an ingenious candle-snuffers, which the author of The Heroic Epistle to Sir William Chambers made the vehicle of a facetious ode that went through eight editions. The title of this *jeu d'esprit* ran thus, Ode to Mr. Pinchbeck, upon his newly-invented Candle-Snuffers, by Malcolm M'Gregor, Esq., 1776 :—

> ' Illustrious PINCHBECK ! condescend,
> Thou well-beloved, and best king's friend,
> These lyric lines to view ;
>   Oh, may they prompt thee, ere too late,
>   To snuff the candle of the State,
> That burns a little blue !'

Pinchbeck published a poetical reply, and the two pamphlets were for a long time the talk of town " (*J. C. Hotten*).—— Inferior, deteriorated.

" Where, in these *Pinchbeck* days, can we hope to find the old agricultural virtue in all its purity ?"—Framley Parsonage.

PINDARIC. An ode in imitation of Pindar, prince of the lyric poets, a contemporary with Æschylus ; an irregular ode (*Addison*). " There is nothing more frequent among us than a sort of poems entitled *Pindaric* odes, pretending to be written in imitation of the manner and style of Pindar, and yet I do not know that there is to this day extant, in our language, one ode contrived after this model " (*Congreve*).

PINDARIC HEIGHTS. Studying the odes of Pindar. —*Oxford* (*J. C. Hotten*).

PINITE. A mineral found in prismatic crystals, of a greenish-white colour, brown, or deep red, and occurring also massive ; from Pini, a mine in Saxony.

PIRAKOFF OPERATION. The operation of partially removing the foot ; named after Dr. Pirakoff, one of the most celebrated operating surgeons in Russia, who first made this sort of amputation.

PISONIA. A plant of five species, natives of Jamaica, Domingo, Antigua, Hispaniola, &c. ; named by Plumier in honour of William Piso, physician at Amsterdam, author of the Natural History of Brazil, 1648.

PISTOL (Fr. *pistole, pistolet;* It. and Sp. *pistola*). A small firearm, held and fired by one hand. The word is said to be derived from Pistoia (anc. Pistori), in Italy, where this weapon was first made. Stephens says, "*Pistole* and *pistolet* are from Pistoia, a little town near Florence, where they made little poinards, which being newly imported into France were called first *pistoyers*, then *pistoliers*, and finally *pistolets*; that shortly after harquebuses were invented, to which were given the name of these little poinards, and that this poor little word, having for such a length of time travelled from place to place, was at last imported into Spain and Italy for the purpose of signifying crown pieces, &c.'

PISTOLE (Fr.) A gold coin of Spain, but current in the neighbouring countries; equal to about 8s. 6d. sterling (*Ogilvie*).——A coin of different values in Germany, Italy, and Switzerland. See PISTOL.

PISTOLET. A little pistol.

> " Those unlickt bear-whelps, unfill'd *pistolets*,
> That, more than cannon-shot, avails or lets.''—*Donne*.

A diminutive of *pistol*, q.v. The French use the word *pistolet* not only to denote a pistol, but also a small kind of bread made somewhat in the form of a crescent.

PISUM (Gr. πισον). The pea, a plant now classed as a genus of plants, nat. or. *Leguminosæ;* so called, it is said, from Pisa, in Italy, where it abounded.—*Crabb*.

PITAYA BARK. " One of the false barks obtained from the mountain of Pitaya " (qu. where ?).

PLASTER OF PARIS. A composition of several species of gypsum, dug at Montmartre, Paris ; used in building and in casting busts and statues. In popular language, this name is applied improperly to plaster-stone, or to any species of gypsum.

PLATONIC. Pertaining to Plato, or to his philosophy, his school, or his opinions. The *Platonic* bodies are the five regular geometrical solids—viz., the tetrahedron, hexahedron or cube, octahedron, dodecahedron, and icosahedron. The *Platonic* year is a period of time determined by the revolution of the equinoxes. *Platonic* love is a pure spiritual affection subsisting between the sexes, unmixed with carnal desires, and regarding the mind only and its excellencies ; a species of love for which Plato was a warm advocate.

PLATONISM. The doctrines of Plato and his followers. "The cupid of the Hôtel de Rambouillet affected strict Platonism."—For. Quar. ii. 313.

PLATONIST, PLATONIZER. One who professes to be a follower of Plato, and to philosophize as he did.

PLUTONIC. Designating the system of the Plutonists or Plutonians, who adopt the theory of the formation of the world from igneous fusion; from Pluto, god of the infernal regions. The Plutonian theory of the formation of rocks and mountains is opposed to the *Neptunian*. *Plutonic* rocks are granite, porphyry, and other igneous rocks, supposed to have consolidated from a melted state at a great depth from the surface; *Plutonic* action is the influence of volcanic heat and other subterranean causes under pressure.

POGRAM. A dissenter, a fanatic, formalist, or humbug; so called from a well-known dissenting minister of this name. —*J. C. Hotten* (slang).

POINT D'ESPAGNE. Gold or silver Spanish lace so called.

POITEVIN (formerly POICTEVINE). An ancient French coin struck at Poitiers. The annotator of Rabelais thinks the appellation "*Red Poitevins*," by which the people of Poitou were for a long time known, was given them from this coin, which, consisting of a small quantity of silver, mixed with a great deal of red copper, its colour was apparent upon being ever so little handled.

POIVREA. A genus of plants, nat. or. *Combretaceæ*; named after Poivre, the celebrated French naturalist, Intendant of the Mauritius in 1766.

POLACCA (Fr. *polaque*). Another name for the dance air called *polonaise*; probably the same word as polka, *q.v.*

POLECAT. Popular name of a small European quadruped nearly allied to the weasel. Some derive the word from Fr. *poule*, a hen, *chat*, a cat, a hen cat, because it feeds on poultry, eggs, &c. Bailey says, q.d., "*Polonian* cat, because Poland abounds with them."

POLEDAVY. A sort of coarse cloth (*Ainsworth*). Poledavies, a coarse canvas (*Bailey*). Pouldavis, a sort of sail-cloth; obs. (*Webster*). It was probably first made at Poldavid (formerly Pouldavy), a town of Bretagne, on the Douarnenez water. This seems to be confirmed by Anderson (Hist. Commerce, vol. 2, p. 174): "We have the best authority for fixing the date of the first manufacturing of sail-cloth in England to this year (1590), being the preamble to an Act of Parliament, 1 James I. c. 23, reciting that whereas the cloths called mildernix and *powl-davies*, whereof sails and other furniture for the shipping and navy are made, were heretofore altogether brought out of France and other parts beyond sea, and the skill and art of making and weaving of the said cloths was never known or used in England until about the thirty-second year of the reign of Queen Elizabeth—that is, in the year 1590— about which time, and not before, the perfect art or skill of making and weaving the said cloths was attained to, and since practised and continued in this realm, to the great benefit and commodity thereof, &c."

POLKA. A fashionable dance said to have been brought from Hungary. The word is probably derived from the Polish word *Polka*, a female Pole. "A species of dance of Polish origin; also the air played to the dance" (*Ogilvie*).

POLONAISE or POLONESE. A long robe or dress edged with fur, adopted from the fashion of the Poles; sometimes worn by ladies.

POLONOISE. In music, a name given to an air in which the movement is slow or moderate; used in Poland both for songs and dances; in instrumental music, the name of certain pieces with an animated movement.

POLONY. A sausage; corruption of *Bologna* sausage.

POMARD. A fine wine made from grapes grown near Pomard, a village of France, dep. Côte-d'Or.

POMPADOUR. Now called *cuire*, a brownish-yellow colour; so named as forming the colours of Madame de Pompadour, mistress of Louis XV. The Buffs are called Pompadours, from the colour of their facings (*S. F. Creswell*). Pompadour and the saucy Pompeys (short for Pompadours), a name for the fifty-sixth regiment of foot, from their purple facings, the favourite colour of Madame Pompadour.——A name given by the French to the peculiar style of architecture, &c., which prevailed throughout nearly the whole of Europe about the middle of the eighteenth century; so called from Madame de Pompadour. It is also called by the French, *Rococo* and *Chicorée*, and by the English, *Style of Louis Quatorze* and *Louis Quinze.* Hope, in his Historical Essays on Architecture, pp. 555, 559, very ably exposes this style, and says its proper name should be "The Inane or Frippery Style." It was not confined to architecture, being found in sculpture, painting, poetry, bronze, porcelain, &c. "Boromini in Archittetura, Bernini in Scultura, Petro da Cortona in Pittura, Il Cavalier Marini in Poesia, sono peste del Gusto, peste ch'ha appestato un gran munero di Artisti" (Miliz. Diz. delle Belle Arti, voc. Boromini, p. 122). The late king George IV., who had the most frivolous, meretricious, gawdy taste, adopted this *rococo, pompadour, chicorée* style in the ornaments of the great ball room at Windsor, and as late as 1837 it was quite the fashion in France, especially in bronze work, ormolu, and porcelain.

POMUM ADAMI (Adam's apple). A protuberance in the anterior part of the neck, formed by the forepart of the thyroid cartilage; so called from a whimsical supposition that a part of the forbidden apple which Adam ate stuck in his throat, and thus occasioned the protuberance.

PONS VAROLII. An eminence of the medulla oblongata, first described by Varolius.

PONTAC. A sort of claret, used in England in the manufacture of what is called by wine merchants, and believed by the public to be, *port wine;* named from Pontac, dep. Basses-Pyrénées, where it is made.

POONAHLITE. A mineral, according to C. Gmelin, consisting of silica, alumina, lime, soda with a trace of potash, and water; found with apopyllite at Poonah, in Hindustan.

POPE JULIUS. An old game, possibly similar to the modern game of pope-joan (*Halliwell*). A game of cards greatly in vogue at the court of Henry VIII., and which was probably the origin of the vulgar round game called in modern times pope-joan. The various points in that game, such as matrimony, intrigue, pope, and the stops, appear to have borne

significant allusion to the relative situations in the royal drama
of the divorce and the interference of the Pope and his agents
in preventing the king's marriage with his beautiful favourite,
Anne Boleyn. It is supposed to have been named in mockery
of Julius II. (elected Pope 1 Nov., 1503, died 21 Feb., 1513),
the copy of whose breve of dispensation had been lately produced by Catharine of Arragon as an important document in
favour of the legality of her marriage with Henry VIII. See
Life of Anne Boleyn, by Agnes Strickland, pp. 227, 228. It
might have even been named after Clement VII. (elected Pope
10 Nov., 1523, died 26 Sep., 1534), whose name was *Julius* de
Medicis, who refused to grant the divorce between Henry and
Catharine. He was natural son of Julian de Medicis, cousin
of Leo X.

POPERY. The religion of the Roman Catholic Church,
comprehending doctrines and practices; so called from the
Pope, in L. *Papa.*

POPE'S NOSE. The extremity of the rump of a roast
fowl, devilled as a dainty for epicures.

POPLIN. A stuff made of the finest wool and silk, first
introduced into Ireland by a French emigrant family named
Latouche (who founded there a manufactory of Papelines or
Popelines) upon publication of the Edict of Nantes by Louis
XIV. (22 Oct., 1685). It was first made at Avignon, in
France, which was formerly part of the Papal territories, and
was on that account called *Papeline*, from *Pape;* Med. L. *Papa,*
the Pope. For further information see Dict. des Sciences,
new Ed. 1847, 4o, pp. 328, 419.

PORT. A dark purple astringent wine made in Portugal,
and drank there; so called from Porto or Oporto, whence it
was formerly shipped.——A wine made in Portugal for British
consumption, and shipped from Oporto.——A wine made in
England from cider, logwood, and common British brandy,
drunk by the middle classes. Ford says benicarlo (a Spanish
wine), familiarly called "black strap," is much used to concoct
what the trade call *curious* old port.

PORTEGUE. A gold coin equal to 3*l.* 10*s.* (*Bailey*);
doubtless coined in Portugal.

PORTITE. A mineral, a hydrous silicate, from the gabbro rosso in Tuscany ; named after M. Porte, of Tuscany.

PORTLAND STONE. A yellowish-white calcareous freestone, much used in building ; from the Isle of Portland in England.

PORTO RICO. A tobacco much smoked in Germany ; brought from Porto Rico, one of the Spanish West India islands.

PORTUGAL. A light and elegant carriage ; so named from having been sent to the King of Portugal.

POUPART'S LIGAMENT (*Fallopian ligament*). In anatomy, the tendinous attachment of the external oblique muscle of the abdomen to the superior and anterior spinous process of the os ilium and os pubis ; named after Francis Poupart, a celebrated French physician and anatomist, who was born at Mans in 1660, and died in 1709 ; author of Chirurgie Complete, and of several papers in the memoirs of the Academy of Sciences.

POURRETIA. A genus of plants, trees, natives of South America ; named by Wildenow in honour of the Abbé Pourret, a French botanist, who wrote on Spanish plants in the memoirs of the Academy of Toulouse.

POYNINGS' LAW. An act passed in the reign of Henry VII., by which all legislation in Ireland was confined to what had previously been approved by king and council in England; so called from Sir Edward Poynings, then Lieutenant of Ireland.

POZZUOLANA, POZZOLANA, or PUZZOLANA. Volcanic ashes, used in the manufacture of mortar, which hardens under water ; from Pozzuoli, in Italy.

PRADO (VERDE DI). A green marble occurring near the little town of Prado, in Tuscany.

PRE-ADAMITE. An inhabitant of the earth before the time of Adam.

PREDAZZITE. A mineral consisting of carbonic acid, lime, magnesia, water, alumina, red oxide of iron, and silica ; found at Predazzo, in the Tyrol.

PREHNITE. A pale green mineral, consisting of silica,

alumina, and lime, with some water; named by Werner after Colonel Prehn, who first found it at the Cape, and brought it to Europe.

PRE-RAPHAELITISM.   A system of painting said to be founded on truthfulness to nature only, as opposed to the teaching and practice of schools founded on laws derived from the works of great painters; truthfulness to nature irrespective of any conventional rules of painting.   It was founded by Rossetti about 1849-50, and was first introduced into England by Millais, Holman Hunt, &c.   Pre-Raphael simply means "before Raphael;" because, before his time, painters had no other guide but that afforded by the study of nature.

PRESTONIA.   A genus of plants, the only known species of which is *P. tomentosa*, a twining downy shrub, found near the banks of the Rio de Janeiro, in the Brazils; named by Mr. R. Brown in memory of Dr. Charles Preston, a correspondent of Ray.

PRESTON SALTS.   Salts prepared by adding a few drops of liquor ammoniæ fortior and some volatile oils to coarsely-powdered sesqui-carbonate of ammonia; originally from Preston Pans, in Scotland.   The monks of Newbottle, who obtained a grant of Preston before 1189, from Robert de Quincey, and who discovered coal within their lands, established a salt work here, which gave rise to the name of Preston Pans, and at the beginning of the last century it was commonly called Salt Preston.

PRINCE'S METAL.   A mixture of copper and zinc, in imitation of gold; also called Prince Rupert's metal, because it is said to have been invented by him.

PROCRUSTEAN.   Resembling Procrustes, or his mode of torture.   "Procrustes, called by Pausanias Polyphæmon, was, in Grecian mythology, a robber, who placed on an iron bed travellers who fell into his hands, which their stature was made to fit by cutting off the projecting limbs, or by stretching them to suit its dimensions: hence the metaphorical expression, 'the bed of Procrustes.'"   "He is obliged, *Procrustes*-like, to cut off some letter from the beginning, middle, or end; or, by the touch of his magical wand, to make the letters of the radical change place, or start above their fellows, before they will suit his purpose " (Ed. Rev. iii. 317).

PROMETHEAN. Having the life-giving quality of the fire which Prometheus stole from heaven.

" Whence doth spring the true *Promethean* fire."—Love's Lab. Lost.

" I know not where is that *Promethean* heat that can thy light relume." —Othello.

——A glass tube containing sulphuric acid, and surrounded by an inflammable mixture, which it ignites on being pressed.

PROSERPINACA. A genus of North American aquatic plants. Linnæus derives the name *à proserpendo*, from its creeping habit. According to others, it is an ancient name in Apuleius, and is the Proserpina of Pliny, and is so called after Proserpine, queen of the infernal regions, because it grows in low places infested with frogs and newts. Cf. Gronovius and Miller's Dict.

PROTEA. A genus of plants, shrubs, chiefly natives of the Cape ; named by Linnæus after Proteus, in allusion to the great diversity of habit in the different species. See PROTEUS.

PROTEAN. Readily assuming different shapes ; lit. pertaining to or resembling Proteus, *q.v.*

" Change shapes with *Proteus* for advantages."—3 Hen. VI.

" I am not, however, very sanguine as to the result of the experiment in Turin, knowing how strangely *Protean* are the forms of prejudice, and how curiously and unexpectedly they manifest themselves in different countries."

PROTEAN STONE. A material invented by Mr. Cheverton ; manufactured from gypsum, which, by various modes of treating it, is made to resemble ivory, granite, or different kinds of marble. See PROTEUS.

PROTEUS. One who easily changes his form or principles; so called from Proteus, son of Oceanus and Tethys, whose distinguishing characteristic was the faculty of assuming different shapes.——A genus of batrachian reptiles, allied to the sirens, salamanders, and frogs.——A genus of homogeneous infusoria.

PRUSSIAN BLUE. A bisalt of a beautiful deep blue, much used as a pigment ; from Prussia.

PRUSSIATE. A name first applied to Prussian blue, but subsequently to numerous salts in which the protocyanide of iron is the acid. See PRUSSIAN BLUE.

PRUSSIC ACID. An acid, a deadly poison, obtained from Prussian blue (*q.v.*), in which it forms the colouring matter.

PTOLEMAIC. A system maintained by Ptolemy, who supposed the earth to be fixed in the centre of the universe, and the sun and stars to revolve around it. This theory was received for ages, but has been rejected for the Copernican system.

PUNCH AND JUDY. Supposed to be a corruption of *Pontius Pilatus cum Judæis*, represented in some miracle-play (*S. F. Creswell*). Theobald, in a note to Shakespeare, says, " There was hardly an old play till the period of the Reformation which had not in it a devil, and a droll character, who was to play upon and work the devil." " Perhaps," says a correspondent of N. & Q., " Judas was often introduced as a fit representative, and so in our street exhibitions we generally see both characters (Judas corrupted in Judy), and Punch victorious over both. Galiani, in his vocabulary of the Neapolitan dialect, has bestowed a great deal of learning upon the subject. He fixes on Pucchio d'Aniello, at Acerra, near Naples, as the original Punch, and says that after his death a Polecenella, or young Puccio, succeeded him." Another correspondent of N. & Q. says, " The name of Punch in Italy is Poncinello, a very easy corruption of Pontiello or Pontianello; Judy is certainly very like Giudei (the Jews) or Giuda (Judas). There are certainly two places in Europe where traditions respecting Pontius Pilate still survive—Avignon, where some say that he died, and Mount Pilatus, near Lucerne. The story at the latter place is, that he threw himself into a lake on the top of the mountain. It would appear from this that traditions respecting him were afloat during the Middle Ages, and nothing is more likely than their embodiment in a mystery play." Again, another writer derives the name from πολυ κινεω, to move much, " which seems to me at least plausible.

considering that the founders of Neapolis were a Greek colony, and that their descendants still retain very many features of their original country." The most probable derivation is that from *Punchinello*, from *Pulicinella*, a character in the Neapolitan drama ; so called from *pullicinus*, a little chicken, because his nose resembles the disproportioned beak of a young pullet. The name *Judy* is exclusively English. But see Notes and Queries, 1st S., v. 610 ; vi. 43, 184 ; 2nd S., ii. 430, 495-6 ; Rev. des Deux Mondes, vol. 20, p. 823, 1 June, 1840 ; and voc. PANTALOON in this Dictionary.

PUNIC. Faithless, treacherous, deceitful; lit. pertaining to the Pœni, Phœni (*i.e.* the Carthaginians), Carthage having been settled by Phœnicians. The Latins used the term *Punica fides* (Punic or Carthaginian faith) to denote unfaithfulness, treachery, perfidiousness.——The ancient language of the Carthaginians, of which Plautus has left a specimen.

PURBECK STONE. A limestone from the isle of Purbeck, a peninsular district, co. Dorset ; possessing excellent quarries of stone, slate, and marble.

PUSEYISM. The principles of Dr. Pusey and others at Oxford, as exhibited in " The Tracts for the Times." They propose to carry back the discipline and doctrine of the Church of England to an imagined period, when there would have been no ground of separation from the then Church of Rome. —*Smart*.

PUSEYITE. One who holds the principles of Puseyism.

PUSSEY-CATS. A corruption of *Puseyites*, a name constantly, but improperly, given to the "Tractarian" party in the Church ; from the Oxford Regius Professor of Hebrew, who by no means approved of the Romanizing tendencies of some of its leaders.—*J. C. Hotten.*

PYRRHIC. An ancient military dance, said to have been invented by Pyrrhus.——In *poetry*, the foot so called.

PYRRHONISM. Scepticism, universal doubt ; from Pyrrho, founder of the Sceptics. "Launched into a dark shoreless sea of *Pyrrhonism*, what would remain for us but to sail aimless, hopeless; or make merry, while the devouring Death had not yet engulfed us ?" (*Carlyle*).

PYRRHONIST.   A sceptic; one who doubts of everything.   See PYRRHONISM.

PYTHAGOREAN.   A follower of or belonging to the
philosophy of Pythagoras, founder of the Italic sect of philosophers.

PYTHAGORISM.   The doctrines of Pythagoras.

PYTHIAN.   Delphic; pertaining to Pythia, priestess of
Apollo, who delivered oracles.

PYTHIAN GAMES.   One of the four great national
festivals of ancient Greece, celebrated near Delphi (an old
name of which was Pytho), in Phocis, in honour of Apollo,
conqueror of the dragon Python: hence Apollo himself was
called Πύθιος, Πύθων.

PYTHONESS.   A sort of witch;·any female supposed to
have a spirit of divination; so called from the priestess who
gave oracular answers at Delphi.   See PYTHIAN.

PYTHONIST.   A conjurer.—*Webster.*   See PYTHONESS.

Q.

QUARRINGTON.   A Devonshire apple so named, but
whether from the cultivator or from locality is doubtful.
There are places called Quarrington in cos. Durham and
Lincoln.

QUASSIA.   A genus of plants, at present comprising but
one species, viz., *Quassia amara* (Linnæus).   It was once
much employed as a bitter tonic medicine, but, the supply not
equalling the demand, the Picræna excelsa (Lindley) was gradually substituted, under the same name, and is the article now
incorrectly called *Quassia* in the shops.   The former is a
native of Surinam, Guiana, Colombia, and Panama; and the
latter of Jamaica.   The wood and bark, both of the root and
top, of both of these articles are the parts employed in medicine.   The Quassia amara had its name from a negro named
Quassi or *Quash*, who used it with remarkable success in curing
a malignant fever which prevailed at Surinam.

QUASSINE or QUASSITE. The name given by
Wiggers to the bitter principle of Picræna excelsa; from
quassia, q.v.

QUEEN BESS. The queen of clubs; perhaps so called
because that queen, history says, was of a swarthy complexion.
—*North Hants.* See Gentleman's Magazine for 1791, p. 141.

QUIDDANY. Marmalade; a confection of quinces prepared with sugar; from L. *cy̆dŏnium*, quiddany; *cy̆dŏnĭtes*,
marmalade; *cydonia* (sc. mala), quinces. Gr. κυδώνιον (μῆλον),
a quince; from κυδωνέα or κυδωνία, the quince-tree; from
Κυδωνία, Cydonia, a town of Crete; thus κυδωνία, κυδώνιον,
cydonium, cydonio, cydoni, cydani, quidani, quidany, Quiddany.

QUINCE (Fr. *coin* or *coing*; Armor. *avalcouign*; G. *quitte*,
quidden, quittenapfel; D. *kwee, quee, queeper, queepeerboom*, the
quince-tree). A fruit much used in making pies, tarts, marmalade, &c. Webster renders the Armoric word, " the cor-
nered apple or wedge-apple," and he says one species of the
quince is of an oblong shape, from which, probably, it has its
French name. Again, Bescherelle derives *coing* from Celt.
coin, fruit. But all forms of the word are more probably
corrupted from L. *cy̆dōnia* (mala), quinces (Gr. κυδωνία, the
quince-tree), from Κυδωνία, Cy̆donia, a town of Crete, famous
for abounding with this fruit.

QUINCEITE. A hydrated silicate of magnesia tinged red
by oxide of iron; found near Quincey, in France.

QUININA, QUINIA, QUININE. An alkaloid obtained
from various species of cinchona, and one of the active principles of these trees; a very important article of medicine,
much used in the treatment of fevers, agues, certain sorts of
mortifications, &c.; properly cinchonina, cinchonia, cinchonine,
or cinchona. According to some, it had its name from the
Countess de Chinchon, wife of the viceroy of Peru, who was
cured of a fever in 1638 by this medicine. The Condésa del
Cincon or Chincon (perhaps from Chinca, in Peru), wife of the
viceroy of Peru, brought some of this powder with her to
Europe in 1639. Soon afterwards Cardinal de Lugo, a
Jesuit, brought it to Rome, where it was called Jesuits' bark,
otherwise Jesuits' powder, Pulvis Cardinalis de Lugo, Pulvis

Patrum, and Pulvis Comitissæ (countess's powder). It was subsequently employed in France by Sir Robert Talbor, whence it was called Talbor's powder, or the English remedy.

QUIXOTISM. Romantic and absurd notions; schemes or actions like those of Don Quixote, the hero of Cervantes.

R.

RABEL WATER (*Eau de Rabel, Aqua Rabelliana*). A water consisting of one part of sulphuric acid and three of rectified spirit of wine, constituting a sort of sulphuric ether; named from its inventor, the empiric Rabel.

RABBI WATER (*Rabbi wasser*). A chalybeate water from the baths of Rabbi, Val di Rabbi, Tyrol; much frequented by the Trentines and Tyrolese.

RABBINIC, RABBINICAL. Pertaining to the Rabbins, or to their opinions, learning, and language.

RABBINISM. A rabbinic expression or phraseology; a peculiarity of the language of the Rabbis.

RAFE or RALPH. A pawnbroker's duplicate (*Norwich; J. C. Hotten*); doubtless from the name of a pawnbroker.

RAGUSINA. A silver coin of Tuscany, Ragusa, and Venice; so named from Ragusa, where it was the highest silver coin, worth 3s. 1¾d. sterling. It was also called *talaro* (dollar) and *cislino*.

RAJANIA. A genus of climbing plants, nat. or. *Dioscoriaceæ;* called after Ray, the celebrated naturalist.— *Crabb.*

RAMILIE. A cocked hat, worn temp. George I.; named in commemoration of the famous battle of Ramilies.——A wig worn as late as the reign of George III.——A long gradually-diminishing plait to the wig, with a great bow at the top, and a smaller one at the bottom. See Planché.

RAMIST or RAMEAN. A follower of Pierre Ramée (Peter Ramus), professor of rhetoric and philosophy in Paris temp. Henry II., who perished in the massacre of St. Bartholomew. His system of logic was opposed to that of the Aristotelian party, between whom and his followers there raged a vehement contest during the latter half of the sixteenth century. The dispute rendered essential service to science, by exposing the absurdities of the schoolmen.

RANDAL'S-MAN. A neckerchief, colour green, with white spots; named after Jack Randal, the pugilist.—*J. C. Hotten.*

RAYNES or RENNES. A table cloth supposed by Mr. Douce to have been manufactured at Rennes, in Bretagne; "A cloth of reines." "Thenne the Kerver shall go into the Cupibord and redresse and ordeyne Wafers into Toweyles of Raynes or fine Napkins," &c. (Notes to a Relation, or rather Ane account of England, an. 1500, &c., translated from the Italian by Miss Charlotte Augusta Sney, published by the Camden Society in 1847).

REAUMUR. A method of graduation on the thermometer, which is still the only one used in France and many parts of the continent; invented by Reaumur. See REAUMURIA.

REAUMURIA. A plant, so called in honour of the great French naturalist, the Sieur de René Antoine Ferchault Reaumur (born at Rochelle, 1683), principally known as a botanist by his examination of the fructification of *Fuci*, but chiefly celebrated as a philosophical inquirer into the history of insects, and their transformations, &c. Linnæus mentions Hasselquist as the author of the name *Reaumuria*, of which no traces are found in his book.

REDOWA. A fashionable dance, doubtless brought from Poland. The official gazette of Poland is called the *Gazeta Redowa*. Both names are probably derived from Radow, in Poland; or perhaps from a surname.

REINSCH'S TEST. A test for the detection of arsenic in mixed solutions, consisting in boiling slips of metallic copper in a portion of the filtered liquor; invented by Reinsch.

REMOLINITE. A mineral consisting of hydrochloric acid, chlorine, copper, water, and silica; found at Los Remolinos, in Chili; also in Peru; in Saxony; and on the lavas of Vesuvius and Ætna.

REUSSINE (also *reussin* and *reussite*). A salt of sulphate of soda and magnesia, found in the form of a mealy efflorescence ; discovered in the neighbourhood of Sedlitz, in Bohemia. According to some, it was named in honour of M. Reuss, the German mineralogist, who first analysed it and made it known. Others derive the name from the principality of Reuss, in Germany, where they say it was found.

REYNOLDS'S SPECIFIC. A nostrum for gout and rheumatism, consisting of the fresh bulb of colchicum and sherry wine ; invented by Reynolds, who is said to have killed himself by taking an over-dose of it.

RHABARBARUM. Rhubarb. Forsyth derives this word " from *Rha* and *barbarus*, wild; so called because brought from the banks of the Rha, now the Volga, in Russia." See also Isidorus, and Littleton's Lat. Dict.

RHAPONTICUM. Systematic name of the rhapontic rhubarb. Forsyth renders it the " Rha Pontus, *i.e.* Rha, in Russia, on whose banks it grew." Pliny calls it Rhacoma ; Celsus, Radix Pontica.

RHEUM. A genus of plants, mostly perennials, including the different species which yield the stalks and root called rhubarb ; supposed by some to derive its generic name from Rha (the Volga), a river of Russia, on whose banks some species of the genus abound. It is the Ρηον of Dioscorides, which some, however, derive from ρεω, to flow.

RHINE-GRAVE (G. *Rhein-graf*). The Count Palatine of the Rhine.

RHUBARB. See RHABARBARUM.

RIBSTON or RIBSTONE PIPPIN. An apple brought from Italy by the late Sir Harry Goodricke. It received its present appellation from having been first grown in this country at Sir Harry's residence, Ribstone Hall, in Yorkshire, where the original tree was still growing a few years since.

RICCIA. A genus of plants, nat. or. *Hepaticæ ;* named in honour of P. F. Ricci, a noble Florentine, and a great patron of botany.

RICE (Fr. *riz* or *ris*, It. *riso*, Sp. and Port. *arroz*, G. *reiz* or *reiss*, D. *ryst*, Dan. *ris*, L. *oryza*, Gr. ορυξα, Eth. *rez*). A plant of the genus *Oryza*, and its seed, of which there is only one species.

"Sume hoc ptisanarium *oryzæ*."—Hor. Sat. iii., 155.

The common rice, *Oryza sativa*, is a native of Hindustan, where it grows in a wild state in and about the borders of lakes. The rice plant is also a native of Ethiopia. Webster gives the Arab. *arazon*, from *araza*, to be contracted, or to be firmly fixed; and he says the word is common to most of the Asiatics, Persians, Turks, Armenians, and Tatars. Others derive the word from Orissa, in Hindustan.

RICHARDSONIA. A genus of plants, nat. or. *Cinchonaceæ*; called after Mr. Richardson, an English botanist.

RICHEBOURG. A fine wine from Richebourg, in Burgundy. It is usually called Vin de St. George.

RIOLITE. A mineral, colour lead-grey, composed of silver and selenium; found at Tasco, in Mexico; named after the mineralogist Del Rio.

RITTERA. A plant, native of the Caribbees; named by Schreber in honour either of Albertus, or Joannes Jacobus Ritter, physician in Silesia, born at Bern 1714.

RIVINA. A plant, native of the West Indies; named by Plumier after Augustus Quirinus Rivinus, prof. of physiology and medicine at Leipzig.

RIVINIAN. A name given to the excretory ducts of the glands situated under the tongue; so called after their discoverer, Rivinus.

ROAM. To wander; to ramble; to rove; to walk or move about from place to place without any certain purpose or direction; lit. to wander to Rome for the sake of religion.

ROAN (Port. *ruão*). A sort of linen for handkerchiefs, made at Rouen, found Rouan.

ROBERD'S-MAN or ROBERT'S-MAN. In the old statutes of England, a bold, stout robber, or night-thief; said to be so called from Robin Hood, a famous robber.—*Johnson*.

ROBERT or HERB-ROBERT. An annual plant, of the genus *Geranium*; probably named after the horticulturist.

ROBERT SAUCE. A sauce made of onions, mustard. butter, pepper. salt, and vinegar (*Bailey*); probably named after the maker.

ROBINIA. A genus of plants, nat. or. *Leguminosæ* ; named after J. Robin, herbalist to Henry IV. of France.

ROCHE ALUM (*Rock alum*). A variety of alum, originally brought from Roccha, formerly called Edessa, in Syria. That now sold under this name is common English alum, artificially coloured.

ROCHELLE SALT. Tartrate of potassa and soda, used in medicine as a mild aperient ; from Rochelle, in France. It is also called *Sel de Seignette*. Its classical name is Rupellensisal ; from Rupella, the L. appellation of Rochelle. " So called from M. Seignette, of Rochelle, by whom it was first prepared " (*Crabb*).

RODOMONTADE (Fr. *id.*, It. *rodomontáta*). Vain boasting ; empty bluster or vaunting ; rant.

" It is thus that Lord Palmerston brought to a close the too numerous bravadoes of his career, by a declaration which combines *rodomontade* with *reculade* in a fashion odiously burlesque."—*M. Forçade*.

The word is derived from *Rodomont*, a blustering and boasting hero of Boiardo, adopted by Ariosto.

ROELLA. A genus of plants, nat. or. *Campanulaceæ*, natives of the Cape and Barbary ; named by Linnæus in honour of William Roelle, prof. of anatomy at Amsterdam, who sent many seeds of plants to Linnæus from both Indies, Africa, and Japan ; amongst others the seeds of this plant from Africa.

ROHRIA. A genus of plants, of only one species, native of Guiana ; named by Schreber after Julius von Rohr, who sent many plants to Europe from South America and the West Indies.

ROMAIC. A term applied to the modern Greek language; from *Rouma*, a name by which the Arabs called the Greeks. The Arabic *Rûm* is used to designate alike Rome, Greece, the Turkish empire, Roumelia, and Asia Minor.

ROMAIKA. A national Greek dance which owes its origin to the classical period of Greek history. See ROMAIC.

ROMAN. An epithet for the type now commonly used, in distinction from the Italic.

ROMANCE. A term denoting the dialect formerly prevalent in some of the southern districts of France, which springs directly from the Roman or Latin language.——A fabulous relation or story of adventures and incidents designed for the entertainment of readers ; a fiction ; *as a verb*, to forge and tell fictitious stories; to deal in extravagant stories. "The Latin ceased to be spoken in France about the ninth century, and was succeeded by what was called the Romance tongue, a mixture of the language of the Franks and bad Latin. As the songs of chivalry became the most popular compositions in that language, they were emphatically called *romans* or *romants*, though this name was at first given to any piece of poetry."

ROMANÉE. A celebrated red wine grown at Romanée, dep. Côte-d'Or, famed for its vineyards.——A common Burgundy with a Romanée label, occasionally sold in England.

ROMANESQUE. A term applied in painting to that which appertains to romance, or rather to fable, as connected with objects of fancy ; in architecture, to the debased styles subsequent to, and imitative of, the Roman ; in literature, to the common dialect in some of the southern districts of France, the remains of the old Roman language.

ROMANISM. The tenets of the Church of Rome.

ROMANIZE. To Latinize ; to fill with Latin words or modes of speech ; to convert to the Roman Catholic religion or opinions ; to conform to Roman Catholic opinions, customs, or modes of speech.

ROMANSH or ROMANSCH. The dialect of the Grisons in Switzerland ; a corruption of the Latin or Roman language.

ROMANTIC. Pertaining to romance, or resembling it ; wild, fanciful, extravagant; as a *romantic* taste, *romantic* notions, *romantic* expectations, *romantic* zeal.——Improbable or chimerical; fictitious ; as a *romantic* tale.——Fanciful, wild ; full of wild or fantastic scenery ; as a *romantic* prospect, a *romantic* situation ; from romance, *q.v.*

ROMANTICISM. The state of being romantic or fantastic;

applied chiefly to the unnatural productions of the modern French school of novelists. See ROMANCE.

ROMANZOVITE. A variety of garnet, colour brown or brownish-yellow ; named after Count Romanzoff.—*Cleaveland*.

ROMEINE. A mineral consisting of antimonious acid and lime, colour hyacinth or honey-yellow ; named after the mineralogist Romé de L'Isle.

ROMEPENNY or ROMESCOT. A tax of a penny on a house, formerly paid by the people of England to the Church of Rome.

ROQUELAURE (Fr.) A man's cloak used in the beginning of the last century ; named after the Duc de Roquelaure, renowned for his courage, his military talents, and his genius.

ROS CALABRINUS. A designation of the officinal manna. "Dew of Calabria," a district of Italy.

ROSELITE. A very rare mineral occurring in small deep rose-coloured crystals, associated with cobalt bloom, at Schneeberg, in Saxony ; named in honour of Dr. Gustavus Rose, of Berlin, a learned naturalist.

ROTA. A red wine from Rota, a seaport, Bay of Cadiz ; sacked by the English in 1702.

ROTHIA. A genus of plants, or. *Cichoraceæ*, natives of the south of Europe; named by Schreber in honour of Dr. Albert William Roth, a physician of Bremen, author of Flora Germanica, &c.

ROTTBOELLA or ROTTBOLLIA. An extensive genus of grasses, distributed throughout Asia, and also found in Egypt; named by Linnæus the younger in honour of Dr. Christian Früs Rottböll, professor of botany and anatomy at the University of Copenhagen, author of several botanical treatises, &c.—*Wright*.

ROUENNERIE. Printed cotton manufactured at Rouen, in Normandy, and celebrated all over France.

ROUNCENVAL. A variety of pea, so called from Roncesvalles (Fr. *Roncevaux*), a frontier village of Spain, in a gorge of the Pyrenees.

ROUSSEA. A climbing shrub, of only one species, found by Commerson in St. Mauritius ; named by J. E. Smith, M.D., in memory of Jean Jacques Rousseau, who wrote very elegant letters on botany.   Linnæus, who frequently corresponded with him, had in his MSS. consecrated a plant to his name ; but the younger Linnæus having, by mistake, published that under the name of Russelia, Dr. Smith gave this new, beautiful, and very singular genus the name of Roussea.—*Miller.*

ROUSSEAU'S DREAM.   A celebrated air composed by Jean Jacques Rousseau, and a pantomime tune in his opera *Le Devin du Village.*   See N. & Q., 2nd S. iii., 13, 135 ; and 3rd S. iii. 260.

ROUSSILLON.   A fine red wine from Roussillon, an old province of France, separated from Spain by the Pyrenees.

ROXBURGHIA.   A plant, a native of Coromandel; named in honour of William Roxburgh, M.D., a native of Scotland, who settled in the East Indies, author of a splendid work on the plants of the Coromandel coast.

ROYAN.   A species of sardine caught in autumn, a table delicacy furnished by the Bordeaux markets ; perhaps named from Royan, a seaport at the mouth of the Gironde.

ROYENA.   A genus of plants, natives of the Cape ; named by Linnæus in honour of Adrian van Royen, prof. of botany at Leyden.

RUABON.   A coal from Rhuabon, North Wales.

RUBICON.   The name of a small river which separated Italy from Cisalpine Gaul, the province allotted to Cæsar. When Cæsar crossed this river he invaded Italy, with the intention of reducing it to his power : hence *to pass or cross the Rubicon* signifies to take a desperate step in an enterprise, or to adopt a measure from which one cannot recede, or from which one is determined not to recede.   Some authors make the *Rubicon* the modern Fiumecino ; others the Pisatello, which flows into it.

RÜDESHEIMER.   A celebrated red wine made from grapes grown at Rüdesheim, opposite Bingen, on the Rhine. The best quality grows upon the terraces overhanging the Rhine, close to Ehrenfels.——An inferior Rhine wine with a Rüdesheimer label, sold in England.

RUDOLPHINE.   An epithet applied to a set of astro-

nomical tables computed by Kepler, and founded on the observations of Tycho Brahe; so named from Rudolph II., King of
Bohemia, Emperor of Germany.

RUFFIAN (formerly *ruffin* and *rouffin*, Fr. *ruffien*, a bawd).
A boisterous brutal fellow; a fellow ready for any desperate
crime; a robber; a cutthroat; a murderer.

> "In the meantime a commune and notable *rufyan* or thefe, whiche
> hadde robbed and slayne a manne, was entred into the barne where Gysyp-
> pus laye."—*Sir J. Elyot.* The Governovr, b. ii., c. **12.**

> "His blood a traitor's sacrifice was made,
>   And smok'd indignant on a *ruffian's* blade."
>   *Young.* Last Day, b. ii.

Webster says, "If this word signifies primarily a robber, it is
from the root of *rob*, Sw. *röfva*, Dan. *röver;* in Scottish, *ruffie*
is a worthless fellow; in It., *ruffiano* is a pimp, Sp. *rufian*, Port.
rufiam, D. *roffiaan*, id." Todd says, "Some have thought that
our word is from *ruff*, the bullies and swaggerers of old time
wearing enormous ruffs." Ferrari derives *ruffiano* from L.
rufa, scurf of the head; and he says *rufare* is to rub the head
and remove the scurf, &c. Du Cange derives *ruffiano* from
rufus, red, because the hair of courtesans was ordinarily red,
whereas that of virtuous women was ordinarily black; and
Ménage adds, that the Italian ladies who pretended to gallantry,
when they washed their heads, made use of a wash which dyed
the hair red, and that on account of its colour they called it
la bionda. He says also, "*Rufien* signifie aussi parmy nous un
homme débauché aux femmes; et ce mot en cette signification
est plus usité qu'en l'autre." Nicot says the Fr. word signifies
a maquereau (*i.e.* a pander or pimp); but that at all events
both the Fr. and Eng. words are from the It. *ruffiano*, which
some derive from Rufus, a celebrated pimp, from *rufus*, red;
because pimps wore red garments.

RUIZIA. A genus of shrubs, natives of the Isle of Bourbon; named by Cavanilles in honour of Don Hippolito Ruiz,
a Spanish botanist, who, in conjunction with Pavon, wrote the
splendid Flora Peruviana.—*Wright.*

RUMBLE. See **RUMBOLD.**

RUMBOLD. A carriage of the stanhope kind; either named after the maker, or from one of the Rumbold family: hence, perhaps, *rumble*, the hind seat of a travelling carriage, for servants.——A machine used to clean small works of cast iron, which soon scrub each other bright by friction.

RUMFORD. Name of one of the earliest improvements of the common stove, for the purpose of saving fuel; invented by the celebrated Count Rumford, whose title was conferred on him by the Elector of Bavaria. His real name was Benjamin Thompson, and he was born at Woburn, New England, in 1752.

RUSSELIA. A genus of plants, found by Jacquin about Havana, in close woods and coppices; named by him in honour of Alexander Russel, M.D., F.R.S., a native of Scotland, author of the Natural History of Aleppo, Lond. 1756.

RUTHERFORDITE. A mineral occurring along with rutile, brookite, zircon, and monazite, at the gold mines of Rutherford & Co., North Carolina.

S.

SABAISM or TSABAISM. The name given by Arabic writers to a species of idolatry, which consisted in worshipping the sun, moon, and stars, and which prevailed to a great extent in Arabia and Mesopotomania. Some derive the word from the Sabaei ($\Sigma\alpha\beta\alpha\iota\iota$), a people of Arabia Felix, who inhabited the northern part of the modern Yemen, the Sheba or Seba of Scripture. According to others, *Tsabaism* was derived from Tsabi, son or brother of Enoch; but (says the writer in the P. Cyc.) it is more probably derived from their worshipping the Host of Heaven, צבא-השמים. It is also called Sabianism, and the Sabian, Sabæan, or Sabaian worship or religion; and its followers Sabians, or Sabeans.

SABBATIA. A genus of North American plants, nat. or. *Gentianaceæ*, of several species, all characterized by a pure bitter principle, on which account they are extensively used in North America in intermittent and remittent fevers; named after L. Sabbatia, an Italian botanist.

SABBY. A soft biscuit, probably from *Savoy*, q.v.

SABELLIANISM. The doctrines or tenets of Sabellius, an Egyptian philosopher of the third century, who advanced the doctrine of unity in the Deity, declaring the Son and the Holy Ghost to be mere qualities. These tenets obtained many proselytes, and met with great success, till the opposition of St. Dionysius caused them to be formally condemned.

SABINA (*Juniperus Sabina*). A tree whose leaves form the active ingredient in the ointment used for keeping up a discharge from blistered surfaces ; so called from the Sabines, whose priests used it in their religious ceremonies.—*Forsyth.*

SABINEA. A genus of plants, nat. or. *Leguminosæ*, whose species are Indian shrubs ; named by De Candolle after Joseph Sabine, F.R.S., long time secretary to the Horticultural Society of London.

SACK. Formerly a dry Spanish wine, supposed by some to be sherry ; still applied to a kind of sweet rubbish.

" Go fetch me a quart of *sack*, put a toast in it."—Merry W. of W.

" Wherein is he good, but to taste *sack* and drink it?"—1 Hen. IV.

> " Let me rejoice in sprightly *sack*, that can
> Create a braine even in an empty pan.
> Canary !"   *T. Beaumont.* The Vertue of Sack.

Bailey renders "*sack* (Sax. *sec*), a wine called canary, brought from the Canary Islands ; also a wine brought to us from Malaga, in Spain." Richardson says, " Lat. *saccare* is to strain through a *sack* or bag ; and in Low Lat. *saccare*, per *saccum* colare et exprimere ; and *saccadum*, liquor aquæ fæci vini admixtus, *sacco* expressus (*Du Cange*). For the kind of wine so called, see the commentators on Shakespeare, Hen. IV. pt. i. (*Drake*) ; Shakespeare and his Times, vol. ii., p. 130." According to some, it was called from Xeque, a prov. of Spain, whence it was brought ; but the name of this wine is found written *sherris-sack* or *sec*, i.e. dry sherry : hence, by abbreviation, *sack*. See SHERRY.

SADDUCISM. The doctrine or opinion of the Sadducees.

SAGERETIA. A genus of plants, nat. fam. *Rhamneæ*,

whose species are found in both North and South America, Java, China, and in India along the foot of the Himalayas; named after M. Sageret, a French vegetable physiologist.

SAHLITE. A massive cleavable variety of augite, first obtained at the Sahla mountain, in Westermania.

ST. ANTHONY'S FIRE. Popular name of the erysipelas; so called because supposed to have been cured by intercession of St. Anthony.

ST. CRISPIN'S LANCE. An awl, so named from Crispin, the famous patron of the shoemakers.—*Bailey.*

ST. EMILION. A celebrated wine made at St. Emilion, France, dep. Gironde.

ST. IGNATIUS'S BEAN. Seed of the *Ignatia amara*, having similar properties to those of nux vomica; named after St. Ignatius.

ST. JOHN'S BREAD. A plant of the genus *Ceratonia;* also called the Carob Tree.—*P. Cyc.*

ST. JOHN'S WORT. A name common to plants of the genus *Hypericum*, most of which have yellow flowers.

ST. JULIEN. A red wine, named from a village near Bordeaux.——In England, a wine made of acetic acid, cream of tartar, and coloured with cochineal or some other substance. ——In France, a variety of prune.

ST. MICHAEL. An orange brought from St. Michael (San Miguel), largest of the Azores or Western Islands.

ST. PÉRAY. A fine high-flavoured white Rhône wine from Saint Péray, dep. Ardèche, renowned for its white wines.

ST. PETER'S WORT. A plant of the genus *Ascyrum*, and another of the genus *Hypericum*. See SAMPHIRE.

ST. STEPHEN'S. Parliament House, Westminster; so called because St. Stephen's Chapel was, till lately, used by the Lower House for its sittings.—*S. F. Creswell.*

ST. VITUS'S DANCE (*Danse de St. Guy*). A disease affecting with irregular movements the muscles of voluntary motion, and attended with a great failure of the general physical strength, called by physicians *Chorea Sancti Viti.* The name is said to have been borrowed from some devotees of *St. Vitus,* who exercised themselves so long in dancing that their

intellects became disordered (*P. Cyc.*) This disease first broke
out in the Archbishopric of Trèves and Cologne, and other
parts of Germany, in 1374. The name was derived from a
chapel in Ulm, dedicated to *St. Vitus*, which was greatly in
vogue with those afflicted with the disease, who flocked thither
in crowds to entreat the saint's intercession in their behalf.
N. & Q. 2nd S. ii. 188 ; Lit. Gazette, July 12, 1856. Horstius
says the name was given to it in consequence of the cure of
certain women of disordered mind, upon their visiting the
chapel of *St. Vitus*, and there dancing from morning till night.

SAL MARTIS (*Salt of Mars*). Green sulphate of iron.

SALAM-STONE. A kind of blue sapphire brought from
Ceylon (*Dana*); probably derived from *Sélan* (Port. *Selan*),
the Malay name for Ceylon.

SALIAN. " The original dance among the Romans," says
M. Blasis, " was the *Salian*, taught first by Salius, an Arcadian:
whence the word *saltatio*." Our author is of opinion that the
saltatio was very similar to the Italian grotesque, which was
nearly the same as our modern tumbling, or the buffoonery of
our English clowns (Fosbroke, Encyc. Antiq. Lond. 1840,
697).

SALIC (Fr. *salique*). Appellation of a law of France by
which males alone can inherit the throne. " A law in France
made by King Pharamond, or, as some say, by Philip the Long,
by which females were excluded from the throne" (*Crabb*).
Echard deduces this word from *sala*, a house, and the law from
the circumstance that a male only could inherit his father's
mansion and the court or land enclosed (Cf. Montesq. b. 18);
others derive the word from *sale* (*salle ?*), because ordained
only for the *sales* (*salles ?*) and royal palaces ; or from *sel*, salt,
as though a law full of salt, *i.e.* of wisdom, by a metaphor
drawn from salt. Indeed, D'avisson derives it from G. *saltz*
and *lik* (salt-like). " Hanc legem *Salicam* barbaro vocabulo
nuncupant origine et nomine, à *sale* deducta. Vox enim *Salica*,
solis Gallis usurpata, sunt duæ voces, à vetere Germanico
idiomate corruptæ. *Saltz* quippe Latinis *sal* vocatur. Et vox
ipsa *lik*, similitudinem aut simile aliquid denotans. Unde vo-
cabulum illud barbarum *Salik*. Lex illa conservatrix, seu sali

similis, vulgo *Salica* dicta." Postel says it had its origin from
the Gauls, and that it was called *Salique* for *Gallique*, " pour
la proximité et voisinage que la lettre *g* en viel moule, avait
avec la lettre *s*." According to others, " *Salique* is a contraction of *Salomonique*, because Solomon was the first who practised this law in Judea, in the person of his son Rehoboam."
The word has also been derived from Salogast, one of the
chief counsellors of Pharamond. Indeed, some assert that
Pharamond himself was called *Salique*. " The most reasonable
derivation," says Ménage, " is from the Saliens (Salii), the name
given to the Franks who dwelt on the borders of the Saale
(Sala), in Germany."

SALISBURY. A tree from China; but why so named is
doubtful. " Salisburia, maiden-hair tree, a genus of plants,
nat. or. *Taxaceæ*" (*Crabb*).

SALLY LUNN. " The bun so fashionable, called the *sally
lunn*, originated with a young woman of that name at Bath
about thirty years ago. She cried them on a basket, with a
white cloth over it, morning and evening. Dalmer, a respectable baker and musician, noticed her, bought her business, and
made a song and set it to music in behalf of *Sally Lunn*. This
composition became the street favourite; barrows were made
to distribute the nice cakes; Dalmer profited thereby and retired, and to this day the *sally lunn* cake claims pre-eminence
in all the cities of England " (Hone's Every Day Book, 1826).

SAM. To " stand Sam." To pay for refreshment or drink;
to stand paymaster for anything. An Americanism, originating
in the letters U. S. on the knapsacks of the United States
soldiers, which letters were jocularly said to be the initials of
Uncle Sam (the Government), who pays for all. In use in this
country (England) as early as 1827.—*J. C. Hotten.*

SAMARITAN. A term denoting the ancient characters
and alphabet used by the Hebrews before the Babylonish captivity, and retained by the Samaritans; so called from Samaria,
principal city of the ten tribes of Israel, belonging to the tribe
of Ephraim, and, after the captivity of those tribes, repeopled
by Cushites from Assyria or Chaldea.——The language of
Samaria, a dialect of the Chaldean.

SAMIAN EARTH. A marl of two species, formerly used in medicine as an astringent; named from the isle of Samos.

SAMIAN STONE. A sort of polishing stone used by goldsmiths. See SAMIAN EARTH.

SAMIAN WARE. Vessels, bowls, and dishes of a bright red colour, and of various sizes, fragments of which have been discovered in almost every European country. Cf. Gent. Mag. Ap. 1844, p. 369; and Jan. 1845, p. 23. See SAMIAN EARTH.

SAMPHIRE or SAMPIRE. A herb of the genus *Crithmum*, which grows upon rocky cliffs near the sea-shore, where it is washed by the salt water. It is used for pickling. In the United States the term is applied to what in England is called glass-wort. The name is said to be a corruption of *St. Pierre* (St. Peter).

SAMPSON. An Australian drink. See SAMSON.

SAMSON. A cant name given to gin by some vendors, from its strength; from the Scripture *Samson*.

SAMSON'S POST. In ships, a strong post resting on the keelson, and supporting a beam of the deck over the hold; probably named, from its strength, from the Scripture *Samson*. ——A temporary or moveable pillar carrying a leading block or pulley for various purposes.

SAND, GEORGES SAND. A variety of chrysanthemum, red, gold centre; named after the celebrated French writer.

SANDWICH. Two pieces of bread and butter, with a thin slice of ham or other meat between them; said to have been a favourite dish of the Earl of Sandwich. "Lord *Sandwich* brought into fashion the luncheon of seasoned meat between slices of bread and butter, which goes by his name" (N. & Q. 2nd S. vii. 418, 447).

> " When Tom Macaulay's Indian sits
>   Where London's ruins stretch afar,
> Little he'll think of England's fame,
>   Of Waterloo and Trafalgar.

> " Yet England's earls e'en then shall live,
>   Remember'd by our tawny censor,
> Whilst yet he boasts his ' *Sandwich* ' box,
>   And wraps him in his ' Spencer.' "

———" A human advertising medium placed between two boards strapped over his shoulder. A *toad in the hole* is the term applied to the same individual when his person is confined by a four-sided box " (*J. C. Hotten*). See also SPENCER.

SANTORIN. A dry red wine, with a port wine flavour; from *Santorin*, largest of a small group of islands in the Grecian Archipelago. This island was also called Thera and Calliste: hence Thera, a white wine, full of body, and Sercial Madeira character; and Calliste, a very superior stout wine, equivalent to and resembling Bucellas. Corinthe is also the name of a stout full-bodied wine, of a champagne flavour, from the same island; but probably named from *Corinth*.

SAPPHIC VERSE. The versification used by Sappho, the Grecian poetess. " The *Sapphic* verse consists of eleven syllables in five feet, of which the first, fourth, and fifth are trochees, the second a spondee, and the third a dactyl. The *Sapphic* strophe consists of three *Sapphic* verses followed by an Adonic " (*Brande*).

SARACENIC. Denoting the architecture of the Saracens, the modern Gothic.

SARASIN or SARRASINE (Fr. *sarrasin*). A plant, a kind of birth-wort (*Polygonum fagopyrum*); so called, says Bouillet, because, originally from Persia, it was brought into Spain by the Arabs or Saracens.——In *fortification*, a sort of portcullis or herse; perhaps first invented or copied from the Saracens. The French give the appellation of *sarrasin* to a sort of wheat (*buckwheat*), originally from Africa, and said to have been named from the Saracens.

SARCENET (Fr. *id.*, Low. L. *saracenicum*). A fine thin woven silk. The name is found written *saracennet*, and is supposed to be a corruption of *Saracenic*, i.e. of Saracen or Oriental origin. Bailey gives It. *saracinetto*, q.d. Saracen's silk. Webster says, " Qu. *saracenicum* or *Saracen* silk." Skinner gives *sericum saracenicum*. " *Sarcenet* or *saracennet*, from its Saracenic or Oriental origin, was known about this period (Edw. I.) The robe of Largesse or Liberality in the ' Roman de la Rose ' is said to have been—

' Bonne et belle,
D'une coute toute nouvelle,
D'un pourpre *Sarrascinesche.*' "

Line 1172.   *Planché.*

" Thou tender heir apparent to a church-ale,
Thou sleight prince of single *sarcenet.*"

Beaum. & F.   Philaster, act v. sc. i.

Dufresne gives " *Saracenicum,* pannus *Saracenici* operis, *Sarcenet,* in Inventario Eccl. Eboracensis ann. 1530 in Monastico Anglic. tom. 3, pag. 177 : *Item una capa del Sarcenet, operata cum imaginibus, etc. Saracenicum opus,* ibidem non semel pag. 321, 326, etc. [Vide *Sarantasmum.*]" Also " *Saracenum,* velamen sanctimonialium comput. ann. 1239, ex. Bibl. Reg.: *Abbatissa S. Antonii pro* vi. *supertunicalibus emptis apud Pontisarum, pro Saracenis, camisiis ; braccis, sotularibus, et caligis, etc. Saracenum* dici videtur quod *Saracenis* mulieribus maxime solitum erat caput velamento operire, ut testatur le Roman de la Rose MS. :

' Mes ne quevre pas le visage,
Qu'il ne veut pas tenir l'usage
Des Sarrasins, qui d'estamines
Cuevrent le vis as Sarrasines
Quant il trespassent par la voie
Que nus trespassans ne les voie,
Tant sont plains de jalouse rage.'

Nisi malis vocis originem deducere a *Saracenicum,* quod ex panno *Saraceni* operis erant ejusmodi velamina (*Vide* Gloss. Med. Græcit. v. Σκαρανικον)."

SARD, SARDOIN.   A variety of chalcedony, colour rich brownish-red; from the same root as *sardel,* q.v.

SARDEL, SARDINE (L. *sardius,* Gr. σαρδιον).   A precious stone ; from Sardis, now Sart, in Asia Minor.   One of the kind was set in Aaron's breastplate (Exod. xxviii).

SARDINE or SARDEL.   A Mediterranean fish, often prepared, like the anchovy, as a delicacy ; so called from being caught near the island of Sardinia.   Ménage (quoting Isidore, xii. 6) seems to think that the *Sardine* (It. *sardina, sardella*) was so named from resembling a fish called the *sar,* which abounded in the neighbourhood of Tyre, formerly called Sarra from that circumstance.

SARDINIAN. A graceful vehicle, named after its patron, the King of Sardinia.

SARDONIA. A kind of smallage; from *Sardonia* (where?), its native soil.—*Forsyth.*

SARDONIC. An epithet applied to that forced, heartless, or bitter laugh or grin which but ill conceals a person's real feelings; so called from the *Sardonic* laugh (*Sardonicus risus*), a spasmodic affection of the muscles of the face, in which the lips are drawn involuntarily apart, giving it a horrible appearance of laughter; frequently met with as one of the symptoms of *tetanus* or locked jaw, or as an attendant on other convulsive affections. It is said to have been originally caused by eating the *Herba Sardonica* or *Sardoa*, a species of ranunculus (*ranunculus sceleratus* of Linnæus) growing in Sardinia.

SARDONYX (Gr. σαρδονυξ, L. *sardonyx, sardonyches*). A stone or gem, nearly allied to onyx ; colour reddish-yellow, or nearly orange; so called from *Sardis* (hod. Sart) in Asia Minor, and ονυξ, a nail, claw, &c.; "from the resemblance of its colour to the flesh under the nail" (Plin. lib. 37, 6). Bailey says, "Partly of the colour of a man's nail, partly of a cornelian colour." According to others, the sardonyx had its name from *Sardo*, the Greek name of *Sardinia*, whence the Carthaginians are said to have exported it.

SARRACENIA. A genus of handsome plants, nat. or. *Sarraceniaceæ* or *Sarracenice*, of four species, natives of North America; named by Tournefort in honour of Dr. Sarrazin of Quebec, regius prof. of anatomy and botany, who sent this plant to him from Canada.

SARSAPARILLA (O. Fr. *sarzepareille*, Sp. *sarsaparilla*). A plant, a species of smilax, whose root is valued in medicine for its mucilaginous and farinaceous or demulcent qualities (*Encyc.*) Much used in medicine to counteract the effects of mercury. Some derive the word from Sp. *zarza*, a bramble, *parilla*, diminutive of *parra*, a vine. Forsyth says it is of Spanish origin, and signifies " red tree." Joseph Scaliger says *saza parilla* is the true *smilax aspera*, well known at Montpellier, and was so named from Sp. *çarza* (*zárza*, a common thorn), and *Parillo*, a Spanish physician who first made use of it as a medicine, and who introduced it into France ; and that the doctors of Montpellier always make sarsaparilla from the roots of the smilax.

SASSOLIN, SASSOLINE. Native boracid acid, found in saline incrustations on the borders of hot springs near Sasso, in Italy.

SATIRE. A composition strongly seasoned with raillery. By some derived from *Satyr;* but most probably from *Satura lanx,* an olio, a medley.—*S. F. Creswell.*

SATURDAY. The last day of the week ; the Jewish Sabbath; from A. S. *Sæternes-dæg,* Saturn's day. See SATURN.

SATUREIA. A genus of plants in the Linnæan system ; so called from the lustful *Satyrs,* because it makes those who eat it lascivious (*Blanch*).——The pharmacopœial name of the summer savory.

SATURN. One of the planets of the solar system, next in magnitude to Jupiter, but more remote from the sun ; so called from *Saturn,* one of the oldest and principal deities, son of Cœlus and Terra, and father of Jupiter. The Gr. name was Κρονος, which at a later period was made equivalent to Χρονος, time.——*Saturnus.* In the *ancient chemistry,* a name given to lead.——Another name for the sable colour in coats of arms.

SATURNALIA. Among the Romans, the festival of Saturn, celebrated in December as a period of unrestrained licence and merriment for all classes, extending even to the slaves. See SATURN.

SATURNALIAN. Loose, dissolute, sportive ; *lit.* pertaining to the *Saturnalia,* q.v.

SATURNIAN. Golden, happy, distinguished for purity, integrity, and simplicity.

" Th' Augustus, born to bring *Saturnian* times."—*Pope.*

Lit. pertaining to *Saturn,* whose age or reign, from the mildness and wisdom of his government, is called the *golden age.*——A verse, a kind of iambic used by the Romans, consisting of six feet and a syllable over.

SATURNINE. Child-devouring ; so called from *Saturn,*

who devoured his sons as soon as born, because he dreaded from them a retaliation of his unkindness to his father.

"The Revolution, struck to save the Republic, has displayed its old *Saturnine* voracity, for the majority of the newspapers devoured by it were Republican."

——Supposed to be under the influence of *Saturn :* hence dull, heavy, grave, not readily susceptible of excitement, phlegmatic; as a *saturnine* person or temper.——In *ancient chemistry*, pertaining to lead ; as *saturnine* compounds.

SATURNITE. A metallic substance, separated from lead in torrefaction, resembling lead in its colour, weight, &c., but more fusible and brittle (*obs.*); so called from *Saturn*, an old appellation of lead.

SATYRIASIS (Σατυριαςις). Immoderate venereal appetite (*Coxe*). "From σατυρος, a satyr, because they are said to be greatly addicted to venery " (*Forsyth*).

SATYRIUM, SATYRION. A plant, supposed to excite salacity (*Pope*) ; so called from the *satyrs*. See SATUREIA ; also Forsyth's Med. Dict. under " Satyrion."

SAUSSURITE. A mineral, colour white, greenish, or greyish, consisting of silica, alumina, lime, and oxide of iron ; named after M. Saussure, who discovered it.

SAUTERNE. One of the best white wines of the Bordelais, made from grapes growing at Sauternes, dep. Gironde, situate in the midst of vineyards. It may occasionally be had in England.

SAVITE. A mineral; a hydrous silicate, occurring in the gabbro rosso of Tuscany ; named after M. Savi.

SAVOY. Common name of a hardy cabbage, much cultivated for winter use; so called from the duchy of *Savoy*, whence it was first brought.

SAVOYARD. In Paris, a sweep; *lit.* a native of *Savoy*, whence the Paris sweeps chiefly come.

SAWNEY. Nickname for a Scotchman, from *Sawney*, a common Christian name in Scotland ; corrupted from *Alexander*.——A simpleton ; a gaping awkward lout.

SAXON BLUE. A deep blue liquid used in dyeing, and

obtained by dissolving indigo in concentrated sulphuric acid ; so called from *Saxony*, whence it was first brought.

SAXONISM. An idiom of the *Saxon* language.

SCALLION. A young onion ; so called in the North of England ; from *Ascalon* (*S. F. Creswell*). See Gerarde's Herbal, and cf. SHALLOT.

SCAMANDER. To wander about without a settled purpose ; possibly in allusion to the winding course of the Homeric river of that name.—*J. C. Hotten.*

SCARBOROUGH WARNING. A warning too shortly given to be taken advantage of. When a person is driven over, and then told to keep out of the way, he receives *Scarborough warning.* Fuller says the proverb alludes to an event which happened at that place in 1557, when Thomas Stafford seized upon Scarborough Castle before the townsmen had the least notice of his approach.—*J. C. Hotten.*

SCARBROITE. Hydrated silicate of alumina, occurring in beds of sandstone covering the calcareous rock near Scarborough.

SCHÆFFERA. A small tree or shrub, native of the West Indies, discovered by Jacquin about Carthagena in New Spain ; named by him in honour of Jacob Christian Schæffer, superintendent of the church at Ratisbon, author of Studii Botanici Methodus, 1758, &c.

SCHEELE'S GREEN. A pigment obtained by mixing arseniate of potassa with sulphate of copper ; perhaps first mixed by Scheele. See next.

SCHEELINE or SCHEELIUM (Fr. *scheelite*). A name sometimes given to the metal tungsten, in honour of Charles William Scheele, an eminent chemist, who was born in 1742 at Stralsund, and who discovered the oxalic, fluoric, malic, and lactic acids.

SCHEFFLERA. A genus of plants, of only one species, native of New Zealand ; named by Forster in honour of Scheffler, physician and botanist at Dantzic.

SCHEUCHZERIA. A genus of plants, natives of Lapland, Siberia, Sweden, Denmark, Germany, Prussia, and Dauphiné ; named by Linnæus in memory of the brothers Scheuchzer, the one professor of mathematics at Zürich, author of Itinera Alpina, the other professor of physics at Zürich, author of a celebrated treatise on grasses.

SCHIEDAM. A name for hollands gin; so called from *Schiedam*, in Holland, which contains upwards of one hundred distilleries, and is the chief seat of the manufacture of Dutch gin. The town has also a large trade in pigs, 30,000 of which are said to be annually fattened on the refuse of the distilleries.

SCHMIDELIA. A tree resembling *Rhus trifoliata*, native of the East Indies; named by Linnæus in honour of Casimir Christopher Schmidel, author of Icones et Analyses Plantarum, Gesneri Botanica.

SCHNEIDERIAN MEMBRANE. The pituitary membrane, which secretes the mucus of the nose; named after Schneider, who first described it.

SCHNEIDERITE. A mineral found with sloanite in the gabbro rosso of Tuscany; named after Schneider, director of the mine of Mount Catini.

SCHOEPFIA. A genus of plants of only one species, a small tree, native of Santa Cruz and Montserrat; named by Schreber in honour of Johann David Schoepf, president of the medical college at Anspach, author of Materia Medica Americana, &c.

SCHOTIA. A genus of plants of only one species, native of Senegal and the Cape; named by Jacquin after Richard Van der Schot, companion in his travels.

SCHOTTISCHE (" Scottish "). A celebrated dance of German origin.

SCHRADERA. A genus of plants of two species, the one discovered by Ryan in the island of Montserrat, the other native of Jamaica; named by Vahl after Hen. A. Schrader, author of Spicilegium Floræ Germanicæ, Hann. 1794.

SCHREBERA. A genus of plants of only one species, a large timber tree, native of the Rajahmundry Circar; named in honour of Joseph Christian Dan. Schreb, professor of physic, &c., at Erlang, editor of Linnæus's Genera Plantarum, and author of many works on botany.

SCHRÖTTERITE. A mineral found in nodules between granular limestone and clay slate on the Dollinger Mountain, near Freienstein, in Styria; analysed by Schrötter.

SCHWALBEA. A genus of plants of only one species, native of North America; named by Linnæus after Schwalbe, a physician.

SCHWEINFURTH GREEN. A compound of arsenious acid and oxide of copper, resembling Scheele's green; probably named from Schweinfurt, in Bavaria.

SCHWENKIA. A biennial plant, native of Guinea; named by Van Royen after Martin Wilhelm Schwencke, physician and professor of botany at the Hague, died 1785.

SCOTTICISM. An idiom or peculiar expression of the natives of Scotland.

SCYTHICUS. A name for the liquorice-root, or anything brought from Scythia; from *Scythia*, its native soil.—*Forsyth.*

SEDAN. A portable chair or covered vehicle for carrying one person, and borne on poles by two men (*Dryden; Encyc.*) Some derive the word from L. *sedeo*, to sit; others from the town of *Sedan*, in France, where this article was first made. " It was in 1634 that Sir Saunders Duncombe first introduced *Sedan* chairs. Sir Saunders was a great traveller, and had seen these chairs at Sedan, where they were first invented " (*Pulleyn*).——A sort of cloth from Sedan.

SEIDLITZ WATER. A saline mineral water from Seidlitz, in Bohemia, often taken as an agreeable aperient. Seidlitz powders are intended to produce the same effect with Seidlitz water.

SEIGNETTE'S SALT. A neutral salt consisting of soda, potash, and tartaric acid; prepared and made known by a Frenchman named Peter Seignette, an apothecary of Rochelle, about the end of the seventeeth century, when it was employed in preference to many other medicines long known, which had been equally serviceable.—*Forsyth.*

SELLA TURCICA (*Ephippium*). A cavity in the sphenoid bone, containing the pituitary gland, surrounded by the four clinoid processes; from *sella*, quasi *sedda*, from *sedere*, to sit,

and *Turcica*, from its supposed resemblance to a Turkish saddle.
—*Forsyth.*

SELTZER WATER (Properly Selter's Water ; G. *Seltzer wasser*, Fr. *Eau de Seltz*). A mineral water containing much free carbonic acid ; named from a spring near the village of Nieder-Selters, in the duchy of Nassau.

SEMOLINA (It.; Fr. *semoule*). This substance, as well as soojee and manna croup, are granular preparations of wheat, deprived of bran. The word is said to be derived from *Semo*, a tutelar deity of sown corn. Others derive it from *semi-moulu*, half-ground.

SENEBIERA. A genus of plants, nat. or. *Crucifera* ; named in honour of John de Senebier, of Geneva, a vegetable physiologist.

SENEGA or SENEKA. The plant called snakeroot, rattlesnake-root, and *Polygala Senega*, growing in the mountainous parts of the United States. It was so named from having been employed by the Seneca or Senegaw Indians as a remedy for the bite of the rattlesnake.

SENEGIN. A name given to polygalic acid, the native principle of the senega root. See SENEGA.

SEQUIN (found chequin, zechin, and zequin ; Fr. *séquin*, It. *zecchino*). A gold coin of Italy and Turkey. The average value at Venice and in other parts of Italy is 9*s*. 5*d*. sterling; in Turkey the *sequin fonducli* is valued at 7*s*. 7*d*. sterling. Webster, under " Zechin," says, "If named from *Zecha*, the place where minted, this is the correct orthography." Bailey, under " Zechin, Zachin," says, " So called from *La Zeecha*, a place in the city of Venice, where the mint is settled ;" probably from θηκη, a repository ; thus θηκη, *theca, zeca*, Zecca. The Spanish has, however, *zequi*, a zechin, an Arabic gold coin formerly used in Spain, and the Arab. has *zuwak*, argentum vivum.

SERAPIAS. Helleborine. A genus of plants, nat. or. *Orchidaceæ* ; " from *Serapis*, a lascivious idol; so called because it was thought to promote venery, or from the testiculated shape of its roots " (Hooper, Lex. Med.)

SERGE (Fr. *id.*; O. Fr. *sarge*; Sp. *serja, sarja*; It. *sargia* a coverlet; Sp. *xerga, jerga*, coarse frieze, and *jarjon*; D. *sergie*).

T

A woollen twilled stuff. *Silk serge* is a twilled silk fabric, used mostly by tailors for lining men's coats. Skinner derives the word from G. *serge*, *teges*, *tegmen*; in D. *sargie*, a coverlet; others from *sarica*, a tunic (*Sarica misticia cum manicas curtas valente siliquas aureas duas. Sarica prasina ornata, valente solido uno*); "and," says Ménage, "as tunics are made ordinarily of *serge*, the name may have been taken for the stuff itself; that the Italians derive it from *sargia*, milled counterpane (*lodier*); others from *serica*." In the supplement he adds, " Although this stuff (*sarge*) is made of wool, it may still derive its name from *sericum*, silk, from being a twine, à la façon des étoffes de soie. Eckchardus le jeune, Moine de S. Gal, *De Casibus Monasterii S. Galli*, ch. 3. *Missus est Magontiam utique pro panis laneis emendis, quos* sericales *aut* punicas *vocant.*" Woollen *serges* are called in France " cadis de Montauban," from Montauban, where they are made. See also SILK.

SERIANA (more commonly Serjania). An entirely tropical South American and West Indian genus of the natural family *Sapindaceæ;* named by Schumacher after Serjeant, a French monk and botanist.

SERICEOUS. Pertaining to silk; consisting of silk; silky; from L. *sericeus*, from *sericum*, silk, muslin; from *sericus*, of or belonging to the *Seres*, or their country. See SILK.——In *botany*, covered with very soft hairs pressed close to the surface; as a *sericeous* leaf.

SERIPHIUM. Flax-weed; from *Seriphus*, name of the island upon which it grew.—*Forsyth.*

SESLERIA. A grass which in its manner of flowering resembles the genus *Aira*, but having the appearance of *Anthoscanthum;* a native of Europe in mountainous and boggy pastures; named by Scopoli in honour of Dr. Leonard Sesler, a botanist, who formed the genus in the island of St. Helen.

SEVERITE. A silicious hydrate of alumina, colour white; found near St. Sever, in France.

SÈVRES. A porcelain made of a clay consisting of felspar in its different states of decomposition, with small quantities of silica and chalk ; so called from Sèvres, a town of France, cap. caut. Seine-et-Oise, where it is manufactured.

SEYD or ZEID. The name of a slave of Mohammed, who was one of the first to acknowledge the divine mission of his master, was adopted by him, and received Zeinab, a cousin of Mohammed, as his wife. The prophet, however, having fallen in love with her himself, Seyd was ready to resign her. Voltaire, in his *Mahomet*, makes Seyd an innocent but blindly submissive youth, who at the prophet's order, kills a person, who turns out to be his own father. *Seyd* is, therefore, sometimes used to denote a man blindly devoted to the will of another. Thus St. Just is called by Mr. Nodier the *Seyd* of Robespierre; and the Duke of Rovigo says in his Memoirs that he has often been taken for the *Seyd* of Napoleon.

SHADDOCK. A large species of orange, *Citrus decumana ;* named after Capt. Shaddock, who first carried this fruit from the East to the West Indies.

SHADRACH. A mass of iron, in which the smelting has failed of its intended effect; probably called from Shadrach, one of the three men who were preserved in the fiery furnace.

SHAKO, CHAKO, or SCHAKO. A military cap. Some derive the word from O. Sp. *zaco* (now *jaco*), a short jacket, formerly used by soldiers ; corrupted from *Jacobus*, i.e. James. Cf. JACKET.

SHALLOON (*ras de Chalons*, Sp. *chalon, chalun*). A slight woollen stuff, the great staple of Halifax, where about 10,000 pieces are annually made for shipment to Turkey and the Levant. The name is said to be derived from *Chalons*, in France, where it was first made. Bailey writes the word *shallons* and *shaloon ;* and Chaucer uses *shalons* for blankets.

SHALLOT (found shalot, shalote, eschalot ; Fr. *échalote* for *eschalote*, It. *scaglogno*, Sp. *escaluña*). A plant, the *Allium Ascalonium*, a species of small onion, the mildest cultivated ; named from Ascalon or Askelon, a city in the land of the Philistines, between Azoth and Gaza, on the Mediterranean coast, where it grows wild, as it does also in many parts of Syria. It was from Ascalon that the Romans imported the *Allium Ascalonium*. Calmet says, " The ancients praise the *shalot*, which takes its name from Askelon." See also Athen. lib. ii. cap. 28 ; Plin. lib. xix. cap. 6 ; Strabo, lib. xvi. ; Stephens, and Ménage. *Ascalonium, ascalonio, ascalone, ascalote, aschalote, eschalot,* Shallot.

SHANGHAI. A tea from Shanghai, in China.——A sort of domestic fowl.

SHAWL. A cloth of wool, cotton, silk, or hair, used by females as a loose covering for the neck and shoulders. This article of dress is said to have been originally manufactured in the heart of India, from the soft woolly inner hair of a variety of the common goat reared in Thibet. The best shawls now come from Cashmere, but they are also manufactured in Europe. According to some, it had its name from Shawl, a town and valley in Beloochistan, the centre of the traffic between Shikarpoor, Kandahar, and Kelat. The town is not now celebrated for its shawls, but carpets and blankets are made there in considerable quantities. Moreover, the Persian *shál* means not only a shawl of goat's hair, but also a coarse mantle of wool and goat's hair worn by dervishes, a tunic without sleeves, a small carpet, &c.

SHELTIE. A Shetland or Zetland pony, a small but strong horse in Scotland ; so called from Shetland, where it is produced. Dr. Edmonston (Zetland, ii. 207) says the *shelties* are very sagacious, so much so, that, in crossing the mossy hills they of themselves select the best "road," though there be not " the vestige of a footprint." See also Ed. Rev. xvi. 152.

SHEMITIC or SEMITIC. An absurd appellation given to the languages called Chaldee, Syriac, Arabic, Hebrew, Samaritan, Ethiopic, and Old Phœnician ; from *Shem*, son of Noah.

SHEPARDITE. A mineral, colour brownish-black, found in small grains in the Bishopville meteorite ; named after Professor Shepard. It was formerly called schreibserite ; doubtless derived from Schreibser.

SHERARDIA. A genus of plants, nat. or. *Rubiaceæ ;* whose only species is the *S. arvensis*, found on sandy soils in Great Britain, continental Europe, and the Crimea ; named by Dillenius after his patron, William Sherard, LL.D., consul at Smyrna.

· SHERRY (formerly Sherris). A strong wine of a deep amber colour, and having an aromatic odour ; so called from Xerez, now Jerez, near Cadiz, where it is made.——A similar wine made at Jerez for the English market.——A wine made in England of *Je ne sais quoi.*

SHILLALY, SHILLALAH, SHILLELY, or SHILLE-LAH. An oaken sapling or cudgel ; so named from a wood, famous for its oaks, near the " Meeting of the Waters," in the county of Wicklow, Ireland. " Four miles from Tinehely is Coolatin Park, residence of Earl Fitzwilliam, well-cultivated fields and comfortable homesteads abounding around the mansion. On this estate is the famed wood, or rather what remains of it, of Shillelah, which gives its name to the solid oak sapling so renowned in Milesian song and story. This wood, which covered the southern portion of the county, was cut down in 1634 by Lord Lieutenant Strafford, who wrested it from the original proprietors, the O'Byrnes, because they were unable to produce any written titles to their lands. Some of the oak was used to roof St. Patrick's Cathedral, and Westminster Hall, it is supposed, was roofed from the same source. Tourist's Handb. for Ireland.

SHIRAZ. A celebrated tobacco, brought through Bushire, from Shiraz, a city of Persia, capital prov. Fars, and formerly capital of Persia itself.——A wine whose flavour is by no means attractive to the European palate, notwith-standing the praises of the poet Hafiz.

SHRAPNEL SHELL. In *gunnery*, a name given to shells filled with musket-balls, which when the shells explode are projected in all directions ; so called from the name of the in-ventor. " Shortly after the siege of Gibraltar Lieut.-Gen. Henry Shrapnel invented the spherical case-shot, which con-sists of a hollow globe of iron, filled with musket-balls and gunpowder. When the shell explodes these balls are projected about 150 yards, and do as much injury as the same number of muskets, in addition to the effects produced by the splinters of the exploded shell. On the adoption of these shells by the artillery, General Shrapnel was granted a pension of £1200 per annum, in addition to his regular pay. He died in 1842" (*T. Wright, M.A.*)

SIBBALDIA. A genus of plants, class *Pentandria:* named after Robert Sibbald, M.D., author of Scotia Illustrata.

SIBERITE. A mineral, a sort of red tourmaline, found in Siberia.

SIBYLLINE. Pertaining to the Sibyls; uttered, written, or composed by Sibyls; like the productions of the Sibyls, who, in pagan antiquity, were certain women said to be endowed with a prophetic spirit, and who resided in various parts of Persia, Greece, and Italy. They are pretended to have written certain prophecies on leaves in verse, which are called *Sibylline verses*, or *Sibylline oracles*. Hence the term is applied to a gipsy or fortune-teller. Hence also *Sibylline books*, or documents of prophecies in verse, supposed to contain the fate of the Roman empire, and said to have been purchased by Tarquin the Proud from a *Sibyl*. *Sibylline* oracles are universally allowed to be spurious, but it is evident that the Romans in particular revered these productions as sacred, and on all important occasions consulted them. Ten, or, as Gellius and some others affirm, fifteen eminent Romans were appointed to superintend and examine them. The *Sibylline* books were preserved till the times of the civil wars between Sylla and Marius. Cf. Aulus Gellius, Attic Nights.

SICILIANO. In *music*, a composition in measures of 6-4 or 6-8, to be performed in a slow and graceful manner; so called from Sicily, where it originated. "*Sicilienne*, sort d'air à danser dans la mesure à six-quatre ou six-huit, d'un movement beaucoup plus lent, mais encore plus marqué que celui de la gique."—Rousseau, Dict. Mus.

SICILIAN VESPERS. The era of the general massacre of the French in Sicily, in 1282, on the evening of Easter Tuesday, at the toll of the bell for vespers.

SIEBERA. A genus of plants of one species, *S. pungens*, native of the Levant; so called after Henry Sieber, a celebrated botanical collector.

SIENNA. Clay coloured by the peroxide of iron and

manganese, known as raw and burnt sienna, according to the treatment it has received (a good artists' colour); from *Siena*, in Italy.

SILESIA. A sort of linen cloth; so called from Silesia, in Russia, where first made.

SILHOUETTE (Fr.) A profile; a representation of the outlines of an object filled in with a black colour. Etienne de Silhouette (who was born at Limôges in 1709, was successively counsellor to the parliament of Metz and master of requests, and who held other important appointments, and was author of several works) greatly occupied the public attention during his short administration by recommending rigid economy. Immediately after his fall everything that was brought out at the time was called *à la Silhouette:* hence the term *Silhouette*, which was in vogue at this time, and was applied in derision to the cheap picture above described.

SILK (A. S. *seolc*, Sw. and Dan. *silke*, Russ. *schilk*). The fine soft thread produced by various species of caterpillars, particularly by the larve of the insect called *silkworm* or *Bombyx mori*. Webster gives the Arab. and Pers. ﺳﻠﻚ *silk*, properly any thread, from Arab. *salaka*, to send or thrust in; to insert, to pass or go. Others derive the word from Gr. σηρ, a silkworm. Rees says, "The ancients were but little acquainted with the use and manufacture of *silk*; they took it for the work of a sort of spider or beetle, who spun it out of its entrails, and wound it with its feet about the little branches of trees. This insect they called *ser*, from *Seres* (Σηρες), a people of Scythia, whom we now call the Chinese, who, as they thought, bred it; whence the silk itself was called *sericum* (σηρικον); but this *ser* of theirs has very little affinity with our silkworm (*Bombyx*), the former living five years, the latter dying annually." Virgil evidently alludes to *silk* in Georg. ii. 121, "Velleraque ut foliis depectant tenuia seres?" Braunius is of opinion that there is no mention of *silk* in the Old Testament, and that it was unknown to the Hebrews in ancient times (De Vestitu Heb. Sacerdotum, lib. 1, cap. viii. sec. 8). The only text supposed to denote that material, and therefore rendered *silk* (מֶשִׁי *meshi*, *sericum*) in our common version, is to be found in Ezek. xvi. 10; but which, it is thought, refers more probably to some valuable article of female attire. Aristotle (Hist. Anim. v. c. 19) is the first ancient author who affords any evidence respecting the use of *silk*. The art of weaving *silk* was first practised in China 2600 years before our era (*vide* Du Halde's Hist. China, vol. ii. 355-6, 8vo ed. Lond. 1736), to which country the labours of the silkworm were wholly confined until the time of the Emperor Justinian. Long before the latter period, however, the Chinese had largely exported the raw material to Persia, Tyre, Berytus, &c., where it was wrought into various forms. The name seems to be derived from the country where it was doubtless first produced, viz. Serica. Serica, in ancient geography, was an eastern country, whose frontier is very vaguely indicated by ancient writers, but which has been more precisely ascertained by Ptolemy. According to the latter, it is bounded on the west by Scythia, on the other side of the Imaus; on the south by unknown territories, and by a part of India beyond the Ganges and the Sines. M. d'Anville refutes the opinion of those who assert that the Serica described by Ptolemy corresponded to the northern part of China, and he adopts that of M. de Guignes (Hist. of the Huns), that it belonged to the conquests of the Chinese towards the west; and he says that, with the exception of a small angular territory at the extremity of the province of Chen-si, towards the north-west, China formed no part of Serica. According to some, the metropolis of Serica (the Sera of Ptolemy) is now known under the name of Can-cheou, the first considerable town that occurs at the entrance of the Chinese province of Chen-si, which belongs to a country known to orientals under the name of Tangut, which, says Rees, may therefore be the country anciently inhabited by the Seres, of which Sera was the capital. The word would come thus: *sericum, seric*, by mutation of *r* into *l, selic, selik*, Silk. "Such, indeed, was the importance of *silk*," says Tomlinson, "that the very people and their country are named Seres and Serica in ancient writings, from the Chinese word *se*, which signifies *silk*. *Sze keen* is the proper orthography, but if the name of the country is of

Chinese origin it might also be from *Sze-e*, an appellation applied to foreigners on all sides of China." Cf. Yates Textrinum Antiquorum, 8° ed. Lond. 1843 ; Wilkinson, Ancient Egyptians, iii. 125, 8°. Lond. 1847, quoting Thompson ; Smith, Dict. of Gr. and Rom. Ant. v. " Sericum," 860 ; and N. & Q. 2nd S. vii. 456, and 500-1.

SILKSTONE. A coal from Silkstone, near Barnsley, Yorkshire.

SILLERY. One of the best sorts of champagne, a non-sparkling wine. Sillery, near Rheims, is not the locality which produces this celebrated champagne. It derives its name from Sillery by a secondary process. Under its name is comprehended the produce of all the vineyards of Verzenay, Mailly, Raument, &c., situated at the north-east termination of the chain of hills which separate the Maine from the Verle, and formerly belonging to the Marquis de Sillery, husband of Madame de Genlis. Having been originally brought into vogue by the greater care bestowed upon its manufacture by the Maréchale d'Estrées, it was long known by the name of *Vin du Maréchale*.

SILLIMANITE. A mineral, colour dark grey and hair-brown, composed of silica and alumina, with some oxide of iron, found at Saybrook, in Connecticut ; named in honour of Prof. Silliman, of Yale College.

SILURIA. A term applied to the fossiliferous strata below the old red sandstone ; so named from the portion of England and Wales in which the successive formations are clearly displayed, and wherein an ancient British people (the *Silures*), under their king Caradoc (Caractacus) opposed a long and valorous resistance to the Romans.

SIM. One of a methodistical turn in religion ; a low churchman ; originally a follower of the late Rev. Chas. Simeon.—*Cambridge ; J. C. Hotten.*

SIMON or SIMPLE SIMON. A credulous gullible person ; so called from a character in a song.—*J. C. Hotten.*

SIMON PURE; " the real Simon Pure," the genuine article. Those who have witnessed Mr. C. Matthews's performance in Mrs. Centlivre's admirable comedy of *A Bold Stroke for a Wife*, and the laughable coolness with which he, the *false Simon Pure*, assuming the Quaker dress and character of the *real one*, elbowed that worthy out of his expected entertainment, will at once perceive the origin of this phrase. See act v. sc. 1, and Hotten's Slang Dict., especially the preface, p. 36.

SIMONIAC. One who buys or sells preferment in the church.—*Ayliffe.* See SIMONY.

SIMONIOUS. Partaking of simony; given to simony, *q.v.* —*Milton.*

SIMONY. The buying or selling ecclesiastical preferment, or the corrupt presentation of any one to an ecclesiastical benefice for money on reward. By stat. 31 Eliz. c. vi. severe penalties were enacted against this crime. So named from Simon Magus, who wished to purchase the power of conferring the Holy Spirit. Acts viii.

SIMPLE SIMON. See SIMON.

SINGLO (*Songlo-tcha*). A species of green tea from China; so called from the Mountain Song-lo, prov. Kiangnan, where it is cultivated.

SIREN (L. *siren*, a mermaid, music, melody; Fr. *sirène*; It. *sirena*). In modern use, an enticing woman, a female rendered dangerous by her enticements.

> " Sing, *siren*, to thyself, and I will dote."—*Shak.*

The *Sirenes* were the three daughters of the River Achelous and one of the Muses, half human, half bird, who by their sweet singing tempted sailors on shore to their destruction. They derived their name from Heb. שׁוּר *shur*, to sing.——Pertaining to a *siren*, or to the dangerous enticements of music; bewitching; fascinating; as, a *siren* song.——A batrachian reptile of Carolina, constituting a peculiar genus, destitute of posterior extremities and pelvis.

SISAL HEMP. The prepared fibre of the American aloe, used for cordage; named from Sisal, a port in Yucatan, whence it is doubtless brought.

SIVATHERIUM. An extinct animal, whose skull and other bones were recently discovered in India. It had four horns and a proboscis, was larger than the rhinosceros, and must have resembled an immense antelope (*Mantell*) ; so called from Siva, an Indian deity; Gr. ϑηριον, a wild animal.

SLAVE (Dan. *slave, sclave;* Sw. *slaf;* D. *slaaf;* G. *sclave;* Fr. *esclave;* Arm. *sclaff:* It. *schiavo:* Sp. *esclavo;* Port. *escravo;* Ir. *schlabhadh;* Gael. *sglàbh*). One wholly subject to the will of another; one who has no freedom of action, but whose person and services are wholly under the control of another; one who surrenders himself to any power whatever; as, a *slave* to passion, lust, or ambition; a mean person; one in the lowest state of life; a drudge; one who labours like a *slave:* hence to *slave,* to drudge, to toil, to labour as a *slave;* so called from the Slavi, or Slavonians, a people who were made *slaves* by the Venetians. The name of this people, however, is said to be derived from the Slavonic word *slava,* praise, glory. "The word acquired its present signification in consequence of the great number of prisoners made by the Germans among the Slavonic nations, and whom they reduced into servitude." Gibbon says, "The national appellation of the *Slaves* has been degraded by chance or malice from the signification of glory to that of servitude. This conversion of a national into an appellative name appears to have arisen in the eighth century in oriental France, where the princes and bishops were rich in Sclavonian captives. From thence the word was extended to general use, to the modern languages, and even to the style of the last Byzantines. Jordan subscribes to the well-known and probable derivation from *slava,* a word of familiar use in the different dialects and parts of speech, and which forms the termination of the most illustrious names." See Gibbon, Decline and Fall, vol. x. 197-8, ed. 1797, text and note; De Orig. Sclav. part i. 40, part iv. 101-2; Journal des Débats, 19 April, 1839, in a note by De Xivry.

SLOANITE. A mineral, a hydrous silicate, from the gabbro rosso of Tuscany; doubtless named after Sloane.

SLONEA. A genus of liliaceous plants, trees, natives of South America; named in honour of Sir Hans Sloane, founder of Chelsea botanical garden.

SMITHIA. A genus of leguminous plants; named after the late Sir James Smith, the celebrated botanical writer.

SMYRNIUM (Σμυρνιον of Diosc.) A genus of plants, now of the nat. or. *Umbelliferæ*, of seven species, natives of Africa and North America; so named, according to some, from the city of Smyrna. Others say from σμυρνα, the same with μυρρα, because the root yields a juice very similar to myrrh.

SNOOKS. An imaginary personage often brought forward as an answer to an idle question, or as the perpetrator of a senseless joke (*J. C. Hotten*); corrupted from *Sevenoaks*, in Kent, but why is doubtful. *Snooks* is an existing surname.

SNOWDON PUDDING. A pudding made of fine raisins, butter, minced beef, kidney suet, bread crumbs, salt, rice flour, lemon marmalade, pale brown sugar, whisked eggs, and grated rinds of lemons; so named from being constantly served to travellers at the hotel at the foot of *Snowdon*, in North Wales.

SOBIESKI'S SHIELD (*Scutum Sobieski*). A modern northern constellation, consisting of eight stars; doubtless named after Sobieski, the patriot King of Poland, surnamed the Great.

SOCINIANISM. The tenets or doctrines of Socinus, a native of Sienna, in Tuscany, founder of the sect of *Socinians*, in the sixteenth century. He held Christ to have been a mere man inspired, denied His divinity and atonement, the doctrine of original depravity, and kindred doctrines.

SOCRATIC, SOCRATICAL. Pertaining to Socrates, or to his language or manner of treating or philosophizing. The *Socratic* method of reasoning and instruction was by a series of questions leading to the desired result.

SOCRATISM. The doctrines or philosophy of Socrates.

SODOMY. A crime against nature; so called because committed by the inhabitants of Sodom, one of the five cities in the land of Canaan which were utterly destroyed by fire.

SOLANDRA. A genus of plants, nat. or. *Solanaceæ*, native of Jamaica; named by Linnæus the younger in honour of Daniel Charles Solander, M.D., D.C.L., a Swedish naturalist, disciple of Linnæus, under-librarian of the British Museum, companion of Sir Joseph Banks in his voyage round the world with Captain Cook.

SOLECISM. Impropriety in language, or a gross deviation

from the rules of syntax; incongruity of words; want of correspondence or consistency. "Any unfitness, absurdity, or impropriety" (*B. Jonson*).

"A barbarism may be in one word; a *solecism* must be of more."— *Johnson*. From Cicero.

"Cæsar, by dismissing his guards, and retaining his power, committed a dangerous *solecism* in politics."— *Middleton*.

From Gr. σολοικισμος, impropriety of language, barbarism; said to be derived from the Soli, a people of Attica, who being transplanted to Cicilia, lost the purity of their language. Hence the Gr. σολοικια, impropriety of language; σολοικιζω, to speak like the Soli, to speak ungrammatically or incorrectly; Σολοικος, an inhabitant of Soli, of Athenian origin, who spoke in a corrupt dialect. "*Solecism* (*solœcismus*, σολοικισμος), a grammatical term which is used by the later Greek and Roman writers, and by modern grammarians also, though in a somewhat different sense. It is defined by Sinnius Capito (Gell. v. 207) as an unequal and improper arrangement of the parts of speech; that is, as a violation of the rules of syntax. Quinctilian (i. s. 28, &c.) specifies four kinds of *solecisms* : the first consists in the addition of a superfluous word; the second, in leaving out one that is necessary; the third, in perverting the order of the words of a sentence; and the fourth, in using an improper form of a word. The ancients also used the word in a wider sense, understanding by it any kind of fault, error, or mistake, whether made in speaking, writing, or acting. Modern grammarians designate by *solecism* any word or expression which does not agree with the established usage of writing or speaking. But, as customs change, that which at one time is considered a *solecism* may at another be regarded as correct language. A *solecism*, therefore, differs from a barbarism, inasmuch as the latter consists in the use of a word or expression which is altogether contrary to the spirit of the language, and can, properly speaking, never become established as correct language. The term *solecism* was supposed by ancient grammarians to be derived from Soli, a town of Cilicia, where the language of the original Greek settlers, who were few in number, became corrupt through the influence of the people by whom they were surrounded " (*P. Cyc.*)

SOLFATARA. A volcanic vent from which sulphur, sulphureous, watery, and acid vapours and gases are emitted; so named from Solfaterra, the celebrated mountain of Naples, called by the ancients Phlegræi Campi.

SOLFERINA or SOLFERINO. The new pink; a pink of a dark bright colour; named from Solferino, in Italy, scene of the battle between the French and Italians and the Austrians in 1859.

SOLOMON'S LEAF. A plant so called.

SOLOMON'S SEAL (*Sigillum Salomonis*). Popular name of several plants belonging to the genera *Polygonatum, Smilacina, Streptopus*, &c., the fresh rhizome of which is used as an outward application for bruises. Dried and powdered, it is said to be antidysentric; and is so called from having upon its root the resemblance of an impression made by a seal.

SOMERVILLITE. A Vesuvian mineral related to gehlenite; doubtless named after its discover Somerville, or in honour of one of that name.

SOMMITE. Rhomboidal felspar, occurring in granular limestone at Monte Somma, and in the lava of Capo di Bove, near Rome. It is also called nepheline (from νεφελη, a cloud), because in nitric acid its transparent fragments become cloudy.

SORBONIST. A doctor of the Sorbonne, a theological college in the University of Paris, founded by Robert de Sorbonne, A.D. 1250. *Sorbonne* is properly the name of the building, from which the theological faculty are called the *doctors of the Sorbonne.—Murdock.*

SORDAWALITE. A mineral, colour greyish or bluish-black, in appearance resembling pit-coal; found near Sordawala (Sordawald, *Webster*), in Wibourg, Finland.

SOUBISE. A particular way of serving up cutlets (*côte-lettes à la Soubise*); so named after the Prince de Soubise, marshal of France.

SOUTHDOWNS. Name given to a celebrated variety of sheep bred on the South Downs, in Sussex.

SPA. A general name for a spring of mineral water; so

called from Spa, a town of Belgium, famous for its mineral springs. Spa water is the lightest and most subtle of all the mineral waters, and is said to give great relief in all disorders of the kidneys, ureters, and bladders, whether occasioned by stone, gravel, or ulcerations.

SPANIEL (Fr. *épagneul*, L. *hispaniolus*). A dog used in sports of the field, remarkable for his sagacity and obedience. Some derive the word from *Hispaniola*, now Hayti; but it is rather from *Spain*, whence the breed (*canis Hispanicus*) were first brought. Indeed, the Spaniards themselves were anciently called *Spaniels* by the English. See also P. Cyc.; Duchat's Notes on Rabelais; Maturin Corderius; Pennant; and especially Ménage.——To follow like a *spaniel*, to fawn, to cringe, to be obsequious; a mean, cringing, fawning person.

SPANISH BROOM. A shrub of the genus *Spartium*, thickly set with verdant flexible rush-like twigs; from Spain.

SPANISH BROWN. A species of earth used in paints, whose colour depends upon the sesqui-oxide of iron; from Spain.

SPANISH CHALK (French chalk). A variety of steatite or silicate of magnesia; from Spain.

SPANISH FLY (*Cantharides*). The blister-fly; so called because the best are brought from Spain.

SPANISH NUT. A bulbous plant, the *Moræa Sisyrinchium* of the south of Europe (*Miller*); originally from Spain.

SPANISH WHITE (white bismuth). Nitrate of bismuth; also called pearl-white, magistery of bismuth, &c.; a white earth from Spain, used in paints.

SPARMANNIA. A genus of plants, nat. or. *Tillaceæ*; called after Sparmann, the Swedish botanist, who accompanied Captain Cook in his second voyage.—*Crabb.*

SPARTAN. Hardy, undaunted; as, *Spartan* souls; *Spartan* bravery; so called from the ancient Spartans, who were celebrated for their hardiness and bravery.

SPENCEAN SYSTEM. A plan devised and published by one Thomas Spence, a political enthusiast, by which the human kind could be provided with sustenance without pauperism. He died in October, 1814.

SPENCER. A short over-jacket worn by elderly gentlemen.

> " Two noble earls, whom if I quote
>   Some folks might call me sinner,
> The one invented half a coat,
>   The other, half a dinner.

> " The plan was good, as some will say,
>   And fitted to console one,
> Because in this poor starving day
>   Few can afford a whole one."

It is said that Lord Spencer told his tailor to cut off the tails of his coat, and he would get some custom by it: hence the name. " This article of dress originated with the late Lord Spencer. His lordship, when Lord Lieutenant of Ireland, being out a hunting, had, in the act of leaping a fence, the misfortune to have one of the skirts of his coat torn off, upon which his lordship tore off the other, observing, that to have but one left was like a pig with one ear. Some inventive genius took the hint, and, having made some of these half-coats, out of compliment to his lordship gave them the significant cognomen of *Spencer*" (*Pulleyn*). "*Spenser*, from Lord Spenser, who introduced the short round overcoat, from under which the swallow-tails protruded. Hence, to '*spenser*' a man was to tear off his coat-tails, so that he would appear as in a jacket. This is a word in the mouths of old electioneering or fast men" (*S. F. Creswell*).——A sort of jacket formerly worn by women.——Among *seamen*, a fore-and-aft sail set abaft the fore and main masts ; a trysail. See also Notes and Queries, 2nd S. vii. 418, 447.

SPIELMANNIA. A plant of only one species, native of the Cape ; named in honour of Jas. Reinbold Spielmann, professor of medicine and botany at Strasbourg ; author of Prodromus Floræ Argentoratensis, &c.

SPIGELIA. Worm-grass ; a genus of plants ; named in honour of Adrian Spigelius, professor of anatomy and surgery at Padua ; born at Brussels, 1578.

SPINACH, SPINAGE (L. *spinacia*, It. *spinace*, Sp. *espinaca*). A plant of the genus *Spinacia*, whose leaves are boiled for greens and used for other culinary purposes. See SPINACIA.

SPINACIA. Spinach, spinage. A genus of plants, nat. or. *Chenopodiaceæ.* "From Ισπανια, Spain, whence it originally came; or from its spinous seed" (*Forsyth*). "From *spina*, a thorn, on account of its prickly fruit" (*P. Cyc.*)

SPINOZISM. The form of Pantheism taught by Benedict Spinosa, a Jew of Amsterdam, who maintained that God is not only the maker, but also the original *matter*, of the universe, so that creation was only a development of Himself by the Deity.—*Murdock.*

SPRUCE. Nice, trim, neat without elegance or dignity; formerly applied to things with a serious meaning; now applied to persons only (*Webster*).

" He is so *spruce* that he never can be genteel."—Tatler.

" Now, my *spruce* companions, is all ready, and all things neat ?"—Tam. of the Sh.

> " Beware of men who are too *sprucely* dress'd,
> And look, you fly with speed a fop profess'd."
>
> *Congreve.* Ovid Imitated.

"Salmacis would not be seen of Hermaphroditus till she had *spruced* up herself first."—*Burton.* Anat. Melanc. p. 335.

Minshew derives *spruce*, in the sense of neat, trim, *a purus*. Skinner from Fr. *preux*, valiant. Junius says the well-fed and strong are called *spruze* and lustie young fellows, from A. S. *spryttan*, to grow, to spread. Dr. Johnson says, " I know not whence to deduce it, except from *pruce*. In ancient books we find a furniture of *pruce*, a thing costly and elegant, and thence probably came *spruce*." The word is doubtless corrupted from *Prussian* leather, found written *Spruce* leather, and also *Pruce*. (" The leather was of *Pruce*." Dryden's Fables). A *spruce* person was one dressed in the Prussian fashion. Hall, the chronicler, describing the appearance of Sir E. Haward and Sir Thomas Parre, says they were "appareyled after the fashion of Prussia or *Spruce*" (Hall, Chron. 513; N. & Q. 3rd S. v. 385). "Perhaps," says Richardson, "the quotation from Hall will show the true origin of the word. It was the custom of our ancestors, on especial occasions, to dress after the manner of particular

U

countries. The gentlemen who adopted that of Prussia or *Spruce* seem, from the description of it, to have been arrayed in a style to which the epithet *spruce*, according to our modern usage, might have been applied with perfect propriety. Prussian leather (*corium Pruscianum*) is called in Barett by the familiar name of *spruce*." The beer called *spruce* is probably from a totally different root; perhaps from the German form of the word, viz. *sprossen-bier* (*sprossen-fichte*, the spruce tree); from *sprossen*, sprouts; *sprossen*, to sprout, to bud; because *spruce* is made from the twigs and buds of the tree; or it may be from Gr. πευκη, a pine or fir. The term *spruce* for a fir-tree is not only applied to all the species of that section of the Linnæan genus *Pinus* which are comprehended under " Abies," but likewise to some that are comprehended under " Peuce."

STAMBOULY. A Constantinopolitan coin, current at Bassora for 20¼ mamoodies; named from Stamboul, the Turkish appellation of Constantinople.

STANHOPE. A light two-wheeled carriage without a top; named after Lord Stanhope, for whom it was contrived. " So called from being introduced into the *beau monde* by the Hon. Mr. Stanhope" (*Pulleyn*).

STANHOPE LENS. A lens, in shape, a cylinder of small diameter, terminated at one end by a hemisphere, the other end being a portion of a sphere less than a hemisphere; named after the late Lord Stanhope.

STANHOPE PRESS. A celebrated press, invented by Lord Chas. Stanhope, who died in 1816.

STEINBERG (frequently called Stein). A wine made from grapes grown at Steinberg, near Biberich, on the Rhine. It is held in as great esteem and is equally priced with Johannisberg.

STEINMANNITE. A mineral, colour lead grey, found at Przibram, in Bohemia, with silver, blende, pyrite, and quartz; named after Steinmann.

STENO'S DUCT. The excretory duct of the parotid gland; called after its discoverer, Nic. Steno, a learned anatomist, who was born at Copenhagen in 1638. He was

author of many works, the principal of which is Elementorum
Myologicæ Specimen, &c.

STENTORIAN. Extremely loud; as, a *stentorian* voice;
able to utter a very loud sound; as, *stentorian* lungs: like
Stentor (Στεντωρ), a herald of the Greeks before Troy (mentioned by Homer), whose voice was as loud as that of fifty
other men; according to the Schol., an Arcadian who con-
tended with Mercury in shouting, and lost his life.

> " Ενθα στασ' ηυσε θεα λευκωλενος Ηρη,
>
>   Στεντορι εισαμενη, μεγαλητορι, χαλκεοφωνω,
>
> Ος τοσον αυδησατχ', οσον αλλοι πεντηκοντα."
>
>   Il. v. 784.

"There standing, the white-armed goddess Juno shouted
aloud, having likened herself to great-hearted, brazen-voiced
Stentor, who was accustomed to shout as loud as fifty other
men."

STEPHANITE. A mineralogical synonym of one of the
varieties of brittle sulphuret of silver, occurring in Saxony,
Bohemia, Hungary, the Hartz, in Mexico, and Peru; named
after the mineralogist Stephan.

STEPHEN or ST. STEPHEN'S DAY. A festival of
the Christian church, observed on the 26th Dec. in memory
of the first martyr St. Stephen.

STERLING. The lawful current money of England; as
a pound *sterling*; a shilling *sterling*; a penny *sterling*. It is
not now applied to the coins of England; but *sterling* cost,
sterling value are used. It was so called from the *Esterlings* or
Easterlings, Saxons who occupied the district of the present
Hanse Towns, and who were the earliest traders of Europe
(Spelman, Gloss. 203; Dufresne iii. 165). "Probably from
Easterling, once the popular name of German traders in England, whose money was of the purest quality" (*Camden*). "So
called from *Esterlings*, i.e. Prussians and Pomeranians, who in
old times were artists in filing gold and silver, and taught it to
the Britons" (*Bailey*). "*Sterling*, *sterlingum*, was and is the
epithet for silver money current within the realm; and took

name from this, that there was a pure coin stamped first in
England by the Easterlings or merchants of East Germany, by
the command of King John, and accordingly Roger Hoveden,
parte poster. suor. annal. fol. 377, writes it *Esterling*" (*Cowel*).
See also Stat. of Purveyors, cap. 13; stat. 31 Edw. I.; Lownd's
Essay upon Coins, p. 14; Kennet's Gloss. in Sterlingi; and
Ruding's Hist. of Coinage.——Genuine, pure, of excellent
quality; as, a work of *sterling* merit; a man of *sterling* wit or
good sense.

STILTON.   A well-known cheese first made at Stilton,
co. Huntingdon, but now chiefly in Leicestershire.   "Stilton,
'that's the Stilton,' or 'it is not the Stilton,' *i.e.* that is quite
the thing, or that is not quite the thing; polite rendering of
'that is not the cheese.'" (*J. C. Hotten*).

STŒCHAS.   French lavender; from Στοιχαδες, the islands
on which it grew.—*Forsyth.*

STOIC (Στοιχος).   A disciple of the philosopher Zeno, who
founded a sect.   He taught that men should be free from
passion, unmoved by joy or grief, and submit without complaint to the unavoidable necessity by which all things are
governed; from Στοα, a porch in Athens where Zeno taught.

STOIC, STOICAL.   Pertaining to the Stoics or to their
doctrines; not affected by passion, unfeeling, manifesting indifference to pleasure or pain.   See STOIC.

STOICISM.   A real or pretended indifference to pleasure
or pain; insensibility; the opinions and maxims of the Stoics.
See STOIC.

STOKIN or STOKEN.   An apple; probably named from
Stoke, in Herefordshire.

STOLPENITE.   The bole of Stolpen, a town of Saxony.

STRADUARIUS.   A violin; named from its maker,
Antonio Stradivarius, most skilful pupil of Amati, born at
Cremona about 1670, died about 1728, whose altos, contre-
bassos, but, above all, whose violins are in the highest estima-
tion.

STRAKONITZITE.   A yellowish green steatite-like
mineral, forming pseudomorphs at Mutenitz, near Strakonitz,
in Bohemia.

STRATHSPEY. A lively Scotch dance, a sort of reel, danced in most parts of Scotland; named from Strathspey.

STRELITZIA. A genus of plants of two species, natives of the Cape; named by Sir Joseph Banks in honour of Queen Charlotte of Great Britain, of the family of Mecklenburg-Strelitz, a patroness of the science of botany.

STROGANOWITE. A mineral, a silicate, from near the River Sludänka, in Dauria; named after M. Stroganow.

STROMEYERITE. A steel-grey ore of silver, consisting of sulphur, silver, and copper (*Dana*); named after M. Stromeyer.

STROMNITE. Another name for bary-strontianite, a compound of carbonate of strontian and sulphate of baryta; called from Stromness, in Orkney.

STRONTIA. A genus of ponderous earths, consisting of strontian earth combined with acids. See STRONTIAN.

STRONTIAN. An earth which when pure and dry is perfectly white, and resembles baryta in many of its properties; named from Strontian, in Argyleshire, noted for its rich lead mines, where it was discovered in 1790.

STRONTIUM. A base of strontian, *q.v.*

STRUMPFIA. A genus of plants of only one species, native of Curaçao; named by Jacquin after Christop. Car. Strumpff, professor of chemistry and botany at Halle, in Germany, editor of Linnæus's Genera in 1752.

STRUVITE. A name given to the crystallised ammonio-magnesian phosphate, found in peat earth in digging the foundation of a church at Hamburg; named in honour of Struve.

STYGIA. A water made from corrosive sublimate; so called, on account of its supposed poisonous qualities, from Styx, a name given by the poets to one of the rivers of hell.

STYGIAN. Hellish; infernal.

> " At that so sudden blaze, the *Stygian* throng
>   Bent their aspect."—*Milton.*

So called from Styx, one of the rivers of hell, over which the shades of the dead passed, or the region of the dead.

SUFFOLK PUNCH. A variety of team horse; probably bred in Suffolk.

SULTAN OSMAR. A turban ranunculus so named.

SULTAN PLANT or SWEET SULTAN. An annual flowering plant, *Centaurea moschata;* named after one of the sultans of Turkey.

SULTANA. A raisin; named in honour of the Sultana. *i.e.* the queen of the Sultan of Turkey.

SULTANIN. A former Turkish money of 120 aspers; also a gold coin worth 10s.; also a name for the Venetian gold sequin; doubtless named after one of the sultans of Turkey.

SURAT. Coarse short cotton grown in the neighbourhood of Surat, in the Bombay presidency (*S. F. Creswell*).——"An adulterated article of inferior quality. This word affords a remarkable instance of the manner in which slang phrases are coined. In the report of an action for libel in the *Times*, May 8, 1863, it is stated that since the American civil war it has been not unusual for manufacturers to mix American cotton with *Surat*, and the latter being an inferior article, the people in Lancashire have begun to apply the term *Surat* to any article of inferior or adulterated quality. The plaintiffs were brewers, and the action was brought to recover special damages resulting from the publication of an advertisement in these words:—'All in want of beerhouses must beware of Beaumont and White, the *Surat* brewers'" (*J. C. Hotten*).

SURIANIA. A plant of only one species, native of the sea-coast of South America and the West India Islands; named by Plumier in honour of Donat Surian, physician at Marseilles, who accompanied him in his travels.

SURINAMINE. A crystallisable principle obtained from the bark of the *Geoffroya Surinamensis* or Surinam bark, *i.e.* from Surinam, in Lower Guiana.

SUSSEX MARBLE. A variety of limestone constituting one of the freshwater deposits of the Wealden group.

SWEDE. A turnip originally from Sweden.

SWEDENBORGIANISM. The doctrines of the followers of Emanuel Swedenborg, who claimed to have habitual intercourse with the world of spirits, and to have received Divine instructions from on high. He denied the doctrine of the Trinity, and maintained that Jesus Christ alone is God. He taught the doctrine of *correspondences*, i.e. that there is a spiritual meaning of the Scriptures lying back of the literal one, which constitutes the only true meaning.—*Encyc. Am.*

SWEETIA. A genus of leguminous plants; called after Robert Sweet, F.L.S., author of several botanical works.

SWERTIA. A plant of six species, natives of Germany, Austria, Switzerland, France, and Siberia, in Alpine bogs, Virginia, Arabia Felix, Canada, and Kamschatka; named by Linnæus in honour of Eman. Sweert, a cultivator of bulbs and flowers in Holland, author of Florilegium in 1612.

SWIETENIA. A genus of plants, nat. or. *Cedrelaceæ*, of three species, one of which is the mahogany tree, a native of the warmest parts of America, and growing plentifully in Cuba, Jamaica, Hispaniola, and in the Bahamas; named by Jacquin in honour of the illustrious Van Swieten, chief physician to Maria Teresa, Empress of Germany, who, at his persuasion, founded the botanic garden at Vienna.

SWISS. A mercenary. This term arose from the hired bands of Swiss soldiers who, in the Middle Ages, and down to our own times, found employment in the armies of foreign states. *Le Suisse*, in a French church, is the verger (from this post being formerly held by Swiss), and is usually a tall man dressed rather more extravagantly than an English dowager's footman, with livery, cocked hat, and staff.—*S. F. Creswell.*

SYBARITIC, SYBARITICAL. Luxurious, wanton; like a Sybarite. " On the 4th I shall get to town, when I hope you will dine with me on a single dish, to atone to phylosophy for the *sybaritic* dinners of Prior Park " (Holland, Plinie b. xviii. c. 30). So called from Sybaris, a town of Magna Græcia, whose inhabitants were noted for their luxury and sensuality. " Sybaris, a Greek city in Lucania, in Southern Italy, situated between the River Crathis (hod. Crati) and the Sybaris (hod. Coscile, Coscilello, or Siburi). It was a colony founded about B.C. 720 by Achaians and Troezenians (Aristotle, Polit. v. ii. 156, ed. Göttling; Strabo, vi. 244). Strabo, without men-

tioning the Troezenians, calls it an Achaian colony founded
by Iseliceus.   In consequence of the fertility of the district
this colony soon increased in wealth and power; for at the time
of its greatest prosperity, about 200 years after its foundation,
it had, according to Strabo, acquired the dominion over four
neighbouring tribes, and had twenty-five subject towns.   The
city itself occupied a space of fifty stadia in circumference, and
the Sybarites were enabled to send an army of 300,000 into
the field, a number which does not appear so unreasonable as
some modern writers have thought (Strabo, Diodorus Sic. xii.
9).   Sybaris itself also became the mother of other colonies,
such as Posidonia, and carried on a considerable commerce,
especially with Miletus, in Asia Minor.   But the prosperity of
Sybaris had a pernicious influence on the people, and within
the short period of 210 years that it existed the effeminacy
and the luxury of the inhabitants were carried to such a pitch
that the name *Sybarite* became proverbial and synonymous
with a voluptuous person.   Many curious particulars in illus-
tration of their effeminate character are mentioned in Athenæus which it would be difficult to believe if they were not
reported on the authority of Aristotle, Timæus, and Phylar-
chus.   Thus it is stated, among other things, that it was forbidden by law to carry on within the city any trade or craft
which made a noise, or might possibly disturb the citizens in
their sleep; and for the same reason no person was allowed to
keep cocks (Athenæus, xii. 518, &c.)   The arts which contributed to the enjoyment of life were prized most highly, and
those who distinguished themselves as inventors in this line
were considered benefactors to the nation.   A Sybarite of the
name of Smindyrides is called by Herodotus the most luxurious man that ever lived; and it is said that when he went to
Sicyon to sue for the daughter of Cleisthenes he was accompanied by one thousand cooks and fowlers (Herodotus, vi. 27;
Athenæus, xii. 511 and 541.   Cf. Perizonius on Aelian,
Var. Hist. ix. 24).   .   .   .   It is probable that all we read
about the effeminacy of the Sybarites applies only to the ruling
aristocracy.   .   .   .   The city was taken, sacked, and razed
to the ground, and most of the inhabitants put to the sword, by

Croton, B.C. 510. . . . The site of the ancient Sybaris is at present unknown, but it is generally supposed to have been situated near the modern Torre Brodognato or Terra Nuova" (*P. Cyc.*)

SYDNEAN or SYDNEIAN. A name given to a kind of white earth brought from Sidney Cove, in South Wales.

SYENITE or SIENITE. A compound granular rock composed of quartz, hornblende, and felspar, colour greyish; so called because many ancient monuments consisting of this rock have been brought from Syene, in Upper Egypt.— *Dana.*

SYEPOORITE. A mineral, a sulphuret, employed by the Indian jewellers to give a rose colour to gold; so called from Syepoor, near Rajpootanah, in North-West India, where it occurs in ancient schists with magnetic pyrites.

SYLVANITE. Native tellurium, a metallic substance discovered in Transylvania.

SYPHILIS. Dr. Mason Good says that this term was probably invented by Frascatorio, from Gr. συν and φιλεω, importing "mutual love;" for such is the title by which he has designated his celebrated and very elegant poem on this very inelegant subject. Others derive it from σιφλος, disgusting; others from the name of a shepherd who fed the flocks of King Alcithous, and who insulted the sun, in vengeance of which the venereal disease was sent upon earth.—Hooper, Lex. Med.

SYRIAC. The language of Syria, especially the ancient language of that country.

SYRIANISM or SYRIASM. A Syrian idiom, or a peculiarity in the Syrian language.

SYRTIS (Gr. συρτις). A quicksand or shelve in the water, made by the drift of sand or gravel; so called from the Greater and Lesser Syrtes, on the north coast of Africa.

T.

TÆNIA TARINI. A yellowish horny band lying over the *vena corporis striati*, first noticed by Tarinus. It is a thickening of the lining membrane of the ventricle.

TAFFY. A Welchman; corruption of *David*, a common name in Wales.

TAFILET. An excellent fig imported into Europe in considerable quantities; from *Tafilelt*, a principality of Marocco, east of the Atlas range.

TAGILITE. A mineral, colour emerald green to mountain green, occurring at Nischnii Tagilsk in reniform masses on brown iron ore.

TAGLIACOTIAN or TALIACOTIAN. Rhinoplastic, applied to the surgical operation for restoring the nose. The Taliacotian operation is a mode of forming a new nose from the integuments of the forehead, or from the arm, &c., of another person; named from the first operator, Gasper Taliacotius (Tagliacozzi), a Venetian surgeon, whose statue stands in the anatomical theatre at Bononia, holding a nose in his hand.

TAGLIONI. An overcoat; so named after Madame Taglioni, the late celebrated dancer.

TALBOR'S POWDER (English remedy). The name formerly given in France to cinchona, from the successful use of it in intermittent fever by Sir Robert Talbor, who employed it as a secret remedy. For a similar reason it has, at different times, received the names of the Countess's Powder, Jesuits' Powder, &c.

TALBOTYPE. A process of photography invented by Mr. Fox Talbot.

TAMARIND (Sp. *tamarindo*, It. *tamarino, tamarindi*, Fr. *tamarin*). A tree which yields the fruit called *tamarinds*. Two species are recognised, one a native of the East Indies, Arabia, and Egypt; the other of the West Indies and South America. It is cultivated in both the Indies for the sake of its shade, and for its grateful cooling acid fruit, the pulp of which, dried either alone or with salt, or mixed with boiled sugar, is imported into northern countries. The word is derived from the Arab. حبذ أ تمر‎ tamru'l Hind, the date of Hind or India. In like manner the Malacca bean is called *tamru'l fahn*. The word *tamr* signifies not only a ripe date (of which there are seventy species), but also a dry or preserved date.

TANTALIZE. To tease or torment by presenting some good to the view, and exciting desire, but continually frustrating the expectations by keeping such good out of reach; to tease; to torment; so called from Tantalus (son of Jupiter, father of Pelops and Niobe), a king of Lydia.

> " Thy vain desires, at strife
> Within themselves, have *tantalized* thy life."—*Dryden.*

Tantalus is represented by the poets as punished in hell with an insatiable thirst, and placed up to the chin in the midst of a pool of water, which, however, flows away as soon as he attempts to taste it. There hangs also above his head a bough richly loaded with delicious fruits, which, as soon as he attempts to seize it, is carried away from his reach by a sudden blast of wind. According to some, his punishment is to sit under a huge stone hung at some distance over his head, and, as it seems every moment ready to fall, he is kept under continual alarms and never-ceasing fears. The causes of this eternal punishment are variously explained. Some declare that it was inflicted upon him because he stole a favourite dog, which Jupiter had intrusted to his care to keep his temple in Crete. According to others, he stole away the nectar and ambrosia from the tables of the gods when he was admitted into the assemblies of heaven, and that he gave it to mortals on earth. Others say, from his cruelty and impiety in killing his son Pelops, and in serving his limbs as food before the gods, whose divinity and power he wished to try, when they stopped at his house as they passed over Phrygia. There are also others who impute it to his lasciviousness in carrying away Ganymedes to gratify the most unnatural of passions. Pind. O. 1; Hom. Od. 581; Cic. Tusc. i. 5, 4, 16; Eurip. Iphig. ;

Propert. 2, 1, 66; Hor. Sat. i. 1, 68; and Lempriere.——A genus of birds allied to the Ibis.——Tantalus's cup is the name of a philosophical toy which amusingly exhibits the principle of the siphon.

TANTALUM (*Columbium*). A metal found in the Swedish minerals tantalite and yttro-tantalite; so named from the insolubility of its oxide in acids, in allusion to the fable of Tantalus. Hence *tantalum* ore (*columbite* of Hatchett), a prismatic ore of tantalum, occurring as a coarse red granite in Finland.

TARANTELLA. See Tarentism and Tarentula.

TARENTISM or TARANTISM (L. *tarentismus*). A fabulous disease supposed to be produced by the bite of the insect called the tarentula, and considered to be incapable of cure, except by protracted dancing to appropriate music: hence the Sp. *tarantéla*, a powerful impressive tune played to cure the bite of the *tarantúla*; whence the celebrated dance called the *tarantella*.

TARENTULA or TARANTULA (It. *tarantella*, formerly *tarantola*, Sp. *tarántula*, Fr. *tarentule*, O. Fr. *tarentole*). A species of spider whose bite on some persons produces no effect, and on others is about equal to the sting of a wasp; so called from Tarentum (hod. Taranto), a city of Naples, in the vicinity of which this insect is said to be found.

TARIFF (Fr. *tarif*, Sp. *tarifa*, It. *tariffa*). A list or table of duties or customs to be paid on goods imported or exported. Some derive the word from the Arab. تعريف *tárif* (Hind. *id.*, Hindi *táriph*, Tel. *tariphu*); lit. determination, ascertainment; from عرف *árafa*, to know; others from *Tarifa*, a town of Spain, at the entrance of the Straits of Gibraltar, where duties were formerly collected.

TARQUINISH. Proud, haughty; like Tarquin, a king of Rome.—*Quart. Rev.*

TARRAGON. The herb dragon-wort; a plant of the genus *Artemisia*, celebrated for perfuming vinegar in France; so called from Tarragona, in Spain, where it abounds.

TARSHISH. In Scriptural times, a precious stone; so called as brought from Tarshish, an ancient, celebrated, and opulent city, which carried on trade in the Mediterranean and with the seaports of Syria, especially Tyre and Joppa. It was doubtless the same with Tartessus, in Spain, which was not far from the Straits of Gibraltar, and near the mouth of the Guadalquivir. The Lxx, followed by Josephus, makes this stone the " chrysolite," *i.e.* the topaz of the moderns, which is still found in Spain. Others suppose it, without reason, to be amber. In the authorised version the word is translated " beryl." Cf. Exod. xxviii. 20 ; xxxix. 13 ; Ezek. i. 16 ; x. 9 ; xxviii. 13 ; Cant. v. 14 ; Dan. x. 6.

TARTAN (O. Fr. *tyretaine*, Mod. Fr. *tiretaine*). A sort of woollen cloth, checkered or cross-barred with threads of various colours (*Jamieson's Dict.*) A checkered worsted stuff, called tartan or plaid, is made in various parts of England (*Encyc. of Dom. Econ.*) Logan derives the word from Gael. *tarstin* or *tarsuin*, " across;" but Planché says the French had the word *tiretaine* for a woollen cloth as early as the thirteenth century, and that the true Gael. term for the Highland plaid or mantle is *treacan-feile*, lit. the " chequered, striped, or spotted covering." *Tartan*, in French *tyretaine*, in Latin *tiretanus*, was a fine woollen cloth, much used for ladies' robes, and generally of a scarlet colour. John de Meun speaks of

> " Robbes faites par grands devises,
> De beaux draps de soies et de laine,
> De scarlate de *tiretaine*."—Roman de la Rose.

From whence, probably, its name, the *teint* or colour of Tyre; scarlet being indifferently used for purple by the early writers, and including " all the gradations of colours formed by the mixture of blue and red, from indigo to crimson" (*Vide* Illustrations of Northern Antiquaries, 4to, Edinb. 1814, p. 36. *Planché*). ——(Sp., It., and Russ. *tartana*, Fr. *tartane*, Barb. Gr. ταρτανα.) A small coasting vessel in the Mediterranean, having only one mast and a bowsprit; now a boat for transport and fishing, says Jal. Ménage, however, seems to think that the name of the vessel was formed from *Tartarina*, i.e. from *Tartary*. He says further that tarida, ταριδες, is a sort of sea vessel, and that *tartane* may have come from *tarida;* thus *tarida, taridana, tardana,* Tartane. Jal says *tartane* may be from Bas. L. *tarta,*

a ship of the Middle Ages, which the continuers of Du Cange
regard as the taride ; and that the form *tarta* is very near the
forms *tareda* and *tareta ;* but that *tartane* may also come from
the old Sp. *tardante.*

TARTAR. A person of a keen irritable temper : hence,
to catch a Tartar, *i.e.* to lay hold of or encounter a person who
proves too strong for the assailant ; so called from the Tatars.
Latin authors of the thirteenth century changed the name into
Tartar, from having, perhaps, the same sound as their word
Tartarus. See David's Turk. Gram. ; Remusat, tom. i. 1 ;
Klaproth, tom. ii. 1.——" A savage fellow, an ugly customer "
(*J. C. Hotten*).

TARTAREAN or TARTAREOUS. Hellish; pertaining
to Tartarus, the name of the infernal regions, over which
Pluto or Hades ruled.

> " And for lightning see
> Black fire and horror, shot with equal rage
> Among his angels ; and his throne itself
> Mixt with *Tartarean* sulphur, and strange fire,
> His own invented torments."—*Milton*, P. L. b. ii.

TARTERINE (O. Eng. *tarteryne*). Formerly, a kind of
silk stuff; said to have been so named because obtained from
the Tartars, properly Tatars.

TARTUFFISH. A term used by Sterne for precise,
hypocritical; so called from Tartuffe, the hero in Molière's
celebrated comedy of the same name ; hence the Fr. *tartufe*, a
hypocrite.

TAURUS PONIATOWSKI. A modern constellation,
consisting of seven stars, situated between Aquila and Ophi-
uchus, formed by the Abbé Poczobut, a Polish astronomer, in
1778; probably named after Poniatowski, King of Poland,
father of the celebrated Polish general.

TAWDRY. Very fine and showy in colours, without taste
or elegance ; having an excess of showy ornaments without
grace ; as, a *tawdry* dress; *tawdry* feathers; *tawdry* colours.
" *Tawdry* implies the gay or gaudy finery purchased at the
fair held in Ely and elsewhere on St. Etheldreda's Feast, on
the 17th Oct." (*Nares, Gloss.*) Thus *St. Etheldreda, St.*

Audry, Staudry, **Tawdry.** "Just as *St. Olave's* Street becomes *Tooley* Street" (*S. F. Creswell*).

TELAMONES. In *architecture*, figures of men supporting entablatures, as distinguished from *caryatides*, which are figures of women. Dr. Wm. Smith says the Greeks called them Atlantes, and he thinks they may refer to the strength of Ajax, son of Telamon. Atlas is also called Telamon in Latin, and Telamon was the name of a town and harbour of Etruria, now called Talamone.

TELEPHIUM. A great ulcer, and of difficult cure; so named from Telephus, who received a wound from Achilles, which proved incurable.——(*Sedem Telephium*). Systematic name of the orpine, "because it heals old ulcers, such as that of Telephus, made by Ulysses" (*Forsyth*).

TEMPLAR. A student of the law in the inns of court called the Inner or Middle Temple. "So called from a house near the Thames, which originally belonged to the Knights Templars. The latter took their denomination from an apartment of the palace of Baldwin II., in Jerusalem, near the Temple" (*Webster*).

TENERIFFE. A wine often sold as Madeira; brought from Teneriffe, one of the Canary Islands, abounding in wine, fruit, cattle, and game. It is also called Vidonia.

TENNANTITE. A blackish lead-grey ore of copper, from Cornwall, consisting of copper, iron, arsenic, and sulphur; named after Smithson Tennant.

TERENTIAN. Pertaining or peculiar to Terence (Publius Terentius Afer), the celebrated Latin comic poet; as *Terentian* measures.

TERMAGANT. A boisterous, brawling, turbulent woman; in Shakespeare used of men.

"She threw his periwig into the fire. 'Well,' said he, 'thou art a brave *termagant*.'"—*Tatler*.

"The sprites of fiery *termagants* in flame."—*Pope*.

"The eldest was a *termagant*, imperious, prodigal, profligate wench."—*Arbuthnot*.

So called from Termagant, a vociferous tumultuous character

in ancient farces and puppet shows. Cf. the Tale of Sir
Thopas, in Chaucer, i. 15,221.

TERMINALIA. Roman festivals, annually celebrated in
February, in honour of the god Terminus; first established by
Numa. Peasants assembled at the principal termini, or land-
marks, that divided the fields, and offered libations of milk and
wine. These termini were a kind of statues without hands or
feet.

TERPSICHOREAN. Relating to Terpsichore, the muse
who presided over dancing.

TERRA SIENNA (It.) A brown bole or ochre, used as
a pigment; from Sienna, in Italy.

TEUCRIUM. A plant, the herb speedwell; now applied
to a genus, nat. or. *Labiatæ ;* so called, according to Dioscorides, from Teucer, a Trojan commander, by whom it was
discovered.

TEUTONIC. The language of the Teutons, the parent of
the German, Dutch, and Anglo-Saxon or native English.——
A military religious order of knights, founded in 1191, in imitation of the Templars and Hospitalers. It was composed
chiefly of Teutons or Germans, who marched to the Holy
Land in the Crusades, and was established in that country for
charitable purposes. It increased in numbers and strength till
it became master of all Prussia, Livonia, and Pomerania.

TEXASITE. Another name for emerald nickel, found on
chromite at Texas, in Lancaster, co. Pennsylvania.

THAPSIA. The deadly carrot, *Thapsia asclepias* of Linnæus ; from *Thapsus*, the island where it is found.—*Forsyth*.

THAPSUS. The great white mullein, or cow's lung-wort ;
from the Island *Thapsus.*—*Forsyth*.

THEBAICA. The Egyptian poppy ; from the country
about the ancient city of Thebes, where it flourished.—
Forsyth.

THEBAID. A celebrated heroic poem, written in twelve
books, by Statius, the Roman poet, contemporary with Domitian. The subject of this poem is the civil war of Thebes
between the two brothers Eteocles and Polynices, or Thebes
taken by Theseus. The author was twelve years in composing

it. Several Greek poets had composed Thebaids before the time of Statius, the principal of which were Antagoras, Antiphanes of Colophon, Menelaus the Ægean, and an anonymous author mentioned by Pausanius, lib. ix.—*Nuttall.*

THEBAN YEAR. In *ancient chronology*, the Egyptian year of 365 days and 6 hours; so called from Thebes, where it was doubtless first in vogue.

THENARDIA. A genus of plants of two species, one a native of Cayenne, the other of Mexico; dedicated by Kunth in honour of his friend L. J. Thenard, who wrote on the chemical physiology of plants.

THEODOLITE. A surveyor's compass furnished with a small telescope for the more accurate measurement of angles. Webster derives it from θεω, to run, δολιχος, long; and several other etymologies will be found in Notes and Queries. It was, perhaps, invented by and called after one Theodulus, a name that occurs more than once in Zedler (Lex.) A writer in Notes and Queries (3rd S. vii. 337) says, "I have before me a copy of Exegeses Physico-Mathematicæ, de momentis gravium, de vecte, &c., dedicated to D. Carolum Theodolum, Marchionem S. Viti, Romæ, 1685. He is described as belonging to a family renowned for their interest in mathematical studies. It is not very improbable that the instrument was named after him, or one of his ancestors. I have less doubt in offering this suggestion, as all others hitherto given seem so manifestly impossible."

THEODOSIAN CODE. An important code of laws promulgated in the Eastern Roman empire, A.D. 438, under the auspices of Theodosius II.

THEOPHRASTA. A genus of plants, nat. or. *Myrsinaceæ*, from the pounded seeds of which bread is said to be made in St. Domingo, where it is called *le petit coco*. It was originally called Eresia by Plumier, from *Eresus*, in the isle of Lesbos, the birth-place of Theophrastus, the celebrated Greek naturalist and philosopher, but was afterwards altered by Linnæus to its present name in honour of Theophrastus.

THERA. A wine. See SANTORIN.

THESPIAN. Pertaining to Thespis, an Athenian poet,

x

who lived in the time of Solon, about 535 B.C., and who is said to have introduced the first rudiments of a tragic stage: hence the art of representing tragedy has been called the *Thespian* art.

THOLOSAN GOLD. When Cœpio, the consul, plundered the town of Tholosa (Toulouse), in Gaul, and found vast quantities of gold in the temples of the place, whoever in this plundering had touched the gold is said to have perished by a miserable and agonizing death. Hence the expression *Tholosan gold* became a proverb by Cicero and Strabo. An account may be found in Herodotus of a calamity which persecuted certain Scythians who were engaged in a similar offence against Venus, by plundering one of her temples. Cf. Aulus Gellius.

THOMAISM or THOMISM. The doctrine of the Thomists or followers of Thomas Aquinas, in opposition to the Scotists, with respect to predestination and grace.

THOMSONITE. A mineral of a glassy or vitreous lustre, consisting of silica, alumina, and lime, with some soda, and fourteen per cent. of water. The mineral comptonite is identical with this species (*Dana*); named in honour of Dr. Thomas Thomson, of Glasgow, the celebrated chemist and mineralogist.

THORIA or THORINA. A white earthy substance, obtained by Berzelius in 1829 from thorite, *q.v.*

THORITE. A massive and compact mineral, found in Norway, and resembling gadolinite; so called from the Scandinavian deity Thor. See THURSDAY.

THORIUM or THORINUM. The metallic base of thoria, *q.v.*

THRASONICAL. Boastful, bragging; so called from Thraso, the braggart in the Latin comedies. But see Terence's Eunuch.

THUGGISM. The practices of the Thugs, in India, robbers and assassins of a peculiar class, who, sallying forth in a gang of smaller or larger numbers, and in the character of wayfarers, either on business or pilgrimage, fall in with other travellers on the road, and, having gained their confidence, take a favourable opportunity of strangling them by throwing their turbans or handkerchiefs round their necks, and then plundering them and burying their bodies. The word *thug*, *thag*, signifies primarily a knave, an impostor, and has also been applied to child-stealing and robbery not amounting to *Dakaiti*; from Hind. *thag*, *thug* a cheat. Cf. Wilson, Ind. Gloss.

THULITE. A variety of epidote, colour peach-blossom, found in Norway; doubtless named from Thule, *i.e.* the Ultima Thule of the Romans, denoting the northernmost and further-most part of the habitable world; probably Iceland.

THUMITE. A mineral, another name for axinite, occur-ring at Thum, near Ehrenfriedersdorf, in Saxony.

THURSDAY (G. *Donnerstag*, D. *Donderdag*, thunder-day, L. *Dies Jovis*, It. *Giovedi*, Sp. *Jueves*, Fr. *Jeudi*). The fifth day of the week; from Dan. *Torsdag*, i.e. *Thor's day*, the day con-secrated to Thor, in *Scandinavian mythology*, the son of Odin and Freya, the deity that presided over all mischievous spirits in the elements, the god of thunder, answering to the Jove of the Greeks and Romans.

TIGER (L. *tigris*, Gr. τίγρις, Fr. *tigre*, It. *tigro*). A fierce and rapacious animal of the genus *Felis*, one of the largest and most terrible of the genus, inhabiting Asia. Some derive the word from Heb. גיר *gir*, a dart, whence תיגר *tiger*. According to others, this animal was so named from frequenting the banks of the Tigris, a river of Asiatic Turkey.——A boy in livery who rides behind his master; probably named from his activity. ——A parasite.——A ferocious woman.

TILBURY. A kind of gig or two-wheeled carriage with-out a top or cover; named from the person who first manufac-tured or let it out to hire.

TILBURY WATER. An acidulous or saline water issu-ing from a spring near a farmhouse at West Tilbury, in Essex. It is esteemed for removing glandular obstructions, and is recommended in scurveys and cutaneous diseases.

TIMOTHY GRASS (*Phleum pratense*, meadow cat's-tail grass). A grass highly extolled by many agriculturists for the profusion of hay which it makes, and also for its rapid growth when depastured; so called from a person of the name, who successfully cultivated it in North America, where it grows more luxuriantly than any other kind of grass.

TINGIS. A genus of insects which for the most part live by pricking the leaves of plants ; named from Tingis (Tangiers), in Africa, where this insect abounds.

TINTAMAR. A hideous or confused noise [*not in use*]. " Bruit éclatant accompagné de tumulte, de désordre. Faire un grand tintamarre. Quel tintamarre ! Il y a trop de tintamarre là dedans, trop de brouillamini " (*Mol.*) Pasquier derives the word from *tinter* (to ring, tingle), and *marre* (mattock); " parce que les vignero*n*s, pour s'avertir mutuellement que le moment de quitter le travail était venu, frappaient, *tintaient*, sur leur *marre* avec une pierre." Ash says Fr. *tintamarre*, L. *tinnitus*, ringing, tinkling ; and *Mars*.

TIRONIAN NOTES. The shorthand among the ancient Romans, the usage of which in France only ceased about the tenth century ; said to have been named after Tullius Tiro, freedman and secretary of Cicero, by whom it was either invented or perfected. In French diplomacy the Tironian alphabet is an alphabetical and explanatory table of the Tironian notes.

TITAN. A calcareous earth ; said to have been so named by Klaproth after the Titans. See TITANIAN.

TITANIAN, TITANIC, TITANITIC. Earth-born ; so called from the Titanes, sons of Cœlus and Terra, who were treated with great cruelty by Cœlus, and confined in the bowels of the earth, till their mother pitied their misfortunes, and armed them against their father.

TITHONIC. Pertaining to or denoting those rays of light which produce chemical effects ; doubtless from Tithonus, son of Laomedon, who was so beautiful that Aurora became enamoured of him and carried him away.

TOBACCO. A plant, a native of America, of the genus *Nicotiana*, much used for smoking and chewing, and in snuff. Some derive the word from Tabasco, in Mexico. According to others, the Spaniards called it *tobacco* from *Tabaco*, *Tabago*, or *Tobago*, an island in the Bay of Panama (discovered by Columbus in 1496); or, as others style it, a province of

Yucatan, where they first found it and first learnt its use. Rees (Encyc.) gives Tobago, one of the Caribbee Islands, in the West Indies; Tobago (Little), a small island near the east coast of Tobago; Tobacco Key, a small island in the Bay of Honduras, near the coast of Yucatan.

TOCCAVIENSIS BOLUS. Bole of Tokay, in the Materia Medica; a fine medicinal earth, dug about Tokay, in Hungary, and esteemed a powerful astringent. Kentman calls it the Bolus Pannonica Vera; and Crato, Bolus Hungarica.

TOKAY. A wine made at Tokay, in Hungary, of white grapes; distinguished from other wines by its aromatic taste. This wine, which is said to be produced in so small a quantity as never to be genuine unless when given in presents by the Court of Vienna, is, however, a common dessert wine in all the great families at Vienna and in Hungary.

TOLEDO. A sword of the finest temper; so called from Toledo, in Spain, once famous for its swords (*B. Jonson*). There is still a sword manufactory there. But see Ford's Spain.

TOLU BALSAM (called in medicine, *balsam of Tolu*). A resin, or oleo-resin, produced by a tree of South America, the *Myrospermum toluiferum*; said to have been first brought from Tolu, in Venezuela.

TOLUOLE. An oily hydrocarbon obtained by distillation from balsam of Tolu, *q.v.*

TOM (OLD). A slang appellation for gin; said to be called from the nickname of a publican.

TOM-AND-JERRY. A low drinking shop; probably some allusion to Pierce Egan's famous characters in his *Life in London.—J. C. Hotten.*

TOM THUMB. A dwarf geranium so called.

TONTINE. An annuity or survivorship; or a loan raised on life annuities, with the benefit of survivorship. Thus, an annuity is shared among a number, on the principle that the share of each at his death is enjoyed by the survivors, until at last the whole goes to the last survivor, or to the last two or three, according to the terms on which the money is advanced.

The term is derived from Lorenzo Tonti, a Neapolitan, who originated the idea in 1635, and who introduced it into France, where the first tontine was opened in 1653. " Tontines have seldom been resorted to in England as a measure of finance. The last for which the government opened subscriptions was in 1789. The terms may be seen in Hamilton's History of the Public Revenue, 210. There have been numerous private tontines in this country, for the purpose of carrying into effect some desirable public improvement, the whole of which derive a considerable profit from their investments *now*, whilst the last survivor becomes the sole possessor of the capital. It has frequently been applied beneficially towards the erection of great hotels, such as the Tontine establishment in Glasgow, of which Mrs. Douglas, of Orbiston, who died on the 28th July, 1862, was the last of the original shareholders. Hamilton (p. 61) remarks that ' tontines seem adapted to the passions of human nature, from the hope every man entertains of longevity, and the desire of ease and affluence in old age ; and they are beneficial to the public, as affording a discharge of the debt, although a distant one, without any payment.' " Cf. N. & Q. 3rd S. ii. 213. " The term originated from the circumstance that Lorenzo Tonti, an Italian, invented this kind of security in the seventeenth century, when the governments of Europe had some difficulty in raising money in consequence of the wars of Louis XIV., who first adopted the plan in France. A loan was obtained from several individuals on the grant of an annuity to each of them, on the understanding that as deaths occurred the annuities should continue payable to the survivors, and that the last survivor should take the whole. This scheme was adopted by other nations as well as France, but was not introduced into England until recently, and then only for the purpose of raising money to carry private speculations into effect, which could not be satisfactorily accomplished without a combination of capital." As to the formation of such a scheme, see Stone's Benefit Build. Soc. 78.

TOORKOMAN. A horse said to be preferable for service even to the pure Persian. It is large, standing from fifteen to sixteen hands high ; swift and inexhaustible under fatigue, and was so called from Turkistan, which has been celebrated from very early times for producing a pure and valuable breed of horses.

TOORKY. A horse, of beautiful form. graceful action, and docile temper; originally from a Toorkoman and a Persian.

TOPHET. Hell; so called from a place east of Jerusalem, where children were burnt to Moloch, and where drums were used to drown their cries; from Heb. תפה *tophet*, from תף *toph*, a drum.

TORGAU. A very fine wine from Torgau, on the Elbe.

TORRELITE. A red mineral from New Jersey, consisting principally of silica, iron, and lime; named from Dr. Torrey.

TORRICELLIAN. Pertaining to Torricelli, an Italian philosopher and mathematican, who discovered the true principle on which the barometer is constructed. The *Torricellian tube* is a glass tube, thirty or more inches in length, open at one end, and hermetically sealed at the other, such as is used in the barometer. A *Torricellian vacuum* is a vacuum produced by filling with mercury a tube hermetically closed at one end, and, after immersing the other end in a vessel of mercury, allowing the enclosed mercury to descend till it is counterbalanced by the weight of an equal column of the atmosphere, as in the barometer.

TOURNOIS. A *livre Tournois* was a French money of account, equal to twenty sous, or a franc; called in distinction from the Paris livre, which contained twenty-five sous; so named from having been minted at Tours. *Tournois* was also the appellation of a sous equal to twelve deniers, the Paris sous being valued at fifteen deniers.

TOURNOSER or **TOURNOVER.** A coin minted at Tours, temp. Philip le Bel and his immediate successors.

TRAPPISTINE. A liqueur, for the manufacture of which the Abbey of Grâce-Dieu, near Besançon, in France, has acquired considerable reputation; so named from the Trappists, a religious order founded in 1140 in the valley of La Trappe, and still existing in Normandy. See *Globe*, 20 Jan. 1865.

TRATTINICKIA. A genus of plants, cl. *Monoecia*, of only one species, *T. rhoifolia*, native of Brazil; dedicated by Willdenow to Dr. Trattinick, a German botanist.

TRAUTVETTERIA. A genus of plants, cl. *Polyandria*, instituted by Fischer and Meyer in honour of E. R. Trautvetter, a distinguished botanist, author of Monographs of Echinops, &c.

TRAVERTIN. A white concretionary limestone, usually hard and semi-crystalline, deposited from the water of springs holding lime in solution. It was called by the ancients Lapis Tiburtinus, the stone being found in great quantity by the River Anio, at Tibur, near Rome. Some suppose *travertin* to be an abbreviation of *trasteverino*, from *transtiburtinus*.— *Lyell.*

TREBELLIANICK. By the *trebellianick* portion is meant the fourth part which the laws appropriate to executors who are charged with a universal fiduciary bequest of the whole inheritance, or of a part of it; which distinguishes the *trebellianick* portion from the falcidian portion; for the falcidian portion relates to legacies, and to particular fiduciary bequests of certain things. It was so called from a decree of the Senate, named after one of the Consuls of the year in which it was made, ordaining that the executor who should be charged to restore the inheritance to the fiduciary substitute should be discharged of all the debts and burdens, and that the same should pass with the goods to the substitute. Domat, Civil Law, part 2, lib. v. tit. iv.

TREMOLITE. A mineral, a white variety of hornblende; called from the valley of Tremolla, in the Alps, where it was discovered.

TREPAN or **TRAPAN.** To ensnare; to catch by stratagem; a snare. Webster derives it from Sax. *treppan*, from *trap* (to ensnare); others from τρυπανον, which Bailey renders a crafty beguiler, but which signifies lit. a borer, drill. The usual derivation is from *Trapani* (anc. Drepanum), a seaport of Sicily, where some English ships being friendly invited in, in stress of weather, were afterwards detained, contrary to the assurance given them.

TRIDENTINE. Pertaining to Trent (Tridentum), in Southern Tyrol, or the celebrated council held in that city.

TRIPOLI. A powder used for polishing metals and stones, first imported from Tripoli, which, as well as a certain kind of siliceous stone of the same name, has been lately found to be composed of the flinty cases of infusoria.—*Lyell*.

TRITON. According to Linnæus, a genus of *Mollusca*, of only one species, having the body oblong, and tentacula or arms twelve, which inhabits the cavities of submarine rocks in Italy; so called from the demi-god Triton, who is represented by poets and painters as half man and half fish.——A genus of batrachian reptiles, or aquatic salamanders, comprehending numerous species.

TROPHONIAN. Pertaining to the Grecian architect Trophonius, or his cave, or his architecture.—*Dwight*.

TROY or TROY-WEIGHT. A weight of twelve ounces in the pound, by which gold and silver, jewels, medicines, &c., are weighed; said to have been named from Troyes, in France, where it was first adopted. According to others, the original name was *tron*.

TUBA EUSTACHIANA. The Eustachian or auditory tube of the ear, first described by Bartholomew Eustachius, an eminent Italian physician of the sixteenth century. His Opuscula Anatomica was published by Boerhaave in 1707.

TUESDAY (Sw. *Tisdag*, Dan. *Tirsdag*, D. *Dingsdag*, A. S. *Tiwæsdag* or *Tuesdæg*). The third day of the week; so called from Tig, Tiig, or Tuisco, the Mars of the Northern nations, who presided over combats, strife, and litigation: "hence," says Webster, " *Tuesday* is court day, assize day, the day for combat, or commencing litigation."

TULBAGIA. A genus of plants, nat. or. *Spathaceæ* ; named by Linnæus from De Tulbagh, Governor of the Cape, patron of botany, who sent the Cape plants to the brothers Burman, in Holland.

TULLE. A kind of silk open-work or lace; said to have been originally brought from Tulle, in France, dep. Corrèze. According to French authors, however, there is not and never was either at Tulle or in the environs any fabric of this sort.

There is, however, a place in France named Toul, on the Moselle, having lace manufactories.

TUNISIAN FALCON.   A hawk from Tunis, in Africa.

TURANIAN.   A name by which the inhabitants of Iran designate the barbarians of the North ; a term frequently but inappropriately used in ethnology and philology.   Max Müller, speaking of the Aryans, says that the etymological signification of Arya seems to be, " one who ploughs or tills," and is connected with the root of *arare ;* and that the Aryans would seem to have chosen this name for themselves as opposed to the nomadic races, the *Turanians,* whose original name, *Tura,* implies the swiftness of the horseman.

TURCISM, TURKISHNESS.   Religion, manners, &c., of the Turks.   " He [Dr. Cox] grounds his following discourse upon the probability of the fall of *Turcism,* and the hopes of the further propagation of the Christian religion ; and the necessity of unity and concord of Christendom " (Strype, Eccles. Mem. Hen. VIII. an. 1536).   " Contemnynge of knowledge and learninge, settinge at nought, and having for a fable, God and His highe providence, will bringe us, I say, to a more ungracious *Turkishnes,* if more *Turkishnes* can be than this, than if the *Turkes* had sworne to brynge all *Turkye* against us " (Ascham, Toxophiles, b. i.)

TURKEY.   A domestic bird, the *Meleagris* of Linnæus ; said to have been so called from being brought from India through Persia and Turkey.   It is, however, a native of America.   Its French name is *dinde, dindon,* from *D'Inde,* i.e. from India.

TURKEY BUZZARD.   In America, a common species of vulture, having a distant resemblance to a turkey.

TURKEY RED.   A fine durable red, dyed with madder upon calico or woollen cloth.

TURKEY STONE.   Another name of the oil-stone ; brought from Turkey.

TURKOPHONE.   A new musical instrument invented by Ali Ben Squalle ; from *Turk,* and φωνή sound.

TURK'S CAP.   A plant of the genus *Lilium ;* and also of the genus *Melocactus.*

TURK'S HEAD. Name of plants of the genera *Mammil-laria* and *Melocactus*.

TURK'S TURBAN. A plant of the genus *Ranunculus*.

TURLUPINADE. A term used chiefly among the French for a low jest or witticism; said to be derived from *Turlupin*, a celebrated comedian of Paris, whose talent consisted mainly in raising a laugh by miserable puns and quibbles.

TURNERA. A genus of plants, of which Miller enumerates two, and Linnæus four species; named after Turner, the naturalist.

TURNERITE. A rare mineral, occurring in small crystals of a yellowish-brown colour, found only on Mount Sorel, in Dauphiné; named in honour of Mr. Turner, in whose collection it was first found.

TURPINIA. A small genus of trees, nat. fam. *Celastrineæ*, common in the West Indies, India, and China; named after Turpin.

TURQUOISE (Fr. *turquoise*). A mineral, called also calaite, of a bluish-green colour; when highly coloured, much used as a gem. Pedro Teneira says this stone was brought from Nixabar, a province of Persia, bordering on Turkistan, whence it was called *Turkoise*. Others assert the Fr. word was named from its blue colour, the favourite one of the Turks, whence the It. word *turchino*, blue. Cf. La Crusca and Scaliger. Webster writes *turkois*. Bailey says, " *Turcoise*, a precious stone of an azure colour; so called because brought to us from the Turks."

TURRÆA. An evergreen tree or shrub, of five species, found by Koenig among heaps of scoriæ or worn-out volcanoes in the East Indies; named by Linnæus in honour of Giorgio à Turre, author of a History of Plants, Padua, 1585.

TUTENAG (sometimes called Tooth and Egg Metal). Chinese copper, an alloy of copper, zinc, and nickel, or spelter. The Rev. Thos. Boys says, although what we now call German silver, which is one of many alloys that have been termed *tutenag*, does not appear to have been made in Europe till about the commencement of the present century, that various alloys resembling in appearance German silver, and known by the name of white copper (*weiss kupfer*), were made in Germany long before; that the Portuguese, meeting with a similar article in their early commerce with India and China, would at once be struck with the resemblance, and, speaking by their own language, would naturally call it *prata Teutonica* (German silver); that *Teutonica* thus becomes the trade name of the Eastern article, and in due time comes back to Europe, transmuted into *tutenag;* that *tutenag* is also called *tutenago* (*Encyc.*, and *Beckmann*) and *tutenaga* (*Moraes*), and that these last two forms represent the Portuguese masculine and feminine:—*metal Teutonico*, m. (German metal); *prata Teutonica*, f. (German silver).——" A watch-maker of Nottingham, named Tutin, made articles from it, whence they are often, but incorrectly, called Tutinic ware" (*S. F. Creswell*).——A name given in India to zinc or spelter.

TWEED. A light woollen stuff, used for summer coating; a milled Scotch trousering or wrapper worn by shepherds and others; said to derive its name from the Tweed, a river of Scotland and England; perhaps because first manufactured on its banks.

TYBURN TICKET. A certificate given to the prosecutor on the capital conviction of a criminal, by virtue of the 10 & 11 Wm. III. c. 23, s. 2, which exempted the prosecutor "from all manner of parish and ward offices within the parish wherein such felony was committed; which certificate shall be enrolled with the clerk of the peace of the county, on payment of 1s., and no more." This Act was repealed by 58 Geo. III. c. 70 (3rd June, 1818), a fact, however, which seems to have been afterwards ignored. A correspondent of Notes and Queries remarks, " In the autumn of 1856 I was on the jury at Newgate. On that occasion Mr. Pratt, armourer, of Bond Street, claimed and obtained exemption from serving on the jury by reason of his possession of a *Tyburn ticket*." The editor of N. & Q. (25 Dec. 1858, p. 529) says, " Mr. George Phillips, late of Charlotte Street, Bloomsbury, and now residing in Kingsgate Street, Theobald's Road, was the last individual who received the *Tyburn ticket* for a burglary committed by two housebreakers on his premises. This ticket was purchased of Mr. Phillips by the late Mr. Pfeil, of Holborn."

TYCHONIC. Pertaining to or designating the system of Tycho Brahe the astronomer, a noble Dane, born A.D. 1546. The *Tychonic* system partly restored that of Ptolemy, concerning the earth remaining at rest whilst the other heavenly bodies moved round it.

TYPHEAN. Pertaining to Typhæus, the fabled giant with a hundred heads.

TYRANT (L. *tyrannus*, Gr. τυραννος). A cruel master; an oppressor. According to Liddell and Scott, τυραννος is strictly Doric for κοιρανος, from κυρος, κυριος, a lord, master. Carr (Lucian) says the Tyrrheni were a mischievous people, very troublesome to the Athenians; and that from their name it is pretended was derived the word *tyrant*, which was, however, in better repute than its original, being for some time synonymous for king. " We will not inquire whether Turk, the grandson of Japhet (who gave his name to the nation), was or was not the Targitaos of Herodotus, and the Togarmah of Scripture. But it is more curious that the name of the people found its way into the language of the Greeks in a sense of prognosticating evil. The ancient Persians, who called their own country Iran and every other country Aniran, gave to the land beyond the Oxus the name of *Turan;* the inhabitants of this country were proverbial among the Persians for their rudeness and ferocity, as the Scythians and Thracians among the Greeks and Romans; from thence the Asiatic Greeks borrowed the word τυραννος, so that the word *tyrant*, traced to its primitive signification, means a *Turk*" (For. Quar. Rev. iv. 239).

TYRIAN. Of a purple colour; so called from Tyre, a celebrated city on the coast of Phœnicia, where the Tyrian dye was made.

TYROLITE. A mineral, colour apple-green, verdigris-green, inclining to sky-blue, found at Falkenstein, near Schwatz, and other places in the Tyrol; also in Hungary, &c.

U.

ULLMANITE. Phosphate of manganese and iron, occurring massive at Limoges, in France; analysed by Ullmann.

ULSTER. A name given to one of the kings at arms. Edw. VI. in his journal makes the following note:—" Feb. There was a king at arms made for Ireland, whose name was *Ulster*, and his province was all Ireland." This must mean that *Ulster* was his title, which he derived from the province of that name in Ireland.

ULTIMA THULE (L.) The utmost stretch or boundary; so called from Thule, the name given, in early history, to the northernmost part of the habitable world; and supposed to refer either to Iceland or to one of the Shetland Isles.

UNION JACK. " The British flag consists of the crosses of St. George, St. Andrew, and St. Patrick, united; but the etymology of the term *Union jack* has never, it is presumed, been explained, for it does not occur in any lexicon or glossary. The word *Union* obviously arose from the event to which the flag owes its origin (the union of Ireland in 1801); the only difficulty, therefore, is as to the expression ' *Jack.*' As the alteration in the banner of St. George occurred in the reign of James I., it may with great probability be supposed to be a corruption of *Jacques*. If, however, this hypothesis be rejected the following is submitted:—English soldiers were formerly accustomed to wear the cross of St. George on their upper garment, and as it appears from early writers that the upper dress of a horseman, and, according to others, a coat of mail was called *Jack*, it admits of the inference that a small flag containing the cross in question was termed a *Jack* when used at sea after the banner, which, more properly speaking, is confined to the field, fell into comparative disuse. The former of these conjectures appears, however, the more probable." Sir Harris Nicolas's Naval and Military Mag. 1827.

URALIC. A name given to the languages of the Finnic tribes, from it being generally supposed that the original seat of such tribes was in the Ural Mountains.

URANIA. A genus of plants, nat. or. *Musaceæ ;* named after Urania, one of the Muses.——A genus of lepidopterous insects.

URANITE, URAN MICA, or **URAN GLIMMER.** An ore of uranium, colour bright green or yellow. See URANIUM.

URANIUM. A metal, colour reddish brown, discovered by Klaproth in 1789, in pitchblende ; perhaps named after Uranus, the same as Cœlus, the most ancient of all the gods, whose children conspired against him because he confined them in the bosom of the earth. But see URANIA.

URANUS. One of the primary planets ; the name now generally given to the planet discovered in 1781 by Dr. Herschell, and by him called *Georgium Sidus ;* by others, Herschell. So called from Uranus, otherwise Cœlus, the most ancient of all the gods, who married Terra. A better name would have been Urania, the Muse who presided over astronomy.

UTOPIA. A word now used in all the European languages to signify a state of ideal perfection ; a term invented by Sir Thomas More (from Gr. ουτοπος, no place), and applied to an imaginary isle, which he represents as enjoying the greatest perfection in politics, laws, &c.

UTOPIAN. Ideal, chimerical, fanciful, not well founded. See UTOPIA.

UTOPIANISM. Chimerical schemes in theory or practice. —*Chalmers.* See UTOPIA.

V.

VACHELLIA. A genus of plants, of only one species, *V. Farnesiana,* the *Acacia Farnesiana,* a small tree, native of India ; dedicated by Wright and Arnott to Rev. H. G. H. Vachell, who has lately made the botany of China better known to Europeans, by means of specimens.

VAHLIA. A genus of plants, cl. *Pentandria,* of seven species, natives of Africa ; dedicated by Thunberg to Martin Vahl, professor of botany at Copenhagen, author of several botanical works.

VALANCE. A piece of drapery hanging round the tester and head of a bed, and also from the head of window curtains (*Swift*).

> "*Valance* of Venice gold in needlework."—T. of the Shrew.

> "Thy face is *valanc'd* since I saw thee last."—Hamlet.

Webster qu. Fr. *avalant*, falling; Norm. *valaunt*, descending. Bailey derives the word, which he writes *valences* and *vallens*, from *Falenzana*, in Italy. Skinner gives " *Valenzana* del letto, from *Valentia* (Valencia), a town in Italy and Spain." There is also Valenza, in Sardinia; and Valence and Valencia are names of several places in Continental Europe.

VALANTIA. An annual with smooth stem and leaves, native of Italy and the south of France; named by Tournefort in honour of Sebastien Vaillant, an eminent French botanist, demonstrator at the botanic garden at Paris, author of several works on botany, who died in 1722.

VALDEPENAS. A red wine from Valdepeñas, between Granada and Madrid; the produce of the Burgundy vine, transplanted into Spain.

VALENCIANITE (of Breithaupt). A mineral, a variety of adularia; named from the Mexican mine Valenciana.

VALENCIENNES. A rich lace, from Valenciennes, a town of France, dep. Nord.

VALENTINE. A sweetheart or choice made on Valentine's Day (*Wotton*).——A letter containing professions of love or affection, sent by one young person to another on Valentine's Day (*Burton*). The term is also now applied to caricatures sent in jest on the 14th February, Valentine's Day, in the Roman Church, a day sacred to St. Valentine. "It was," says Webster, "a very old notion, alluded to by Shakspeare, that on this day birds begin to couple. Hence, perhaps, arose the custom of sending on this day letters containing professions of love and affection."

> "Saint *Valentine* is past, begin these wood-birds but to couple now."—M. N.'s Dr.

In the following passage in Bacon's Descriptio Globi Intellectualis, c. 6, the fantastic speculations of the modern Platonists are compared to " the images and dreams of *Valentine ;*" and some of the customs (the most prevalent of which seems to have been that of drawing lots for lovers) connected with St. Valentine's Day, seem to be alluded to : ' De cœlis vero et spatiis immateriatis, religioni omnino standum et permittendum. Quæ enim a Platonicis, et nuper a Patricio (ut diviniores sili- cet habeantur in philosophiâ) dicuntur, non sine superstitione magnâ et jactantiâ, et quasi mente turbatâ, denique ausu nimio, fructu nullo, *similia Valentini iconibus et somniis ;* ea nos pro rebus commentitiis et levibus habemus ' " (Vol. xi. 21, ed. Montagu). [The Neo-Platonic philosopher mentioned in this passage was Francis Patricius, or Patrizzi, who was born in 1529, and died at Rome in 1597]. A correspondent of Notes and Queries (3rd S. iii. 128) says, " How this Saint [*Valentine*] came to be chosen as the patron of lovers seems to be still a *vexata quæstio*, but I think that some light may be thrown on the subject by the fact that *valantin* is still used in Normandy in the sense of *sweetheart.* Frédéric Pluquet, a well-known Norman antiquary, in a small brochure on the popular Tales, Patois, &c., of Bayeux, explains the word *valantin* as signify- ing ' petit galant ; le *v* pour le *g ;*' and in a tale by a modern French novelist, Emile Souvestre, the scene of which is laid in Normandy, and in which the dialect of that province is occasionally introduced, both *valantin* and *galantin* are used in this sense. There can be no doubt that *galant* and *vaillant* are both derived from the Latin *valens,* and our English word *gallant,* with a distinguishing accentuation, combines both meanings. *Valantin* being thus so closely identified with *galant,* it is easy to conceive how a saint with such a name as *Valentine,* and whose feast occurs at a time when all living nature inclines to couple, should have been fixed upon as the patron of lovers. I have not been able to find any satisfactory reason for believing that he was so honoured elsewhere than in Great Britain and France. The assertion of some writers that the custom of choosing *valentines* had its origin in heathen times, and was attempted to be turned to a religious purpose by the Saint, seems to want confirmation. If this was the case, traces of the custom would surely be found in other Christian countries." Another correspondent of Notes and Queries (3rd S. iii. 169) says, " The assertion that the custom of choosing *valentines* was attempted to be turned to a religious purpose by St. Valentine, seems to want confirmation, or, rather, has no foundation at all. Indeed, there is no connection whatever between the custom of *valentines* and the history of the saint himself. We know but little of him, as is the case with many early martyrs and other saints. He was a priest at Rome, and celebrated as an illustrious martyr under Claudius II. about the year 270, on the 14th February, having been put to death for assisting the martyrs; but nothing is recorded of this saint that could in any way connect him with the observances in question. That the custom, however, of choosing *valentines* had its origin in heathen times may be safely said to need no confirmation. Every one read in Roman history is acquainted with the festival of the *Lupercalia*, on the 15th of February, in honour of Pan, when the young men used to run about the streets and whip all whom they met, and particularly the women, who willingly submitted to the whip, under the belief that it imparted fecundity and promoted safe delivery. But this feast was also kept in honour of Juno, who was called from it Februata, Februalis, and Februlla, as Mr. Douce observes in his Illustrations of Shakespeare. The names of young women were drawn out of a box by young men, and some Christian pastors, though not St. Valentine himself, substituted the names of saints to be drawn instead of those of young women, and fixed upon St. Valentine's Day, as occurring about the middle of the month, the time of the *Lupercalia*. The pagan customs, however, still prevailed, as in too many other instances, though the pastors of the church have repeatedly laboured to suppress them, or at least to divert them to innocent and holy purposes. Thus St. Francis of Sales severely condemned the profane custom of *valentines*, and laboured to substitute for them papers with the names of saints proposed for imitation. In many religious houses these billets are regularly drawn for on St. Valentine's Day, and each member of the community preserves the billet during the year, as an excitement to invoke the saint's intercession, and to imitate his virtues, the principal of which are noted upon the paper. It is stated that the earliest poetical *valentines* known were composed by Charles Duke of Orleans, who was taken prisoner at Agincourt in 1415, and wrote them in the Tower of London. They are preserved in MS. in the British Museum. John Lydgate alludes to the custom of *valentines* in a poem in praise of Queen Catherine in 1440. The day is observed with different practices in different places. In Norwich it has grown into a monstrous and almost universal system of giving and receiving presents, which prevails nowhere else, or is at least of only partial observance in other places."

VALENTINIA. A herb, flowers usually of a deep rose colour, but varying to pale flesh-colour and white, native of France, Switzerland, Italy, the Levant, and Barbary. It was named by Dr. Schwartz in memory of two writers named Valentini, both of whom contributed to botanical information. One of them (Michael Bernhard Valentini) was professor of medicine at Giessen, and author of several works on natural history.

VALERIAN. A plant of the genus *Valeriana*. The root of the *officinal valerian* has a strong smell, is very attractive to cats and rats, and is much used in medicine. The genus *Valeriana* is a native of France, Switzerland, Italy, the Levant, and Barbary. Some derive its name from *valor*, or *valentia*, or from *valere*. According to others, it was so called from Valerius, who first used it as a medicine, or who first particularly described it. See Miller.

VALLANCY. A large wig that shades the face, mentioned by Dryden ; perhaps from same root as *valance*.

VALLISNERIA. A genus of aquatic plants, nat. or. *Hydrocharaceæ* ; named by Micheli after the naturalist Antonio Vallisneri, F.R.S., &c., professor of medicine at Padua, archiater to Emp. Chas. VI., author of Opere Fisico-Mediche.

VALLS. A wine from Valls, in Catalonia.

VALONIA. A species of acorn, produced in the Morea and the Levant, and used by tanners. Rees says, " Velani, sometimes called *valonia*, a name given by the modern Greeks

to the acorns of a species of oak denominated the *Velanida*."
The word is probably derived from Valona, Avlona, Aulona
(anc. Aulon), a town of European Turkey, Albania. On
referring to Blackie, I find I am confirmed in this etymology.
He says the exports of Valona consist chiefly of salt, pitch
from the mines of Selenitza, olive-oil, wool, gall-nuts, and
valonia.

VANADATE or **VANADIATE.** A compound of vanadic
acid and a base. See VANADIUM.

VANADIC ACID. A compound of vanadium and oxygen,
in the proportion of one equivalent of vanadium, and three of
oxygen.

VANADINITE. The mineral vanadate of lead, occurring
in yellowish and brownish hexagonal crystals.

VANADIUM. A metal, colour white, extremely brittle,
much resembling silver ; discovered by Sefström in 1830, and
named after Vanadis, a Scandinavian deity.

VANCOUVERIA. A genus of plants, of only one known
species, native of north-west coast of America ; named by
Decaisne in honour of the celebrated circumnavigator Vancouver.

VANDAL. One hostile to the arts and literature ; one
ignorant and barbarous ; so called from the Vandals, one of
the most barbarous of the northern nations that invaded Rome
in the fifth century, notoriously for destroying the monuments
of art and literature.

VANDALIC. Ferocious, rude, barbarous ; like the Vandals. See VANDAL.

VANDALISM. Ferocious cruelty ; hostility to the arts
and literature; the spirit or conduct of Vandals. See VANDAL.

VANDELLIA. A genus of plants of very many species,
principally natives of the East Indies and other parts of Asia;
dedicated by P. Browne to Dominico Vandelli, professor of
natural history at Lisbon.

VANDYKE. A small round covering for the neck, worn
by females, as seen in portraits by Van Dyck, temp. Chas. I.:
hence articles of dress are vandyked when ornamented with a
kind of notch-work. " At Cambridge University, a drunken

person is said to *vandyke* when he zig-zags from one side of the pavement to another " (*S. F. C.*)

VARINAS. A celebrated tobacco from Varinas, a town and prov. of Venezuela, South America.

VARRONIA. A genus of plants of several species, natives of the West Indies, Santa Cruz, Carthagena, Curaçao, China, and the Caraccas; named by Browne after Marcus Terentius Varro, one of the most learned of the Romans, author of De Re Rusticâ.

VARSOVIENNE. A celebrated dance; named from Warsaw, in Poland, where it probably originated.

VARVICITE. An ore of manganese, occurring massive at Hartshill, in Warwickshire, and in pseudo-crystals at Ilfeld; named from locality, *Varvacite* being a softening of *Warwickite*.

VAUDEVILLE. In the French theatre, a piece whose dialogue is intermingled with light or comic songs; but originally a song common among the vulgar, and sung about the streets; a ballad; a trivial strain. Some assert that the *vaudeville* is a song, *Qui va par la ville;* others derive the word from *voix de ville.* According to others, the " French *aval* or *avau* is a phrase among navigators implying the reverse of *amont; avau de l'eau* is used adverbially to express drifting down a stream (' Personne ne ramoit, nous nous laissions aller à vau de l'eau '); and *vaudeville* was originally applied to designate any song or ballad borne along the current of town gossip or popularity—' *à vau de ville.*' " The correct etymology is from *Vaux-de-Vire*, in Normandy, where the *vaudeville* first originated. Ménage says, " *Vaudeville*, sorte de chansons par corruption au lieu de *Vaudevire.* C'est ainsi qu'on appelloit anciennement ces chansons; parce qu'elles furent inventées par Olivier Basselin, qui étoit un foullon de Vire, en Normandie, et qu'elles furent premièrement chantées au Vaudevire, qui est le nom d'un lieu proche de la ville de Vire." Charles de Bourgueville (Antiquités de Caën), speaking of Vire, says, " C'est aussi le pays d'où sont procédez les chansons que l'on appelle Vaux-de-Vire : comme ces-deux :

' Hélas ! Olivier Basselin,
En la Duché de Normandie,
Il y a si grand' pillerie, &c.'

Jan Vauquelin, Sr. de la Fresnaye, père de Mr. Des-Yveteaux, précepteur de Louis XIII.:

> ' Je ne puis sans horreur ouïr qu'au Vau-de-vire,
> Où jadis on souloit les belles chansons dire,
> D'Olivier Basselin, &c.' "

Du Bois says, " Le Vau-de-Vire (car ce n'est que par corruption que depuis on a dit *Vaudeville*) tire son nom des *Vaux* de la rivière *de Vire*, où chantait si gaîment Basselin. Ainsi c'est encore à la Normandie, qui a vu naître presque tous nos premiers auteurs fameux, que l'on est redevable d'Olivier Basselin et du Vau-de-Vire. Il est incontestable que la *vaudeville* est d'origine Normande." Dibdin, in his account of Vire in Normandy, gives the following note on the Vaudevires of Olivier Basselin:—" The present seems to be the proper place to give the reader some account of this once famous bacchanalian poet. It is not often that France rests her pretensions to poetical celebrity upon such claims. Love, romantic adventures, gaiety of heart and of disposition, form the chief materials of her minor poems; but we have before us, in the person and productions of Olivier Basselin, a rival to Anacreon of old, to our own Richard Braithwait, Vincent Bourne, and Thomas Moore." . . . " Basselin appears to have been a *Virois*; in other words, an inhabitant of the town of Vire. But he had a strange propensity to rusticating, and preferred the immediate vicinity of Vire—its quiet little valleys, running streams, and rocky recesses—to a more open and more distant residence. In such places, therefore, he carried with him his flasks of cider and his flagons of wine. Thither he resorted with his ' boon and merry companions,' and there he poured forth his ardent and unpremeditated strains. These ' strains ' all savoured of the jovial propensities of their author; it being very rarely that tenderness of sentiment, whether connected with friendship or love, is admitted into his compositions. He was the thorough-bred Anacreon of France at the close of the fifteenth century. Vire is the chief town of that department of Normandy called the Bocage; and in this department few places have been, of old, more celebrated than the *Vaux de Vire*, on ac-

count of the number of manufactories which have existed there
from time immemorial. It derives its name from two principal
valleys, in the form of a T, of which the base (if it may be so
called—'jambage') rests upon the Place du Château de Vire.
It is sufficiently contiguous to the town to be considered among
the fauxbourgs. The rivers Vire and Viréne, which unite at
the bridge of Vaux, run somewhat rapidly through the valleys.
These rivers are flanked by manufactories of paper and cloth,
which from the fifteenth century have been distinguished for
their prosperous condition. Indeed, Basselin himself was a
sort of cloth manufacturer. In this valley he passed his life in
fulling his cloths, and in composing those gay and delightful
songs which are contained in the volume under consideration.
Discours Préliminaire, 17, &c. Olivier Basselin is the parent
of the title *Vaudevire*, which has since been corrupted into
Vaudeville. From the observation of his critics, Basselin
appears to have been the father of bacchanalian poetry in
France. He frequented public festivals, and was a welcome
guest at the tables of the rich, where the Vaudevire was in
such request that it is supposed to have superseded the 'Conte,
or Fabliau, or the Chanson d'Amour,' p. xviij:

> 'Sur ce point-là, soyez tranquille :
> Nos neveux, j'en suis bien certain,
> Se souviendront de Basselin ;
> Père joyeux du *Vaudeville*.' "

Among other specimens of the Vaudevire of Olivier Basselin,
Dibdin gives the following :—

VAUDEVIRE II.

> " Ayant le doz au feu et le ventre à la table,
> Estant parmi les pots pleins de vin délectable,
> Ainsi comme ung poulet
>
> Je ne me laisseray morir de la pepie,
> Quant en debvroy avoir la face cramoisie
> Et le nez violet.
>
> Quant mon nez devendra de couleur rouge ou perse,
> Porteray les couleurs que chérit ma maitresse,
> Le vin rent le teint beau.
>
> Vault il pas mieulx avoir la couleur rouge et vive,
> Riche de beaulx rubis, que si pasle et chétive
> Ainsi qu'ung beuveur d'eau."

I believe it is not generally known that it is to one of the
Vaudevires of Olivier Basselin we are indebted for the song
called " Jolly Nose." The original will be found in Vau-de-
Vire xviii., " A son nez," in the edition of Olivier Basselin,
ed. by M. Louïs du Bois, Caen, 1821. It commences thus—

> " Beau nez, dont les rubis ont cousté mainte pipe
>   De vin blanc et clairet,
> Et duquel la couleur richement participe
>   Du rouge et violet."

Cf. Gabriel du Moulin, Discours sur la Normandie ; André du
Chesne, Antiquités des villes et châteaux de France ; Jean
Chardavoine de Beaufort, Recueil des plus belles et excellentes
chansons en forme de Voix de Ville (Paris, 1, 1576); Saint
Julien, Mélanges historiques, 263 ; Callieres, Des Mots à la
mode ; Vaux-de-Vire par Olivier Basselin, poëte Normand de
la fin du 14 siècle, ed. par M. Louis du Bois, 8°, Caen, &c.,
1821 ; and especially Dibdin's Tour in France and Germany,
Vol. i. 289, *et seq.*, Lond. 1829.

VAUQUELINITE.   Chromate of copper and lead, green,
of various shades ; named after Prof. Vauquelin, the celebrated
French chemist.   The French at first gave the name of vau-
queline to strychnine, in honour of the same professor.   Vau-
queline is also the French name of a genus of Mexican plants.
The *Corymbus V.* is a tree thirty feet high.

VENEGASIA.   A genus of plants, or. *Superflua*, whose
only species is a native of California ; dedicated by De Candolle to P. M. Venegas, a Spaniard, who wrote on the civil
and natural history of California.

VENERABLE (L. *venerabilis*).   Worthy of veneration or
reverence ; deserving of honour and respect ; as, a *venerable*
magistrate ; a *venerable* parent ; rendered sacred by religious
associations, or being consecrated to God and to His worship ;
to be regarded with awe, and treated with reverence ; as, the
venerable walls of a temple or church ; from *Venus*.

VENERATION (L. *veneratio*).   The highest reverence ;
respect mingled with some degree of awe ; a feeling or sentiment excited by the dignity and superiority of a person, or by

the sacredness of his character, and, with regard to place, by its consecration to sacred services; from *Venus*.

VENEREAL. Pertaining to sexual intercourse; adapted to the cure of venereal diseases; from *venereus*, from *Venus, eris.*——Consisting of or pertaining to copper, formerly called by chemists *Venus*.

VENETIAN SCHOOL. A school of painting, in which the distinguishing character is colouring, and a consummate knowledge of chiaro-oscuro, in both of which all is grace, spirit, and faithful adherence to nature, so seductive as to lead the spectator away from any consideration of its defects; named from Venice, whence it originated.

VENETIANS. Blinds for windows, doors, &c.; so called from Venice, where they were first made.

VENICE TURPENTINE; vulgarly called Weenus's turpentine; doubtless brought from Venice.

VENICE WHITE (Dutch white, Hamburg white). A pigment consisting of carbonate of lead mixed with sulphate of baryta, brought from Venice.

VENULITE. A petrified shell of the genus *Venus*.

VENUS. One of the inferior planets, but the brightest, and to appearance the largest of all; as morning star, called by the ancients *Lucifer;* as evening star, *Hesperus;* so named from Venus, goddess of beauty and love.——In the *old chemistry*, a name for copper.——A genus of animals, cl. *Vermes*, or. *Testacea*, having a bivalve shell.

VENUS'S COMB. An annual plant of the genus *Scandix;* shepherd's needle.

VENUS'S FLY-TRAP. A plant, *Dionæa muscipula*, which seizes and holds fast insects which brush against its leaves.

VENUS'S LOOKING-GLASS. An annual plant of the genus *Campanula*, allied to the bell-flower.

VENUST (*obs.*) Beautiful; from L. *venustus*, from *Venus*. Hence *devenustate* (obs.), to deprive of beauty and grace.

VERDE DI PRADO. A green marble, marked with spots of a deeper green than the rest, passing into blackish blue; found near the little town of Prado, in Tuscany.

VERNIER. A contrivance attached to the graduated limb

of an instrument for measuring aliquot parts of the smallest spaces into which the instrument is divided (*Olmsted*); named from the inventor, Pierre Vernier, born at Ornans, Franche Comté, 1580; died 1637.

VERNONIA. A plant, named after Wm. Vernon, fellow of St. Peter's College, Cambridge, who, with David Kreig, M.D., of Saxony, collected many new plants in Maryland, inserted in the supplement to Ray's History.

VERTUS. One of the best sorts of champagne, from Vertus, in France, dep. Marne.

VERULAM. A genus of plants, whose only species is *Corymbus V.*, growing in Africa; probably named after Lord Verulam.

VERVISE. Formerly a kind of coarse woollen cloth, otherwise called plonkets; probably from Verviers, in Belgium.

VESTA. One of the asteroids, discovered by Dr. Olbers in 1807; so called after Vesta (Εστια), virgin goddess of the hearth or fire. The Vestals, who were six in number, were virgins consecrated to Vesta, and to the service of watching the sacred fire, which was to be perpetually kept burning upon her altar.——A sort of lucifer match.

V E S T A L (L. *vestalis*). Pure, chaste; pertaining to Vesta, *q.v.*

VESUVIAN. Idocrase; a mineral consisting of silica, alumina, and lime; called from Mount Vesuvius.——A sort of lucifer match for lighting pipes, cigars, &c.

VEVEYSAN. A cigar made at Vevey, Switzerland.

VICHY WATER. A water from the tepid mineral springs near Vichy, in France.

VIDIAN DUCTS. Two small canals at the base of the pterygoid process; discovered by Vidus-Vidius, a celebrated physician of Florence, professor of medicine at the Royal College of Paris, temp. François I. The name is also given to a nerve and to an artery.

VIGANI'S ELIXIR. Sweet elixir of vitriol; or the *sp. ætheris aromaticus;* named after Vigani.

VIGO PLASTER. A plaster used in variola; probably named from Vigo, in Spain, where it was first made.

VILLANOVA. A wine from Villanova, in Catalonia.

VIN-DE-GRAVE. A wine growing upon the Grève, *i.e.* upon the banks of the Garonne, in the Bourdelois.

VIOLA (the violet). A genus of plants, nat. or. *Violaceæ;* "from Iον, because first found in Ionia" (*Forsyth*).

VIOLET-MARIAN. A flower called also Canterbury bells.—*Bailey.*

VIRGILIA. A small, chiefly tropical, genus of the large natural family of *Leguminosæ;* named by Lamarck in honour of Virgil.

VIRGINIA. Tobacco from Virginia, one of the principal kinds imported into England from the United States.

VIVIANITE. A phosphate of iron, of various shades of blue and green, found at St. Agnes, in Cornwall, also in Carinthia, Greenland, Transylvania, the Crimea, New Zealand, the United States, and in Syria; doubtless named after one of the Vivian family.

VOCONIAN LAW. Among the Romans, a law enacted for the purpose of limiting the fortunes that might be left to females. It is recommended by M. Cato in his oration, and was named after its author, Voconius Saxa, the tribune, A.U.C. 584. "It enacted that no woman should be left heiress to an estate, and that no rich person should leave by his will more than the fourth part of his fortune to a woman. This step was taken to prevent the decay of the noblest and most illustrious of the families of Rome. This law was abrogated by Augustus" (*Lempriere*).

VOLBORTHITE. A mineral, colour olive-green, also gray; first discovered by Volborth, with copper ores, in the collection of Dr. Rauch.

VOLCANIC. Pertaining to volcanoes; as, *volcanic* heat. ——Produced by a volcano; as, *volcanic* tufa.——Changed or affected by the heat of a volcano, *q.v.*

VOLCANIST or **VULCANIST.** One versed in the history and phenomena of volcanoes.——One who believes in the effects of eruptions of fire in the formation of mountains. See VOLCANO.

VOLCANO (It.)　In *geology*, an opening in the surface of the earth, or in a mountain, from which smoke, flames, stones, lava, or other substances are ejected. Such are seen in Etna, Vesuvius, &c. So called from Vulcan, the god who presided over fire, &c.

VOLGERITE. A mineral, a white powder or crust occurring with cervantite, and resulting from its alteration ; analysed by Volger.

VOLNAY. A fine light wine, of an agreeable bouquet ; produced at Volnay, France, dep. Côte-d'Or, renowned for its wines.

VOLTAIC PILE. A column formed by successive pairs of metallic discs, with moistened cloth between every two contiguous pairs ; named in honour of Volta, who invented it. The *voltaic* apparatus is used for exciting and accumulating galvanic electricity, a larger specimen being called a *voltaic battery*.

VOLTAISM. That branch of electrical science which has its source in the chemical action between metals and different liquids ; so called from Alessandro Volta, a celebrated experimental philosopher, who was born at Como in 1745. He laid the foundation of his fame by two treatises, which described a new electrical machine ; was for thirty years professor of natural philosophy at Pavia ; was created an Italian count and senator by Napoleon, and died in 1826. Volta directed his attention particularly to the subject of galvanism, or animal electricity, in which science he made many discoveries and improvements; but the great invention which immortalizes his name is the Voltaic pile, or electrical column. His works form five vols. 8º. *Voltaism* is more properly called *galvanism*, from Galvani, who first proved or brought into notice its remarkable influence on animals.

VÖSLAUER. A celebrated wine from Vöslau, near Vienna.

VOUGEOT (Clos-Vougeot). A red wine of the first quality, produced at Le Clos Vougeot, near the village of Vougeot, dep. Côte-d'Or, France.

VULCANIAN. Pertaining to works in iron, &c.; so called

from Vulcan. See VOLCANO.——As an epithet, in *geology*, the same as *plutonian*.

VULCANIZATION. The process of treating India rubber with sulphur, and exposing it to a strong heat to make it more serviceable; so called from Vulcan, "the very first of black-smiths."

VULPINITE. A mineral, a variety of anhydrite, containing some silica, colour greyish-white; from Vulpino, in Italy.

W.

WAGNERITE. A rare mineral, a phosphate of magnesia, resembling the Brazilian topaz; named after Wagner.

WALCHOWITE. A mineral found in yellow translucent masses in brown coal at Walchow, in Moravia; formerly called Retinite.

WALKERIA. A genus of plants, allied to *Gomphia*, of two species, shrubs; the one a native of Malabar and Ceylon, the other of French Guiana; dedicated by Schreber to Richard Walker, D.D., founder of the botanic gardens at Cambridge.

WALLENIA. A genus of plants, of only two species, small trees, the one a native of Jamaica, the other of the East Indies; dedicated by Swartz to Matthew Wallen, who cultivated both indigenous and exotic plants in Jamaica.

WALLERITE. A variety of clay, found in small compact masses, white and opaque, yellowish and translucent; named after Waller [not used].

WALLICHIA. A genus of plants, of only one species, a palm, native of the East Indies; named by Roxburgh after N. Wallich, Ph.D., superintendent of the East India Company's botanic gardens at Calcutta.

WALLOP. To beat or thrash. Mr. John Gough Nichols derives this word from an ancestor of the Earl of Portsmouth, one Sir John Wallop, K.G., who in Hen. VIII.'s time distinguished himself by *walloping* the French.

WALLROTHIA. A genus of plants, of a few species,

trees; dedicated by Roth to F. Wallroth, M.D., a German botanist.——Also a genus of only one species, the *W. tenuifolia*, a native of the Central Pyrenees; dedicated by Sprengel to the same botanist.

WALLSEND. The coal so called. "Wallsend, so called as being the spot where the celebrated Wall of Severus terminated on the northern bank of the Tyne, a few miles below Newcastle, has in modern times been chiefly known as the site of a colliery yielding the most valuable description of coal. So important, indeed, is the appellation in the market that, although the high main seam which afforded the original coal has long been worked out, the designation has not only continued to be applied to some other sort, as the best, but to several sorts which the dealers wish to recommend."

WALPERSIA. A genus of plants (identical with the *Trichocephalus* of Brogniart), small heath-like shrubs, natives of the Cape; dedicated by Riessek to G. G. Walpers, author of Repert. Botan.

WALPURGIS NIGHT. According to popular superstition, the witch festival held on the summit of the Brocken, in the Harz Mountains, on the 1st of May, a festival of St. Philip and St. James. The superstitution is said to have originated in the rites performed by the pagan remnants of the Saxons to their gods, when their nation was forcibly converted to Christianity, and which, being secretly celebrated in remote places, were supposed by the vulgar to be supernatural orgies. St. Walpurga was an English lady, sister of Boniface, the apostle of the Germans. Her festival falls on the same day with that of the above-mentioned saints, and is a common day in Germany, like Lady Day in England, for the commencement of leases, &c.

WALSALL-LEGGED. Said to be equivalent to baker-legged, which Bailey renders straddling with the legs bowing outward. A correspondent of N. & Q. says, "I have heard similarly-fashioned people called '*Walsall-legged*,' their formation being accompanied with a peculiar outward motion of the knees when the person is walking, like to that made in descending stairs; and I have been told that this arises from the natives having to walk up and down so many steps when going to and from their houses." Another correspondent of the same journal says, " The natives of Walsall are, or at least used to be, looked down upon by their neighbours as peculiarly uncouth. This circumstance is well illustrated by an anecdote that I remember to have heard of a gentleman living in the last century, who, in walking through a street in Birmingham, happened to jostle against a passer-by. The man jostled against vented his wrath upon the stranger by calling after him that he was ' A Wa'sall tyke, that had never been in Brummagem before.'" Another correspondent says, "Formerly several years resident in various parts of Staffordshire, in- cluding the old-chartered town of Walsall, the epithet *Walsall- legged* I have repeatedly heard orally from persons Walsall- born, whose family, relative, and official positions for three generations in the locality rendered them tolerably well ac- quainted with its traditions ; a hearty welcome and prolonged stay being often accorded to visitors or friends by saying, ' till you begin to get *Walsall-legged.*' The comparatively great elevation of the parish church at the head of the town, its foundations nearly on a level with adjacent house-tops, on the west entered by ascending a number of steps, and diverging from the main street, itself a tedious incline; on the south- west, its approaches, formerly rugged and dilapidated, being fragments of crumbled out-of-the-hill sort of steps, partly earthen and partly hill-side shale, causing consequent exertion and precariousness of ascent—these are local traditionary par- ticulars for the jocose saying, *Walsall-legged.* Recent years' improvements of the approaches by removal and otherwise of surrounding property afford but partial evidence of its anterior tendency to leg-deformity of the natives, though its present considerable number of modern steps leading to the sacred edifice still frequently give rise to the old saying, ' Don't get *Walsall-legged.*' " Another correspondent of the same journal says, " Walsall parish church is built on a very steep hill, and there are many steps from the street to the church. Black Country people affirm that Walsall men became bandy-legged through ascending and descending the hill and steps : hence

the terms, '*Wa'sall-legged*,' and 'He's bin [been] up Wa'sall
steps.' A local rhyme says—

> ' Sutton for mutton,
>   Tamworth for beef,
>   Walsall for bandy-legs,
>   And Brummagem for a thief.' "

WALTHERIA. A genus of plants, of many species, small
shrubs, principally natives of the tropical parts of America;
dedicated by Linnæus to Aug. Fred. Walther, a German
botanist, professor of medicine in the University of Leipsic.

WARWICKITE. Borate, a mineral occurring in granular
limestone near Edenville, New York; probably named from
its discoverer Warwick, or from one of the several places in
America so named.

WARWICK'S (COUNT) POWDER. A powder, consisting of scammony, oxide of antimony, and cream of tartar;
much extolled by Baglivi and Van Swieten as an efficacious
purgative in intermittent fevers.

WATERFORD. A sort of over garment. Stanihurst,
who wrote in the reign of Elizabeth, and whose account of
Ireland is published in Holinshed's chronicles, speaking of
Waterford, says, " As they distill the best *aqua vitæ*, so they
spin the choicest rug in Ireland. A friend of mine, being of
late demurrant in London, and the weather, by reason of a
hard hoare frost, being somewhat nipping, repaired to Paris
Garden clad in one of these Waterford rugs. The mastifs had
no sooner espied him, but, deeming he had beene a beare,
would fain have baited him; and were it not that the dogs
were partly muzzled and partly chained, he doubted not but
that he should have beene well tugd in this Irish rug; whereupon he solemnlie vowed never to see beare-baiting in any such
weed " (*Planché*).

WAVELLITE. A phosphate of alumina, consisting of fine
radiated fibres; named after Wavel, who discovered it.

WEBSTERITE. The sub-sulphate of alumina, a white or
yellowish mineral, occurring on the coast near Newhaven, in
Sussex; doubtless named from its discoverer, Webster.

WEDGWOOD-WARE. A kind of semi-vitrified pottery,

without much superficial glaze, but capable of receiving all kinds of colours by means of metallic oxides and ochres. Admirable imitations of Etruscan and other vases have been executed in this ware (*Ure*). Named from the inventor, the celebrated Josias Wedgwood, who was born July, 1730, and died in January, 1795, at his house in Staffordshire, to which he gave the name of Etruria, whence the place of that name.

WEDNESDAY (Sw. *Odensdag* or *Onsdag*, Dan. *Onsdag*, D. *Woensdag*). The fourth day of the week; from A. S. *Wodnesdag*, Wodin's day, from Woden, Wodin, or Odin, a deity or chief among the northern nations of Europe, said to correspond to Mercury of the ancients.

WEHRLITE. A mineral consisting of silica, red oxide of iron, protoxide of iron, oxide of manganese, lime, alumina, and water; found on the Kecskefar mountain, near Szutraskö, in Hungary; analysed by Wehrle.

WEISSIGITE. A mineral occurring in the cavities of a porphyritic amgygdaloid, with chalcedony and quartz, near Weissig, in Saxony.

WELLINGTON. A boot; named after the late duke.

WELSH RABBIT. Cheese melted into a mass, and usually spread over slices of toasted bread; properly Welsh rare-bit; and doubtless so called from having been first made in Wales.

WELTER'S TUBE. A safety tube introduced into a Woolfe's bottle, to prevent retrograde pressure; named after the inventor.

WERNERIA. A genus of plants, nat. or. *Compositœ;* so called after Werner, the mineralogist.

WERNERIAN. Pertaining to Werner, the German mineralogist and geologist, who arranged minerals in classes, &c., according to their external characters, and advocated that all the geological strata were originally in solution in an aqueous fluid, from which they were deposited or precipitated.

WESLEYANISM. Arminian methodism. The doctrine and discipline of the Wesleyan methodists, a sect founded by John Wesley, who was born at Epworth Rectory, co. Lincoln, 17 June, 1703, and died 1791.

WESTRINGIA.   A genus of plants, nat. or. *Labiatæ* ; called after Westring, physician to the King of Sweden.

WHARTON'S DUCT.   The excretory duct of the sub-maxillary gland ; named after its discoverer, Wharton.

WHITECHAPEL.   Low, mean, paltry; so called from the district of same name at the east end of London.——" The upper-cut, or strike" (*Pugilistic*).——" In tossing, two out of three wins" (*J. C. Hotten*).

WILDING OF CASSOY or BESI DE CASSOY.   A pear named from the Forest of Cassoy, in Bretagne, where it was discovered.   It is also called Rousset d'Anjou and Petit Beurré d'Hiver, *i.e.* small winter butter pear.

WILLEMITE or WILHELMITE.   A mineral, a silicate of zinc, colour yellowish ; found at Moresuet, in Belgium, and in New Jersey ; doubtless named after its discoverer (Willem or Wilhelm ?)

WILLIAM (SWEET).   The name of several species of pink, of the genus *Dianthus.*

WILSON'S MUSCLE.   The perpendicular portion of the compressor urethræ, described by Mr. Wilson.   The transverse portion was discovered by Mr. Guthrie, and bears his name.— *Hoblyn.*

WINCHESTER BUSHEL.   The original English standard measure of capacity, established by Henry VII., and ordered to be kept in the town hall of Winchester.   It contained 2150 cubic inches, and is the one generally used in the United States.

WINDSOR PEAR.   A pear from Windsor, in Berks.

WINTERA AROMATICA.   A tree, whose bark, called Winter's bark, is used as an aromatic tonic, native of the Straits of Magellan, Peru, Chili, &c.; named in honour of Capt. Winter, companion of Sir Francis Drake in his voyage round the world, who brought some of this bark from the Straits of Magellan.

WINWICKED.   A slang term used in Cornwall for *over-reached* ;   said to have originated from the last male repre-sentative of the Winwick family, who, from tradition, was celebrated for making good bargains.   Have you been *win-nicked?* as they pronounce it in the west.

WIRSUNG'S DUCT (*Canal de Wirsingus*). Another name for the pancreatic duct ; named from Wirsung, who first demonstrated it in 1642.

WITHAMITE. A variety of epidote, colour red or yellow, found in Scotland; doubtless named in honour of its discoverer, Witham.

WITHERINGIA. A genus of plants, of only one species, native of South America ; named by L'Heritier in honour of William Withering, M.D., F.R.S., author of " An Arrangement of British Plants, &c."

WITNEY. A very superior blanket made at Witney, co. Oxford. The colour is said to be attributable to the peculiar properties of the water of the Windrush. In the time of Queen Anne the manufacturers had 150 looms in full operation, affording employment to more than 3000 persons. Of late the trade has greatly declined, and most part of the fabrics now sold as Witney blankets are made in Glamorganshire and elsewhere.

WITSENIA. A genus of plants, of only one species, native of the Cape; named after Nicholas Witsen, author of Descriptions of Shells found in East Indies, and of Observations in New Holland, both printed in the Philosophical Transactions.

WOLFFIAN BODIES (false kidneys). A name given by Rathke to the substance by which the kidneys are preceded in the embryo ; first remarked by Wolff.

WOLFRAM or WOLFRAMIUM. An ore of tungsten, colour brownish or greyish black ; named from Wolfram, a ferruginous mine in Sweden.

WOLLASTONITE. A mineral, a variety of tabular spar, found in the Banat, in Finland, Sweden, Italy, Germany, the United States, Canada, Ceylon, &c. ; named after William Hyde Wollaston, M.D., a celebrated chemist and natural philosopher, who died in 1828.

WOODEN WEDGE. " The last name in the classical honours-list at Cambridge. The last in mathematical honours had long been known as the *Wooden Spoon* ; but when the classical Tripos was instituted in 1824, it was debated among the undergraduates what *sobriquet* should be given to the last on the examination list. Curiously enough, the name that year which happened to be the last was *Wedgewood* (a distinguished Wrangler): hence the title."—*J. C. Hotten.*

WOODSIA. A genus of ferns, of two species, the *woodsia* of the Isle of Elba, and the hyperborean *woodsia ;* named after the English botanist, Wood.

WOODVILLE. A cigar imported from Cuba; named from an estate there.

WOODWARDIA. A genus of ferns, of seven species; named after Prof. Woodward, of England.

WOOLFE'S APPARATUS. An apparatus for impregnating water for medicinal purposes with carbonic acid ; so called from the name of the inventor.

WORMIAN BONES (*Ossa triquetra*). A name given to triangular bones sometimes found in the course of the suture of the parietal and occipital bones ; so called from Olaüs Wormius, physician of Copenhagen, who first described them.

WORSTED. Yarn made of wool drawn out into long filaments by passing it, when oiled, through heated combs ; supposed to take its name from Worsted, in Norfolk, where it was first manufactured. Stow says, " Soon after this [sixteenth century] Wm. Rider, then apprentice to Tho. Burdet, at the bridge foot, opposite the church of St. Magnus, seeing a pair of knit worsted stockings at an Italian merchant's, brought from Mantua, borrowed them, and, having made a pair like unto them, presented them to the Earl of Pembroke, which was the first pair of worsted stockings knit in this country." This says nothing against worsted stockings having been afterwards manufactured at Worsted, and having had their *name* from thence. From the following passage in Anderson's History of Commerce, it may, however, be still doubtful whether the original name was not *Ostade,* which is both a surname and a local name. Anderson says, " Guicciardini likewise ascribes to the Netherlands, but without assigning the times when, among other arts, that of making says, serges, fustians, ostades (worsteds) and demi-ostades, woollen cloth napped (à friser), and many sorts of linen cloth, besides a great number of lesser inventions."

WOTHLYTYPE (*votely type*). In photography, a new process by which permanence is secured; lately invented by Herr Wothly.

WRISBERG. Another name for the lesser internal cutaneous nerve, the smallest of the brachial nerves; named after its discoverer.

X.

XAINTONGE or SAINTONGE (pucelle de Xaintonge). A pear named from Saintonge, formerly Xaintonge, in France.

XIMENIA. A genus of plants, of three species, natives of the West Indies and New Caledonia; named by Plumier in honour of Rev. Francis Ximenes, a Spaniard, author of the Animals and Plants of New Spain, 1615.

Y.

YANKEEISM. The *ism* of the Yankees, the popular name for the citizens of New England, but applied among foreigners to all the inhabitants of the United States indiscriminately.

YARMOUTH CAPON. A bloater or red herring.— *Ray's Proverbs.*

YENITE or JENITE. A mineral, colour black or brownish-black, occurring massive and in prismatic crystals; first obtained at Elba, and called jenite, in commemoration of the battle of Jena.—*Dana.*

YORKSHIRE. "To Yorkshire," or "come Yorkshire over any person;" to cheat or bite them (*North*). The proverbial overreaching of the rustics of this county has given rise to this phrase, which is sometimes pronounced *Yorkshar.* "*Yorkshar*, to put *Yorkshire* to a man, is to trick or deceive him" (Lancashire Dialect, 1757).——Every man pays his share (*Sporting*).

YTTRIA.   A metallic oxide, in appearance of a fine white powder, without taste or smell; discovered in 1794 by Prof. Gadolin in a mineral found at Ytterby Quarry, in Sweden.

YTTRIUM or ITTRIUM.   The metallic base of yttria, first obtained pure in 1828 by Wochler.   See YTTRIA.

Z.

ZANONIA.   A genus of plants, of one species, native of Malabar; named by Linnæus after Giacomo Zanoni, prefect of the botanic garden at Bologna, author of Istoria Plantarum, Bol. 1615, edited in Latin by Monti, 1742.

ZANNICHELLIA.   Pond-weed, a genus of plants, nat. or. *Niadaceæ*, native of Europe and Virginia; named by Micheli after Giovanni Geronimo Zannichelli, apothecary of Venice, author of Laboratorium Zannichellianum, &c.

ZANY (It. *zanni*, a buffoon).   A merry-andrew, a buffoon; *v.a.* to mimic.

"Marry, you may bring Frisker, my *zany*; he's a good skipping swaggerer."—*Ben Jonson.*   Poetaster.

> " Talking of stones, stars, plants, of fishes, flies,
>   Playing with words, and idle similes,
>   As th' English apes and very *zanies* be
>   Of every thing, that they do hear and see,
>   So, imitating his ridiculous tricks,
>   They speak and write, all like meer lunaticks."—*Drayton.*

> " Reads her asleep a-nights, and takes his oath
>   Upon her pantoffles, that all excellence
>   In other madams do but *zany* hers."—*Beaum. & F.*

From *Zan*, the Italian nickname of *John*, in Dutch *Jan*. Casaubon derives it from Gr. σαννος, a fool; Skinner from L. *sanna*, a scoff.   " But," says Bailey, " it rather is of *Zane*, Ital., a contraction of *Giovanni*, i.e. *John*, as we use *Jack* often by way of contempt."   Richardson gives, " It. *Zane*, the name of John.   Also a *sillie John*, a gull, a noddie.   Used also for a simple vice, clowne, foole, or simple fellow in a play or comedy (*Florio*); and Skinner seems inclined to favour this etymology; and Ménage also considers it to be a corruption of *Giovanni*. Tooke supposes *Sanese* (an inhabitant of Sienna) was used to denote a fool; and that the first part of the word *Sane* has given us *zani*, and the latter, *neze, nizzy.*"

ZANYISM. The state or character of a zany, *q.v.*

ZAPANIA. A genus of plants, or. *Angiospermia*, dedicated by Jussieu to P. A. Zappa, an Italian botanist.

ZAUCHNERIA. A genus of plants, or. *Monogynia*; dedicated by Presl to the botanist Zauchner.

ZELTINGER. A very good wine made at Zeltingen, centre of the wine districts of the Moselle, in which all the best sorts are produced.

ZENONISM. The philosophy of Zeno, the celebrated Greek philosopher, founder of the Stoics.

ZEUXITE. A zeolitic substance, found in Huel-Unity Mine, near Redruth, in Cornwall; doubtless named after Zeuxis, one of the most celebrated painters of antiquity; but why is doubtful.

ZIERIA (Fr. *ziérie*). A genus of Australian plants, one species of which is cultivated in French orangeries; named by Dr. J. E. Smith after John Zier, F.L.S., an indefatigable botanist.

ZINKENITE. A steel-grey ore of antimony and lead; named after M. Zinken.

ZINN. A genus of plants, of five species, natives of Peru, North America, and Mexico; named by Linnæus in honour of John Godof Zinn, pupil of Haller, and professor of botany at Göttingen after him; author of Hortus Goettingensis, 1757.

ZION. The theocracy or church of God; so called from a hill in Jerusalem, which, after the capture of that city, became the royal residence of David and his successors.

ZOEGEA. A handsome plant, flowering in summer and autumn, found by Michaux in the Levant; named by Linnæus after Johann Zoega, M.D., author of Flora Islandica.

ZOISITE. A greyish variety of epidote; so called from Baron Von Zois, its discoverer.

ZORGITE.   A mineral found in granular masses at Tilkerode and Zorge, in the Harz.

ZWINGERA.   A genus of plants, of only one species, a shrub, native of Guiana; named after Theodorus Zwinger, prof. of anatomy and botany at Basel, author of Theatrum Botanicum, Basel, 1696.

Additions and Corrections.

ABERNETHY. A biscuit named after the late celebrated surgeon, John Abernethy.

ACADEMY. At p. 1, l. 9, for *Academe* read *Academia*. Donnegan gives Ακαδημια, the Academy, a garden so called after an ancient hero, *Academus*, near Athens, where Plato taught (Aristoph. Nub. 992) : hence the school of Plato. Etym. properly, a fem. of ακαδημιος, α, ον, of, or pertaining to *Academus*.

ALABASTER. " A white stone used for ornamental purposes. The name is derived from Alabastron, a town of Egypt, where there appears to have been a manufactory of small vessels or pots made of stone, found in the mountains near the town. These vessels were employed for containing certain kinds of perfumes, used by the ancients in their toilets, and with which it was the custom to anoint the heads of their guests, as a mark of distinction, at their feasts. There are in Horace many allusions to this custom. In like manner, Mary, the sister of Lazarus, poured upon the head of our Saviour, as He sat at supper, ' very precious ointment' from an *alabaster-box*. The terms αλαβαστρον among the Greeks and *alabastrum* among the Romans were applied to those vessels even when they were not made of the white stone ; for, although they may have imitated the original form of the vessels made at Alabastron, they appear from Theocritus (Idyl. xv.) to have been sometimes made of gold. They were of a tapering shape, and without handles ; and from this circumstance, Adam (Lat. Dict.) gives as the etymology of *alabastrum*, α without, λαβη handle, a derivation which certainly cannot be assigned to it consistently with the formation of the Greek language. It appears from a passage in Demosthenes (Oration on the Embassy, ch. 68), that one of the brothers of Æschines, the orator, was employed in painting these alabaster-boxes. Pliny says (lib. xxxvi. 12, and xxxvii. 54) that the stone, which he calls *alabastrites*, was got from Thebes; but Mannert (Geographie der Griechen und Römer) places the town of Alabastron in Heptanomis, or Middle Egypt, in the hills between the Nile and the Red Sea, about thirty English miles east of Acoris; and states that the stone of which the *alabastra* were made was brought from Mons Alabastrinus, about thirty miles south-east of the town. Mr. James Burton, who has been long resident in Egypt, has determined the site of Alabastron to be latitude 27° 43′, longitude 31°, not far from the east bank of the Nile, a few miles south of the ruins of Antinoë."—*P. Cyc.*

ANACREONTIC.   At p. 6, l. 10, for *anapest* read *anapæst.*

ASSASSIN.   At p. 10, l. 10, for *plant* read *preparation of hemp.*

ATHANASIAN.   At p. 10, l. 11 from bottom, for *of faith* read *of the orthodox faith.*

ATLANTES.   At p. 11, l. 2, for *Zelamones* read *Telamones.*

ATLAS.   At p. 11, l. 13, for *vertebra* read *vertebra.*

BANTING or BANTING SYSTEM.   A treatment for the cure of corpulence first resorted to by Mr. Wm. Harvey, a London surgeon; so called from Mr. Wm. Banting, of Kensington, who was the first person cured by it.

> " What combination of anti-Banting, engineering, and sartorial jargon have we here? What does this worthy gentleman actually mean by ' widen without weakening.' "—*D. Tel.*

BASSORINE.   At p. 16, l. 16, for *constitutent* read *constituent.*

BAYONET.   At p. 17, l. 3, for 1814 read 1714; and at p. 18, l. 4 from bottom, after *Madrid*, add, " The word is still vulgarly pronounced *bagganet.—S. F. Creswell.*"

BENEDICT.   See also Notes and Queries, 3rd. S. viii. 210, 276, &c.

BERENICE.   At p. 20, l. 11, for *Evergetes* read *Euergetes.*

BERTHOLETIA.   At p. 21, l. 5, for *Brazil nut tree* read *Brazil-nut tree.*

BESSEMER.   At p. 21, for *a steel invented by M. Bessemer* read *a process of making steel invented by M. Bessemer.*

BILBO. At p. 22, for *Bilboa* read *Bilbao*.

BISANTIUM. At p. 22, l. 9 from bottom, for *ducane* read *ducat of.*

BISHOP. Among *horse-dealers*, to use arts to make an old horse look like a young one, or to give a good appearance to a bad horse (*Ash ; Encyc.*). " Dishonest dealers in horses have been said to resort to a method of prolonging the mark in the lower nippers. It is called *bishoping*, from the name of the scoundrel who invented it " (Lib. Usef. Knowl.; *The Horse*). ——A cant word for a mixture of wine, oranges, and sugar (*Swift*).——A part of a lady's dress (*Webster*).

BISTOURY. At p. 22, l. 6 from bottom, for *Pistoria* read *Pistoja.*

BOCK or **BOCK BEER.** A strong beer now much drunk at the Paris cafés. Ure says, "*Bock*, a favourite double-strong beverage of the best *lager* description, which is so named from causing its consumers to prance and tumble about like a buck or a goat (because it makes one capricious);" but the word is more probably derived from the place where it was first brewed. Meyer (Das Grosse Convers. Lex.) says simply that it is a beer from the Bockkeller, in München (Munich); but in the supplement he gives a long notice of it. He says it is a strong malt-rich Bavarian beer, that was first brewed in the little Hanoverian town of Einbeck, and that it is in great repute. He states that Friedrich, Elector of Saxony, called the Wise, was in the habit of sending Martin Luther a mass (over an imperial quart) of it daily, in order to strengthen him. He speaks of a Bavarian princess who was cured by it after a serious illness of several months, and mentions the following words in connection with it :—Bier und Bockfreund, Bock-hallen, Bockkur, Bocksaison, Bockschäffler, Bockwalzer (a melody), Bockwappen, Bockzeit, Bockzeitung. Since writing the above I have found the following notice of this celebrated beer in the Bayerisches Wörterbuch von J. Andreas Schmeller (Stuttg. 1827, vol. 1, p. 151-2), " Der Bock, Aïmbock, eine Art besonders starken Bieres, das nur in den Staatsbrauereyen zu höherem Preise, als dem des gewöhnlichen Märzenbieres verschleisst werden darf, in soferne also der Gegenstand eines

Monopols ist. Die kurze aber rauschende Epoche, die dieses Getränk, besonders bey den mittlern Volksklassen Münchens, jährlich macht, tritt gewöhnlich um die Zeit des Fronleichnamsfestes ein. Bock mit Bockwürsten (einer eignen Species) ist an diesen Tagen ein beliebtes altmünchnerisches Frühstück. Der Bockkeller, eine für den Beobachter des Münchner niedern Volkslebens nicht ununterrichtende Spelunke. Im Reichsarchiv zu München findet sich noch eine, auf den Erfurter Bürger Cornelius Gotwalt, unterm 2ten März, 1553, zum Transport von 2 Wagenschwer *Ainpeckhisch Bier*, von *Ainbeck* aus, nach München oder Landstrut ausgestellte herzogliche Vollmacht. 'Einbeckisch Bier, so die Nürnberger dem gnädigen Herrn gelifert' kommt auch in einer Münchner Hofrechnung, v. 1574 (Wstr. hist. Calender, v. 1788, p. 195), vor. Wie aus Einbecker oder Embeckerbier gemeinen Mann, der in jeden, ihm fremden Ausdruch gern einen handgreiflichen Sinn legt, Ainbock und endlich gar Bock werden konnte, ist begreiflich. Diese volksmässige Umformung ist indessen schon ein paar Jahrhunderte alt, denn in der Land und Policey Ord.v.1616, f. 532, ist auch von einem Bock-Meet die Rede, welcher nicht anders als zur Nothdurft ' der kranken gesotten werden solle.' Als gegenstück zu diesem (stärker stossenden) Bock gieng, besonders aus den Bräuhäusern der Jesuiten, die etwas sanftmüthigere Gaiss hervor." Einbeck, or rather Eimbeck, is a town of Hanover, gov. Hildesheim, on the Ilm, forty miles S. Hannover. It was a place of considerable importance in the fifteenth century, and early embraced the Reformation. It still contains, among other factories, several brandy distilleries and breweries.

BORDEAUX. At p. 2, for *made* read *exported from*.

BOSWELLIA. At p. 27, l. 13 from bottom, for *Catholic Church* read *and Greek Orthodox Churches*.

BOUGIE. At p. 28, l. 14, for *Corruvias* read *Covarruvias*; and transfer to p. 27 after " Boswellism."

BRAGATIONITE. At p. 29 read *Bagrationite*; at l. 7, for *Bragation* read *Bagration*.

BRAG. To boast; from *Bragg*, a Scandinavian deity who sang the praise of the heroes in the Hall of Odin (*J. Power*).

Bragi or *Brag* was the god of poetry: hence it was sometimes bestowed as a proper name on a poet. There was a celebrated Icelandic bard called Bragi Skalld.

BRUM (*nearly obsolete*). A counterfeit coin; from Brummagem, *q.v.* (Slang. *J. C. Hotten*).

BRUMMAGEM. Trashy, common.

> " Diluted history and *brummagem* lore."—*Sat. Rev.*

So called from Brummagem, *i.e.* Brumwycheham, ancient name of Birmingham, the great emporium for plated goods and imitation jewellery.

BURPORT DAGGER. A periphrase for being hanged, in allusion to the ropes for which the manufacturers of Bridport were once famous, and with which Newgate and other places were supplied. See the Old Morality of *Hycke Scorner*, in Dr. Percy's Collection, dated 1520 (*circ.*) " Once a yere the inmates of Newgat have taw halts of Burtporte."

CABAL. At p. 34, l. 15 from bottom, after *councils* add, " This accidental circumstance may have introduced or extended the foreign meaning of the word.—*S. F. Creswell.*"

CÆSIA. At p. 35, l. 15, for *Frederico* read *Federico*.

CALATRAVA. At p. 35, l. 4 from bottom, after *from* add *St. John of.*

CAMBO. A fragrant Chinese tea with a violet smell; its infusion pale; so called from the place where it is made.

CANNIBAL. At p. 37, l. 9 from bottom, after *Islands* add *S. F. Creswell.*

CANTABRICA. At p. 38, l. 14 from bottom, for *north-eastern* read *northern*.

CARLINO. At p. 39, l. 12 from bottom, for £51 read £5.

CAROLINEA. At p. 40, l. 13, for *Sterculiacæ* read *Sterculiaceæ*.

CARP-MEALS. At p. 40, l. 9 from bottom, after *English coast*, add, " probably from Cartmel, in North Lancashire.—*S. F. Creswell.*"

CARTHUSIAN POWDER (*Poudre de Chartreux, Pulvis Carthusianorum*). A designation of Kermes mineral, or amorphous tersulphuret of antimony ; so called from its successful use by a Carthusian friar named Simon.

CHARTREUSE. A liqueur probably named La Grande Chartreuse, a celebrated monastery in France, dep. Isère. The French word is also used for a little isolated country house ; also, in conchology, horticulture ; and frequently in the culinary art.

CHESSY COPPER. Another name for the mineral called azurite, which occurs in splendid crystallizations at Chessy, near Lyons.

CHILTERN HUNDREDS. Appellation of a nominal stewardship under the Crown. Chiltern is the appellation of a chain of chalky hills, separating the counties of Bedford and Herts, and running through the middle of Bucks, from Tring. Herts, to Henley-upon-Thames, Oxon. They are covered, in various parts, with woods, and some of the eminences are of considerable height, and afford rich prospects. To these hills, which belong to the crown, is annexed the nominal office of steward of the Chiltern Hundreds, by the acceptance of which a member of the British Parliament is enabled to vacate his seat.

CHRISTMAS. At p. 49, for *the festival* read *the principal festival.*

CIRCENSIAN. Pertaining to the Circus, in Rome, where were practised games of various kinds, as running, wrestling, combats, &c. The Circensian games accompanied most of the feasts of the Romans, but the grand games were held five days, commencing on the 15th of September. From L. *Circenses,* games of the Circus.

CLAUDETYPE. A process of photography invented by M. Claudet.

CLAYTONIA. At p. 50, for *Pontulacaceæ* read *Portulaceæ.*

CLIONIDÆ. At p. 50, l. 5 from bottom, for *peteropods* read *pteropods.*

CLYDESDALE. Name of a good draught-horse, especially for farming business and in a hilly country; so called from the district on the Clyde, in Scotland, where it is principally bred.

COACH (p. 51). Adelung (Mithridates), under the Hungarian word *kotsi*, says, "Kutsche doch vie leicht ist das deutsche wort aus dem Ungarischen entstanden, weil die Kutschen in Ungarn erfunden seyn und von dem Marktflecken Kots ihren Nahmen erhalten haben sollen."

COLBERTEEN (p. 51). "Lace so called after the celebrated French minister, M. Colbert. Swift mentions the 'pinners edged with colberteen' (temp. Jas. II. and Wm. & Mary), as the lace streamers were called."—*Planché*, Hist. Brit. Cost. 395.

CONGREVE. At p. 56, last line, for *engine of war* read *rocket*.

CORUNDOPHILITE (p. 59). Delete this paragraph.

CORYDON. An old classical term for a shepherd ; so called from the name of a shepherd in Virgil.

> " Nerine Galatea, thymo mihi dulcior Hyblæ,
> Candidior cycnis, ederâ formosior albâ :
> Cum primùm pasti repetent præsepia tauri,
> Si qua tui *Corydonis* habet te cura, venito."
>
> Bucol. Ecl. vii. 37.

COZAKEE. A horse, patient and docile, deep in the girth, powerful in the fore-arm, but with large head, and sadly cat-hammed ; hardy, and calculated for long journeys and severe services. The name would seem to be a corruption of *Cossack*.

CRETISM. At p. 60, l. 13 from bottom, after *deceivers*, add, "St. Paul thus characterizes them in his epistle to Titus i. 12 : 'One of themselves, even a prophet of their own, said, The Cretians are always liars, evil beasts, slow bellies.'— *S. F. Creswell.*"

DAVILLA. At p. 66, l. 14 and 15, for *Davilla* read *Davila.*

DIGBY CHICKENS. "The neighbourhood of Digby appeared to me particularly eligible, for the town was a thriving little sea-port ; boats of a large size were built in her docks, and the sea abounded with several good sorts of fish. A small species of herring afforded the inhabitants almost a staple commodity. They are extremely delicate, and are salted in great quantities every year. They have gained the nickname of *Digby Chickens*, and are exported to different parts of the province in barrels."—Forest Scenes in the Wilds of North America, by Geo. Head, Esq., Lond. 8⁰· 1829. See Quar. Rev. No. 83, p. 82.

DRACONIC. "The most *draconic* repressive statutes." So called from certain laws made by Draco, a celebrated Athenian lawgiver, who succeeded Triptolemus as legislator, B.C. 623. On account of their severity they were said to be written in letters of blood. Idleness was punished with as much severity as murder, and death was denounced against the one as well as the other. Solon abolished all except that which made murder a capital offence.

ELEUSINIAN. Relating to Eleusis (now Lepsina), in Attica, or to sacred rites in honour of Demeter (the Roman Ceres), there celebrated; as, *Eleusinian* mysteries. The *Eleusinia* was celebrated on the 15th of the month of Boëdromion, lasted nine days, and was held by the Athenians in great reverence. Everybody was obliged to pass through the ceremonies once in the course of his life. Strangers, slaves, bastards, prostitutes, &c., were excluded from these rites; and so superstitiously were they observed that, if any one revealed any of the mysteries or applied to private purposes any of the hallowed solemnities, it was considered a capital crime. See Dissertation on the Eleusinian and Bacchic Mysteries, by Thos. Taylor, Amst. 1792, 8⁰·; Essai sur les Mystères d'Eleusis, by Ouvaroff, Par. 1816, 8⁰·

EOLIC. At p. 79 read *Æolic;* and at last line, for *Eolia* read *Æolia*.

FAIRNTOSH. The name of a whisky in very great repute up to 1761; so called from the lands of Fairntosh, in Scotland, where it was distilled. For an interesting account of this beverage see Ed. Rev. No. 94, pp. 505-7 (May, 1828), in an article on Jamieson's Scot. Dict.

FALLOPIAN. At p. 83, l. 3, for *Versalius* read *Vesalius*.

FENIANISM. The political principles of the Fenians, an association of natives of Ireland or their descendants in the

United States, having for its avowed object the separation of
Ireland from the government of Great Britain, and the establishment of the former as a republic. The name *Fenian* is said
to be derived from Fion, a hero in Ossian, famous for his victories
over the Scandinavian and German invaders. In the Edin.
Rev. (July, 1805, p. 429) I find the following :—" It is allowed,
on all hands, that numberless traditions were current in Ireland
concerning the Fenij or Fions, a species of militia inhabiting
Leinster, and commanded by Fin Mac Coul, named by Ferguson, Fingal, the son of Conhal." F. K. Meyer, in a late
work entitled " The still existing Celtic People, Languages, and
Literatures," gives the following on the name of the Fenians:—
" Many traditions of the primitive history, contests, and migra-
tions of the Celts had been preserved, as on the British Islands,
so principally in Ireland. These were finally revived and re-
modelled in the second and third century of our era by the
latest Irish-British immigrants; the Scoti, that came from the
north-east, calling themselves by the Irish name Fiona, Fena,
i.e. the blond or white, from the singular Fion (Kymri *gwen*,
guend, ancient Celtic *vind*, as in Vindobona, &c.) This tribe
was distinguished both by beauty, wisdom, poetry, and valour,
and thus widely differed from the contemporaneous, likewise
East-Celtic, tribe of the Picts, or, according to their indigenous
name, Cruithne, the Dubh Taratha Cruithne (black people of
the Cruithne) of the Irish Annalists, and the Llu Dhu (black
host) of the Welsh bards and triads. Eminently celebrated,
however, among the blond Fena for beauty and wisdom was
the so-called light or noble family of the Ua-sin, or Uaffin
(from ' Ua,' the O' of the Irish family name—family ' Sippe,'
and ' sin' or ' ffin,' clear, white). After many sanguinary fights
the Fena were conquered and destroyed towards the end of the
third century, by the Belgian king Cairpre Cinncait, in the
great (half-mythical) Battle of Cath. This destruction, it
would appear, became the origin of the new Fion or Fin Gall
(of Ossian's poem of that name). The ancient hero of the
tribe who bore that name arose anew in the course of centuries,
enlarged as it were into an historical primary type, and a
religious and historical expression, not merely for the one East-

A A

Celtic branch of the Irish-Scottish population, but for the whole complex of its West and East-Celtic portions. He became the Divine king who had immigrated either from north or south (hence, perhaps, his name Gall = stranger), son of Cumhal, *i.e.* the Picts in the north, grandson of Basc, *i.e.* the Iberians in Spain; the type and beginning of all ancient Irish history and culture, civilization and legislation, and, more especially, from his epithet of Miledh (warrior), the ancestor of all ancient Irish families that date their descent from the East, the so-called Phœnico-Milesians."

FEVILLEA. At p. 84 read *Feuillea.*

FORTUNATUS'S CAP. "Fortunatus had a wishing hat, which, when he put on and wished himself anywhere, behold he was there. By this means had Fortunatus triumphed over space, he had annihilated space; for him there was no *Where*, but all was *Here*. . Were a hatter to establish himself in the Wahngasse of Weissnichtwo, and make felts of this sort for all mankind, what a world we should have of it! Still stranger, should, on the opposite side of the street, another hatter establish himself, and, as his fellow-craftsman made space annihilating, make time annihilating. Of both would I purchase, were it with my last groschen; but chiefly of this latter. To clap on your felt, and simply by wishing that you were any *where*, straightway to be *there*. Next to clap on your other felt, and simply by wishing that you were any *when*, straightway to be *then*." — *Carlyle*, Sartor Resartus. For Fortunatus's Purse, see N. & Q. 2nd S. vii. 21; xi. 72.

FRAUNHOFER LINES. Fraunhofer was an eminent optician residing at Munich, who, having prepared some glass of great purity, repeated the experiments of Newton on the analysis of white light. His researches showed that not only are the rays of light of very different refrangibility, but that some of the rays are wanting in the spectrum. It has been reserved for the recent discovery of spectrum analysis to show that their spaces—these Fraunhofer lines—are due to the absorption of those rays in their passage through the sun's atmosphere by the vapours of those metals, which, in a state of incandescence, would emit rays of the same refrangibility.

GAGG. "A foolish fellow. 'And Agag came unto him delicately.' Hence *gaggish*."—*J. Power*.

GOLGOTHA. At p. 100, l. 12 from bottom, for *the place of skulls* read *facetiously identified with the place of a skull*.

GRASSINI. At Turin, a kind of bread in long crispy sticks, for easy digestion; named after the inventor.

HECTOR. At p. 115, l. 4, for αγς read αγανας.

HOCUS-POCUS. At p. 120, l. 11, after *Transubstantiation*, add, The priest, however, says, *Hoc est enim corpus*.

IRVINISM. At p. 126, for *rving* read *Irving*.

ISTHMIAN GAMES. One of the four great festivals of Greece; so called because celebrated on the Isthmus of Corinth. "The prize was an ivy-wreath" (*S. F. C.*)

ISTHMIAN SCHEME. The French scheme of cutting through the Isthmus of Suez for the purpose, it is said, of gaining a preponderance in the East.

ISTHMUS OF VIEUSENS (*Isthmus Vieusenii*). The ridge surrounding the oval fossa, or remains, of the foramen ovale in the right auricle of the heart; so called from Vieusens, the anatomist, who discovered it. He was born in 1641, and was author of several works on anatomy.

LETHEAN. At p. 151, l. 14 from bottom, for *letheed* read *lethe'd*.

LIEBERKÜHNIAN GLANDS. At p. 153, l. 14, for *Lieberkühnn* read *Lieberkühn*.

LINNÆA. Add, "It is remarkable as having received its name in honour of the great Swedish naturalist, who, as appears by the journal of his 'Tour to Lapland,' chose this plant to transmit his own name to posterity."—*T. Wright, M.A.*

LINNÆAN SYSTEM. At p. 154, l. 19 from bottom, for *Linne* read *Linné*.

LOCHABER AXE. At p. 155, l. 7, for *and farewell my Jean* read *farewell to my Jean*.

MAÇON. At p. 163, ll. 2 and 3 from bottom, for *Maçon* read *Macon*.

A A 2

MAYONNAISE. A superb sauce, compounded of yolks of unboiled eggs, oil of the purest quality, French or Tarragon vinegar, cayenne, and salt; properly *Bayonnaise*, so called from Bayonne, where it was first made. The term is usually applied to a pyramidical dish composed of boiled or roast chicken delicately carved, served up with hearts of small lettuces, hard eggs, jelly, &c., and covered with this sauce.

MOGUER. A wine mixed with sherry, and forming that inferior kind of which a large quantity is exported; so called from Moguer, on the Guadalquivir, where it is produced.

MORAVIANISM. At p. 190, l. 19 from bottom, for *to the* read *in the*.

MOSS-LAIRD. A name given to the tenants in the great improved Moss of Blair-Drummond.—*Carlisle.*

MOSS-TROOPERS. A term applied to certain bandits that formerly infested the border country between England and Scotland. The name is derived from the character of the country over which they "trooped," it being extensively *moss* or morass.—*Webster.*

NABOTH'S GLANDS. At p. 201, l. 10 from bottom, for *ovula* read *ova*. Add also, "Some small glands situated between the folds of the membrane lining the cervix uteri. An anatomist named Naboth, finding them morbidly enlarged, mistook them for ova, whence they were called *ovula Nabothi*, or *glandulæ Nabothi*."—Hooper, Med. Dict.

PARADISE. A garden, library, or study. See Britton's Arch. Dict.—*Halliwell.*

PARAMATTA. At p. 220, l. 15, for *where it is manufactured* read *which produced the wool from which it was manufactured*.

PHÆBE. At p. 230, l. 5 from bottom, for *Phœbe* read *Phœbe*.

ROQUEFORT. A superior French cheese resembling Stilton in flavour; named from Roquefort, dep. Aveyron, where nearly 1000 tons of it are annually made.

ST. JULIEN. At p. 261, l. 16 from bottom, after *prime*, add, " In England, a kind of pear."

TÆNIA TARINI. At p. 298, l. 2, for *vena corporis striati* read *corpus striatum.*

TINTAMAR. At p. 308, l. 8, after *grand tintamarre*, add, " " ; and at l. 11 for *vignerous* read *vignerons.*

TOKAY. At p. 309, l. 16, add *Tempora mutantur.*

TYRANT. At p. 317, l. 13, for *Tyrreheni* read *Tyrrheni.*

FINIS.

WITHDRAWN